Surviving th

All Screv

5.5 Years Pleasur...y ..s Majesty

ALEX BELFIELD

Published by Belfield Book Company

Mush Manor
Tattyfilarious Lane
Likiend
Cockfosters
AB1 VOR
Bangkok

alexbelfield.com

Special Thanks To:

Big Boned Jean – Manuscript Mule & Common Law Assistant
Dame Jan– Tippy-Tappy Typist
Network Nick – SVoR Tech Wizard
Angel Tigger – Proof Reading
Al & Mr A – Head of Legal Blame
Dolittle and Diddleum - Legal
Tim C – Dotting 'i's' and Crossing 't's'

ISBN – 978-1-918006-30-8

Dedication

I dedicate this book to my Mum, Dad, Sister, Nephew, God Sons, Beloved Friends, Miss Doddy, Absent Friends, My man sausage admirers with palatial jelly wobblers and <u>YOU</u>.

Yes - YOU! my SVoR friends and family who collectively have saved my life and made my dreams come true.

I especially thank all of the trolls, medicated mentals and haters in their mother's back bedroom for paying their good earned dole or PIP money reading about my blessed life I blame care in the community.

NO REFUNDS!

A huge thanks to my PA and hug monster Big Boned Jean who has visited every shithole slammer in Britain to collect these books page by page. Huge credit to Delicious Dame Jan for transcribing my incomprehensible, illegible and shambolic scribbles. I'm indebted to tech wizard Network Nick who kept SVoR alive. And finally, huge thanks to my producers James N, Hayden and James B for their solidarity.

I hope you like my epistles.......

You're all Diamonds!

I would not be alive without the collective love and kindness.

Contents

About the author

Alex Belfield is the UK's most notorious convicted talker! He's been entertaining the nation - WITHOUT fear, alarm, or distress – for 30 years as of 2024!

Alex is a comedian, entertainer, journalist, and sex symbol for the visually impaired. He has worked for 80+ radio stations around the world and has toured the UK extensively since the age of fourteen. After 15 years at the BBC, he became the nonce factory's #1 whistle-blower, writing for the Mail, Sun, and Mirror.

Alex is arguably YouTube's most successful UK reviewer, theatre critic, and investigative journalist. His influence made him the #1 target for the far-left mafia. In 2020, he shot to fame with 'The Voice of Reason' – his no-holds-barred YouTube chat show, where he amassed 500,000,000 hits and was selling out theatres across the UK, from Glasgow to Bournemouth via his spiritual home in Blackpool.

In 2022, Alex was sentenced to 5.5 years for 'Stalking' people he hadn't met, been near, threatened, or - in two cases - didn't even know – under a new 'on-line' [s]talking law. It all started with an anonymous email from a BBC employee who wanted to 'close him down.' The BBC presented the entire witch hunt to the police.

Officials at the MOJ calculated him to be a 0.17% risk. Alex's stretch cost the taxpayer £150,000 and £3 million in legal fees. This political prisoner didn't qualify for any rehabilitation due to his almost-zero risk to the public. HMP unlawfully prevented his progress to an open prison.

Alex wrote his six books, including this, whilst Pleasuring His Majesty He did not use a tippy-tappy or a ghostwriter; just a pen, paper, and a lot of brain power over 33 months! What you read here is warts and all. No airs and graces. It's not 'nice' – it's a series of memoirs covering over 40 years of a media mogul's life and the establishment's finely choreographed witch hunt to 'close him down.'

His books were all handwritten and edited whilst in prison at HMP Lincoln, HMP Stocken, HMP Five Wells, HMP Erlestoke, and HMP Fosse Way between 2022 and 2025.

So, enjoy Alex's scribbles, written whilst held hostage by the state. If you spot a mistake in this epistle, keep it to yourself – Alex is no Stephen Hawking!

To the thousands of fans who have kept Alex's heart and soul alive during his kidnapping - this book is dedicated to you.

We hope you enjoy Alex Belfield – Surviving the Slammer.

Chapter 1

Political Prisoner

16th September 2022, 11am

"Mr Belfield is sentenced to 66 months," said High Justice Saini at Nottingham Clown Court.

I did not react. I did not flinch. This was entirely inevitable. They hadn't gone to this much effort to give me a tickle. A serenity enveloped me. I felt 100% protected. But by whom or what?

The establishment had taught me <u>the</u> ultimate lesson. I'd been made the proverbial example with an unheard of consecutive – not concurrent sentences. Five and a half years is a high price to pay for free speech, telling the truth, and standing up for what you believe. The inevitable harsh bird was a result of my refusal to plead guilty or be sorry. This is not acceptable to the CPS (Crooked Persecution System) or the cuntstables who pushed this through via the MOJ (Ministry of Injustice). "Send him down" the judge said. Well, that's that then. Now what? The witch hunt worked, and I got a two-year nine-month sabbatical. I'd never had a day off in my life - so finally, I could become the ultimate state-funded benefits slob. Their ambition to 'close me down' since 2019 had been handed down from on high and the mission was complete. No point in crying over spilt milk, hey? I now had to hunker down. Stoic British Bulldog spirit would be my only salvation. I might as well get on with it and try to cope with the next half a decade of authoritarian dictatorship and control. As God is my witness, I was totally calm, and my blood pressure did not rise above 'inspiringly perfect.' I was comforted by the tsunami of love from my nearest and dearest, as well as the truck load of messages, letters, and emails of support I had received in the weeks leading up to this hostage situation, all underscoring that <u>THIS WILL END</u> - before it had even begun. From second one, I never viewed this as a prison sentence. It was an establishment gagging order to shut down their most outrageous critic until the public had forgotten me. I saw it as a research project Pleasuring His Majesty during the most catastrophic period in prison history. My timing was impeccable; within weeks the entire system was in a state of collapse! I'm old and ugly enough to realise that many people are in 'prison' in real life, 99% will never be behind a prison wall, they're simply captured by their own mental illness, a health condition, or abuse for example. The majority of the country is imprisoned by financial restrictions, and some are simply trapped by their piss poor and dopey dull jobs. Why should I be any different? I'd had forty-two fantastic years of joy and showbiz, who am I to moan? It's time to man up and take it on the chin.

I was (and still am) totally pragmatic about the reality of my situation. This is not a time to boohoo, or woe is me. My life was now going to be two years and nine months of public silence on-air......but not privately. I view this as working abroad. Look, we all know this sentence was totally disproportionate in comparison to others. Nonces get suspended sentences and indeed Rolf

Harris got an identical bird after being found guilty of the <u>sexual assault of ten women</u>. No risk paedos like BBC's highest paid journo Huw Edwards got fack all! I'd ruffled feathers after an undeniable and orchestrated witch hunt to 'close me down.' I hadn't been within a hundred miles of my 'victims' to commit WHD – (Wandering Hand Disease). However, my manufactured, brand-new conviction of 'online stalking' would sentence me to the same time behind bars as rapists - on a stretch longer than if I'd beat up my accusers with weapons, not words! As the prosecution made clear, I was to be the first person ever sent down for stalking people I'd never met, never been near, or attempted to go near. They didn't even attempt to accuse me of proper professional stalking – just tippy-tappy name calling. Conjecture is now pointless; you have to be philosophical. I'm not stupid. I knew, after the bomb squad were sent by the corrupt and inept NPMGM (Nottingham Police Mob & Goon Mafia), that they weren't going to stop until I was intimidated into silence or incarcerated - to get me off air. My palatial stretch was inevitable and deliberate - to avoid me getting a tag or a suspended stretch. Who gets arrested five times and raided three times (with no warrant) by imbecile bizzies who extended bail illegally, changed witness statements, and carried out an investigation that found ZERO evidence from my police interviews or my tech/house? All evidence was handed by the evil BBC who coerced the witnesses to file complaints, as admitted in court. This collectively hums like a pound of Stinking Bishop on the coffee table next to the fire.

We had a trial with the local judge removed, and a High Justice -who normally deals with terrorism and mass murder - sent in from London to sort me out, as the case was so 'high-profile.' Yet NEVER in the trial was my thirty-year unblemished career, VoR, or my 500,000,000 views mentioned. The judge's wife was given a job at the BBC just days after my conviction - according to The Guardian and her LinkedIn. He directed, on day one, that I was banned from mentioning any of the corruption and incompetence from the cuntstables at Notts Police in its entirety. He wouldn't allow me to self-represent and cross-examine the witnesses, refused a forensic psychologist's opinion, and oversaw the circus of protective curtains - normally only used in horrific child abuse or extreme rape cases - to shroud the indignity of my accusers. ALL of my accusers were connected – mostly by the evil BBC - who I'd been exposing for corruption in the national press for over a decade. I was their #1 whistle-blower, after fifteen years in custody at the noncy corporation - a sentence three times worse than the one I'd been given today! This doesn't come near the almost entirely hearsay evidence, the missing 'thousands of emails,' and the classic 'I hope you die of Covid' tape - given by a witness's 'friend' (later denied as a friend), who is in fact a disgraced ex-Met Cop. Shushy shushy. Nothing to see here. All of the BBC woman types were completely disbelieved by the jury and, at the time of writing, are apparently no longer working for the corporation. Two men - one of whom was the most high-profile victim - secured my conviction for 'stalking WITHOUT fear, alarm, or distress.' Yet the key term 'WITHOUT' was completely absent from every moment of the trial and sentencing. Deliberately, the case was framed as 'Simple Stalking' - a term echoed in courtrooms and plastered across media outlets. It wasn't until 2024 - when the Police National Computer, via my SAR request, finally disclosed the charge in full - that the missing 'WITHOUT' was revealed. So, if you're not feeling alarmed and distressed reading this book - I'm probably stalking you and will get another 13 weeks in prison. Now, can you see why I can't take this Clown Court circus seriously? The 'system' was incandescent with rage that I had mocked and ridiculed this entire farce from day one. Now was not the time for respect and reverence.

Look, it's a joke. It's unprecedented. And to top it all, I was convicted of a new crime - a crime explained to the jury as 'not normal stalking. Mr Belfield is not accused of going near any of his victims.' Well, it's not stalking then, is it, numb nuts?! Give me strength. Stalking is described in the dictionary as 'with stealth' - i.e. in secret. Mine was broadcast to half a million people on a channel that had 500,000,000 hits a year – therefore it's very hard to lose sleep over the laughable and untenable credibility of my crime. By the way, what journalism doesn't cause alarm and distress? I'm a pain in the arse yes! Stalker – turn it in!!! I pleaded not guilty, which infuriated the 'powers that be,' and I refuse to be sorry to this day - AS I'M NOT. You can't mount a witch hunt to close someone down anonymously and then cry like a baby when they want to know who said it. So, deal with it! I have nothing to be sorry for. I did not lie! So, here I am - after two years of legal hell, designed to break me - with unprecedented arrests and raids intended to drive me to suicide, to end up on the roof and vanished. I had fought on, day by day, since October 2019 when this started, remaining shamelessly proud of my true character - backed by my angel audience, who knew exactly who I am and what I stand for. I remained defiant on-air - even reporting on my own trial - so that every single word of importance was broadcast, unedited, to the nation for the public to decide. They're the ONLY opinion that truly matters. My tenacity and resilience infuriated the establishment even more. My fortitude and strength defied their relentless assassination attempt. In my heart, I knew that the public are smart - and despite the mainstream media's obsession to destroy me (and similar patriots on our side, identical to me) at <u>any</u> cost - the truth would always <u>set</u> me free. The fake news hates me. YouTube is whooping their ass, and TV and Newspapers are dead in the water. We also know how sanctimonious journalists are - believing they're beyond reproach. Not anymore - since the BBC's chief news paedo was outed. They clearly did not report the trial fairly, having left the courtroom whenever we spoke or challenged. But I had done everything I could to expose the blatant lies by an unbeatable establishment opposition and collective mafia. Remember, it was *R vs Alex Belfield* - the state, NOT individuals. They were mere puppets, acting as the bullet in the shushy establishment gun.

<u>Take Him Down!!!!</u>

I stood up from my chair in the dock as all of the appallingly dressed journalists rubbed their sweaty hands with glee - some were so excited, their gimp masks had steamed up and their nipple clamps slipped off with excitement at my imminent incarceration. I didn't look at the gallery. My dearest friends were there, and that was not an image I wanted in my head as I began my au revoir. Two very polite officers took me into the side room, and then the media circus truly began in earnest on civvy street. Now I couldn't defend myself - they'd have a no-holds-barred free-for-all! For me, the torture of the career and financial assassination was over. I was at peace, away from toxic lawyers and the crooked police mafia. It was my Maundy Thursday – not a Good Friday! But would I ever rise again? This was my only ambition and focus.

I have to admit, most of the officers seemed more shocked than I was. You didn't need to be Mystic Meg to see this coming. No one could fathom the sentence. I explained they weren't meant to understand. You can't argue with stupid or explain the inexplicable. It was deliberately unprecedented. I've since done a lot of research. Here's why I got five and a half years. The 'consecutive' element is the most astounding and the biggest part of the stitch-up. There was no way - given the complete lack of physical contact - that the judge could have handed me more than two and a half years (the minimum) for stalking WITHOUT violence. No violence was accused on ANY count. Violence is two counts above 'alarm and distress,' and four levels above 'without fear, alarm, and distress' - the specific charge for which I was convicted. My sentence is already an embarrassment to 'real' stalking victims, who have openly spoken out about the grave injustice. However, the sentence is absurd by comparison - as stalking with violence averaged a two-year custodial, often suspended (i.e., let off). So, how did I get five and a half years WITHOUT fear of violence? Women have been violently hounded for years, and their attacker doesn't get anywhere near this length of incarceration. So - shenanigans are clearly afoot, and the judge had to do some clever jiggery-pokery and creative accountancy to get this over the line. So - let me explain...

My bird had to be over four years to prevent me getting a tag. Why is this so important? A tag would've allowed me to be back home with my family, get back to normality, return to my job (talking), and live a normal life far too quickly for my troll's satisfaction. It's now a year on tag - back then, it was a maximum of six months. So, let's do the maths. You only serve half your sentence. Now, 40% for nearly all. If I got two years, for example, that would mean you could get a tag with only three months behind the door. What's the point of that? That wouldn't teach me a lesson - barely a slap on the sphincter! I'd be back on-air before the lunatics on X had finished their MDMA and poppers party in celebration of my departure. So, the judge did something that defied any legal expert's comprehension. He made my sentences consecutive. This is unheard of - unless there is proof of conspiracy – trying to cover up your crime. That was never alleged - and certainly not accused - considering my girthy-sized puntership! If you're sentenced to over four years bang-up, you're not eligible for tag - guaranteeing that, if the MOJ played it right, I'd be invisible for nearly three years if they could stitch me up for five. They hoped this would be enough time for me to be completely forgotten - or lose the will to live and jump off HMP Nottingham's roof. So why a stalking charge, when I was arrested on 'malicious communications?' They couldn't get me on harassment, as the sentence would've been collectively under a year - suspended (i.e., no jail time) - and would not succeed in getting me off-air or resolving the 'problem' of my online influence and popularity.

I maintain, whoever is behind this witch hunt needed me pushed to the brink in the hope this would break me, end me, and hopefully I'd give up and top myself. I believe they hoped the pressure of the endless arrests and raids from the corrupt 'cuntstables' alone would be enough to land most humans ten toes up and ten feet under. My defiance and stamina staggered the establishment mafiosi, which led them to relentlessly pile on the pressure and up the odds to the final bomb squad raid. Lest we forget, I was 'no further actioned' four minutes after they invaded my house to steal my microphone. Let's face it, the mentals had no idea how perfect my life was. The BBC too were compelled by the narrative that I was a sad loner, living in my mother's back bedroom. Little did they know - when the Notts Police mob goons burgled my house without a warrant THREE TIMES - they found 'a beautiful home' (as one of the non-binary, tattoo-clad, mincy, closeted truncheon lovers whispered in my shell-like, in a very effeminate voice). They hoped to expose me for paedo, dark web porn, weapons, drugs, and any other embarrassment they could find during their illegal raids. That would have been the end of my public life. THEY FOUND THE SQUARE ROOT OF FACK ALL! Not ONE piece of evidence. I'll leave that to other highly paid disgraceful journalists at the nonce factory!

They simply found a baby grand piano, a cockapoo, wigs, and fake knockers in my 'props' cupboard - and a shameless, unflinching gobshite in a house they could never afford in their wildest dreams! I was the most boring man they'd ever met, and up to nothing. I'd spent forty years working my arse off to pay for my palace. My HOME - that they soiled with their seedy sanctioned, scum sucking pondlife intentions - that totally backfired. I was shameless in explaining to the knuckle-dragging rozzers how I'd paid for most of the bricks......which was selling stories to the Daily Mail exposing corrupt civil serpants like them! These BBC protected mafia were the very people who had sent the mob to close me down! Coincidence? I learned a very good lesson on day one - when their pig's trotters crossed my doorstep. They're deaf. They do not listen. They've already decided. NOTHING you say makes any difference - so say NOTHING! You're completely wasting your time!!! The irony that you're now reading a book exposing the police, Clown Court, and HMP! What an own goal! Hey Ho, if you lock up an investigative journalist – that's what you get nobheads!

When you enter the MOJ vortex, you undergo an assessment of your risk and safety. At no point did these buffoons ever suggest I was an escape risk - or even 'high risk' - given a clean criminal record and a first offence of words. 'Perfect character,' as was known for forty-plus years of my blessed, bizzy-free life! Zero violence, no weapons - therefore, no risk. So - I was never handcuffed or taken by force throughout the entire process, in court or even to prison. I cannot accuse 'the' system of giving me a kicking, as they have not. Many of my pokey colleagues tell a much different story. It's much more dark, evil, and insidious than that. It's mental torture and relentless sabotage, conducted with total impunity - signed off at the highest level, and choreographed by all agencies in cahoots.

My years of reading psychology and books on 'coping,' processing subvert malice, and handling pressure came up trumps. It was now all about acceptance - and writing EVERYTHING down to profit from later. Turning their kidnapping into an HMP research project is the only way to keep this tomfoolery in perspective. This is entirely a game of strength - drawn from 100% contempt and utter derision. 100% mental fortitude and tenacity is the only way to survive. To this date, my only anxiety - I hate that bullshit word - is for my friends and family, who are being punished far worse than I. I'll never forgive myself for what these evil manipulators have done to them – TOTALLY INNOCENT GREAT PEOPLE! I'll take my just deserts on the chin, but my nearest and dearest didn't deserve this. So, on their behalf I had to survive the slammer! I was 'taken down' the stairs at Nottingham Clown Court to the custody suite area. Big Boned Jean (my common-law assistant) had taken my bag - containing my toothbrush, clothes, pens, paper, and shoes - into court prior to my arrival. This was all pre-arranged. The 'much hacked' line from the mentals is that I was shocked and unprepared for jail. Bollocks! I knew exactly what was going to happen. I'd spent weeks preparing. I was told I was facing five years, despite probation recommending community service. I knew exactly what this High Justice had in mind! The judge never referenced this 'pre-sentence report.' Equally, he chose to ignore all my raving references from doctors, teachers, MPs, and even disabled people who I cared for. This good character did not fit the narrative or agenda. The five-and-a-half-year sentence meant I would only serve two years nine months - and have the same 'on licence.' Curiously, you can go to 'D CAT' (open conditions) with a sentence under three years, so this would be interesting. Would I qualify immediately, or would the dark forces keep me under lock and key as a serious risk to the public for the full stretch? Their only justification for not letting me go to 'open' (home) is public protection. Technically - by law - I could be sent straight there immediately. But obviously, in this very clear, PR-driven case of 'let's make an example of him,' that was never going to happen!

So - my job now was to literally waste time and write six books, preparing for my second coming - costing YOU (the taxpayer) £48,000 a year.

If only I was a BBC comedian nonce like Tom Binns, who had over a hundred child rape videos and 30,000 images on his tippy-tappy, I'd have been at home right now on a suspended sentence – deemed a zero risk to your kiddies. So silly, isn't it? If only I were the BBC's number one news gobshite - one who enjoys watching Class A child rape videos, paid for with good BBC money to a convicted paedophile - I'd be enjoying my hot tub and freedom. There's a pattern already, isn't there? So obvious and transparent. The question - from a public protection point of view (the only purpose of HMP) - is this: if a person's risk is so low they don't qualify for any rehabilitation, what is the crime, and what's the point of them being there in the first place? This is what my time in the hoosegow will establish. What courses would HMP force me to 'rehabilitate' with? Do they have a 'pain in the arse' course for trappy know it all's? We shall see.

Anyway, that's not why you called... I had my bag searched, and my personal areas - and man sausage - poked and prodded. Every cloud. This was my first raised-eyebrow moment... What is it with the police, court, and HMPerverts wanting to grope my gentleman's area? They're all molesting meeskites!

There's no time for self-pity. I now needed grit, determination, and a heart full of chutzpah to survive until 2025! I will not surrender to this foolishness. I still believe (even now in my darkest moment) that the TRUTH WILL SET ME FREE......

Chapter 2

Pointless Searches and Driven to Insanity

Since my very first search at court, I've never seen the point. Through this entire charade, I've had hundreds of molesters trying to grab my gonads - they're all a complete waste of time. Officers aren't allowed to touch private parts or anywhere near them. To be honest, if half of these people (of limited capacity) want to have a grab of my man sausage....help yourself. Times are hard and friends are few. Any intimate touching at my time of life is welcome. I repeat my old line 'if you've nothing to hide, you've nothing to fear.' None of this stuff ruffled my feathers. Of course, the cons stick anything they want to get past security up their jacksy, making the entire circus pointless.

Like the entire system – it's all window dressing. All over custody suites - at police stations, courts, and prisons - are signs about 'dignity,' 'human rights,' 'respect,' and 'duty of care.' These are all lefty, woke buzzwords that mean bugger all in the real world -least of all to institutionalised, brainwashed civil serpent robots whose job it is to find half a kilo of crack up your crack, or behind your sack. I was so fascinated by the process and this type of bullshitery - that I hadn't got time to be worried, scared, or overcome by self-loathing. I was in sensory overload - having a blast thinking of gags I'd shove in my Rolodex, not out of my gob. Little did I know, the professional smuggler used their schmuck as an Amazon Prime collection point that screws would go nowhere near. So inventive – why didn't I think of hiding some Parma ham and Châteauneuf-du-Pape up there? I'm told SD cards can be concealed perfectly. Who's the bellend now? Christ, I won't even put a condom on mine, let alone a smegma flip phone secreted up my Johnson! Anywho, more about bellends later – you can't like all the screws! So - they searched my bags, and I had pens, paper, underwear (Calvin Klein, naturally - to enhance and point my half an inch and a dozen wrinkles in the correct direction), as outlined in the PSI (prison law) framework. With all these daily searches, I wanted to look my best when I was identified - should their wish come true to bring me out in a body bag. Curiously, there seemed to be an awful lot of staff to 'handle' me - at one point I nearly offered selfies. I think I was the most exciting thing to pass through the Nottingham Custody for Cons since Robin Hood!

I was then put in a cell and a very nice lady brought me a coffee and offered me a sandwich, crisps, and a chocolate bar. I thought 'this is marvellous!' During fifteen years at the BBC - including my last year in the sewer of Leeds, on the naughty step, facing seething bosses spewing 'policy,' 'editorial guidelines,' and 'how to be dull' training - I was never given this level of hospitality! She then very kindly handed me a copy of The Guardian newspaper. I quipped, 'Is that to wipe my arse with?' She tittered and said, 'It won't be long, the bus is on its way!' 'Oh,' I thought, 'they've booked me a minibus!' I'd never suit one of those mucky riot police vans. I didn't want to be rude. I said, 'No rush. I'm having a lovely time. Do you have a KitKat? Could you give two fingers to the judge?' She laughed.

You've always got to offer something she can gossip with back at the desk. I have never blamed any of the government-financed operatives for this hostage situation - they're just doing their job. However, the newspaper was an indignity too far, so I handed her back *The Guardian*, explaining: "Things are bad enough! That lefty vomit will push me over the edge, and you don't need another death in custody this soon after sentencing - it would look suspicious." She laughed, "You are a card, Mr Belfield." I think she said 'card!'

Moments later, the door opened again, and I was invited to see my KC, David Aubrey. He was still dressed to the nines in wig and frock. I couldn't help but break the mood: "You didn't need to go to all this effort for me, David." He smiled. "Are you OK?" he asked cautiously. I said, "Well, I've had better days. Can you just get a message to Mum and Dad and let them know I'm OK - and I will ALWAYS be OK! We'll always be OK! Bullies and liars never win. Tell them that." He replied, "Of course I will." This was my only heartache. Causing my family upset is the hardest punishment of all. Prison is fine, I've stayed in shitty Premier Inns, but to attempt to hurt my family is unforgivable. My only heartache is the worry of others far and wide, including my Voice of Reason punters, who were beside themselves with legitimate worry. Prison is undeniably dangerous - there's no question the authorities were intentionally putting me at real risk. It would be weeks before I could truly comprehend the pain this had caused to so many angels. I said, "Five and a half was a bit steep, wasn't it?" KC said, "It's ludicrous, I'll file the appeal immediately. Don't worry you'll be fine. You're strong, you've got incredible support, and this will end – you will get through this and come out stronger." Wow. Platitudes that were humbling on one hand and terrifying on the other. What a responsibility, that 'I'll be OK!' One can't help but think 'it's easy for you to say'…...but I took it to heart in the sincerity it was given and said, "I did warn you that this was a stitch-up." Mr Aubrey, a very caring and religious man, said, "You have my number - you can call me anytime." I said, "Thank you!" He said, "At the very worst, you'll be out at forty-five, with the best of your life and career ahead of you! You'll turn this around - I know you will." I was mortified. I'm only twenty-seven! Forty-five is very old and verging on a midlife crisis. I'd prefer to see this as a blip caused by the innocence of youth!!!! Mr A shook my hand.

That was that - nothing else to say. There haven't been many weeks during this book-writing sabbatical that I haven't spoken to him. About half an hour later, after I'd had my afternoon tea, the door opened, and the nice Guardian–Andrex lady walked me to one of those nine-seater prison vans. I was seat 1A - that's first class on British Airways. I was cock-a-hoop they'd got my memo about travel requirements. I promise you; I was totally calm - as a wave of armistice and peace from my attackers descended over me. The bravado had gone. I no longer needed the stiff upper lip or defiant courage, as I was now 100% safe and free from my enemies, liars, establishment manipulators, and the court's ludicrous aspersions. I was FREE - finally - and protected from the witch hunt that had haunted and hounded me daily, from the BBC and the private security force, NCP - Notts Corrupt Police. More than two years of taunting had ended. I had a lovely view of Nottingham as I was driven away. My town - forty-plus years of memories and my dreams coming true. My recurring sadness was that I couldn't let my loved ones know I truly was OK - regardless of where I was going. The last thing I told my audience was: 'Whatever happens, I'll be back.' No crocodile tears or temper tantrums from me - ever! The narrative now was 'tick tock' to my second coming. Little else mattered, other than the health of any beloveds. The pearl clenching and gloating from the mentals and media would only draw more focus on the injustice. I wasn't averse to ANY of it in this HMP sweatbox/bubble.

The van didn't hang about. They're not allowed to tell you anything once you're in custody – but they do. Word was incoming that I was off to HMP Lincoln as HMP Nottingham was full. I don't believe that BTW. I would have been too well-known in my hometown pokey - by staff and cons. This was the first 'intel' -based decision by the dark forces at HMP. Little did they realise, thirty miles down the road in Lincoln, it would make ZERO difference. I'm told HMP Nottingham is an even bigger shithouse than Lincoln... which is like saying being shot is worse than being eaten alive by a tiger. Impossible to believe. It felt like I was being given a guided tour of my hometown. The sat nav was clearly off its tits - again, all entirely deliberate in 'high-profile' cases to throw off any prowling paps or twatty trolls. We headed towards the M1 via Radcliffe-on-Soar power station, which is completely the opposite direction to Lincoln. I smell a rat. As we crossed the M1 at Junction 24, I had to smile - the times I've done that journey to fly off from East Midlands Airport to somewhere fabulous. Now I'm the top story on the MSM propaganda fake news, being driven to my new (more private) life in the slammer - presumably lying on top of a fella called Dave for the next two years and nine months..... bunk beds, you understand. This ain't an Oxbridge swinging weekend. Do you remember when - woe is me - Prince Harry buggered off to America to invade his own privacy? It felt like Meghan the Manipulator being exorcised by the establishment - to give some much-needed peace and quiet. Megs and I are identical, except I don't have teeth like Mr Ed, a chip on my shoulder, and I don't boohoo like a cracked record! But that's not why you called.....

I suddenly looked down under my seat as we entered the M1 North and I thought 'fack me how crap are their security checks, someone's left their shopping on the bus.' A bag was next to my seat, I opened it - and blow my bloomers it was another sandwich, water, crisps, and chocolate bar! Good Lord, hospitality on *The Bill* or *Prisoner Cell Block H* ain't this good! Well, I never look a gift horse in the ass - so I ate this as well. Who knows when I'd eat again? I felt better treated than an illegal immigrant on the Bibby Stockholm! We turned off at Junction 25 to Derby. It turned out that we had to pick up another co-star from Derby Clown Court. How I didn't bollock the driver for going twenty minutes south to then head thirty minutes north is beyond me. He must have been a London taxi driver in a previous life. I was fascinated by how little room my chauffeur-driven cubicle had. I tittered to myself; I do hope Alison Hammond never goes to jail – she'd never fit in this broom cupboard! Eventually, another fella hopped on the Big White Loser Limo - and off we went to Lincoln... via Newcastle, it felt. Not good for the environment. Greta would be whizzing her tits off with this smack in the gob to 'Just Stop Oil.' Next came a scream from the rear: "I need a piss!" Ouch. I wonder if the nice driver would stop at Tibshelf services? A cackle came back from the cockpit: "She'll shove you a piss bag under the door." Blimey. This hasn't happened since I last flew Ryanair. It was the height of summer and warm, but naturally, my carriage had air con - a bit chilly, actually. I did request 72 degrees. That's the only temperature for air <u>con</u>.

I was wearing my cheap jacket from Burtons and a pair of old gig trousers, as I didn't want my nice stuff creased on this wild goose chase. Throughout the trial, I'd worn my Armani (Salvation Armani) posh jacket - but we all knew which direction this was going. There ain't no flies on me. That was safely back in the wardrobe for when I'm ejaculated back to the North Pier 'Second Coming' tour. The most bizarre thing was that I couldn't stop thinking about KC Aubrey's words: 'You're strong.' Ermm... what does that mean? I'm no Hulk Hogan - and I'm more grab the flab than pinch an inch. I guess it means that, at times of crisis - when all those around you are losing their heads - you will keep yours. I was about to be flung into a world of nightmares, with seriously dangerous people, yet I did not feel scared. But why? Is that 'strength?' Encouraging, but an intimidating and MASSIVE responsibility not to let him and many others down - who believe this HMP cruise contract would be my biggest life challenge ever! Somehow, my curiosity - feeding my journalistic nosiness - kicked in. This is now an exclusive three-year investigation exposing His Majesty's Prison and Probation Service. HMPPS, by their own admission, is in collapse and BROKEN! What a time to be inside this 90,000-men operation - the biggest prison population per capita anywhere civilised. I did feel an inner power from others, believe me. I know exactly who I REALLY am - not the fabricated bollox the judge PR'd to his media congregation of soulless drones, revelling in the lies and distortion. I told myself, 'You WILL be OK.' Could this be my nemesis, having this oxygen removed. Lest we forget - 342 people died in custody last year alone. You don't need to be Diane Abbottcus to work out that's almost one every day. I know I was so lucky to have more love in my life than I could handle or comprehend - but I also have so much love to give. My need for human contact is insatiable. My love for conversation is my lifeblood. Could this be my nemesis - having this oxygen removed? I felt like a fireworks finale on Bonfire Night, about to fizzle out in a downpour of dimwits. I prayed again that my family and loved ones would be OK. If they were OK, I'd be OK. Not sure who I was praying to, but it can't hurt... worth a shot, hey?! Surely the Big Man can do me a good turn?

Chapter 3

Just a Number A4747EW – Not Alex Belfield!

Eventually, we arrived at the mammoth Victorian frontage of HMP Lincoln. Blimey 'mammoth frontage' – isn't that Carol Voderman's twitter handle? This is what's known as a CAT-B 'local remand' prison. Basically, you're only there either awaiting trial - if you're a high-risk defendant on remand - or if you're awaiting allocation to your new home, like me. They call that 'dispersal,' which takes two or three weeks. The rest littering the place are social derelicts caught between CAT-As (lifers) or CAT-C holiday camps. We pulled in with what felt like an inch either side of the bus. You'd have thought someone would have thought about the size of the vans when they built the entrance in 1872! It reminded me of trying to get a word in sideways with one of those gobby lefties, ranting about non-binary or ULEZbian issues. Tight as a duck's arse! HMP Lincoln, like so many Victorian monoliths, looks like a castle. Like HMP itself, they're generally outdated, rat-infested, and not fit for purpose. I'm told they regularly get knocks on the door from passing tourists, requesting 'two tickets to look around.' Trust me, my Japanese friends, this is one of the UK's oldest public toilets - I'd pass by immediately if I were you, chunky! Lincoln Market is far more interesting and entertaining - and you're far less likely to catch the plague.

Eventually, the door opened and they let me off first. I said to the darling dear woman in black and white - who had the look of

Sarah Millican's ugly fat sister – "Can I have my bag, please?" Ahhh, she smiled: "No, lovey—it's at reception." I couldn't resist: "Well, do tip the porter for me. I haven't got any cash!" She laughed. I mentally told myself 'Belfield, you'll have to stop this, being witty and charming is what got you into this mess in the first place!' There were four other co-stars on the Whacko Winnebago, and one by one we went through the rear stage door. I was grateful for all the security - this was no time for autographs! Joking aside, one of the things I had to get used to over the last year or so was being recognised in Tesco's. However, fame is one thing - but infamy is quite another. I believe it was the great Su Pollard who said, 'Infamy, infamy - they've all got it in for me!' – never had this beautifully crafted gag rung more true, as I began my thirty-three months locked up and starved of public attention. We were all in for a shock! A very nice senior officer greeted me at reception: "Mr Belfield, are you OK?" Wow. "Yes, I'm fine, thank you. Do you have any super-king ensuites available tonight?" He smiled. As you're being processed, it all takes a while - but it's very relaxed and civil. I only had one request: "Can I call my mum and dad - to let them know that I'm OK?" I begged. The officer said, "No, you can't." This was my first lesson in prison life. There's no point in arguing. You have to give up immediately, no matter how heartbreaking. Begging, pleading, or kicking off ain't going to change anything. Most lunatics, crackpots, and unhinged whackos fall at this first hurdle. This Captain Peacock had clearly been ordered that I had to remain totally incognito……including from my folks. This was beyond cruel and actually against prison guidelines. They don't care about them - as I was about to find out.

Contrary to belief, I'm not stupid. Despite the bullshit claims that I'm a loose cannon, a gobshite, and an irascible big mouth – I'm actually not. In fact, most of the time, I'm incredibly quiet and don't look for any trouble or confrontation whatsoever. Can I stick up for myself? You have to, in this business! When people are tricky and try closing you down – you have no choice but to send them on their bike and put them in their place! This wasn't the time or place for a tête-a-tête. You are entitled to one call on arrival into custody – just not me! Russell Brand taught me, 'no means no.' I was not getting a call - that's that! Heartless and evil, but it is what it is. Computer says no! I quickly accepted the biggest reality of being a prisoner is that YOU ARE POWERLESS! You're completely and utterly beholden to a man (or butch women with a voice like Dot Cotton and more tattoos than a docker) who is right - even when they're completely wrong. They have a set of keys and ten weeks training – often straight out of nappies or Aldi - but they are now the Gov! Generally, they have no communication or life experience, but my job was to smile sweetly and say nothing. Know when you're on the backfoot. They call the shots, so arguing is a fool's errand - and hoping for logic and compassion would be as stupid as going through a revolving door on skis! I went into a little side room to wait for step two and the box-ticking to begin. The next officer had the most curious Freddie Mercury moustache. He went through my bag for my 'prop card.' What you can't have goes in your 'prop box' - including the bag my items were carried in! I couldn't help but visualise him mincing with a hoover to 'I want to break free!'

Lesson 1: There's a secret language in prison, not dissimilar to palare – the underground chatter the gays used prior to 'it' being legal in the UK:

Lallies = legs, Mincing = walking, Bona = good, Eeek = Face

With 67% re-offending, very few men come in for the first time, so they presume you know the game. Why can't they offer you a welcome brochure - like I get at the Ritz Carlton? So, to help, I put together a lag's (prisoner's) dictionary - full of words that, in real life, you'll never use. Here, it's the only vernacular.

No one explains ANYWHERE. This secret language is endless. So, the prop card is basically a list of your checked and permitted bits and bobs - that you can sue for if they go missing. All done on paper. This was my first realisation that this monolith, HMP, was as outdated, laborious, and frankly redundant as all the other bureaucratic and institutional wastes of money - like the BBC, Police, and NHS. They're all still living in 1975 – the height of Jim'll Fix It. It's always the pyramid of shit. HMP is full of middle managers walking around like Celia Imries, with folders under their arms, achieving the square root of fack all, making everyone's life miserable and getting in the way of anyone who wants to be efficient. Another publicly funded shambles. Why on earth isn't this on your file – called NOMIS? Everything is there digitally. It would save hours of time and paperwork when things go wrong. Within seconds of meeting the first fella, I could feel his palpable frustration with the outdated and broken system. Sadly, this would sum up my entire experience in custody. It gets a lot worse......

I was now no longer Alex Belfield. I'M NOW A4747EW for the next five and a half years!

For the second time today, my pens, book, paper, pants, socks, and the all-important flip flops (essential) were registered on a meaningless handwritten file. What was the point of doing it the first time if they didn't pass it on? I've touched NOTHING since. We had a nice chat though. I asked again when I could ring the family. He said with embarrassment, "You'll have to fill in a form" - here we go – "But it's Friday, and no one will be in until Monday." He lowered his head. "I know." Next, I tried a different tactic: "Well, if I can't ring, can you?" He said, "No, sorry - security have to sign off your approved numbers on your PIN." (Prison phone system). Next, I had to get changed. This was the bit that fascinated me. I'm still intrigued by the psychology. What is the purpose of the dreadful grey clothes that they give you? How did this aid rehabilitation - or reduce the current, inevitable likelihood of coming back to jail? It doesn't, does it? Private jails give you your own clothes to avoid this unnecessary humiliation. Why are the two systems so different - and why do non-private pokeys want to dehumanise you? Within seconds of arriving, they rip away any last self-worth you might have. It makes you identical to the next guy, removing any pride and self-respect that you might have left. So, did I kick off and make a scene? No, I put on my <u>costume</u> to play the part of a prisoner - to enable me to write this chapter of my life. Seriously, how else could I view this pantomime and nonsense?

The screw said to me, "Don't worry you can buy clothes as soon as you settle in." What? I couldn't resist: "So, if you've no money and can't afford clothes, you have to stay in 'greys' - whilst rich people like drug dealers - are walking round in £200 Gucci jeans?" He raised his eyebrows, laughed, and said, "You've got it. Welcome to prison!" A big lesson from day one is that life - and prison - isn't fair. We are not all born equal!!! Very quickly, I'd see the hideous reality of the haves and have-nots. Amidst this cost-of-living crisis, I'll have to wear Gucci for kids = Gucci Gucci Gucci Goo!

I officially signed into the Temple of Twats - full of those who had killed, raped, and destroyed lives. Was I equal to a rapist? Well, in the eyes of the delusional, deranged, and bonkers nutters, who created this narrative, <u>YES</u>! Those who didn't have skin in the game could see I'd been made the poster boy for having the audacity to take on the VERY powerful BBC and police (riddled with wrong 'uns). This officer was in no rush - mind you, nor was I! I'd got nearly three years to talk shite. We chatted for twenty minutes. He said, "You know, you're top story on the news." I said, "Surely I'm not on that dreadful Toy Town Central News?" "Oh no" he said, "You're top story on all national channels." I said, "Wow! Must be a slow news day." He chuckled. Awkwardly, I said, "Yes, this is a magnificent day for the BBC, but they forget it will end." This camp tashed three-stripe (Senior Officer) said, "I'll give you this advice – they can turn the lock, but they can't stop the clock. You'll be fine." He packed away my cheap jacket, trousers, and shiny shoes into my black prop box - and then asked me where I wanted to be located. I said, "What do you mean?" He said, "There are some seriously dangerous people here, I'd like to protect you on VP." I thought, 'WOW – there's a VIP wing?' NO, no – VP = Vulnerable Person = Nonce wing. Lord, take me now!!! WHY ME???

Let me be clear, CAT-Bs can be very perilous and risky. They're old, tired, and not fit for purpose – just like Sleepy Joe Biden. As well as sex offenders, VPs are often police officers, high-profile convicts, or – ironically - corrupt prison staff and bent judges who've been caught taking whopping backhanders to put people behind bars. You'll meet a lot of them in due course throughout my incredible journey at HMPontins. I smelt a rat that VP wasn't going to be the Dorchester of Lincoln Nick, so I raised my eyebrows and said, "Where do you recommend?" Officer Handlebars said, "Listen you are high-profile. They've painted you as a monster, so I can't protect you on the normal wing with lads who just won't understand. You don't need me to explain. You'll be far safer on VP, it's not for long anyway, you'll be out next week and you're behind your door nearly all day." My hands were tied, "OK, VP it is." In hindsight, it was absolutely the right move. Despite the stitch-up, the prison, clearly had a duty of care. Let's face it - the word 'stalker' was used to paint the illusion that I was some creepy lefty cyclist, or Guardian-reading, champagne-sipping type, with binoculars hiding behind bushes. So, in the eyes of a twenty-year-old convict - off his tits on spice - who's looking for acclaim in prison, or being paid by others to get out of debt, beating up a 'famous' stalker could bring huge kudos. It would also deliver great joy to the trolls and the mentals, gleefully self-touching from the sidelines. I'd rather not give them the satisfaction. Also, I didn't want to explain to every imbecile and knuckle-dragger what had happened. On VP everything (for obvious reasons) is on the DL!

VP means you are basically secure - as you're all in the same boat, away from other 'mains' prisoners. It should be noted that a remand nonce could have been <u>accused</u> of rape by a disgruntled ex-Mrs – it doesn't mean it happened! For the record, I've <u>never</u> been a VP prisoner. However, in the far more lively CAT-Bs this was the safest bet for now. This did ultimately work in my favour - as nonces, it turns out, have more gym sessions and separate secure moves, avoiding all other prisoners for safety. That'll do me (for now)!

BTW, more Prison Palare: NONCE comes from slammer slang meaning 'Not on Normal Courtyard Exercise,' i.e. could not socialise with other non-noncy prisoners for their own protection - it does not necessarily relate to paedos. The two groups of cons will <u>NEVER</u> meet in this jail, although they do mix in 'offence neutral' private pokeys that they're trialling at Five Wells and Fosse Way – two jails I'd visit next year! 'Mains' hate nonces = wrong'uns. Before I left reception, Freddie got me a big bag of biscuits, crisps, juice, cereals, milk, coffee, and toiletries for the pad. I couldn't believe my eyes. It was like a bloody food bank. I can assure you I wasn't getting special treatment – all prisoners get this hospitality.

The final step of the reception process was medical. A very nice big-boned lady of colour did my vitals. I think she fancied me - she said I was 'perfect.' What a lovely review! My blood pressure and sugar levels were exceptional... but then again, I'm not off my tits on smack! She said, "I can't believe how calm you are!" I replied, "First rule of showbiz: you can't worry about what you can't control." Compared to a Sheffield working men's club, this was Disneyland. I've overran the bingo and buffet at Chesterfield Miners Welfare – I can handle fear - don't you worry about that! I was just glad that for the next two years and nine months I didn't have to pay council tax or have to worry about my leccy bill! I knew that this 'local remand' prison was as bad as it was ever going to get. I would now have to use my forty plus years of learned decorum, patience, and fortitude to survive this career and literal assassination attempt. I now need to view every experience and picture in my minds' eye as an experience to profit from for the rest of my life via this epistle. The keys clinked, the door lock rattled, and moustache man (perfect for a YMCA musical) said, "Right you're all set, Officer Adams will take you to your pad." That he did..........

Chapter 4

Checking into My Lincoln En suite with Phone & TV

I stood up from the chair and slung my bin bag over my shoulder - like a convicted Santa Claus. On top of the carbs, they'd given me a bed sheet, top sheet (with holes in), pillow (made of concrete), and cup, plate, plastic cutlery... plus some noodles, chocolate, and a sandwich for my tea. Three BLTs in six hours is a stretch - even by my ample manboobage! It was now about 6.30pm. Clearly, nothing good was made in a rush in this hellhole. Why did I even care what time it was? The clock now has little worth. It was almost silent as we walked the endless corridors to the VP wing. By this point, the entire slammer was banged up and in 'Patrol State' - so it was all very spooky. The awkward silence would be a pattern repeated daily with the screws (officers) I didn't know. These are not your friends. Remember: loose lips in the clink sink ships. However, loose lips in a strip club have 50% off! (So I'm told).

I'm not one for idle chatter. One thing I was very aware of - was that anything I said would be taken, written down, and used against me - it wasn't paranoia. I'd done quite enough schtick for one day. I was now in the 'system' - and despite my media circus, I'd done many interviews over the years with horror stories of how the 'service' swallows you up and refuses to spit you out once you're captive. Re-offending is off the scale - and it mustn't be forgotten that someone kills themselves every four days at HMP. It's a staggering statistic, reflecting the darkness of this vortex. From day one, I never lost sight of the fact that I had a determinant sentence which would end - but a wrong move could have dire consequences for the second half of the licence period. However, for now, they'd got me by the bollocks - and my only plan was to be squeaky clean, to prevent them from making further mountains out of molehills. I knew I wasn't (and couldn't be) a CAT-B prisoner, as my 'crime' wasn't violent - although the judge made a lot of 'words are weapons.' Another level of dangly old bollocks from a depressingly woke world. I couldn't help but jest with the big-boned officer. "There're an awful lot of doors, aren't there? Do you think the council got them in a job lot sale?" Nothing. Silence. OK, I'll do it for myself. "Have the fire brigade checked these? All of those gaps between the bars would be a nightmare in an inferno!" Silence. OK, I'll pass. He led me, for a few minutes, to my cell on the 'Vulnerable Person's' wing - safe from the generic prison riffraff, which I would become once ejaculated from this CAT-B world of deadly pointlessness. I always imagined prison would be relentless racket. Not true. Not a peep! There was no one around, not a soul. It was like being on the set of *Porridge* or *Cell Block H* – it definitely hadn't been decorated or cleaned since they were first filmed. HMP Lincoln had entered lockdown over an hour ago, with every door cross-checked and double-checked by two officers - like final checks aboard a Fokker 100 or Boeing 747. All other prisoners were tucked up for the night with their Xbox, bag of groceries, and enough sniff to keep them buzzing until GMTV.

Despite being mid-September, it was still quite warm, but just a month before it had been forty plus degrees in these cells. I'd dodged a bullet by coming in at the end of the summer, before the long cold winter. Hopefully, I'd be out before this notoriously freezing clink had pads like igloos. These hellholes are like greenhouses in August and a chest freezer by Christmas. Finally, we reached my new temporary abode. The door opened and in I went. I was greeted by a young gentleman of colour. My first reaction was total relief as it doesn't smell like a port-a-loo at Glastonbury! The size of my mother's back bedroom, I was aghast to see a TV (with remote), kettle, and most importantly a phone - what more would I need? In that moment, I knew I could do this. I WOULD be OK! "Night" the maudlin officer said, and slammed the door shut for comic effect. You know what they say? Loud bang, small bulge! I haven't heard that much clattering since the current Mrs Belfield threw a saucepan of tripe and onions at me when I got convicted!

You might not believe this but, as God is my witness, for the first time in months I felt safe. No one could 'get' me now. I put my bag on my bed – well plank. I said, "What's your name?" He said "Vinnie, what's yours?" At that exact moment I looked at the TV and there I was on BBC *East Midlands Today* - with some dopey low rent journo crowing about my demise. I pointed. He looked and said, "Oh, they love a celebrity in here. I saw this earlier. I can't work out what the fack you did." I rolled my eyes: "Me neither." Being on the news, on the front of newspapers, and top story on the wireless is a very weird thing - as you know it's all theatre and word vomit – not reality. It's just clickbait and ratings - and tomorrow's chip paper. I was at peace that it's a game and this was my saboteur's moment to shine and crow. This ain't my first rodeo and I've been part of hundreds of pile-ons – so it was now my turn to get schtupped. It's truly an outer-body-experience and bizarrely doesn't feel personal. I had spent twenty years talking about everyone else, so this was indeed a taste of my own medicine. At these moments of insane noise and drama, the best thing to know is who you are - focus on who and what matters, and wait for the tsunami of shitstorm to pass... it always does (mostly) - as it did in my case, within 24 hours. The disproportion was frankly hysterical and raised more suspicion than hatred from the average punter. I made Fred and Rose look like Rosie and Jim. You can't let the freak show get in the way of sticking up the tent. You HAVE to remain grounded 'whilst all of those lose their heads....!' It's tomorrow's loo roll. I've never looked at comments on YouTube. As my mentor Sir Ken Dodd taught me, if you believe the good, you have to believe the bad. Neither do you any good. Opinions are like arseholes – everyone has got one and nearly all stink!

I later found out that the national news and internet - especially YouTube - went into meltdown, with all of the whack jobs, mentals, and bisexual, bifocal, and bipolar frog-faced loons finally getting more than thirty viewers riding off the back of my name. I was big business - and ironically, became my so-called enemies' only means of getting an audience. There's a compliment in there somewhere. I, of course, was blissfully unaware. Vinnie asked if I wanted a 'brew.' I said, "I'm not ambivilacious, I don't drink tea, but I'd love a manly coffee." I didn't want any blurred boundaries so early on. I didn't even know if I was top or bottom (bunk) or if we'd have to top and tail. I'd not had anxiety this electric since my last BBC audition. I was so curious to look round this tiny rabbit hutch and see Fairy Liquid at the sink, Jay cloths to clean, and a loo brush 'just in case.' Wow - you don't get that at a Holiday Inn! Well, not since the dinghy divers moved in. He had Nescafé coffee, Pot Noodles, and Cadbury's chocolate - what kind of a slammer is this?

The nosey parker in me couldn't help but find out more about who my new common-law partner was - after all, he'd be lending me his soap for a shower until my supplies arrived. He was twenty-four and on remand for a domestic with his girlfriend. When you're on remand, you're not guilty - so you cannot be treated as such. They have unlimited 'spends' - money in their prison purse for food and calls - and boy, did he take advantage! He was so generous. I was amazed. He couldn't have been more gracious. What I was most thrilled about was that he didn't puff on those stick suckers......or vapes as they're advertised. It's sickening to see how many grown men are addicted to these modern-day dummies. It's like being in an eighties disco every time you're in a public area in these cesspits of sin. They're like walking steam trains. At private prisons, even the dopey officers walk round sucking on them like their nanny's left boob. So childish - and I believe they'll be proven deeply unhealthy and dangerous in the future. These people rattle like a snake when they cough. Just wait for the 'vape lung' court cases. #MysticBelfieldPredicts. Anywho…….

Vinnie and I hit it off and his ugly Uncle Alex was giving all kinds of advice on life matters. He was lost, but never mind about doing my Claire Rayner act, I broached the awkward conversation about the most important 'pad' issue – no not shitting in front of each other! Faecal issues don't usually bother me - I've interviewed hundreds of politicians - but I'm awfully squeamish with bodily functions. I won't even show my arms in public, let alone push out a doozy in front of a chap I've known for ten minutes! I haven't got to forty-two to start being present during another human's clenching and ablutions. Seriously though - never mind crapping, let's get cracking! I'm talking about the #1 issue – the remote control. Shockingly, this dear hearted young man didn't seem to care. I was staggered. He explained he'd been very depressed since being incarcerated in Lincolnshire's 'Home for the Bewildered' - and the NHS immediately stuck him on a high dose of antidepressants and ADHD tablets, knocking him out a good 22 hours of the day. You could argue this is ideal with 23 hours bang-up! He had no formal diagnosis by the way. Like all GPs - just dish out happy pills like smarties. Like thousands at HMP, they stuck him on them to keep him sedated, asleep, and therefore quiet and compliant. It worked - what a blessing. This whipper-snapper slept all day, leaving me to watch *Loose Women*, *The One Show*, and *Naked Attraction* at my discretion. I'd basically struck gold. I unpacked my few bits, cleaned the bed top to bottom, and made it ready for however long I was going to be held captive in this human dustbin. The metal bed was so old, it had a big slump in the middle - perfect for the ergonomic contours of my back. So thoughtful! I looked at the telephone that, very soon, would be my lifesaver. But for now, it was useless without a 'pin code' to call my beloveds. Without the pin being activated the blower is useless. Vinnie very rarely used the phone...not sure he would appreciate me gobshiting to all and sundry for four hours a night. We'll cross that bridge when we come to it.

As the more observant Voice of Reason punter may have noticed, I'm quite fastidious. I don't like clutter or mess, and I certainly don't appreciate bodily functions, nasty smells, or indecent mucky marks on my glass tables. Thankfully, my cleaner Formaldehyde is marvellous at low dusting and having a squirt and a wipe. I fear my standards may have to recalibrate at this Penitentiary of Pricks. Thankfully, you don't get many crystal chandeliers or baby grand pianos in this Sewage Centre for Shitheads - so cleaning wasn't a big problem. I once again told myself, 'Don't worry - none of this matters.' Everything I stood for and cared about yesterday no longer matters. Thankfully, Vin was very clean - as most prisoners are. They take surprising pride in their pads - which I'm sure was less so twenty years ago, during the slop bucket halcyon days of proper pen punishment! Let's be honest, HMP Lincoln is very old, dirty, outdated, and disgraceful (not dissimilar to the evil BBC) - like nearly all CAT-Bs.......but it's still not torture, I expected much worse. I reminded myself of this every single day. I must be an optimist. At no point did I spare one second worrying about living conditions. You have a toilet (with discretion curtain), a sink with hot and cold water, along with soap, shampoo, and conditioner - this is hardly Guantánamo Bay! We had over thirty Freeview TV channels to keep me busy, whilst the walking Mirtazapine snoozed all day.

Here's the bravado free truth, I was physically and emotionally drained. I had worked for two years non-stop to create one of the biggest Talk YouTube channels in British history - and it had taken its toll. Add to that the obscene abuse from the Police Mafia, whose 'cuntstables' relentlessly hounded me, along with the sicko trolls who made my skin crawl with their loser, twirly, medicated, unhinged fixations... it was a lot to juggle, on top of family and a national tour. Now it was finally over. I was as relieved as a gazelle escaping the lion's clutches in the Masai Mara. I was captive - but free at the same time. No pressure. No expectations. I was untouchable from the cuckoos. All they could do now was scream at themselves and keep my name alive - and that they did, whilst matron upped their meds! Their power and control had gone. They couldn't threaten me or haunt me with their lies and threats of more raids and arrests. It was done. The weight this instantly took off my shoulders was astonishing. My heart was broken for my friends and family, but I knew we'd get through it together. Love will force you to climb any mountain. Light always kills darkness. Karma would sort out the rest. I knew the phone would eventually work, and my loved ones would visit - sooner rather than later. I knew my punters wouldn't flinch at the stitch-up - and no matter how many interviews narcissistic, self-promoting, do-gooding sociopaths did, the truth was still the truth. They'd be waiting for my return. My fans lived every word and second. The wild imaginations of saboteurs were dismissed. Those who knew – knew! Those who didn't know wouldn't care. The crackpots' malicious and distorted spin on their loopy reality doesn't count tuppence to me. I got in bed and watched *Gogglebox*.

I pondered on the old notion that at first, they ignore you. Then jealousy makes them ridicule you. Next, they want to kill you. Only then – if you survive – you comeback stronger. It's so true! This had to be my focus. I laughed at the darling *Gogglebox* couple in the caravan and the two old queens in Brighton. It's the same show whether it's in my front room or in a slammer. It felt so normal. I felt safe. This would be my mantra: that despite new surroundings, the world continues to spin - and everything I knew yesterday was still true today. This kidnapping was only on paper. I HAD to keep perspective. I knew in my heart I'd cope - but would everyone else?

My only ambition now would be to make sure my people were OK, and coping as well as me. Prison is much harder for those who imagine it, but don't live it. How could I convince my people that I was absolutely fine, and that this temporary HMP exposé gig would eventually pass? Mum and Dad had to stay well though, if they broke, that would push me over the edge. This was my only kryptonite, not a few bars and officers in panto costume with cuffs! Every single night before I go to sleep, I'd pray that my loved ones would stay well until this evil nightmare is over. With Dad approaching eighty, this was a terrible toll and blow he didn't deserve. He's my hero. Mum is a fighter, knocking seventy - it'll take more than some horseshit actors in a court of law to finish her off! Please God, keep them stoic, strong, and safe. We've got each other. That's all that truly matters.

Chapter 5

Day One Surviving the Slammer

I woke up at about 7.30am on Saturday, 17th September 2022, and that was it - the drama was over, and this was my new life, indefinitely. No pressure, no work, no phone, no distraction, and thankfully, no lawyers. The relief was almost exhilarating. I remember Hopkins telling me that when she went bust, after the vultures took everything, she felt 'free.' Once it's all gone, there's no fight left and nothing to lose. It's remarkably freeing. It's the weirdest feeling to know nothing matters. It's <u>all</u> beyond your control. Even the pressure of touring was a strain - I love it, but it's a lot of work making sure you never disappoint. All of this neurotic dedication and devotion had been taken away. All I had to do now was stay alive; nothing else was expected of me. It was like being a student! Also, the pressure cooker of notoriety is a lot to stomach. I LOVE the public - but the relentless cuckoo arseholes who want to bring you down (entirely because of jealousy) are a woeful strain. None of that now matters.

At 8am, the door opened - and I shit you not - a young fella said, "Do you want some toast?" WTF - toast delivery? What kind of Travel Lodge for Twats is this? "Errr, yes please. Two brown, please," I said. "There you go," he said as he looked up. "Oh, it's you, Alex. I heard you were here. My dad loves you." BANG - door slammed. <u>This rocked me</u>.

Only twenty minutes earlier, I'd been swimming in a sea of anonymity and my newfound obscurity - yet the first toast chef I met knew exactly who I was. Alex Belfield was meant to be dead! I was supposed to be A4747EW... well, that didn't go very well, did it? Balls! Maybe I wasn't going to be quite as invisible as I'd hoped. This kind chap gave me an extra slice - talk about VIP treatment.

OK, before I get started and go off on one, I can only tell you my story – my experience. I have to be clear that my crime is non-drug, violence, or sex related, so my category of risk is almost zero - similar to fraudsters and other 'white collar' crimes. The screws and cons don't even take this type of foolishness seriously. Prison is a pecking order. Cons have a gentleman's agreement based on what you did. They collectively decide if you're an outcast - not a state-funded judge. So, I knew I was never going in Belmarsh or HMP Wakefield to be segregated. Contrary to the sentencing remarks, there is no evidence that I'm a risk or at risk. I was never going to do 'proper' jail - as a lot of lags have told me. That means 'high-security,' endless bang-up, and brutal jails. I simply didn't deserve it, and therefore HMP couldn't justify it... no matter how much noise there is from Twatter. This was a brief period of transition before I'd be sent to a 'soft' CAT-C - the lowest-risk prison before open prison or release. For now, this was just a lot of bang-up (behind the door) until I was processed to where I needed to be. Every single con goes through this. So, I calmly accepted my reality and got on with it. The most important word any prisoner can learn is ACCEPTANCE. Without it, you'll be angry and stuck in self-torture 24/7 - achieving absolutely nothing but continued self-flagellation and inner torment.

I waited for Vinnie to wake up - my first mistake. Thankfully, I'd be lucky to see him before the 1pm News. Very fortuitous. This kid was living my old life. If I was up before *Loose Women*, it was a busy day. So now what? Well, there is no 'what now.' This is it. At 9am, the door opened. It was left open, but I had no clue whatsoever what to do or where to go. Again - no one tells you anything. You have to work it all out for yourself. The screaming reality was that there's no prison Bible, no HMP guidebook, or cruise-ship-style schedule. For a new boy like me, I'd need allies - and quickly. I walked out onto the landing... it was exactly like you'd expect from an old, shitty Victorian prison they always use in the movies. They're certainly not built for glamour. There's a deliberate coldness and clinical atmosphere, so from day one, I told myself I would stick to my pad working or be in the yard walking. VPs are escorted everywhere, which I found comforting. It put me in mind of security walking me down the North Pier to stage door at the Joe Longthorne Theatre on 10th September - just a week ago. What a difference seven days makes, hey? My true fear isn't Crackhead Bob on G3 - it's the risk of getting heckled in Blackpool and looking like a dickhead in front of a thousand punters halfway over the North Sea! That's when you find out adrenaline is brown. If you bomb, there's always a risk you might be tossed off the pier - which is a lot more humiliating than being chucked off the 'twos' at Lincoln Loo

Lock-up. Nasty business. I was now being escorted by a screw, alongside fifty paedos and rapists, to walk around a slammer yard in one big circle. To my amazement, I very quickly met 'nice,' chatty people - many of whom were my age or younger. This has shocked me more than anything in jail. It becomes so 'nice' and immediately normal.

OK, full transparency: 90% of the prison population you avoid like the plague. Not that they're 'evil' or dangerous - that's a given for most - but it's prison! These people are from a different world, spitting every five yards and calling each other 'bro' in a bizarre Caribbean accent. I'll pass, dear. I felt like an alien amongst halfwits, similar to my time at BBC Yorkshire. The first thing I promised myself was that, at no point, would I compromise who I was. I would not change or try to fit in - it fared me well. I would remain me and just keep myself to myself. To this day, I've kept that promise and survived brilliantly. I was fascinated by everyone. The days of army-style lines and screaming in your face have long gone. "Good morning, Mr Belfield," the gov said as I passed. I wasn't expecting to meet a dear old boy called Eric, who was ninety-two years old. He would be my first wake-up call that you can't judge a book by its cover. Eric had just been convicted of raping a woman back in the sixties, for which he was given a twenty-five-year sentence. Like me, he was awaiting a transfer to his resting place - literally, in his case. I'm no mathematician, but 92 + 25 = doomed. Can you imagine? What's the point? To save £50k a year, shouldn't we try an injection if we're so sure of his guilt? If

52

not, wouldn't a tag suffice for an unprovable set of accusations sixty years ago? Mind you, HMP is still cheaper than your average care home.

You'll hear lots of stories through this book of men who wake up every day knowing they'll never see freedom again. I know I couldn't do it. Why would you torture yourself? I'd be off to Dignitas. Surely there's a very good argument - in the extreme cases like MET cop Wayne Couzens - to put them out of their misery and save £70k of taxpayers' money per annum for scum like him.

I find the psychology of my colleagues infinitely intriguing. Eric felt much the same as me - and I believed him. "I didn't stand a chance! How can I disprove something that didn't happen sixty years ago?" It's a good point. Hearsay appears to be the backbone of justice during a climate of 'all victims have to be believed'... a woeful Tony Blair legacy. This leaves all good, honest, and law-abiding citizens open to vindictive attack - as I know too well. How can that be just? We have to be so careful of crazies with an agenda and vendettas, who seem to have carte blanche to imprison those they want silenced and/or banished. Social media proves the world is littered with them. Without any doctor's notes for sanity... let alone evidence, these people are putting thousands of men behind bars in some evil game of affirmation and power. This is, of course, the biggest travesty to real victims. It's terrifying. Despite the nut grabbers, vape puffers, insane lunatics, druggies, and general weirdos - you can meet the (very rare) old, sentient, calm, 'kind,' and interesting human in jail. Eric had been a top businessman and had his own mansion and Rolls-Royce, which now sat aimlessly, waiting for him to return home aged 117 - when his sentence ended - or 105 if he got parole. Ouch! He was a Godly man, and he invited me to the chapel tomorrow. He was a true gentleman... and convicted rapist. Who am I to judge? I guess he's your ideal grandpa. Having reported on Yewtree and seen the stitch-up and blatant lies about so many innocent stars - like Jim Davidson, Jimmy Tarbuck, and Paul Gambaccini - these kinds of accusations stick in my craw. How can anyone remember anything after so long? I was utterly intrigued. There are two sides to every story. This curiosity defined my entire time in custody. I hadn't even been in the hoosegow 24 hours, and I'd already worked out that ANY opportunity to leave the cell and occupy the mind was a bonus - providing it was around the right people.

It was still only 9.30am, and by 10am, we'd be banged back up until 3pm. This is CAT-B life: two hours' freedom MAX at the weekend, and just sixty minutes Monday to Friday. I went back to the wing to have my shower. I'd been given a change of clothes and accoutrements. I quickly did my ablutions and popped up to the office to see the bosses. Ranking is clearly as important in prison as it is in the Clown Court. The place was full of rankers -one big pissing contest and ego wank of importance. Reverence is <u>everything</u> here, but I tend not to blindly respect authority. No-stripe kangas (officers) are work experience. One stripe is a regular door-locker - pointless asking anything. Two stripes might help you, if they can be arsed. And three stripes are the bosses who actually have some power and influence - equivalent to the regional boss of a Happy Shopper or a Bejam. Asking 99% of <u>anyone</u> in prison for anything is absolutely and completely pointless. Screws are not in a position to help and are too busy to care - generally. Prisoners are far more helpful and honest by a mile. You'll notice at the Lincoln slum I don't really talk about <u>any</u> screws. Unlike CAT-Cs, you literally get no time at all to interact. No bad thing - but remember, they're not your friend. Little fruit comes off the tree of Gov gossiping. I saw them as identical to Lib Dems: to be avoided at all costs, unless absolutely necessary. This never changed - other than a few rare exceptions.

Everything at HMP is still paper and 'app'-driven. It's torturous. I asked a two-stripe, "How do I call my friends and family?" He said, "Mr Belfield, you have to fill in a written app." My first curiosity was: how do you know who I am? My next question: where do I get that form from? This sums up daily life in the slammer - it's relentless 'passing the buck' and filling in forms. Beyond tedious. I was sent downstairs, and there was a set of drawers with thousands of forms. Dear God, I'm in bureaucracy HELL! I took ten phone 'application' sheets and three hundred 'general apps' for everything else. Urggg - 'God take me now.' All this radical-left box-ticking makes me want to puke. Any question about anything is on a general app. Within hours, I realised that sadly - most (not all) officers are so broken by the system, they just don't care. They have morons asking them questions all day. They bug the shit out of them, and they become tired. It's every man for himself. What's scandalous about this Neanderthal paper trail is that the average literacy rate in jail is eleven years old, and ADHD and autism account for over 60% of the prison inmates. This, therefore, tells me that nearly all of the prison population are at a HUGE disadvantage in getting anything done - as they'll simply give up before they've started. No one offers to help. You're entirely alone. You wouldn't believe how many hundreds of forms and apps I've filled in for other lads. It's cruel how the system punishes the least able. Furthermore, how many braindead whippersnappers have their loved one's full name, address, postcode, and telephone number to hand - to get them added and activated by the system? That's, of course, if they're even able to fill in the form in the first place! You can't phone anyone to ask... because you don't have their details. It's an intentional circus - and a circle of shite.

The man-hours wasted processing this crap must be infinite. I had nothing better to do, so I took the reams of A4 back to my pad and meticulously filled them in. You have to be tremendously organised to have this info to hand. Who even knows anyone's landline? One mistake and it's rejected. I made sure that, prior to being sent down, I had everything written down to guarantee I would reunite with my loved ones - the only oxygen I needed to survive. On my way back up to the pad, a fella stopped me on the stairs. This man had very long hair, was unfeasibly tall, and worryingly shifty. This was the first time I had THAT creepy feeling. You know when you know. Light-on-their-feet people have Gaydar - I have Noncedar! You can't unsee it. You quickly develop a sixth sense for perverts. He said, "I'm Pete. I love your show. If you need any help, just shout. My dad won't believe you're in here. We used to listen together." "Oh, thank you," I said - dying inside. If two guys in an hour knew who I was, this obscurity and anonymity wasn't going to be as easy as I thought behind bars. I genuinely believed that, being an 'online star,' I'd be safe from cons who don't have internet. Little did I know that most have phones and secret USB sticks - with twenty-two hours a day to listen to the ramblings of tits like me on their dodgy iPhones, shoved up their arse when searched. Surprisingly, everyone was very polite and not aggressive at all. At no point did I have any fear, or that bollocksy 'anxiety' that lefties thrive off. How could I judge these people, when I was one of them? That was my frame of mind. We've all got our own story, and injustice certainly wasn't unique to me - so why not them too? My first hour 'out' in HMP Lincoln had flown past uneventfully. It was all a bit of an anti-climax. There were far more Fletchers than Hannibal Lecters!

I went back to the pad, and Vinnie Snailpace was waking up. He had learned that rushing in the slammer is pointless. Wise chap! Time is no longer my captor or enemy. For twenty-five-plus years, I'd been obsessed not only with seconds, but with planning tours weeks, months, and years ahead. Time was my obsession. I used to book Christmas tours in January, and the seconds were crucial when hitting the news on radio. Suddenly, 'doing' time - I was free of all that precise discipline and obsession. NOTHING mattered. One of the common and accepted philosophies for survival is: don't fight what you can't control, and accept the cards you're dealt. Years ago, I would never have been able to do this - I was far too impetuous. Now, I had no choice but to give in to the bullshit and just get on with it. Self-pity, fury, or anger would achieve absolutely nothing. NO ONE (in here) cared, wanted to hear my crowing, or - more importantly - could do anything about it even if they did. So my fate was set, and I had to just swallow my bitter pill... without getting bitter! It was my job to find a spoonful of sugar to take the edge off it. Keeping counsel would fare me well. Smiling sweetly (with total insincerity), with patience and peace, would be the only way to survive mentally and get through this almost three-year book-writing project. For now, I was in no man's land - and no matter the inner distress and turmoil of not being able to reassure the folks, nothing would change until at least Monday.

At 10am, the door slammed with that incessant jingle-jangle of keys locking the line of doors - by a grunting officer who had made the ridiculous decision to put himself in prison for life. I'll never understand why any sane person would make this choice, considering the risk and never-ending shifts. It's a very bizarre way to earn a living - as you'll discover. This job appears to attract the most peculiar type of person. Even after a few hours,

I'd rather be in prison than work in the clink. We're <u>FAR</u> better treated and respected than screws!

All I wanted to do was find out as much about prison life as possible. I was like an excited puppy, drinking from the Pedigree Chum bowl. I felt like I'd been given an insight into a secret world. My curiosity was relentless - it still keeps me going every day. There's never a dull moment. I still cannot believe 'they'd' be stupid enough to open the pokey's Pandora's box to a big gob like me. I guess twenty-five years as an investigative journalist was about to pay off.

I'm a glass-half-full kind of guy. What option did I have? I hadn't got time to boohoo or worry about myself. I made notes from day one. So, what next? "We get lunch at 11.30am," Vin said. "Oh marvellous," I said "We'll be back in time for *Steph's Lesbian Lunch on Channel 4*." He didn't laugh. So, I sat in my chair and started filling in more phone apps. I felt like Rain Man, trying to recall second names and postcodes. Do you know your partner's mobile digits? Why would you - it's in your phonebook! 'Siri, call Gladys' doesn't work in jail. This was the first stark realisation that I was now living in North Korea. Prison isn't torture - it's just intentionally facking frustrating. The UK has been heading that way since Covid, so I'd got some practice of totalitarian control through lockdown - but now it was for real! We were all in prison for two years from 2020, so a bit longer won't make much difference. It was now all about intel from the MOJ dark forces. My every step, move, conversation, and 'observations' were monitored and written down by the establishment Gestapo drones. All of this was in the hope of catching me out with something – in fact, ANYTHING! I knew 'they' would need to paint me as mad to keep this character assassination going. I equally knew they would try to trigger and provoke me, to justify incarcerating me as a risk to the public - something even probation did not believe. If they could paint me as 'far-right' (that tired old slur), or off my head, angry and ranting, they could prevent release under licence. I had to play very smart and give them nothing!!! I truly was in the Big Brother Shithouse. However, as I told the cuntstables and goons at the Thought Police - if you're up to nothing, you've nothing to hide or fear! I've remained in this mindset ever since.

My next shock was the 'canteen' that came under the door. Canteen = shopping list. This is astounding - hundreds of items to make a three-course meal. This is prison Amazon! Literally, once a week, you can order anything from Hellman's mayonnaise to evaporated milk, herbs, blueberries, and every snack you can think of in between. Six pages of items - including hair gel and moisturiser with cocoa butter. By the time I got to CAT-C, I could see why they needed bags of onions, tins of broad beans, Lurpak, and extra mature cheese for their master baking sessions. There are no kitchens at HMP Lincoln, but there are Nigella's eateries strewn with George Formby grills and Fanny Craddock muff-makers on every corner in CAT-Cs. For me, now, though, my priority was coffee. They had 'Lyons Gold' for £1.89 (pot head cheap shite), but that won't compare to my three pints of Lavazza in the percolator at home. There was a coffee called 'Redemption Roasters,' which I was particularly partial to - at £4.99. Now here's what you need to know - everything in prison becomes about ten times more expensive than 'real life' - as you are limited on 'cash.' Once set up, you can get money sent in - but it is capped. At £5 for coffee, which is the equivalent of £100 to a prisoner, it's literally gold dust. The underground value of normal 'stuff' in the slammer is so precious. Sugar is the most in demand - as it's needed to make hooch. If you can afford it, everything is at least 'double bubble' once lent to a less fortunate con for repayment next week - which leads to a lot of debt, and then serious violence if not repaid. Thankfully, this would never affect me - but it was the demise of many a smackhead. Drugs equally go for ten to fifty times the value on civvy street. This was the moment I realised: even in jail, there are 'the haves and the losers.'

I ordered Alberto Balsam shampoo and conditioner, some chocolate chip cookies for £1, fruit and nut chocolate, and some dental sticks - heaven forbid I should end up with bad breath whilst sharing my ensuite with the Vinster. Trust me, prison isn't renowned for dental deliciousness... just like Parliament. Oh, I also ordered 'Pooper Star,' the 'after party spray' to keep our penthouse potty smelling like a nun's freshly soaped lady garden. I'd gone from my ten Airwick plug-ins a month at Château Dodster at £5 a go - to wafter 'shit spray' at HMP Lincoln for 99p! Life can be unfeasibly cruel. How the mighty fall, hey? I took it all in good spirit and treated it with the contempt it deserved. My life had officially changed! In the old days, batteries and tobacco used to be the currency of exchange in the slammer. Not anymore - now everything is about vapes. Even I had to succumb to buying them, to get the odd underground remote control, extra pillow, or indeed three for a short back and sides and a blow from the front at the wing barbers. More on these indulgences later.

Saturday in the slammer was racing ahead. I hadn't had this much excitement since Barrymore's pool parties in the '70s! It was now lunchtime, and with quite a bit of curiosity, I went downstairs to the servery for food. Lunch at the weekend is your main meal - but to the joy of the long-timers, it was an all-day breakfast. At precisely 11.30am, the chorus of doors being thunderously unlocked rammed the wing as men rushed to the front of the queue. Why the urgency? "You've still got seven years left to serve, Cedrick!" Hey-Ho... I couldn't help but quip, "What are we rushing for, Vinnie?" He answered, "Well, in this place it's every man for himself. First come, first served. When it's gone, it's gone." Ahhh. A <u>HUGE</u> clink lesson. It wasn't until many months later that I understood this entrenched paranoia. If you're old or alone - with no family, friends, phone calls, letters, future, hope, or support - the only thing to look forward to in your day is food and TV. I quickly learned that you don't mess with people's food. Contrary to belief, the idea of prisoners spitting in your food just wouldn't happen... well, unless it was a nonce being taught a lesson on a mains wing. The consequences would be fatal - to tamper with a lifer's food. However, the servery workers are a clique - and a mafia. They reminded me of custody at Mansfield Police Station! They'll <u>always</u> look after themselves first, which leads to a lot of argy-bargies and the odd punch-up. Even on day one, I knew I'd have to make friends (bribe) the servery lads for the odd extra portion. They always look after their mates first. If you're last in the queue, you'll be lucky to get a couple of beans - let alone a halal sausage. Officers stand by to avoid trouble, BUT these guys are like Fagin, secreting a vegan turkey twizzler in areas not dissimilar to a wizard's sleeve.

This was now my second time out on the wing, and what shocked me was that the majority of men were younger than me. Despite the odd ninety-plus anomaly, a lot of the lads were in their twenties……. on a <u>VP wing</u>. I must enquire……but maybe not today. Put it this way: the internet will be the biggest strain on HMP resources in coming years. Victims seem to come in all shapes, ages, and sizes - but this wasn't the monster mansion I was expecting! Accusations are rife, and vendettas - armed with a colostomy bag of disprovable claims - are clearly the new weapon for a sick and manipulative generation, who've been told they will be believed no matter how fanciful their claims or devious their motives.

Nothing is left to chance in jail. As you leave the pad, you're directed left - but the servery is right. Why? Was I being wound up? No. In a CAT-B, they walk in the same direction to avoid crossing paths on the stairs. Attacks with shanks (= prison blades) are far easier to choreograph when people pass each other. There's no question: CAT-Bs are the most violent, volatile, and unpredictable of all slammers. The population is so transient (I don't mean chop off your man bits), and rife with gang and debt revenge. Your personal risk is automated on a system called OASYS, based on your offence, history, and behaviour in custody.

I've since learned it can be overruled manually by the jail or judge - should they want to give you a hard time. Regardless, you can't challenge any HMP decision. Nothing can be deleted once written either. Your risk will determine which category you need to be in. I'm very surprised the Notts Police Mafia didn't try to stick me in a CAT-A slammer at the other end of the country, sharing a double pad with Lucy Letby or Ian Huntley. They missed a trick there, didn't they? They would if they could - trust me. Anywho, CAT-Bs are full of violent offenders who wander freely, so you cannot truly relax; it's a melting pot of crackpots, crackheads, and fart heads. It's a bit like an Amy Winehouse concert in the '90s! This explains the VERY restrictive regime. Thankfully, VP wings are much quieter - which suits me... despite the prowling nonces.

Back to Belfield's Bang-Up Brunch. I was on a 'default' menu, as I hadn't filled in the menu sheet - which comes once a week through your cat flap. Basically, it was what the lads didn't want... all the lefty, vegetarian, non-binary filth like couscous pie and courgette flan. The servery is the dream job for many lads who fixate on food - it's all they've got. Quality control was now irrelevant to me; it was simply about survival. Everything I'd taught myself about avoiding carbs was out the window. There're no M&S gastroenteritis delights here!!! Calories were no longer an issue. Now I'd have to eat any old shit to stay alive until my canteen - tins of tuna, a lettuce, tomatoes, and cucumber - arrived for a makeshift chopped salad. I reached the front of the queue, and there was no white bread left - but tons of wholemeal loaves of Mother's Pride. Bloody hell, I'd struck gold! "Help yourself," one of the screws said, so I took a loaf back to the pad. I couldn't believe the sell-by date was 25th September. This was my first lesson in surviving the slammer. NEVER say no! I have had a fresh loaf of bread every day since I've been in jail - JUST IN CASE. You can't starve if you're a few slices short of a loaf! The lads are incredibly selfish - BUT if it doesn't affect them, they don't care and will help. No one eats brown bread. Day after day, loaves were thrown away. I got lucky. As for personal hygiene - well, they're given gloves and a servery jacket, but......listen, when in Rome......

I was given bacon, sausage, beans, egg, and two hash browns. Again, I couldn't help being surprised! This wasn't half a pound of caramelized onion Cumberland sausage with a gammon steak from the farm shop, but I've had worse in Skeggy B&Bs! Honestly, I was impressed. The old fable that it's 'porridge and slop' was clearly a thing of the past. I gave two thumbs up to this Little Chef! My mate Dean's last words were, "Don't get fat - keep fit." Judging by the portions, I didn't see any risk of becoming a salad dodger. The only sugar and carbs were from the canteen, keeping lads quiet with tins of mackerel and a box of Coco Pops. That iconic HMP blue plate and bowl will be forever sketched in my memory. This will keep me alive. I trolled back to my box where Vinnie - who clearly respected his elders - allowed me to sit on the chair at the desk whilst he sat on his bed, devouring a Pot Noodle and refusing to touch his scran.

"Do you want this?" he enquired. Does Carol Vorderman sleep on her back?!! I now realise how lucky I was with Vinnie. This could have easily been a bloody nightmare. If you're padded up with a spice head, imbecile, or basket case, it can literally be deadly!!! Our window had the famous bars across it - you could only see the rooftop of the slammer. Thank God bars in jails are now deemed a thing of the past. They hurt rapists' feelings and dehumanise stabbers! I found out much later that CAT-Bs don't allow you to see over the fence, whereas CAT-Cs do - to 'acclimatise' you for the 'community.' These places have more manipulation and mind tricks than a Las Vegas casino.

As quickly as we'd both returned to our feast, the door slammed and was locked again. I asked, "What happens next?" He answered, "At the weekend we get out again at 2pm - for 'SOCE' (pronounced sosh)" – this was a second opportunity to get out and go to the yard for exercise, which doesn't happen Monday to Friday. Very generous, I thought. It was still twenty degrees and dry. Those cell windows don't open in the summer and won't seal in the winter. Vinnie told me, "If you think the heat is bad, try being here during lockdown - when we only got out for fifteen minutes per day for a shower, one by one. The food was even delivered to the door." I would love to see the HMP suicide rates during that period; I imagine they're nearly as high as the rest of us who were kept hostage behind our front doors at home! I asked, "How come you were in then?" Calmly, Vin replied, "Oh, I had another fall-out with the missus, so I was on remand then too." I said, "But I thought you were on remand now." He smiled. "No, I'm on recall now - having given her another slap after she punched me. It was self-defence. The judge found me not guilty, but I'm waiting for probation to release me." WTF. He was neither a first-timer nor a Botticelli angel! However, the red flag was his damnation of probation. I wonder if they'll be kinder and more professional to me in two years and nine months' time?

Dear God. Not only is this a 'local' prison, 'remand' prison, and 'dispersal' prison - but it's also a 'recall' prison. I felt like I was on *University Challenge*, trying to remember all the new jargon. Apparently, 'recall' is the name for the second half of your sentence - after you've been released on licence. If you break the terms of that licence, you can be 'recalled' and banged up again - no questions asked - until probation signs you off. The process to sort it out and get re-released can take six months to a year - this is worrying. Recently, the government announced a twenty-eight-day max re-release, but like everything else in this broken system, it's more likely to be twenty-eight weeks... or months. Oh, my assassinators will love that - trying to catch me out in June 2025 (halfway) - to get me back in the pokey whilst the paperwork mysteriously goes AWOL. Urggg... this ain't going to be easy, as it's all so open to dark forces and box-tickers' interpretations.

What this did teach me was that not only is life not fair - but the prison system is intentionally hopeless. Like the entire legal system, it's completely on its knees and backlogged to the point of buggery. He said, "My probation officer is 23." Oy vey... an unqualified apprentice whippersnapper defining your freedom. Terrifying. Once you're in, you're facked - completely beholden to their mistakes and convenient excuses. When I said this is the HMP Vortex - I'm not joking. They make the rules up as they go along and can move the goalposts at any time. It was amazing that he was so matter-of-fact - he was resigned to 'what will be, will be!' I've come to see a lot of this throughout my custody: lads just give in to the system, which is based on bullying, brainwashing, and 100% compliance. Only yesterday, it was described by their own governing body on the news as 'broken, not fit for purpose, and it lets down the most vulnerable prisoners - which isn't good enough.' Time and time again, the most vulnerable lads are totally abandoned and left without a safety net. Lads mess up big-time, but no one tells them how to behave properly. Mega fail in my book. They stand no chance in life - and even less chance of navigating this inept system, run by inexperienced and under-qualified imbeciles who operate with 100% impunity.

I hate to admit that your boundaries of taste, with regards to TV, go quickly to pot once you're inside - as literally any old shit will do. There are just too many hours in the day NOT to watch cack. Even now, I regularly watch the delights of HGTV - Home and Garden TV. You wouldn't believe how quickly an hour can pass watching someone paint their kitchen or put up a curtain rail in the bathroom. How on earth did it come to this? I used to be the West End's #1 reviewer and now I'm watching a woman having a boil removed on *'Skin A&E.'* This morning, I watched a woman running something up her boyfriend's trellis, whilst a camp fella was pruning his foreign-looking wife's bush - on an Alan Titchmarsh special. Could it get any more depressing? Equally, I find myself watching articles on catheters or psoriasis on *The One Show*. Lord, take me now!

I'd often been found watching *Judge Judy* (ironically). I love hearing the queen of common sense screaming at morons and twazzocks. The reality check she dishes out to conspiring, broken snakes and dopes inspires me to keep going against the conspiracy of diarrhoea that I've endured. I'm still amazed how many people will just lie under oath and genuinely believe they can pull the wool over people's eyes. That would never happen in a British court, of course... Yeah, right. I love it when Judith slaps a few liars - especially those who can't remember anything - around the mush with a Vileda mop. 'Ermmm is not an answer' is her classic catchphrase. She knows that buys time for fantasists to create their next fabrication. She wouldn't stand for half the weasel bullshit in my trial - including Nottingham Police, who also appeared to have dementia and 3,900+ missing and invented emails. This modern court culture of remembering in forensic detail how you feel - yet having total amnesia for the facts - is astonishing. It seems a plague at all recent public enquiries too. If caught out, just say 'I don't recall' and you're off the hook. More like off their heads! Makes my teeth itch! Maybe If I'd lied to the rozzers and had amnesia for the rest, they'd have dropped the case or given me a suspended - like BBC paedos get. Why didn't I play the 'woe is me' mental health card? Silly Belfield. What a load of old manure. In jail, you now have to say sorry to progress. Well, I am not sorry. I refuse to say it. So, stick that in your pipe and smoke it. This will be a HUGE battle with the Celia Imrie box-tickers. If you can't beat them, join them. I pleaded NOT guilty for a reason - now piss off and let me get on with watching *Jude*, *Come Dine with Me*, and Jane McDonald on a cruise somewhere... costing you, the taxpayer, £48K a year for my entertainment. The cheeky buggers charge us 20p a day for the BBC rape tax! At least Dick Turpin wore a mask!

Anywho, Vinnie went straight back to sleep after lunch. He'd be out now 'til long after the six o'clock news. If only all house guests were this respectful! This is marvellous - they'd put me in with a walking Tramadol! So, after a couple of episodes of *A Place in the Sun*, the door was unlocked again. A busty lady of a certain age said, "Do you want to go to the gym, Mr Belfield?" "Yes please," I said, "but I haven't got any kit." She replied, "Go and ask Sid up on the 'threes,' and he'll get you some shorts -

don't piss about!" Heaven forbid! I went up to see a 6'5"
imposing man who looked like he'd lived a life - and had a
terrible accident with a frying pan. Turns out, that's what
fourteen years at HMP Lincoln will do to you. This ain't a
Champneys weekend retreat! Put it this way: if his passport
photo looked like his face, I don't think he'd be fit to fly. BTW, I
kept these comments to myself - I'm not daft. You try telling a
triple murderer that he's as visually disadvantaged as Ed
Sheeran's ball sack. Good luck with that! As if I'd ever risk my
good looks with this zinger! One smack in my gob and my
modelling career is curtains. I was a big hit in *Fisherman's
Weekly* in the '80s - don't you worry about that. I won awards
for my scallops. I used to model door knockers in the B&Q
Christmas catalogue. Anyway... that's not why you called...

I said, "Alo mate, Olive from *On the Buses* asked me to get
some kit." I got a smile - good start! Sid said, "What do you
want, lad?" I told him, "I've just come in, I only have one
change of clothes, and I want to go to the gym." Sid replied, "No
problem." As kind as he could've been, he handed over more
clothes than I needed - five pairs of undercrackers, five pairs of
new socks, three T-shirts, jumpers, joggers, etc. Top man. I'll
tell you, what he lacked in teeth and cheekbones he made up for
in generosity. Then he said, "I saw you on the TV last night."
Here we go. The blood ran from my face into my bollocks.
"They've facked you over, haven't they? Five years for hurty
words. You can't even call someone a C**T these days without
getting a life sentence" – WOW. The relief. Here's how I saw it.

If <u>he</u> could work this out, then HOPEFULLY others would too. I thanked him for being so kind. Then I dropped the biggest bollock ever. "What are you in for?" I asked. He laughed. "Mate, bit of advice - NEVER ask anyone that question. Especially on this wing. Firstly, my friend... let me explain the rules of jail."

1. Everyone is innocent.

2. Everyone is stitched up.

3. They all did a bit of shop lifting in 1982.

4. Don't borrow anything – they'll want double…...three times if it's you, as you've got a bob or two.

5. Trust me, no one will suck you off in the showers - unless you're in a private jail! Just give a female screw three boxes of vapes and Bob's your Auntie Fanny.

6. You'll be fine. I can't even work out what you did other than piss off a load of powerful people. It'll blow over. What doesn't kill you makes you stronger!"

Profound hey. I've never forgotten Sid's six-point rule book. He wasn't wrong. The days of soap on a rope are <u>LONG</u> gone! Phew...

As I walked away, he shouted, "Ere Belfield – I killed my parents, but they deserved it." To this day, I have no idea if he was joking - and I certainly wasn't going to ask anyone else. I was just grateful he'd shown such solidarity. He might be the nicest mass murderer I've ever met. So smiley... or maybe that's just what happens when you're toothless after decades of prison heroin. BALLS! What a tit!

As I walked downstairs, I'd been so carried away with 'building relations and bonds with my co-stars' that I forgot to ask for shorts - the only reason I went up to the 'threes' in the first place! So, I went back to the pad to drop off my ASDA George clothes (of greyness), and then ran back up. "What now, for fack-sake?" Sid screamed. "Sorry mate, I came for gym kit and ended up looking like someone from the Bronx with baggy trousers halfway down my arse but no shorts." He paused, raised his eyes, and said, "Good job I feel sorry for you. There you go - do you want some slippers as well?" SLIPPERS! Is Sid taking the piss? Nope - out came a camp pair of blue grandad slippers, size 10. It was all so ludicrous, I couldn't help but look down on myself in a ridiculous out-of-body experience and laugh. Again, another pattern you'll see throughout this book is that one minute you're up against the profound isolation and inhumanity of prison - but you're surrounded by comforts many can only dream of, like underfloor heating, £7 Nescafé Gold coffee, and free slippers! I rushed to get changed and joined the queue for the gym.

My only frustration in this gaff is the volume of the knuckle-draggers. This wouldn't change. Sadly, the estate is riddled with under-25s (known as YOs - Youth Offenders) who are mostly fighting for attention and status, and are a massive, annoying pain in the tuchus - just like in real life. They're like chest-beating gorillas at Lincoln Zoo. Deafening. Insufferable. Facking annoying! Old farts like me aren't impressed by all this bloody peacocking and showing off. Sadly, the gym often attracts the worst lanky streaks of piss who think they're Hulk Hogan - a load of pimple-popping, moronic imbeciles competing and vying for affirmation whilst grabbing their dangly bits. My life has moments of spotlights, mics, and attention - but 99% of it is private, quiet, and, contrary to popular belief, respectfully shushy and douchebag-free. I don't like big-mouths, and I HATE show-offs more than drag queens in libraries. I don't like willy-waggling, fluffed-up baby buffoons trying to be top monkey. The prison corridors are 100% the worst thing about these asylums. Over time, I've found ways to avoid the brain-dead - but brawn-blessed. The bovine 'conversation' is excruciating. I learnt you have to say 'like' after every third word - like. Surprisingly, though, the gym has been my daily saviour. I stick to the cross-dresser and treadmill, miles away from the Justin Bieber lookalikes. Even now, I go five times a week, and it has been a sanctuary for sanity. I do some of my clearest and most creative thinking on the rower!

What I never would have guessed about prison life is that someone like me is invisible to twats. I have a cloak of invisibility by being on the verge of a gammon. Seriously - they're too busy flooding the jail with spice, the deadly drug of choice for people with an IQ lower than their shoe size. On the out (i.e. not in jail), it's known as Mamba - the zombie drug. These people can't see beyond the end of their nose, let alone a

YouTube gobshite like me who'd dumbfound their obnoxious stupidity. I simply don't exist - which is wonderful! Prisoners find their own tribe and world. 'Birds of a feather' defines the slammer.

I guess just like real life, it's fair to say you create your own jail. It can either be torture - or - you just get on with it and exorcise and delete all the pilchards and donuts that surround you. I was on a cross-dresser next to two silver-tops who were perfectly pleasant. The whippersnapper steroid types were miles down the other end, lifting their own body weight with their pinky. Imagine being blessed with abs but no ability to link a sentence. Prison is clearly identical to *Love Island*! The ONLY thing that scared me was how normal this all felt. Why wasn't I terrified? Why didn't I feel violated? How was I able to take it all in my stride? I'm meant to be crying hysterically - not cavorting to Daft Punk's 'One More Time' in the 'nasium.

I promise you, on my parents' lives, that walking into a toxic cesspit of a BBC newsroom - with a toilet full of journalists - is a hundred times more stress and anxiety-inducing (and intimidating) than walking onto, through, or off the wing. At least here, you have a clear knowledge of what crimes these people have committed - and what they're capable of. I saw this first 24 hours as I have every day since: simply a social experiment to test my tenacity, character, and strength - to create content for these HMP exposés and, quite simply, survive. The separate gym building has showers, CV, weights, and tennis/badminton courts. It's basically David Lloyd without the toffee-nosed receptionist and £60-a-month subscription. You even get a full-on disco to help with the chafing on the inner thighs. I was up down, up down... and then the other eyelid. I did forty minutes running on the spot - I'd got my handcuffs trapped on the elliptical! One of the more recent realisations of the Ministry of Justice is that punishment doesn't work. So, the system now tries to pacify, distract, and basically bribe you to behave - through luxuries that some would argue should never be given in a prison in the first place. Exercise for the millennium man is paramount. Mental 'elf and all that jazz. I've never seen so many effeminate, well-groomed, pristine-looking fellas. It's like the *Next* catalogue on most wings. I guess the generation below me are brainwashed by the David Beckham types - the kind who seemingly take longer in the bathroom than their once hot and previously attractive, now rather dour wives... whose downstairs area resembles, well, a dolphin's beak.

The gym is truly one of the safest places in the slammer, as it's a benefit the lads do not want to lose. They take it very seriously and won't let halfwits sabotage their workout. Any dopes with shenanigans are quickly put in their place. I have to admit - from day one - you tend to find a more intelligent breed of prisoner in the gym, as you have to have a level of discipline and decorum to be there in the first place. Whereas spice losers and smackheads are too lazy and medicated to even get out of bed. For me, it was an obvious escape - to some form of social interaction, normality, and of course, literally getting out of the cell. The byproduct of 'wellbeing' was a Brucie Bonus. Why wouldn't you use this hostage situation to get fit? Over time, I've met some top men in there. I'm up to five kilos on the leg press! I can now bench-press the equivalent of three bags of anthracite! I'll keep at it. Maybe I could use this time to get fit. I get out of breath playing *Scrabble* since the trial! I've never seen one fight, scuffle, or even an argy-bargy in the gym - ever. It's far safer than collecting your afternoon tea at the servery! The screws who work in there are normally great too, as Personal Instructors are civvies - not civil serpent types, brainwashed on Prison Service courses and tarnished by the evil of the clink.

Solidarity amongst men is inspiring. I was amazed how there is an undeniable honour amongst thieves. They stick up for each other, and in many cases have absolutely nothing other than this world to live for. No family, no true friends - just their community! This is their world. I'm not going to pretend for a moment that my situation was remotely normal or average - it was not. But I guess you quickly have to find your own clan. Like magnets, you instinctively sense who you can connect with - and equally who to avoid like the plague. You can see evil, BTW. Yep - blatantly obvious who the complete nasty and deranged bastards are. AVOID!!! However, I have to admit they're few and far between. You learn to read people in a heartbeat in here. You have to! Fight or flight. I'm no Mike Tyson......I need other means to assert respect. Prison has a pecking order. The weak and feeble are bullied. I was having none of that nonsense! What a baptism of fire – and it's not even 3pm!

Regardless of their crime, as a nosey parker I was endlessly fascinated by their story. My lesson from day one was that, in most cases, it was never as simple as it appeared. The law is often nothing to do with justice. Even the idea that you can be held hostage on remand - before being found guilty - is spine-tingling and terrifying! What power of the state, hey? Who decides that? Why should we trust them, knowing how corrupt and inept so many government agencies are? I looked around me, and I was surrounded by Panting Peacock Peters, Muscle Marys, and Tattooed Tommys - all having another out-of-body experience, like in any gym in the world. I couldn't help but wonder why these men went to so much effort. Who were they trying to impress? What purpose or function did this serve, other than <u>distraction</u>? Prison is entirely about remaining alive and human. At my medical, I was weighed in at 86 kilos. No, me neither - can I have that in stones, please? What would I be in 2025? Would prison literally eat me alive? The sheer strength of these brutes was astonishing. They took their diet and physicality <u>very</u> seriously. I found this inspiring - that they keep the faith and hope. This did beg the question: how many screws could handle these bonny lads and hench brutes if they kicked off? Isn't this a total own goal for HMP? Bizarrely though, these Gladiators were out of breath walking back to the wing. Fitness, I guess, is all in the eye of the beholder. The one thing the MOJ have worked out is that, for HMP to avoid hourly riots - keeping men busy, fit, and fed - is the key to keeping prisons calm and self-regulating. Trust me - without the help of stud muffins, officers would be in great danger and prisons would collapse! One thing is for sure: the lads are a thousand times fitter than the laughable screws, who seem to do a passable impression of Peter Kay. The appalling fitness of 70% of the HMP staff is hysterically woeful. It's like *The Benny Hill Show* when things kick off! A bit like hospital doctors and nurses - it staggers me how unhealthy and ill-equipped most are. It's a joke! Of course, in our virtue signalling world, we can no longer test their fitness, as turning down someone because they're a fatty or greedy guts is apparently discriminating. What a load of old bollocks! I've never seen so many unhealthy slobs in my life.

Don't Drop the Soap and Getting Bummed in the Shower?!

After a sweaty work out fifty men need a shower. There was <u>NO WAY</u> I was using those gym showers, so now what? Look, full disclosure, I'm hung like a jelly baby and a penitentiary is no place to audition my micro penis in front of these Magic Mike auditionees. I have many blessings and talents - but my half an inch and a dozen wrinkles ain't one of them! Would the showers be my first reality check of the bromantic and homoerotic rumours of the 'bum boy bang-up club?' I do hope not. What with my bad back and refusal to endure pain, I'm not buggering about! The current Mrs B would be furious - I might enjoy it! I can assure you - I'd have to be the train, not the tunnel. This lifestyle is not for me. I won't even use a communal toilet in case I get the Monkey Aids! You can, you know - if you sit down before the other chunky has stood up...

What this period taught me about the trolls and the mentals is their relentless projection - and fascination with what they believe I am, and, in fact, who they'd like me to be. As YouTube was on fire with my demise, these cuckoo imbeciles went into overdrive. From 'he'll be banned from talking when he comes out' to 'he'll get raped in the showers' - these perversions of perverts couldn't be further from the truth. As my police report proves – I'm the most boring man in showbiz. There's literally <u>nothing</u> to see here. I hate to disappoint the dark web surfing wankers in their mother's back bedroom, but jail in 2022 - is not their creepy fantasy.

My prison pros advised me that one of the most important items in your sin bag was a pair of flip flops. I've got two left feet - so I have a pair of 'Flip Flips.' I've always been a very clean person, and that won't change! Call me talentless, fat, and ugly, and I couldn't give two shiny shites - but say I've got BO or halitosis that could strip the paint off a Nissan Urinator, and I'll kick you in the goolies!

For the record, there are <u>no</u> open showers anywhere in <u>any</u> wing I've ever been on. They're all private cubicles - for total discretion. So sadly, this isn't the noncy fantasy that my creepy hecklers knock one out to! Grow up, get a life, get out of mine, get a proper job, and get matron to up your meds! I hate to disappoint. I have to admit - I've never been one for public nudity. Regardless, in fact, I don't even show my arms in public - what with my excessive back fat and under-moob sweating!

The last thing I want is to bump into some hairy-arsed con dropping his six-foot, pendulous ball sack in front of twenty willy-wagging whippersnappers. Not for me dear heart. Sadly, I have many superior talents and advantages, but my miniscule schlong and droopy gunt ain't one of them! So, I'm glad we've cleared that up early doors. No one can see anything other than my flip flops under the shower flap doors. Sorry to disappoint Gary Glitter fans.

Within days, I timed my ablutions so that I virtually never saw anyone whatsoever in the shower. I still smile that my verruca avoiders are from the St Pancras Hotel Spa. These flip flops have seen every second of this kidnapping - through the good, the bad, and the ugly slammers. A spa couldn't be more incongruous if they were from Captain Tom's hot tub. I told you not to clap for that NHS charity crap, didn't I!!! Another vindication via my cynicism of Piers Morgan–promoted do-gooders! Anyway, that's not why you called... So, I wasn't remotely worried about public bathing, as towel protectors are de rigueur. No - my main (and only) interminable annoyance is the blistering and relentless, adrenaline-fuelled, deafening banter, which would terrify the patience of any sentient human being. The endless cubicle-to-cubicle mass debate is enough to put anyone off showering publicly. Listen, I'm no fun, I'm not! I might have a witty line on-air, or can even captivate an audience for two hours in Blackpool - but the idea of chipping in with a load of heckling hyenas, or man-tit-pounding gorillas all competing for alpha status whilst smothering *TRESemmé* on my gonads ain't for me. I love that old line: 'Are you a man or a mouse?' I say, 'Pass me the cheese!' God, banter is banal. Hideous. Pass me my earmuffs!

My conclusion is that most real gobshites are reserved and never compete for attention. Weak, thick, unconfident, talentless pricks have tribes, packs, and gangs - creating their deafening, inaudible cacophony of racket! Twitter proves you don't need a fortnight in HMP Lincoln to work this out. Group and pack mentality doesn't work for me. I'd rather migrate to two sensible, interesting, quiet, and considerate people than a group of a hundred vying to be the centre-of-attention morons - not my style. Sadly, jail is ALL about which gang you're in. Believe it or not, my preferred clan is unseeable. That way, I can pick and choose who I do - and don't - talk to. On MY terms. Coping with fart heads would be my only challenge in jail.

I think one of the reasons I'm in this mess is that I never wanted to be in with the showbiz 'gang.' I don't enjoy theatre, TV, or radio parties or opening nights - as most journalists and show-offs are boring and creepy. And I can't stomach 'reality' types. I don't want to sip champagne with Eric Gill or Savile to look cool at BBC parties - I never did. There're a LOT of these double-life-living hypocrites around - trust me! Being on the outside looking in is far more powerful and effective than being a brown-noser who schmoozes at powder-snorting parties, blowing smoke up low-rent, medicated luvvies. If they're not shoving stuff up their noses, they're sticking it up their bottoms! Not my bag. Being on the outside, you have far greater leverage for mockery. Once you join the showbiz mafia - you're all in on it together.

There are more blind eyes turned than you can shake a stick at! I just can't play that game. I never have. Pretending, acting, 'playing the game,' and fakeness is my nemesis. I can smell it like a London Marathon port-a-loo. Instead, I'll keep myself to myself in jail - just like I did on the outside. I'll watch, remember, write, and mind my own business! A very smart move. Little did I know that the phoney-baloney probation 'Offender Managers,' who determine your freedom and fecklessly slither through the corridors of HMP, would make BBC weasels and media saboteurs look like UN peace negotiators. I hadn't even been in custody 24 hours and already had the education of a lifetime. What an awakening!

So far, I've learned THE BIGGEST RULE IN JAIL IS never ask permission – just beg forgiveness. If you ask, they'll say no. So, use your judgement and do what you need to do to survive. If it goes wrong, what could they do? I was in prison for the love of God - it could hardly get any worse! I also realised I NEVER wanted any of these goons telling me what to do - EVER - so I'd have to always be ahead of the game! There are strict rules, though - and you don't want to cross the line. The one place no prisoner EVER wants to end up is the 'Seg.' Also known as 'the block,' and CASU - Cell Assessment Segregation Unit. 'The block' is the final port of call before you're either kicked off your wing - and most likely sent to a higher-security prison - or given punishment for something serious. With huge overcrowding and the estate on the verge of collapse, the Seg is much harder to get into. You really have to be violent, or be caught with serious contraband, to end up there. In private jails, there are only sixteen spaces for seventeen hundred men. Most prisoners who aren't bonkers don't go anywhere near this typically rat-infested end of the line in the pokey. At HMP Lincoln, it's seen as 'the dungeon' of the slammer - the highest security part of any prison - which is 23.5 hours a day 'bang-up' (locked door with no TV, no personal clothes, or items)…. well, at HMP. This ain't the case at HMPontins private holiday camps. Food is delivered to your door, and you have no human interaction with anyone - for total social deprivation. Often, drugs and violence are involved, so this makes perfect sense. The Seg can also be used for relationships with officers, which falls under corruption. It happens more than you'd imagine! It's the very end of the line - total sensory starvation. But what does it actually achieve? It seems like a barbaric and outdated punishment. And of course, everyone up in the Seg isn't exactly the sharpest tool in the shed. They know no better. They're often heavily medicated and ill - with very shocking pasts. They're angry and lost. Often, they need serious help, none of which HMP appears to provide. The BIGGEST problem with HMP is that there's no safety net at any stage for any 'head-the-balls.' They don't fix you. When it kicks off, they just keep shifting prisoners around - wing to wing - akin to moving deckchairs around the Titanic.

To get out of the Seg, there is an internal 'court' in every prison - with a board of three senior governors who decide your fate, determined by the seriousness of your actions. Violence against an officer will almost certainly have you moved prisons. A riot will end up in a criminal prosecution, resulting in around five to ten extra years. An argy-bargy between inmates will just get you moved to another wing and a slap on the wrist. In the worst cases, they can even tack on an extra forty days to your sentence - worrying, hey? Especially for someone as high-profile as me! Kick-offs are far too regular to kick up a fuss. They implement 'losses' on your personal account for anything broken and stop your canteen, but frankly this has little or no impact - but why? OK, most of the bad lads are up to shenanigans with drugs or phones. This is worth £1,000s per week. Stopping £33 a week sent in from 'home' is chicken shit. It appears to me prisons have totally given up on the rife drugs issue - both dealing and taking. All I hear is: 'You'll never stop it.' That's because so many staff and officers are the ones bringing it in - and ultimately profiting.

So, the pokey is every man for himself! You come into jail and leave prison alone. The system is like a leaky sieve - where the biggest whack jobs fall through, and the fattest bullies often profit. It's survival of the fittest, and you're either a tiger or a nymphlike gazelle running for your life. Lads can get class A drugs in induction easier than a toothbrush. I'm not working you from behind. It's a woefully inept and broken system. Officers are powerless in this cat and mouse game and are beaten by the scale of the multi-agency failings. My only remaining <u>BIG</u> issue, that I would have to resolve, is the million-dollar slammer question – I'm not bothered about a bag of weed, but how do I get a toilet roll?

Chapter 6

First Day Done

Saturday had come and gone in a flash. It was now 4pm, and Vinnie the snoozy sloth had barely moved. I couldn't resist asking, "Have you done anything today?" He said, "Yes - I got my lunch and had my shower." Fair enough. This was a huge lesson that blew my mind: it's all just a big waste of time. No wonder so many lazy bastards and social derelicts love prison life - nothing matters.

Unlike 'real' life, where you can delude yourself that you have worth, a value, and that what you do matters - in here, the screaming truth is we're all just wasting life until the pause button is un-pressed, and play can resume. I told myself - in the chauffeur-driven sardine truck from the Clown Court - that my entire ethos of efficiency had to stop in that second. I immediately needed a new pace. Having any notion of time, purpose, or productivity was totally out the window for now. Total acceptance and zero rebellion. Give Up - this is literally a complete waste of doing time!

The keys jangled again. Fack me - that door was opened and closed more than Julia Roberts' legs in Pretty Woman! I wonder what delights would be offered now? Once again, we both jumped to our feet in a virtual excitement of the next free meal. "Bring your bowl there's soup" Vinster said. WOW! Soup. Who knew? Hope it wasn't that Heinz lumpy shit. We turned left –

very important to follow the big circle rule to the servery, where I was handed a 'breakfast pack,' milk, a double sandwich (4 slices), crisps, and biscuits. How the hell would I juggle all off this with a bowl of soup? I was shocked, it actually looked like soup. I put the spoon in the huge green thermos gloup cauldron. Was it tomato and basil OR had there been a nasty accident with a carving knife in the kitchens? You'd be amazed how quickly you adapt to food of no specific origin, taste, title, or even identifiable ingredients. I tried to pick up my stash and dropped my milk. A nice young man picked it up for me - as if I was some pitiful pensioner having dropped my dobber at the Gala Bingo. WOW. I was speechless - you wouldn't get that in a Toby Carvery in Wigan if a Yorkshire Pudding fell to its crashing end. Asta-la-Bisto baby! It'd be trampled before you could ask for more sprouts. I carefully climbed the stairs, yards from our pad, praying I didn't make a complete prick of myself again - by dropping my entire 'tea' and falling arse over tit up those metal stairs. I should join a circus with those juggling skills. I managed it. Phew. Last thing I need is forty nonces taking the piss on my opening night debut.

BANG. Door closed – well, slammed - and locked by another anonymous screw that I'd never see again. How many of these penguin-looking key turners are there? I presume there's no turn-down service at this hotel? So that's that - 4.30pm, and the day is done until 9am tomorrow when it starts again. I always wondered what it's like to go to university.

The most miraculous thing about prison life is how noisy and loud the wings can be - only matched by how silent it is once 'roll check' (the 'behind doors' head count) is completed. In the space of five minutes, it goes from frantic rushing and chaos to an oasis of silence and calm - befitting the serenity of a health farm in Hertfordshire. An extraordinary contrast. I now realise how very lucky I've been - as some jails are like an Eminem concert 24/7. HMP have now banned music players big enough to fill Wembley - but if you already had one, you were allowed to keep it. And then, on departure, they're meant to hand them in - but cons naturally sell them on to other gangster types, motivated by an incessant 'N'-word filth pounding with a Radio 1Xtra bassline. Enough to send you crackers - with the 'Big up Beats' making the furniture shake at 7am. Very rarely have I had to endure this excruciating, annoying, selfish nonsense. I'm told it's insufferable in a lot of the London jails.

This was very early days, but already I could see how this place of shushy confinement does have a certain cocoon-like quality - one that could easily become completely comforting by regime. You regress to being a big baby. Everything is about dictated, unmovable, non-negotiable routine. REGIME is the backbone of compliance and discipline. This is a major problem for those who don't like being told what to do. Before long, you're braindead - walking round like a zombie, not knowing if you're in Morecambe Bay or Bombay. The lads LOVE it - and live by it. It's their comfort blanket: every day is identical to the last - to the second! They cannot handle it changing, which is why private jails are a complete disaster for the cons who are disproportionately neurodiverse......which, in my day, meant 'a pain in the arse' or a troublemaker. Without any concern for the cost-of-living crisis, petrol prices, wars in Ukraine or Gaza - this, in fact, could be the dream life for those losers with no ambition or prospects. Everything is done for you. You are required to think about nothing. Zero responsibility. How liberating! Come to think of it - the system doesn't like it when you do think......that totally undermines them. I looked again at the white BT phone on the desk. It was there - but useless. It's like going into a strip club with no money. The tease of an 'old-fashioned' phone sitting in front of you - winking at you, glaring at you, and laughing at you - because you're a forty-two-year-old grown man. Boohoo, baby. Waiting for a twenty-five-year-old lefty, box-ticking, vegan, non-binary 'Public Protection' executive on the minimum wage to activate your numbers so you can phone your mother. What a reality check. This seemed 50% hysterical on the one hand and 60% tragic on the other. I'm no Suzie Dent! The irony was – 'Vinnie the Siesta Fest' had all his phone numbers approved, yet didn't have the energy, inclination, or want to call any of them. Depressing, hey?

For the first time in my life, I had time to properly relax and reflect... not worrying about anything. I hadn't had a single night in forty years with nothing scheduled in the diary, or some issue to resolve. Equally, I'd been so busy I hadn't had a chance to drink in the enormity and success of the last three years. I've never felt the emotion of boredom - or mental freedom from pressure or responsibility - in my life. Even as a kid, I had three hundred hobbies - or the piano - to occupy my mind non-stop. I couldn't comprehend the feeling of nothingness. I had lived this insidiously dark world day in and day out, covering news since 1997 - when I started in radio at *BBC Nottingham*. Finally, staying ahead of the trending news algorithms was someone else's problem - but no longer mine. In times of crisis, you have to be at peace with yourself. You have to rationalise why you're in the situation you're in. You have to own your failings and mistakes and stand back to see the bigger picture. Equally, you need perspective on what you <u>haven't</u> done. Clarity would be my <u>only</u> saviour, and a clear conscience would be freeing. I was steadfast in what had happened - and for what reason. I'd reconciled that LONG ago. I would now use my forty years of survival skills and coping mechanisms to come out stronger, wiser, cleverer - and armed with a series of books to flog down the market to pay for Doddy's Pedigree Chum. If that fails, I might be eating dog food too - and have to sell my body. Tarquin (my producer) reckons I could get £1 an inch......I've got change! I'd better get my *Bic* out sharpish and start scribbling!

In this type of character assassination, witch hunt, and public takedown, you have to ask only THREE QUESTIONS......1) Do your loved ones know the truth? 2) Do they know the full story? 3) Do they still love you? It was a big triple YES for me! I could rest easy, knowing in my heart I'd been royally facked via a new made-up crime. But none of it matters - as no one believed it, other than those in on the conspiracy. I will not surrender to bullies, and I know in my heart the truth will out in the end. I just needed to see this as another laborious showbiz contract and get to the end - not dissimilar to a gig on the cruise ships. At the end of the day... it gets dark.

I made myself comfortable on my bed as the Autumn TV schedules were in full swing. *Strictly* took up two hours. I'd never watched it before. Honestly, I can't see what all the fuss was about. Another one of the BBC's 'private company' programmes that Studios profit from - whilst still pretending the licence fee is their lifeblood. Lying bastards! I've never watched so much unadulterated telly shite in my entire life! I had no idea you could have thirty-five channels - thirty of which repeat the same crap that the others have already repeated the week before. Having led a full, fun, and varied life, I did not have time for guff like Michael McIntyre's *'The Wheel'* - or the relentless creepy drag shows that the MSM appear to be obsessed with - featuring shady, unhinged and seemingly unstable freaks of nature. I shudder at these degenerates. Why do so many end up ten toes up so young? A tragic woke reality! It seems to me that any attention-seeking ambivilacious dope - with no sense of humour or life experience - can pop on their Aunty Fanny's frock, borrow their non-binary brother's handbag....and suddenly appear on Primetime TV with no act. Woeful. Urggg. Shouldn't the Mental Health Act protect us from this mindless cack? I have a feeling Barrymore, Noel Edmonds, and Cilla Black would be turning in their TV graves over this benign, turgid, inane, and inoffensive crap. Vinnie Nytol didn't even ask for the remote, he was already comatosed in the corner. He's the lucky one! As I watched the mincing D listers on Strictly my mind began to wander…...

I couldn't help but recollect that the week before, I was in a dressing room - about to walk out to a sell-out crowd on the North Pier. The most insane, mind-blowing reality in this moment was the incongruous and laughable 'click of my fingers' 360° change in my life and lifestyle just seven days later. The loss of liberty was the least of my worries. The state of this mattress and bedding had much more to be desired. I pondered how, a week ago, I was of no risk to society - allowed to stand in front of hundreds in Blackpool - yet this week, I was behind a locked door: gagged, silenced, portrayed as a danger and a hostage to the state. This foolishness is made even more unbelievable, as the government have today instructed judges to delay sentencing of serious criminals (including rapists) - because prisons are full! So here I am, sat writing this book - paid for by British taxpayers at £48k per year - whilst rapists roam free after conviction. Can a convicted talker really be more dangerous than a violent nutcase or sex attacker? Two-tier justice at its most insane! The answer is a screaming YES……if you're protecting the power, influence, and legacy of unscrupulous establishment associates. How can anyone take such incomprehensible tomfoolery and illogical lunacy seriously?

About 9pm, Rohypnol Vinnie woke for his evening meal of noodles and crisps – I can't see Rosemary Conley approving. I had a thought, 'are we allowed to phone our lawyers?' Vinnie said, "No! They have to be approved as well." Wow! So, you are removed from society, and they miraculously prevent you from speaking to your solicitor - whose full details you're unlikely to have. It gets better - "Oh, and if you don't have phone credit you can't phone them at all. It's not free!" This was the most astonishing revelation so far. How can this onerous codswallop be fair and just? Could I be the first person to notice this flaw in the matrix? What a brilliant way of ripping the carpet from under often broken and desperate men. Those 'up-stairs' will claim they have no idea of this 'damned if you do, facked if you don't' vortex of bureaucracy. Surely legal calls should be free? The cost of phone calls is the next issue. There's no 'all-you-can-use' package for £35 a month like civvies enjoy with BT. Nope - it's 18p a minute on mobiles during the day. At least twenty-minute rip-off calls with your rip-off lawyers are a thing of the past. You know it's bad when your phone bill is more expensive than your barrister! With top HMP wages at £12 a week, you'll have to keep your gossip down to the *Countdown* theme tune. Prison is two-tiered - just like policing. The haves and the have nots. Being alone and penniless in the nick is <u>NO</u> fun. There is literally no safety net - and you're left to sink. For them to weaponize the phone – men's lifeline – is truly astonishing!

By 11pm, I'd had enough of bottom burp tawdry TV. I turned the light off. By the way, a lot of people ask, 'What time is lights out?' - we have our own lights. Human Rights, my friends! We can have the electricity running up the clock 24/7 if we choose - and may do so. The days of 8pm darkness and silence have gone. I'd hate for murderers and terrorists to miss *Open University* on BBC2 at 3am......sorry, I forgot - they'll probably be on their Xboxes, puffing vapes, snorting SPICE, eating Thornton's chocolates, or watching TUG TV on their iPhone.

NONE OF US know what we're capable of until we're pushed to our limits. My achievement of surviving day one was complete. Who knows how I'll climb the other 911 days of this Kilimanjaro test of endurance, but at least I've got off to a good start.

Chapter 7

Darkness of the Deviant Depository

Darkness in jail is much darker than at home - which is strange, as I have posh and pricey blackout curtains (essential for all gingers when horizontally jogging!). I can understand why so many prisoners don't survive jail - they give up, go mad, lose all hope, or are eaten alive by their guilt. You have to have immense inner strength and character to cope with the absolute isolation. The constant obstacles that the institution presents to you daily are a lot to process and reconcile. The paranoia - that the door can open with six tattooed goons waiting to shanghai you to another shithole - never leaves you. I've always had an inner voice to calm my nerves. I guess we all have this right? Please tell me we all have an inner dialogue! 'Hearing' and knowing yourself is essential in life – especially in such captive colostomy bags of shitty times. As a kid, I was so unpopular even my imaginary best friend said he had to draw the line and move on to pastures new. None taken. In life, we talk ourselves sane and rationalise our actions. You can't trust ANYONE 100% in jail – other than yourself. Can we trust anyone 100% in 'real' life? What a responsibility on your own judgement and mind! I've always done this - especially on-air - I'm forever saying to myself 'don't say that Belfield' – in a very stern voice – 'you're in enough shit as it is.' Your inner courage will be your only salvation in the nick - you have to keep hearing yourself, like a parrot perched on your shoulder, screaming the reminder.

For me, the darkness often generates great light, and at the very least, massive clarity and <u>PERSPECTIVE</u>. I felt this during the worst of lockdown and Covid. I could see straight through the treacle of PR - and focused on the holy grail of freedom without distraction. Some people in life pander to negativity, I always look for the dream of better days. Love is the only thing that will save your sanity and life in the slammer.

The prison schedule, however, would re-write all of my life rules. Forty years of waking up at 10am(ish) were over. Now I'd be erect at 7.30am. I had no idea there was two 7.30s in a day! As if things weren't bad enough in my life, now I'd have to watch Naga Manshushy on BBC Breakfast. Total insult to injury! Could things get any worse? Is this what they call restorative justice? If during a nightmare I fell asleep on the remote, I'd wake up to Ed Balls on GMTV – for the love of God, haven't I been punished enough? One day he'll learn how to read an autocue. I'd stick to politics, love. Anywho, TV was dominated by Her Majesty, who had died - leaving many of us questioning our faith in the monarchy. The world was never the same after our glorious Queen passed, ten days earlier.

On a personal level, I would have loved to have gone to London for her funeral. I adored and completely respected her, unlike the rest, who I have little, or no time for. Harry and Andrew, to me, are arseholes - but, as an ideology, I love that we have a faultless and flawless leader who could get us through the very worst of times whilst being 100% consistent. Time will tell if King

Charles (Spaniel) will live up to expectations......in between hugging trees. We certainly didn't have a leader in Boris Johnson, who had now been unceremoniously dismissed as Prime Minister - along with his disgusting, adulterous, and duplicitous Health Secretary Matt Handcock - prior to the Queen's departure from this mortal coil. What a pair of unrelenting hypocritical twunts 'Johnson & Cock' are! A perfect pair. They should be in here – NOT ME! I will never forgive them for the convid lies. What a pair of covidiots!!! I think us naysayers are all now vindicated, don't you?

You can say what you like about me, but I do seem to be a very good judge of character. I'd called out those two sickening slithering vomits two years before - when they lied to our nation over lockdowns and seemingly anything else that excreted from their lips. My cynicism about Baroness Mone, Janette McCranky, and the other WHO/WEF puppets wasn't far off the mark either. Totally unaccountable, our government allowed £5 billion+ in business bonus bollocking fraud - and, it transpires, shamelessly made a lot of their mates, colleagues, landlords, and acquaintances very rich through dodgy PPE deals. Dear God - our country is a laughingstock. You know it's bad - when you feel sorry for Les Truss and Rishi Washy Sunak! His 'Eat Out a Friend' campaign was the only good thing to come out of lockdown! What a time to be alive in September 2022! We had no monarch, a disgraced Prime Minister who was sent packing - and now we have a lucky librarian running the country, who destroyed our economy with 11% inflation! I sometimes wonder if I'm the lucky one - being financed by the state in the Bullshitter's B&B. They can't touch you in here. I've got three fences of protection and two hundred and fifty officers to protect me! You've got Biden, Cameltoe Harris, Putin, and Angela Rayner to contend with!

Prison is not a bed of roses. I'm not going to sugar coat it. If you have a life, loved ones, a brain, ambition, a joy for life – not to mention a creative streak – this is not the place for you. Isolation is cancer of the soul. The entire system is designed to strip you of <u>EVERYTHING</u> - including your self-respect, dignity, confidence, and all aspirations and belongings. So how do most survive in the slammer? Hundreds of people die in custody each year in the UK. How could I be certain that I wouldn't be the star of my own funeral? After all, that's what my establishment assassins wanted, right? They didn't go to all this effort for me to be a martyr - and come out stronger. Just 48 hours into custody, I'd realised that my inner strength was gathered from decades of love and support from the best friends and family in the world. My character, tenacity, defiance, and determination came from forty-plus years of having the best parents in the world, the most supportive and loving sister ever - and, unlike those poor souls above - a heart full of love. Sometimes though, that love has to be managed. Too much love can be like a fireworks display - tormenting and destructive. Since being in custody, I have - for the first time - learned what true heartache is. I mean REAL heartache - not boohoo/woe-is-me attention-seeking victimhood, which so many of the 2020+ lefties rely on.

When the door slams and the key turns, you ain't getting out. If someone you love dies, you ain't going to the funeral. If someone you adore is seriously injured – you're powerless and useless. This is a mega burden and huge strain. You are - by definition, constricted, restricted, contained, controlled, and utterly impotent. These crucifying emotions MUST be managed and monitored. Back in the day you had shit buckets. 'Proper' prison is brutal - and there is no question that I would not have coped. These days, you have Amazon deliveries, fruit and veg, sound systems, PlayStations, and a telephone. It's now a crappy Novotel! I'm not as strong as many believe. Contrary to the mental loons online - I'm only human. Alone, I am useless. Without people, I'm nothing - and without conversation, I might as well give in and be playing at my own 'celebration of life.' There is no question that my forty years of battles with every shithead in Showbiz will not collectively compare to the energy and strength I'll need to get to June 2025 - when the first part of this shambles will be over. The only way I'll do it is by keeping busy. If not, the consequences would be fatal. It's ALL about resilience!

When you arrive in prison, you have to go through a series of inductions - I don't mean like in the army, where you have to pleasure yourself in front of the General and 'arrive' on a Ginsters pasty...No, no! I mean that each department in the clink signs you up to their box-ticking paperwork - so they get paid once you 'engage.' Prison is a BUSINESS! Slowly, but surely, the gym, education, safeguarding, NHS - all came round one by one to get you to sign your life away. Like all corporates in 2020+, everyone is risk averse. Providing they've got you to sign on the dotted line, their arse is covered. Once you've signed on the dotted line 'they' can get paid. Repeat after me – prison is one big business! Prison is one <u>big</u> business. Every conversation is written up on your official file called 'NOMIS.' All this stuff will live forever! Be very careful what you say. There's no neighbourhood watch in prison <u>BUT</u>, there is a snooper's charter that will bite you in the ass for the rest of your sentence. From day one you're being profiled. Every interaction is reported on your record. Stay schtum!!!

Luckily for me, one of the first knocks on the door was from the Chaplaincy. Bums on seats is big business in prison. Everyone is vying for your attention - it's all about funding, and the chapel is no different. If you're not happy with Jesus, there's always a line of other good books to tickle your trout. I was tickled pink. I've always adored churches - they're works of art. Could HMP be on par with Lincoln's glorious cathedral? A lot of what is said (and how it's said) is not my cup of tea - however, it is a 'safe space' and a place where I could avoid so many of the lost souls, imbeciles, and nut jobs who clutter these 'Maisons de Morons.' That blend of irreverence and introspection is pure dynamite. A very nice man invited me along at 10am and I was 'on the list.' Being 'on the list' is <u>critical</u> in the slammer. Security is inconsistent, but you certainly won't get in or out of anywhere without being invited.........or have a <u>very</u> good reason. If you do - and you're caught – even if it's to pop in to see God – you can get in serious shit! You'll be given a 'nicking' and you'll be sent to an adjudication by a top Gov - who will decide your fate for the security breach of being in the wrong place at the wrong time. It doesn't take a rocket scientist to work out that knowing exactly where cons are is paramount to security - especially in CAT-Bs. At 9.45am, the door opened, and I was told to wait by the back entrance. Not what you want to hear on a 'VP' wing! I hadn't had such an obscene request since my fortnight on work experience at *This Morning.* VP guests are escorted separately from the rest of the prison - for their protection. Alas, once in, you still sit together in *God's Big House* - so the plan, like so many, is flawed before the service has even started! You're an easy target on a pew. My concern wasn't being attacked; it was more about which despicable nonce would sit next to me. As for 'blind faith' - sadly, I currently have 20/20 vision!

A lot of people have asked me what it's like to have to live with such animals and scum. Well, the way I viewed it is - you have no idea who is living next door in society. You could argue knowledge is power. At least here, I could be extra cautious - as they're in plain sight. This didn't hit me until twelve months later, when I was sent to my first 'mixed' private jail - HMP Five Wells. I found myself working next to a BBC paedo who'd been sentenced to twenty-two years via 'Operation Yewtree' for raping underaged boys. Is this a sick joke?

Some - like me - were on the VP wing simply because of their profile. Others were evil nonces, shoved into a dustbin of depravity - under the misguided belief that they can be trained not to rape kids and leave rehabilitated. It's a volatile and toxic mix. This tapestry of crackpots puts me in mind of a *Question Time* taping at Media City. You simply can't judge or tell who is what - but my 'third eye' did become powerful! Instinct is *so* important in jail. I was cordial to everyone - but 95% of the time, I didn't give the time of day. Having said that, it doesn't take long for word to spread. The rehabilitation of sex offenders is nonce nonsense. I don't believe any amount of counselling or therapy can change what you are attracted to. Impossible. Makes no rational sense, other than to righteous lefties - who believe everyone deserves a second chance. I do not! It is therefore my belief that these demons will always be a danger to society - regardless of any worthy, virtue-signalling, box-ticking jiggery-pokery by HMP limp-wristed do-gooders. I beg of you to dig deep. In the privacy of your own mind - do you really believe I could convince you to be attracted to something you don't like...let alone a child? Absolutely NOT! If you can, hand yourself into your nearest police station ASAP! I've heard a lot of perverts claim - 'I came across child images on the internet' - did you bollocks! I've Googled all sorts of Tug TV for thirty years and never once found a single inappropriate image of a child - EVER! You cannot be dissuaded from fancying what you are attracted to. This is why 100% proven paedos should be incarcerated for life - or given an irreversible injection. To normal humans, this is obvious. Oh, and no, I don't think nonces are 'normal.' Not PC, but the honest opinion of 99% of normal people – who aren't paedos.

I truly did not get involved with anyone at Lincoln – for two very good reasons: Firstly, there literally wasn't time - we were out for one hour a day, and I was busy cleaning, showering, or exercising. Secondly, I certainly didn't want to get into discussions about my 'crime,' let alone what they had done. This was a burden and distraction I didn't want on my shoulders. Once I moved to a   CAT-C this will be very different. You have no choice but to interact. Unlike the BBC, I was hoping my next clink would be a sex pest or nonce deviant free zone.

Five of us waited to see God – all the others were aged fifty plus. Honestly, they all seemed intelligent, smartly dressed, and very chatty. I dread to think what their eyes have seen. The notion criminals have two heads and seven fingers - is far from the truth. In one way it would be easier if they did. The church is the only place in jail that people are not judged, feel somewhat safe and are treated equally. Sadly, that attracts some of the most despicable men - who make my teeth itch. Curiosity did get the better of me. I guess that's twenty-five years at the coalface of news and investigative journalism. I've always been fearless of evil liars and cheats with dark souls - I think that it comes from working with PR agents and twirlies in the West End for nearly three decades. Intrigue always outweighs intimidation to me. We were taken around the outside of HMP Lincoln's main building – an imposing, old, and tired and rat-infested estate. I'd end up in a 'resettlement' jail - this an unsettlement clink!

Prison is a leveller! Sadly, regardless of your 'brand' of conviction, we're all stuck in this melting pot together. Criminals are often very smart, but manipulative and conniving. Obviously, the men in jail are far less clever than their peers - as they got caught!!!

It was Martin Luther King who said, 'With faith we walk together, to pray together, to struggle together, to go to jail together, to stand up for freedom together, know that we will be free one day.' Politics aside, I think there's majestic strength in those words. Trump once said, 'Never Surrender – fight!' which is more my cup of tea, BUT collectively this advice should get me through my unfeasibly sizable stretch.

Eventually, we arrived at what appeared, to me, to be a lighthouse. We went around and around, up and up this circular series of stairs - I genuinely thought this was a trick and they were escorting me to heaven through the HMP back door. It was astonishing. I had a nosebleed by the time we got to the top of Everest tower. We finally made it. Familiarity at last. That's truly all you really want at this confusing time – to be centred by what you recognised. The removal of everything you know is deliberately disorientating. This is the first test: can you function alone - unaided, unsupported, or unprotected? Most can't. You have to pull every ounce of courage to face the reality of isolation. Maybe the Mother of God can soften the blow - she was marvellous in that stable. I took my pew, sat, and waited for a little heavenly inspiration.

Injustice is hard to comprehend. Keeping your head whilst others lose theirs is paramount. Let's hope my faith cup doth overfloweth! Visitors to the jail help organise the Bibles and generally mingle, as you would in any other holy place. These are usually ladies of a certain age. They often have the most humanity of anyone in the building, as they have no vested interest or axe to grind. Their compassion and kindness exceed that of anyone else in the prison. Occasionally, they're M&M - middle class and meddling - but they're few and far between.

Untarnished by the cynical, clinical, cold, and broken prison system that they can leave until next week - their agenda is usually only to provide warmth and hope. The chapel is about the only place without bars or cameras. The only place for true humanity, regardless of religion or your commitment to it. They take all-comers, while on their knees. It's also the only place officers have a scintilla of reverence, and even the top Govs or security won't mess with this department. The service began, and two things struck me. The sermon was about forgiveness. What a curious topic for CAT-B prison. OK, these places aren't home to the very worst mass murderers, but some pretty despicable and evil men parade every corridor – especially on VP. Forgiveness? You see this is why I could never qualify as a 'proper' Christian. I can't forgive certain people, and I truly believe some people in life should never be forgiven. For crimes against kiddies and pensioners, I would say - even for the church - forgiveness is the elephant in the room, big time! What about rape for the love of God? I looked around me (as I regularly do) thinking this is comedy gold – rapists to the left of me, nonces to the right – here I am stuck in the middle with you! Seriously, this is the stuff of a sick out-of-body experience. So much nodding to 'you must forgive yourself' – errr – no! Not in my book! I just can't play that game. What about the parents of a murdered baby? Should they not take priority over the killer? This is the reality of <u>some</u> of those I've been condemned to sit amongst. Let's not pretty this up or butter our parsnips - you're dealing with the most evil of evil monsters, in some cases. I'm not having that. Forgive? They should never forgive themselves, right - let alone be given that affirmation from us? So many times, I've sat thinking: this ideology, in any other (non-criminal) environment, is genius - but here, it's dangerous! Next, I shit you not - the Bible reading was on injustice. I nearly dropped my vodka and diet coke! I hadn't even been banged up for 48 hours, and God's divine intervention was offering <u>ME</u> solace and comfort - at this time of absurd insanity. The fella in a frock (no handbag – he's not on a creepy drag show) explained the struggles of Jesus, who believed in his cause, and never faltered in his passion to stick by his principles at ANY cost. Now we're talking! I later learned that 'the powers that be' broke thirteen laws to imprison him! I wish I knew who those pesky 'powers' are today. I thought about the pain I was causing so many people - thousands of whom I didn't even know - all of whom saw my passion and unwavering belief in truth and justice for the greater good. Why couldn't I just work at Tesco or wipe arses in care homes? Those are proper jobs of huge value to society. No one got banged up for stacking bananas, and at least you get 20% off your weekly big shop. Emptying catheters never attracted medicated trolls, nor did it whip up a witch hunt - now, did it? Morals and integrity come at a huge price, no matter how many followers on YouTube… or following you up 'The Mount.' The line about the baying crowds who cheered and celebrated as Jesus was nailed to the cross felt most familiar - having seen the two-faced, inbred journos cheering outside the Clown Court at my demise Seeing the joy of the soulless hacks - who edited the facts and deleted the truth to suit their agenda - was beyond ironic. I couldn't help but scream, "Jesus, I hear you brother!" It's like I have a twin! I wonder if I'll be blessed with a second coming.

You know whether you're a Christian or Muslim – white or black - so much of the good book still rings true. You can clearly edit almost everything to fit your specific situation – no matter how unfortunate, grim or indefensible your 'crime.' This has to be the appeal of the chapel in the slammer……you are forgiven - no matter what! You can make it up (and fit your situation) as you please, to get you through the next six days. In a monolith that demands you accept your crime to progress - and forces you to be sorry - it's weird that the chapel totally admonishes you! No wonder the pews are packed. It's either the scriptures getting bums on seats, or the fact there are no cameras and only one officer - so the drug dealers can flog their spice, ket, and MDMA without anyone noticing. So much easier than on the wing! I suppose it's part Bible study, part car boot sale. Either way, I was intrigued by this bizarre collective. Every Sunday since, I've listened to the scriptures - and my biggest takeaway is that we never learn. We think we're clever, but in reality, we're still Neanderthal man: dragging our knuckles and making the exact same devastating mistakes over and over again. Evil wars continue to flare up, and innocent, good people pay the price every single time - whilst politicians and billionaires profit. It's all just a little bit of history repeating, as Shirley Bassey would say!

Bitterness and anger can eat you alive. I guess a good takeaway from the Big Man is to keep the faith and put your heart in people - but that's easier said than done. It would be totally disingenuous of me to claim that my injustice and the disproportion don't stick in my craw and grind my gears. How could I ever forgive what the 'machine' did to my family? I guess I'll have to work on that - every Sunday. The truth always outs in the end, but just like karma - it takes a <u>very</u> long time. From what I'm learning, Jesus would be proud! At the very least, I'm a man of principle. History will be my saviour? One man's terrorist, is another man's freedom fighter - right? The more outrageous and lunatic the accusations made against you (as they did with Jesus), the more people question and ridicule pathetic attempts to profit from the demonisation. At what point do they make you a martyr? Remember, 'Let's close him down' was the request of two 'victims' who got me five years in the slammer - not dissimilar from Jesus's critics during the greatest PR rise, fall, and rise again in history! But I realised, in that moment, that this is my crossbar to bear. This is my test of all tests. It wasn't going to be easy - so let's GET ON WITH IT! I've already done 42 hours - only 24,000 to go! Regardless – I'M OFFICIALLY forgiven!!! Not bad for day two! I can't help but think that the Big Man has put my (relatively) small-time woes into a very powerful perspective. If you feel uplifted and joyful leaving a room - that's a good thing, right? That's why I love a full-body massage. It's always a happy ending to my day. The only room in all slammers where you're not a hostage is the chapel. I sincerely thank God for that. After the service, we walked back down the dizzying staircase to hit the earth like a ton of bricks. From the warmth and kindness - not to mention comfort - of God's house in this heavenly tower, looking down on the sinners of the clink, I was back to the Judas-packed Big Brother shithouse. I guess that mile-high chapel was the air traffic control of HMP Lincoln - home for the bewildered. It was a peculiar pleasure.

Chapter 8

Is there any Hope?

The foundation of faith is hope and belief. So, what hope did I have? Well, let's first start with the facts. A five-and-a-half-year sentence means - in reality - I would 'only' serve two years and nine months 'behind the door' at worst, but that doesn't quite tell the full story. As I've explained, there are different categories of prison. The very worst are in Double A – they're almost never getting out. If you're in an AA like Belmarsh, you're 'on the book' and monitored 24/7. You are 100% risk and 0% trust. Your every move is documented. CAT-B prisoners generally get twenty-three hours of bang-up and are basically in a holding pen for years - until they prove their risk to society is lowered via psychology, bullshit courses, or therapy that, provenly, doesn't work. They will then all move through the system - including murderers and serial rapists - who will get out in ten to twenty years' time. CAT-C prison is next. Generally, you're out most of the day and incentivised to work or learn unmonitored. There're huge amounts of trust by comparison and this should be the key to the door. Let's be clear, this system is not designed for me – or people like me. I knew from day one that I would struggle to find my place... let alone 'my people.' Many are addicted and/or have zero education. HMP is entirely focused on these people as a priority - in this dungeon for dickheads. I couldn't survive in a CAT-B for more than a week or two. It's designed to give you brain damage and intentionally breaks a lot of men.

I'm not going to lie; I quickly realised the next two years and nine months was going to be relentless – BUT – there was one hope. CAT-D is the dream destination of all prisoners, and I was already eligible, being almost zero risk to the public and less than three years left to serve – this is the criteria. CAT-D is 'open' prison. You still have to sleep there and do exactly as you're told under strict conditions – which, for me, was never going to be a problem, as they were mostly drink/drugs/victim related. However, within thirty days, you can do a 'town visit' (go home), and that builds to a week a month - staying in your own bed for <u>five</u> nights a month. MASSIVE difference. HMP claim to make this the ambition of all cons as the carrot to reform.

Listen, all this 'loose cannon' bullshit is exactly that – complete rollocks! I'm not stupid, and despite being dragged up on a pit estate, I'm certainly educated enough to know that arguing (or worse) with a screw or probation - would be the biggest failure since interviewing Kerry Katona and hoping for common sense. We know my fate is sealed and clearly pre-arranged. Nothing I say, or do, is going to make any difference – just like the trial. This was always a game of compliance, of biting my tongue, and of not rising to their bait and provocation. I had to do the same for five weeks in the Clown Court. You can't beat a corrupt system with an agenda. They will never catch me out. I'm up to nothing. My critics wanted to paint me as a rebel. Again, they couldn't be more wrong. I'm defined by my self-discipline, which is innate to any stage and radio artist with nearly thirty years of experience. You won't reach my level of success without tremendous self-restraint, willpower, and stoicism. In fact, the self-control is almost neurotic - to do what I do well, in an unblemished twenty-five-plus-year career. So, regime and compliance were of no concern to me! My issue would be the Celia Imries (with folders under their arms) and box-tickers, cut from the same institutionalized and brainwashed cloth - who are a law unto themselves and have your freedom in their hands! I was warned that probation is broken, and that they'll take any Tom, Dick, or pansy to count paper clips all day - despite having no qualifications, experience, or even knowledge of the job. Devoid of all sense of humour and riddled with corporate sanctimony and dullness, these people would be my only enemy in jail - far more deadly than any murderer! Little did I realise these malicious inbreds would become my nemesis, granted total carte blanche to lie, cheat, and conspire to prevent my progress - with complete protection and impunity.

As we know, this entire circus has been controlled from the very top since day one. I was now in the palm of their hands. Like everyone else, I dreamed of CAT-D - to return home on ROTL, or 'temporary licence.' However, I knew in my head it would not come for a very long time (if at all), as it would be a PR disaster for the CPS - Corrupt Persecution Serpents - if I were back walking my dog within six months... to which I (ironically) was perfectly entitled! They hadn't spent two years trying to bang me up just to let me straight out again. My evisceration was clearly their intention, alongside 'closing me down.' If your recidivism (risk of re-offending) is minuscule, they CANNOT stop open conditions once your sentence plan is complete. Algorithms will determine whether I need to do any courses, based on risk and previous offending - which, in my case, is nothing. I guarantee that if I weren't me, I'd be sent to CAT-D in a matter of months, as it is a non-violent first-time offence. Even HMP magicians, illusionists, and manipulators can't claim I'm dangerous, as probation didn't even recommend jail in the first place. They are the people who sign off your risk. Whoopsie – that's awkward right? What the MSM would never tell you is that I was on bail for over two years and never committed a single crime - while under identical (bail) conditions and restrictions to those imposed by the Robin Red Breast judge!" They could have remanded me immediately had I broken these rules, or if they believed - and could prove - I was a serious risk to the public. My so-called 'high profile' will presumably be their infinite justification to keep me hostage.

Sunday continued with the same rush to get food at lunch - 11.30am, turn left, not right - and for a second day, I was pleasantly surprised. Obviously, hideous by my M&S standards, but perfectly edible by slammer gruel. A fisted chicken leg, two veg, roasties, and gravy. It'll do. I've had worse in £2.89 'all you can eat' Blackpool buffets! I have to admit, 11.30am on a Sunday used to mean a bacon sandwich in my old life - but now, it's the new 3pm meat and two veg. I watched some more dopey TV and had the odd bit of meaningless 'banter' with 'Vinnie the Slow Working Dope' - but I mostly wasted time on the food

Network and Sky Arts - watching re-runs of Rick Stein and Andre Rieu LIVE. I put the 'cult' in cultured you know! I did go for exercise at 2pm, and it was a glorious hour - walking in a big circle and nodding at anyone that didn't appear to be a crackpot. It was at this point I realised how many unstable whack jobs there were in this nick. A terrifying mix of crazy and highly medicated seemed to be everywhere. Yesterday's rose-tinted glasses have quickly turned into turd-tint specs.

As the night progressed and midnight approached, I'd made it through day two. Never in my life had I applauded myself for simply surviving, existing, and breathing – all essential in the 'Travel Lodge for Tosspots.' I know that I've had a privileged life and the best start ever, with such adoring and adorable parents - but this phone staring at me was a killer. I was eight digits away from the voices of those I adored more than anything in the world. They were only an hour away, just over the fence, but it felt like another planet. Could tomorrow reunite my people? And would this blower finally stop winking at me? I turned off the TV, and then something fairly incredible happened. As I reflected on the words in the chapel and the events of the day, I swear on Doddy's life, the most incredible calm, euphoria, and excitement came over me. This feeling didn't leave me for my entire time at HMP Lincoln. I started to think about my future, and suddenly, the two years and nine months turned into two minutes and nine seconds - in my head. I began to visualise what an opportunity (albeit unwanted) I'd been given. It was almost an electrifying feeling of contentment and inspired happiness as to what was waiting for me. My re-birth would be amazing. All I could hear in my head was a chorus of 'never give up,' 'don't give up,' and 'you can do this' - words I'd been told a million times over the last five weeks before sentencing. I truly wasn't expecting this response. I promise you, this happened night after night, as I began to project my own rebirth in my mind's eye, destroying any notion of how they'd conspired to destroy me. It turns out this is rare in prison.

Finding anyone with perspective, let alone ambition, or a dream life to return to, is almost impossible. I began to count my blessings. I still believe I'm not religious - in a party-political way. The sensation of being 'safe' and 'protected' was incredible. If only I could bottle and sell 'that' feeling – I'd be rolling in boxes of vapes. Why wasn't I crying, devasted, angry or even shocked? Why didn't I smash up the cell like so many do - or step on the phone because it wasn't working. I just wanted to scream and let everyone know that 'I've got this. It will be alright!' All of my memories were stacked up in an ever-rotating Rolodex of love and hope. Some magical spirit became my guiding light. I'm a lucky lad. My perspective was clear, and everything was in proportion. Something made me want to wake up tomorrow and have the best day possible - a mantra I've maintained ever since. Ironic that when I had my staff job at the BBC - I wanted to toss myself off an NCP carpark and end up ten toes up - rather than wake up to enter that cesspit of cynical, toxic, and vile nonce venom.

Chapter 9

A New Week – A New Life

Monday morning began just before 8am, but to my amazement you got less time out during the week than at weekends – despite there being more staff. Nope, me neither! Welcome to the crackers and nonsensical world of HMP. It was either morning or afternoon - sixty-minute SOCE or exercise. The coping mechanisms you use to survive are truly fascinating. This is now my home......just a shitty smaller version..... where I sleep on top of a man – a human tortoise who was barely awake, and seemingly had no bodily functions – thank God! Covid was identical to jail, right? Everything was closed, you couldn't see your family, you couldn't travel, and you faced arrest if you didn't comply. We had to come to terms with no travel, theatre, or restaurants during the Old Kung Flu – so what's the difference now? I'm back in lockdown. I'm just confined to a bedroom.

Like anyone else unemployed, off their rocker, or sectioned, I watched Phil and Holly whilst eating my cold toast. Those were the days before Phil did a runner! Cancel culture didn't just wipe out me remember! I'd covered Schofield's double-life two years before the MSM threw him under the bus - after conveniently outing himself. Holly and Phil pushed in the queue for the Queen's 'Lying in State' and the media and public had turned. I knew they (and that show) were doomed. The public are every star's jury. Piss them off at your peril! Shagging young lads is one thing, but rudeness and self-importance will lead you to being brought down a peg or two - don't you worry about that! The showbiz game is brutal! Unlike Phil, at least I can make a comeback! When Phillip came out - there was a Barry Manilow moment. Who knew? Urggg. Who didn't know? More importantly who bloody cares? When Holly claimed she didn't know about the 'young man' Phil was schtupping at *This Morning,* their brand was tarnished forever - finished - and the game was over. Phil's demise was over his duplicity and cover-up - not creepiness. My situation was the opposite. I'd gone above and beyond to tell the world, and my audience, every single detail from the beginning until the daily court reports - slapping it all on the table until the final day. The public ain't daft. Deceive at your own risk! They will never forgive, and quickly send you on your bike if they smell a rat! Would I be given the seal of public approval? It was still way too early to know.

Anywho, another knock at the door. This time it was a Celia Imrie type with a clipboard. Good Lord, save me now! "Can you come down to education?" Now I was finally within the government's clutches. The vortex of 'the process' had now begun. Basically, unless you are 'educated' to a basic level within HMP, you can't progress - and you will literally be behind your door for the rest of your sentence unless you comply. This base level of education is <u>NOT</u> required for officers - astonishingly! Many choose to be left in oblivion – ironically, the ones who are as thick as two short planks and need the most help. They won't force you to do anything; they'll just torture you through isolation and stop all benefits, money, progress, and rewards.

Sadly, a lot don't care. I went down to a small room, which had six computers, where they handed me a ton of printed papers. "Why aren't we doing it on the computer Miss?" I asked. Oh, I forgot to tell you, from the second you're behind bars you're infantilised and back to school. 'Miss' and 'Sir' to everyone. Equally, they call you 'Mr Belfield' (to your face). It's so silly and childish. With the greatest respect - half of these people could be my child (even though I'm still only twenty-seven). It's all façade, fake nonsense, and ridiculous theatre...but it is what it is.

No matter what, you're required to take a test, provide your educational history, and determine whether you qualify to 'progress' without being sent back to school. Only when you're Level 1 can you get a 'job' and opt out of education. Now, I have to be very careful here - because it's going to come across as pompous - but I was astounded by how thick so many of them were. I'm talking about the officers and staff! Sorry 'thick' isn't PC, is it? I mean 'hard of thinking.' Right, let's agree on 'limp under the cap!' The con's lack of smarts is a result of their circumstance and environment, which explains why they had little else to turn to but a life of crime. They didn't stand a chance. They know no better. Listen, I was dragged up on a pit estate, but even I know bad parents are worse than no parents. Many of the stories came back to the same answer: drugs and abuse from their folks. It's woeful. When your parents don't care, it's so hard - near impossible - to ever find your feet in life. How can you blame the child? Wasn't I lucky to have two angels who were besotted with my sister and me? Suppose I'm now meant to feel bad and guilty about that in this broken Britain - am I? I'm aware I'm certainly in the minority. We're not money people, but Mum and Dad both worked tirelessly to give us a life filled with fun, happiness, and bags of endless support. To be surrounded by so many people who have no idea about this level of love and compassion is shocking - and hugely depressing. I was brought up in a deprived area of Notts. I mention that because, throughout my life, I have been surrounded by social challenges and obstacles. There certainly weren't any silver spoons in anyone's gob on the Gedling Colliery pit estate - I wish there had been. Perhaps I wouldn't be so tenacious, principled, and driven by a sense of duty to champion the truth - and to stand up for the working man and the underdog, unfairly disadvantaged by the elite establishment. I'm not well educated. In fact, when my headmaster asked how we could improve my dump of a comprehensive school, I suggested turning it into a sweatshop and giving teachers whips instead of pens and paper. It's since been knocked down and turned into a cemetery - best thing for it! Only a large fire could have improved it, back in the nineties when I was there.

Prisons are full of people who slip through the net of life. You can't blame someone for being stupid, but you can blame them for not knowing right from wrong. That's why I say to grandparents, 'it's all your fault!' If they didn't teach your parents, yours can't pass on empathy and smarts to you. The worst line in life is, 'I don't care.' If you don't care, you won't try - you'll give up and there's no consequences to your actions.

Prison is littered with these people. I was suddenly surrounded by what can only be described as the underclass - people who quite literally DO NOT CARE! OK, wokesters' heads will be spinning - how about calling it the underbelly of society? The kind with tits dragging across a laminated floor like a pregnant sausage dog! A generation of people with whom I can neither communicate nor truly understand. Think Jeremy Kyle auditions - or the man himself - bereft of all moral conscience. Their world is alien to ours. They're addicted, angry, uneducated, uncaring - and they're selfish, the most unattractive curse of any human. What happened next shocked me. Education at HMP Lincoln seemed to be struggling with its educators. I was desperate to ask for their qualifications, but now wasn't the time for my levity and undermining shenanigans - I'll save that for probation! I couldn't believe how disorganised they were, but I was about to be blown away by their staggering ineptitude - which could have been catastrophic.

I explained I had eight (worthless) GCSEs and three pointless A Levels - all done reluctantly and under duress - that have made no difference to my life. They were all distinctly average Cs, with the odd B for some bullshit woodwork class. I was too busy working on-air from seventeen to pursue education, which had no benefit or relevance to my life or job whatsoever. How on earth would these people begin to understand me? I had worked non-stop for twenty-five years, never claimed a penny in benefits, and didn't get up the duff with my cousin when I was thirteen! I had to do the English and Maths test regardless, as do all prisoners whether a moron or dripping in PhDs. What I didn't know was that more than half of the prison population are neurodiverse - i.e., living with ADHD or Autism. Most have primary school literacy. The priority of the system is to make uneducated and uncouth social derelicts capable of being civil - and find a job that is more profitable than crime! This impossible ambition of HMP fails at every hurdle. So, where does that leave the 1% club in jail - those who are blessed with family, had a comprehensive education, and DON'T have addictions? Teams of box-tickers spend all day running around like headless chickens, trying to cure these people of bugger all - to pretend to have 'fixed' them.

After finishing the test, I handed over my papers to the big-boned fella with one of those enormous beards and a chip on his shoulder. He was so discombobulated; he didn't know if he was Arthur or Martha. This guy was a Category B prisoner - not staff! He was tasked with inputting the results of the tests onto the only tippy-tappy that was working. He was a 'trusted' and banded prisoner, presumably considerably more educated than the two staff members who couldn't find their arsehole with both hands, let alone discern it from their elbow. Something at the end of the session made me want to check what he'd written, as I knew the con couldn't care less. Thank God, I did. This pilchard had mixed my test results up with another lad's illegible scribble. He'd confused our pokey numbers (mine is A4747EW) on the prison database called NOMIS. This, therefore, gave me a new criminal record, conviction, and sentence - not to mention the intellect of bovine intelligence. According to education, I was a crack addict from a broken family, unemployed, twenty-three, 5'6", blonde hair, eight and a half inches downstairs, from Wigan (where all the lads have a big'un), dyslexic, and incapable of reading and writing! How on earth do you handle this situation without screaming out loud, in true Catherine Tate style, 'How very dare you?' This was an ENORMOUS lesson for me - and a staggering wake-up call to HMP, on effectively day one. <u>DO NOT TRUST ANYONE</u>. They're nearly all imbeciles, with no pride or professionalism to do anything properly! Double-check EVERYTHING. The system is totally broken - and the consequences of this 'innocent' mistake, this galactic fack-up, could have stayed with me and destroyed my 'progress' indefinitely. How could this 'genuine mistake' happen in EDUCATION??? Cock-up or conspiracy? You decide.

To begin with, Bearded Bigshot argued with me that he couldn't have made a mistake - that I was, in fact, trying to deny my crime, and that the reason I was there was out of embarrassment. In front of everyone - including the poor dope he'd confused me with - he continued to read out all of this guy's private details, declaring, "Accept who you are, or you will never progress, Alex." This was one of those comedy moments where you just can't beat stupid. "OK," I said, "if I can't read or write, how did I fill in my own test and get 86%? Also, do I look like I was born in the latter part of 1999? I could be this kid's grandfather - where he's from!" The other box-ticker then stood up. I continued, "Do I look five foot tall with blonde hair?" as I flapped the script under his grubby, hairy nose in a petulant Piers Morgan style of disbelief. I realised all HMP pen-pushers look identical. There are a few chromosomes missing - if you know what I mean. Is there a school for blandness. Another box-ticker interrupted - Minjita, who was the height of a Diddy Man, had strange, wacky, multi-coloured hair, and piercings in places on the face where they weren't intended. She said, "Ahhh, Mr Belfield, we seem to have a 'copy and paste issue' here - I'll sort it out before you leave Lincoln." I raised my eyebrows, "No you bloody won't dear – that needs correcting <u>NOW</u>! If not for my sake, then for this Justin Bieber lookalike - who has suddenly been re-categorised to 'monster, evil, raving gobshite terrorist 2022' on his records. I'm sure he's done nothing that compares to my crime, and he doesn't want the records to suggest - for the rest of his criminal career - that he's hung like an iPhone ear pod and identifies as a foghorn with a rusty roof and a damp basement!" I made this funny, which is my wont. BUT I was raging inside - that this could happen - and this daft Minjita thinks I'm going to risk her correcting it at some point before my sentence ends in 2028! Little did I know this was the first of hundreds of totally innocent mistakes the inept imbeciles at HMP would unfortunately make - endless and shamelessly. How many others wouldn't notice or care... and pay the price later? There are no flies on me - that needs changing NOW!" The other lads were pissing themselves! "Oh, I see" it said – presumably with twelve pronouns on her/it's/them email signature. Apparently, this one was pansexual. Why you'd want to shag your Le Creuset steamer is beyond me! Urggg. If these people spent more time doing their jobs than worrying about everyone knowing what they do in the bedroom - maybe these 'mistakes' wouldn't happen! I do not believe any of these cretins know who I am - or even care. However, what an opening number by HMP! Twenty minutes later, the errors were corrected - and I'd grown a foot, gone from Bieber to Ed Sheeran 'upstairs,' and didn't have ten years of previous convictions, driven by insatiable addiction on par with Amy Winehouse's left nostril! My first HMP bullet avoided, but imagine if I hadn't spotted it? This stuff lives with you forever. It lingers longer than Trevor Nelson on Radio 2! Most men would never check anything, let alone question the alleged smartest educators in the clink. What a shambles. NOTHING can be deleted off your record BTW - it can only be corrected afterwards. They see everything forever - even if it's bummocks, just pure human error, or no fault of your own. This would be fatal and define my incarceration at the 'Asylum for Arseholes.'

Any staff at your prison can access your most private details, and ANYONE can comment on your file. Data Protection allows you to see who is snooping... I wonder if they'd eventually reveal this illuminating information - to which I (and every other prisoner) am entitled? Blimey, was I learning quick. Trust no one. Double-check everything. Believe NOTHING! Presume everyone is a pilchard and of remedial cognitive ability. You quickly realise it's only luck - not judgement - that the entire system doesn't implode. I am currently sat with my door unlocked and open - when it's meant to be locked. Someone forgot, because I'm simply not on their radar. Does it matter to me – no - but it's a prison. This shouldn't happen. It turns out 'they' can make as many mistakes as they like; however, we of course, have to be impeccable and faultless.

This was also the first time that I was confined in a classroom with eight men - only six computers - and five of them not working. Openly and proudly, they'd brag about drugs and their various achievements profiting from them - in front of staff who say nothing. Who knew cocaine came from the cocoa plant? So, it's basically basil or oregano, hey? 'Bruv, you know to make spice they just mix Domestos with diesel and cement mix.' WTF - CEMENT MIX? I wonder what goes hard? Sounds delicious. Mind you, can't be worse than the current Mrs B's cooking. This monstrosity and waste of skin continued, "I don't do cannabis anymore since they've started spraying it with glass - to make it heavier." I'm glad I'm only into Fruit Fancies and Apple Turnovers at M&S - this would all be a bit much for my delicate disposition and palate. I think diesel would leave my guts for garters - similar to vegan cheese or a couscous salad. We'll leave the cement mix for hardened criminals! I thank you! The benign, bragging, 'big-up' bullshit balls these boneheads splutter is nauseating. Surely there have to be a couple of prisoners who don't call everyone 'bruv' and fist each other instead of offering a polite peck on the cheek. I don't think this prison malarkey is for me.

Chapter 10 - Day 4 Tuesday

HATCHET JOB ON BBC News and Newsnight

Day four was just like any other. I went for 9-10am exercise and tried to avoid getting eye contact with any of the window lickers who were my new neighbours. I timed it perfectly to get my shower five minutes before bang-up. I rushed back into the pad, dried off, got dressed, and stuck on the TV. I wasn't going to risk daytime TV for fear of dying of boredom, so I switched on BBC Two, hoping for *Homes Under the Hammer* (needs must). It was BBC News - as Aunty doesn't have money for original daytime programming, despite its £3 billion TV rape tax. I was about to have an out-of-body experience...

As the channel came to life, while my remote was still in my hand, my face was on the TV! A 'victim' was giving an exclusive interview to Victoria Derbyshire. For the record, I've never met, spoken to, or gone near either of these BBC paid journalists. So, we've got a BBC person interviewing a BBC person. Ermmm! Now remember, it was a different BBC presenter who began the witch hunt to 'close me down.' It was, indeed, BBC legal who orchestrated my arrest and conspired with the Nottingham Corrupt Police to silence me (as their #1 whistle-blower having worked there for fifteen years). They handed the file to the police - which was the only evidence used in court. So, here I am, watching BBC News - which is meant to be balanced, impartial, and verified. Instead, it's airing a twenty-minute hatchet job that was first broadcast on *Newsnight*, then repeated all day on their 6pm and 10pm broadcasts, and hourly on their rolling news shambles. Who knew, being 'stalked' could be such a valuable PR opportunity personally......oh, and a ratings winner for the BBC? It should be made absolutely clear that this person got me convicted and sentenced to 13 weeks (6.5 weeks to serve) for 'Stalking WITHOUT fear, alarm, and distress.' In court, this was only ever described as 'Simple Stalking' - that is to say, the jury did not believe they suffered ANY fear, alarm, or distress. Yet at NO POINT did your publicly funded *BBC News* make this known. In fact, on the contrary, this person painted me as a monster - in line with the twin brother of Adolf Elizabeth Hitler (that was his middle name – ask Mel Brooks!). They appeared to take the glory for the entire five-and-a-half-year sentence, despite only being responsible for 10% of it.

In some extraordinary hysterical WTF moment, I literally roared with laughter at the sheer OTT craziness of this Victoria Derbyshire premeditated character assassination. For the record, I can't stand Derbyshire. I believe her to be classless, charmless, and talentless - but as for her professional conduct, ask her producers at 5 Live if she's a bed of roses to work with – that's none of my business. She who casts the first stone hey? Vicky wallowed in the disproportion of the outrageous claims - made without challenge. I noticed she didn't question why this man had presented evidence by a corrupt and disgraced ex Met police cop. Evidence which was EDITED to say "(A victims name and) Victoria Derbyshire is a CUNT I hope they die of Covid." The judge ordered the jury to 'forget what you heard' - as the tape was pieced together from nearly twenty of my YouTube videos and was a total LIE! In a proper trial, this sort of thing is often classed as perjury, but not in mine! Do you think Vic had skin in the game - to destroy me on the BBC's behalf? Remember, these are the very people who set out to end my career and silence their biggest critic. SHAMEFUL abuse of *BBC News* airtime. No mention of the eighteen trolls, including '@fackyouAlexBelfield' - this 'victim' followed - all referenced during cross-examination on public record. When asked under oath they said, "I don't know." When asked if they personally added/followed them they said, "I can't remember." No mention of the security cameras the person was given by the BBC - at YOUR expense - that were never fitted and GIVEN AWAY. Equally, no mention of BBC security's TWO investigations, confirming I was 'no threat to anyone at the BBC.' How is any of this balanced or impartial Vicky?

As we know, the BBC never lie! They are the bastions of truth, facts, and non-noncy jiggery pokery. So, there I was – the 'feature' twenty-minute interview!

So why am I in prison, you may ask yourself? These direct quotes from the victim confirmed: "The danger came from the online traffic, not the individual." Ermmm... so I'm in jail for someone else - someone who didn't exist - as nothing actually happened. Had they ever met me? "So, the fear (not believed by the jury) was that someone MIGHT attack them by proxy" - even though it DIDN'T happen nor was accused of happening. What alarmed them the most? "With 400,000 people watching those videos, at some point someone is going to take a knife or acid to my face" - this victim said on the BBC. OK, hang on a second. THIS DIDN'T HAPPEN either. It wasn't accused either. So, it was just an undeniable fantasy that was not reality, but simply invented to put words like 'acid' and 'knife' into the public's head. Is that fair? This blither continued; "If the courts hadn't stopped Alex Belfield someone would have died?" Excuse me? That's like saying we close all restaurants in case someone chokes to death and kills themselves. ABSURD!

The best line of FACT that I do agree with is: "Someone who stalks in person hides in the shadows, but Alex Belfield and his army were in plain sight." No shit Sherlock! So, if I was in PLAIN SIGHT how is that stalking (defined with stealth)??? They confirm; "Everyone could see it on Twitter and YouTube." So as for distress; "Were you afraid," Vic asked. This was revealing. "I was afraid of what he could do to my family, as we've seen before with knife attacks and MPs being killed." WOW! That escalated quickly! From I 'wouldn't have been threatening' to I could kill family members BASED on NO interaction whatsoever or knowledge of where they live – let alone any attempt to go anywhere near any of them......for which I was NOT accused. How on earth did anyone fall for this contradictive claptrap? Later this 'without fear' victim described me on twitter as 'unhinged' and 'believed' I'd lost all of my money. Wishful thinking! Is all of this the definition of projection - or just pure fantasy and imagination? I'm no threat but 'unhinged' – how can you be both? The excitement of a slot on *Newsnight* whipped up more insanity and even greater disproportion and delusion. "His channel was a fountain of hate." Blimey! I'm now an ejaculate of the word jizz – give me strength! For the love of God – who signed off this vitriolic vomit? They continued; "He wants that hatred to be so great that someone pays me a visit. I can't be casual about it, I was scared for my two daughters" – Ermmm, yet they chose to give away the security cameras given by the BBC - and paid for by the licence payers! A hate crime was <u>NOT</u> part of my charge, let alone believed by the jury. I wasn't even <u>accused</u> or charged with <u>any</u> fear of violence. Most curiously, the final confessions that journo genius Vic slapped on the table resulted in this Bobby Dazzler; "I'd be looking for (his) followers to block," having conceded; "In a way it took me into his weird brain. He pulls people into his dark orbit." Blimey, my punters never stop pissing themselves! So now, I'm responsible for people tuning into me, right? It's all my fault that people become consumed by my COMEDY and LOVED tuning in! What distortion hey? How am I not being stalked??? How can I take this foolishness seriously? So far, I still don't know what I did. All I'm hearing is what other people didn't do - when nothing happened. Most peculiar.

Further unchecked BBC LIES excreted through the *Newsnight* and *BBC News* screens; "He was convicted, and YouTube demonetised him and closed him down." NO THEY DIDN'T. In fact, I'm still on YouTube and they never pulled a <u>SINGLE</u> video over the trial (or after) - as they couldn't find a single violation.

Then it became more revealing; "He's still got a Twitter account – what the hell!" they petulantly stormed. Errrr. Let me explain, I'm still on YouTube and Twatter, as I have not been found in breach of <u>a SINGLE issue</u> with these two social media goliaths. Curiously though, the BBC mafia forgot to bring this to the public's attention. Hopeless. The final fury was "Belfield's already put a video up from prison saying he's going to be right back, up and running." I obviously hadn't recorded this in prison; it was recorded at Alex's Acres moments before Tarquin drove me to sentencing. At least there is one true FACT in this BBC hatchet job - that I will never surrender to liars, cheats and bullies - or stop fighting for my free speech. Sadly, for my assassins, I was not given a life sentence, therefore, it's my human right to take advantage of free speech when this is over. Does this impartial journalism (funded by the licence fee) seem fair and balanced to you? Where were the sanctimonious and supercilious 'BBC Verify' goons over this appalling so-called impartial journalism, where both parties had a vested interest and skin in the game.

What do you expect from the nonce factory. No mention of 'let's close him down' from THE BBC EMPLOYEE NOW WAS THERE? I'm very happy to do an interview with Victoria Derbyshire in 2025 - to promote the books. I wonder if she'd have the balls, and be quite so economical with the truth, if I were sat in front of her face-to-face. What that gal lacks in looks and charm, she makes up for in bitterness and her personal agenda - that's for sure!

<u>Wing Life goes on – Ring Life does not!</u>

Five days into the slammer and still no sign of my 'telephone pin' being activated. Without a PIN you cannot ring anyone – even if you're approved to ring them. Within seventy-two hours of being banged up, I'd worked out that the most critical, important, and number one thing to remember in prison is that you HAVE to be ahead of the game and fight for what you need. It's every man for himself, and there's no safety net for the lackadaisical! OK, for example, toilet rolls. I get Amazon to deliver thirty-six Andrex (x2) to the house, and shove one in the cupboard upstairs and one downstairs - to never be caught short. When I'm down to ten, I order another thirty-six. I'm always covered! Life in the slammer is all about planning, organisation, and being on the ball. You don't get a second chance, and there ain't no Amazon drone deliveries... just drone deliveries of Class A sniff. You quickly become very canny and clever, so as not to be left out of anything you're entitled to. Once that door is locked, you're facked! No one cares about you. No one from staff has time to manage you, and everything relies on your own smarts and organisational skills to survive. This is ironic, bearing in mind 90% of my co-stars couldn't organise a hand job in a brothel! They're too busy being off their tits on some zombie sniff, or grabbing their nuts singing ghetto BLM music.

Over time, you become more and more disciplined - but what about the morons who don't care or, more often than not, are not capable of looking after themselves? Sadly, nothing. They're left to flounder and squander in their filth. If you don't get your food, for example, it will be days before someone notices. It's every man for himself - military style. I was shocked that prison is, in fact, very generous with shampoo, razors, toilet rolls, deodorant, and even shaving gel – I shit you not. There is no excuse to live like a pig......but you have to care. They give you gloves for cleaning, as well as J Cloths, disinfectant, and even spray air freshener. It's not dissimilar to my suite in the Dorchester. Providing you're not a prick and ask nicely they'll give you as much as you need......but that relies on you being arsed to go and get it. I was hot to trot with this stuff. From day one, officers were very kind, giving me as much paper and pens as I needed – which at times was <u>A LOT</u>! This was my priority above blue roll and a fresh shower curtain.

OK let me slap it on the table. Prison is full of lads playing the big man, bragging about their pathetic crimes and justifying their convictions. "I robbed the little old lady because..." These fell under the bracket of the reoffender, turn-style convicts - who are, frankly, hopeless and totally shameless. The Prime Minister could personally attempt rehabilitation, and it would fall on deaf ears. Mind you, Kia Cars Starlin seems more likely to turn a blind eye than sort out a convict - from what I've read during his time running the CPS (Corrupt Persecution Service). #Savile #Al-Fayed.

Overhearing cons' despicable conversations, justifying their lifestyles, is the most sickening thing about prison. It's a world that 'normal' people simply cannot comprehend. Their instinct is to form a band of brothers, which creates worrying gangs - that seemingly no one at HMPPS does anything about. They'll argue, 'what can we do?' The consensus is that the Prison Service is basically a training school for turnstile twits - to learn new tricks and become better criminals. A total own goal, and everything they claim they do not want to be.

I'm told over the fence, in the real world, it was carnage online – all noise and little substance. Blimey, did the mentals love to gloat and come up with their own version of reality……not dissimilar to the trial. What it quickly exposed was the sheer obsession and fixation on details of my life - that they had invented via their warped minds - that they could now exaggerate, unchallenged, for their own attention-seeking ego. I've since been told that the biggest revelation - and irony - was that these class A twazzocks wrongly believe they could replace me, proving my theory about jealousy: the root of all evil. However, they forgot that they were 'feeding the beast' and exposing how they were, in fact, stalking me. Their obsession with every second of my private life, content, and world (that they genuinely believed was real and true), was beyond revealing. Proper psychos. One fruit made videos about my brother being furious in court. Sadly, I don't have a brother. Another bi-curious and bipolar Mogadon told the world I'd stalked him, despite not a single communication EVER being exchanged. I've never met him – but that's a given. It was a free-for-all, for loony toons to claim their five minutes of fame. How revealing. Of course, my punters were having none of it. It was all jealous misfits, having their moment of reflective glory, in the belief they could inherit my 350,000 subscribers and steal my hard-earned success. FAIL! Woefully exposing and pitiful. I still find the whole torture of being consumed by someone you think you hate to be one of the most worrying psychological developments in our culture. It's prolific! It's all Simon Cowell's fault. His reality show format of being the perennial victim has become a lifestyle for the elbow lickers! They genuinely believe they know you - oh, and that you care. You could start a conference with their distorted realities - riddled in total hypocrisy, of course - born out of an unrequited desire to be wanted, successful, rich, famous, and popular. Instead, they're loners, loopy, and self-touching to the dark web in their council flat!

Prison is like a leaky tap. On VP wing there were now five fellas whose parents watched me. They'd all sent beautiful messages of support which was so encouraging. They were not only devastated, but furious at the ludicrous disproportion and injustice of my pithy case. Bit by bit, they'd tell me what was going on. Bizarrely, the consistent line was that - despite 99% of YouTube wacko trolls rejoicing, getting a little too excited 'downstairs' - 99.99% of the sane commenters did not agree. This was so inspiring and uplifting. Over time, this became a pattern. The public would once again be my saviour. The punters aren't stupid, and will not be convinced by some bonkers, desperate, miserable, and highly medicated wannabes - who celebrate their own mental frailties for pity - to suddenly change their minds about their mate off the tippy-tappy. This gave me so much hope, and a real boost. Arguably these nutters would keep my name and notoriety alive.......no matter how many lies and fantasies they spouted. Their obsessive scrutiny only exposed their infinite weaknesses and unhealthy obsession. The more outlandish and wilder their fantasies were, the less people - who aren't crackers - believed a word they said. The jungle drums on the wing truly were a lifesaver. No one was falling for this noise and foolishness. Giving me a kicking became a sport, but only highlighted how many media and theatre losers had skin in the game - despite having <u>never</u> met me! Sadly, it said more about these social retards than it did me. MATRON!!!!

Who knew - the very people I was told to fear would bring me such solace. My con colleagues had become my eyes and ears. There was no question, though, that I'd gone down quietly. Online was on fire. How would my saboteurs extinguish these flames? Remember, I'd already been convicted, and I remained on-air for six weeks before sentencing. None of my thousands of SVoR subs had cancelled - in fact, we'd gone up fifteen hundred subs over the trial. YouTube remained constant at 350,000. You have to remain steadfast and run into the fire at times of attack. You NEVER give in - or negotiate with terrorists! Running away never works, and was not even an alternative for me. I just needed to find a strength I never knew I had - to weather the shit storm and tsunami of crackpots - knowing that in just 33 months, I'd have my say. Then, all the creepy big mouths would head for the hills, delete their content, and pretend it was all just a BIG misunderstanding.

All you want to know during any crisis in life is, 'Is it going to be alright?' The thrill would be whether I'd be given a second chance by the public - the only jury that matters to me! I've never earned big money, despite the company making a fortune in 24 months. VoR paid me £800 a month to cover the mortgage - and still does. NOT a penny more. The rest went to expenses, taxes, legal fees, and paying for my eight staff. What was left would be the miracle to support me throughout this hostage situation. We know that the only aim of the dark forces was not only to close me down on-air, but also to bankrupt me - forcing me to lose my gorgeous house. This is known as lawfare! I'd worked and saved for 30 years to pay for my palace. All I cared about was my loved ones' peace of mind - and eventually, getting back in touch with my VoR family, which I very quickly did thanks to Network Nick, via the website that was still thriving. My tech genius updated the website with the address and my prison number, so people could write and email. MY community of sweethearts didn't flinch, and naturally couldn't wait to send their love and solidarity. This would be my life saver - total escapism and distraction. A daily check to keep me infinitely busy and focused. Be under no delusions - this wasn't going to be easy! HMPPS can do what they like, when they like, with total impunity. Reasoning with, arguing, or begging will get you nowhere. I knew that the more I kicked back - and the more the public supported me - the worse it would get. I wasn't wrong. All of my bags of mail would, without question, put my head above the parapet - at a time when they needed me isolated, inaccessible, and cut off from my friends, family – and most importantly my punters. The Prison Service try to break you, and is known for shanghaiing - being tricked into doing something you don't want to do, or being sent somewhere you don't want to go - to keep you in constant upset and agitation. I'd need fortitude to survive. This was a long old haul!

In my mind's eye, I'd become Alfie Boe in *Les Mis*. Like Jean Valjean, my prison number was tattooed on my man breasts for the rest of my life. Every day, you wake up and sing 'One Day More,' whilst me mammy belts out 'Bring Him Home' down the blower. The truth is: NOBODY CARES once you're kidnapped by the state! And repeat... nobody cares. Every man for himself. I would have to manage the officers so as to avoid any 'deep' conversations. How could I trust anyone? Up to now, my general interaction with the few officers I encountered was that they were normal gals and fellas - who often were misfits and outcasts themselves. I'd never met a stranger bunch of characters. Obviously, those ten-hour shifts are as palatial as the size of their bottoms. There's a lot of time to eat custard creams in between 'nickings!' Strange peacock or multi-coloured parrot hair appeared a contractual necessity. Facial piercings and ghastly tattoos defined the millennial generation of 'a few fisted chicken legs short of a KFC boneless bucket!' OK, I'll slap it on the table - I haven't seen so many lesbians in one room since Sandi Toksvig's wedding!!! Lady-screws are a unique breed, that's for sure. I'm king of the lesbians BTW. I used to be one myself - before I was sent down! Fortunately, I'm a people person, so I'll whistle Dusty classics and hope for the best!

The old-school chaps were great - they had a cynicism about the system and weren't fooled by the posters claiming to care about mental 'elf, insisting you have dignity and everything to which you were entitled. Trust me, when you enter that courtroom, ALL of your human rights, equality, and dignity are immediately removed - and all of your life's experience no longer counts. Oh, and if you happen to be smarter than the screws and box-tickers, it will 100% work against you - just like in real life with bosses. Some of the screws want to chat, but they don't have time. They are not your friend. In fact, they aren't even each other's friend. You can never be lulled into this false sense of security - once convicted. Befriending your kanga (= kangaroo/screw) would be as daft as believing your solicitor is on your side, cares, or is your friend! These boundaries need to be etched in stones the size of Stonehenge. 'Befriending' a screw = corrupting an officer. That could very easily extend your sentence. All of these red flags and bear traps - I need to be wary of!

A silly thing happened last night, I forgot my milk and breakfast pack, so I went back. I quickly realised when there're extras, take them! Every man for himself. Some lads won't eat from 4pm yesterday to midday today because they weren't on the ball. You snooze you lose! Screws will shrug their shoulders.

'That's your own fault, fella!' I always have ten cereal packs extra, 'just in case.' Incidents happen all the time in the pokey - and if it's really serious, you may not escape your pad in the morning, or even for the rest of the day. BE PREPARED! Once that cell door closes and is locked, its game over. No one is doing anything for you. From 7pm, when the jail - and every prison - is put in 'patrol state,' you ain't getting out unless you're 99% nearly dead. You have a heart attack - good luck! By the time the ambulance arrives, you're ten toes up and brown bread. One man, called 'Oscar One,' sits in the centre of the prison with all the cell keys (obviously, he hasn't got a thousand keys - one fits all). It's only he - with permission from #1 Gov - and in absolute extreme circumstances, such as 'code blue' (not breathing), that he will be allowed to open that door, with five other officers behind him... by which point, it's too late. This is the definition of solitude. In one way, it's not dissimilar to being a pensioner in a care home. A lot of lads can't handle the emptiness and sheer loneliness of bang-up - it drives them cuckoo. That's when they start 'cutting up' (= self-harm), to force the prison to give them attention... or an Xbox. Oddly, on reflection, I'm grateful to Snorefest Vinster. Coming into this alone, and with no phone, may have been a step too far. Many lads choose to be double padded forever - to avoid the deafening silence and emptiness.

The Pen is mightier than the Sword!
What has single-handedly <u>saved my life </u>in prison is the pen and paper. Days are very long. Some days, there can be twenty-four

hours to waste - so what could I do to keep busy? Very soon, my mail sack would be bulging, and my time would be well spent indulging in absolute distraction and 100% love and support. So, during an episode of 'Botched' (the shit you watch in the slammer) – I pondered about how to keep my brain active and my creative (comic) juices flowing. I realised this could go on for years, and I needed to leave with something I could be proud of - something I would never have been able to do at home. A book!!! I told myself - whilst heavily puffing on the cross-dresser in the gym, in one of those 'duh da duh' panto-style moments - that I could never be arsed to write an epistle in real life, as it's tedious, laborious, never-ending, and takes far too much time. I'd had a stroke…. of genius! My incarcerators and shushy assassins had inadvertently given me the TIME (whilst doing TIME) to set the record straight, and forensically tell my side of this unbelievable dystopian nightmare. Time was no longer my enemy - so this could keep me focused and busy, and offer something for my cancelling haters to get furious about on my eviction from the Big Brother Shithouse. 'By Jove, he's got it!' I'm once again employed… at the taxpayers' expense. If anyone cares to buy and read the books, it might start paying off some of my £400,000 legal bills!

I started writing my autobiography and have never stopped scribbling since. It is therapy! I have never written anything in my life other than news scripts, gags for shows, and my annual Grand National bet. Now I would work my flabby white arse off to become an author. What a turn up for the books hey?

Literally! Another string to my bow - that would send the spectrumed nut jobs incandescent with rage - that the taxpayers commissioned my scribes costing you £48K a year! I never realised that writing is all consuming. I'd recommend it to anyone struggling with life, as you cannot double-think during an epistle - your brain is 100% committed and focused to the pen. Any anxiety - I hate that word more than non-binary - drains away from your eyeballs to the end of your pinky. So, my next 2 years and 9 months would go from talking shite to writing shite. Same difference, right? All men need a purpose to avoid insanity or a midlife crisis. Writing would now be my new full-time job...

Chapter 11

A Big Girl's Blouse & Mummy's Boy Reunite

The week progressed far quicker than I imagined. If I'm being totally honest, my curiosity was in overload - and I was drinking in the unbelievable sights and sounds that I was seeing, like I was at Chessington World of Lag Adventures. My journalistic sponge was dripping moist! It was like Centre Parcs for convicts - learning how their roller-coaster lives function and their unique brains work. This patchwork quilt of paedos, rapists, murderers, and gang bangers are a never-ending cacophony of unbelievable observations and revelations.

By Thursday morning, there was still no sign of my numbers being activated - and my piss was beginning to boil. Was this the first of hundreds of baiting triggers to get me to kick off? Nar! Just total incompetence, as always. 'They're' not clever enough to be this devious. I had not been allowed to make contact with anyone for nearly a week. Not only was this cruel, but I'm told it was exceptional - and not lawful. My first test of 'now you're ours' punishment. I went up to the Gov's office for the first time - not the big Gov, the wing boss. You'll NEVER see the proper bosses in an HMP. In private jails, you have lunch with them! I explained that I had not had a call to my parents, which shocked him: "You should have." I said, "Well, I did ask twice." Again, this proved you just can't believe anyone. They'll fob you off quicker than a BA call centre handler located in Bangladesh - when your flight has been cancelled. The BIG lesson - keep asking until you get the answer you need. 'No' in prison is the easiest way to shut down an issue a screw can't be arsed to deal with. It's also the safest option for under-trained and over-promoted security guards - who, two weeks earlier, were tossing burgers in McDonald's. I have to say, this Gov was a venerable fiftyish fella who, true to his word, called the phone people immediately to chase up my apps. He put the phone down and said, "They'll be on shortly - not all, but most!" I hate to sound like a big girl's blouse, but it brought a tear to my glass eye. It had been a week since I'd seen Mum and Dad - the most important of my heroes - and I just wanted to put their minds at rest. If they knew I was alright, they would be at peace too. Once my folks realised that I was fine then word would spread quicker than the new rash on my left bollock. I reckon it's the cheap bedding. No 'White Company' at HMP Lincoln. Family is EVERYTHING to me. I'm old-school. I'm a mother's son. We're so close, as I am with my sister. My nephew is my hero, and to be torn apart from him and my God-kids was unimaginable - but you have to reality check. Lots of people go away to work, so what's the difference? It's all about frame of mind. Once this week of 'shock' was over, we'd all calm down - and it would all be OK.

Whilst I was there, I asked for a job to keep me busy. I deliberately over-egged my omelette, saying 'I won't cope behind the door.' The kind dear said he'd help. Of course, I now realise, I had ZERO chance of getting a gig at Lincoln. They knew I'd be off soon, so it was more trouble than it was worth to do anything with me. I prayed the PPU (Public Protection Unit) would do their job and sort out my calls – not a lot to ask is it? I later found out that PPU doesn't even exist - it's just another name for the nosey bastards in probation. My sister was ahead of the game, and was so smart to work out I'd need money to make calls. You get 50p a day in prison, 'unemployed' - it would be two weeks before I started my new career, on £15 a week IF I was lucky. I'd spent hundreds of thousands of pounds on lawyers so far, and now I'm begging for a few quid for the blower.

The first reality check of being in this sausage factory – money, power, and popularity counts for <u>NOTHING</u>! Deal with it! I've worked my arse off over the last thirty years to pay my way. I've never really been on the bones of my arse, as I always got another job. My Dad's working-class ethic: pull your socks up and get on with it! NEXT! Now I would be entirely reliant on my beloveds to keep me afloat via the tippy-tappy. It shouldn't be forgotten that many nitties (losers) have no one and nothing. They don't have a pot to piss in - or a barred window to throw it out of. Life's not fair, hey?! Despite the leveller of jail, there's still a huge class system and pecking order.

Throughout my life I've never borrowed money off anyone – ever. I have that pit estate pride and will do anything to pay my own way. Money obviously isn't my problem now, but the issue is getting it! My darling sister worked it all out and had already sent £100 into my 'private' account via A4747EW - which was immediately online at the HMP website. It was approved in 24 hours, and one of the few things that works perfectly. All you need is the prisoner's name. Lifesaver! Can you imagine being in the slammer prior to the internet? A hundred pounds is worth a thousand in jail - but it still didn't matter. It turns out you have two accounts in the slammer. 'Privates' and 'Spends.' You can only spend what's in your 'spends' - nothing gets past me! However, this has to be 'dropped down' (= sent from privates weekly) at a limited amount of £22 initially, then up to £33 when you are trusted, well behaved, and become 'enhanced.' The bad lads with 'negatives' or adjudications go on 'basic' - this is lower than the average TOWIE star's IQ. It usually takes three months - unless you offer a backhander to a bent screw. I've never seen a more complicated/convoluted and ridiculous system. However, good behaviour would get me another tenner......but not until Christmas – three months away. It's bonkers. You need to be Rain Man to get your head around all the anachronisms, systems, and rules. How could any newbie possibly grasp all of this confusing, mind-boggling, and bureaucratic twattery? Perhaps it is better to be a re-offender. I tried my best to make notes - and not look like a wet wipe to my contemporaries. What I did know was that I was in no-man's land, until I was transferred to a 'proper' prison. I never lost sight that nothing could be worse than this first week Pleasuring His Majesty. I was now almost halfway through my CAT-B introduction.

What I can tell you - from the bottom of my bottom - is that the 'system,' post-conviction, is designed to break you, bankrupt you, and send you out homeless, penniless, and entirely dependent on the state. 'They' love it when you're 100% desperate and beholden to them. Remember, I was <u>so</u> lucky to have a team of angels keeping me afloat. In the hoosegow, you have no access to pay your mortgage or bills - let alone get yourself a few quid. You can't even pay ghastly lawyers or court orders! You're entirely reliant on loved ones to save you from collapse. HMP sets you up to fail. I was so lucky to have so much support. Even then, it was infuriating - almost impossible at times - with so much security on every log-in and account. It took weeks to get everything accessed and in order. Thank God for my sister! The feeling amongst all men is that it is the deliberate intention of HMP to ensure that, by the time you leave, you are entirely helpless - therefore, 100% monitored and controlled for as long as possible by the state. You're not allowed <u>ANY</u> internet access - EVER – regardless of crime, to sort out <u>ANY</u> bills or business. That's why most lads have to buy an iPhone 5 off a bent screw for £2,000 on day one - to survive, Facetime the kids, and watch Tug TV on YouJerk.

Every hour, I would check the phone to see whether my numbers were working. I tried two or three, including Mum and Dad's - nothing. Next, I tried my Aunty Dorothy's number. I'd been her carer for ten years, although I've never done any personal care - I don't do private parts or wet flannels - but I cooked every night and happily did her shopping. I was her rock. For a decade - I called her every single day (as I have my parents) - no matter where I was in the world. This was never a

148

chore. In fact, it was the least I could do. Sometimes, we'd chat under a minute - but it was my pure pleasure, and comforting to know she was OK. It was a duty I loved and was grateful for. I owe these people everything - they're my lifeblood. She was isolated because of MS, and effectively imprisoned by her condition. I pressed her numbers and dialled my private pin code (774211) to activate the call. Instead of the 'you cannot dial that number' pre-recorded guff I'd heard a thousand times – the phone rang! I could have cried with pure joy and absolute elation. The love in my heart was pounding. No longer was I alone. As far as I was concerned, my captors had failed! I could finally reveal: I WAS OK! My heartbeat returned to its natural rhythm.

It was like having the biggest and best hug of your life. Utterly electrifying! BUT I only had £2 on phone credit. That would equal twenty three-minute calls. "Alo, my darling," I said. "ALEX!!!!" - as she burst into tears. "I'm OK, I'm OK! I'll be fine! I'm OK - don't worry," I excitedly extolled. "Are you OK?" she asked again. "YES! Doll, we never give in to bullies, liars, and cheats. This is an evil test. No one has died - it's all nonsense! I promise you, eventually this wicked bullshit and witch hunt UNDERLINE WILL END." I had to underscore the reality repeatedly. "Now Dorothy, I can't get hold of mum and dad. Can you ask them to come to yours at 6pm sharp and I'll call" - I begged. Dot excitedly replied, "Yes of course Alex." "Right well I'll have to go for now, but we're back together and we'll never be parted again. Tell everyone I'M OK. Spread the good word! I'm just………on a road trip to nowhere to write a few books that I'd never do at home love!" She laughed as I said, "Love you." - "I love you more," she replied. This went on for another twenty seconds, wow! The second best 10p I've ever spent.

The best 10p was at 18:00:15hrs - when I called back. Same process, pin went in, and it rang. Thank God for that! Then Mum answered on loudspeaker. You can imagine: "We've been so worried. We love you so much. Everyone thinks this is ridiculous - you're the kindest man on earth," she cried. "One at a time, please, Mum - you haven't given me a chance to answer. You're answering your own questions like Boris," I quipped. Dad laughed. We all need a bit of levity. "Listen, I love you and Dad more than words. How's my Doddy?" Mum laughed. "She's a lifesaver. She's here listening - she's great. Dad sends his huge love, and your sister will talk after work." Thank God for that! Then Mum answered on loudspeaker. You can imagine: "We've been so worried. We love you so much. Everyone thinks this is ridiculous - you're the kindest man on earth," she cried. "One at a time, please, Mum - you haven't given me a chance to answer. You're answering your own questions like Boris," I quipped. Dad laughed. We all need a bit of levity. "Listen, I love you and Dad more than words. How's my Doddy?" Mum laughed. "She's a lifesaver. She's here listening - she's great. Dad sends his huge love, and your sister will talk after work." I left that call feeling like the New Year's Eve fireworks display! I was cock-a-hoop, fizzing like a can of pop shaken up before opening. It was magical and an elation (and relief) I don't think I'll ever feel again!

Over the coming days, I added twenty of my best F&F (friends and family) on earth. That is the limit. Boy, I'll need a cockamamie scheme to talk to the other thousand-plus peeps in my life - but I'll worry about that later. Don't worry, nothing gets past me. Trust me, I can outwit the dopes in security - it's not hard! A prisoner was recently sentenced to another decade behind the door - for running a drugs empire from his cell, ON THE PRISON PHONE! Oy vey, this is a joke. One by one, all of my calls worked. Chatting is my oxygen. It's my entire life and soul. If the establishment wanted to kill me - just stick me in solitary confinement with no phone, I'll be on the roof by teatime! Contrary to belief, I can see myself from a hundred miles on a foggy day. It's more than just being a nosey parker, gobshite, and wanting to talk the hind legs off a donkey. I can't live without human interaction. Solitude is my nemesis! I don't want to be dramatic, but whilst I have my phone I can cope with ANYTHING. When I was in Africa in 1998 and went a week in between phone calls, it was hideous. I was eighteen years old, living in Nairobi - the 'star' of Capital Breakfast - but dead inside. I promised myself I would not let that happen again. So, I was back! I was re-energised! My batteries were full - just knowing my parents, sister, and loved ones knew I was OK, would be fine, and could hear I wasn't faking it. They could hear that I was utterly intrigued as to why they'd given me this exclusive access to this ridiculous world. Over the next few days, I spoke to everyone I needed to - and the rest were contacted by proxy (proxy is my common-law PA).

My dear friend, merch lady, and head of security 'Big Boned Jean' was the most dramatic. She'd gone out of her mind with worry - even been to her local police station to find out at which funeral home I was 'resting.' No one would say a word as to where I was. Almost as if the Prison Service enjoy torturing loved ones - speaks volumes about how personal my takedown is. Another tactic to bait and push the weak over the edge. Again, I was living it - but I think the worry was far worse for my few but loyal. Eventually, BBJ was added on the blower and the panic was over. My joyous palatial pal became my manuscript mule, and single-handedly got every handwritten page of these books out of jail - direct to Dame Jan to be transcribed. What a team! We've spoken daily ever since, as I have with so many of my angels - without whom I'd be pushing up daisies. I kept two lines free for friends, which I'd swap every few days. HMP were infuriated that I had the audacity to file App after App, working their fingers to the bone. Fack 'em - not my problem!

It was a huge amount of work that they deserved. Sorry HMP, you started it! There were many tears of relief over those next few days - that I hadn't done something stupid, my saboteurs' only hope and sole intention. Aside from the palpable drama, there was mega solace in knowing I was keeping perspective - still me - and could see the light. It wasn't going to be easy, but I knew I could cope in this dustbin of humanity, as long as I could hear the heavenly voices from those I trusted, adored, and who were my rocks. Very soon, they'd start to visit - even better! Emotions come and go in phases in the clink. The only dark shades I wanted to avoid, at all costs, were bitterness and anger. Anything else was fine. I had to be human. I'd earned the right to be absolutely real and honest.

I BEG OF YOU! If you ever have anyone in this situation do anything you can to get on their call list! Do whatever it takes to write/email and give them your details. It's the #1 lifesaver for sanity and keeping lags grounded and focused. Thank God, I wasn't jailed prior to Covid - there weren't any phones in cells prior to 2021. Can you imagine queuing for a call to your loved ones, with forty men tutting and waiting behind you - muttering 'hurry up' every twenty-five seconds? I can't imagine they'd be too pleased with my back-to-back half-hour calls to Tarquin the Producer and my sister Veronica. I call her Vera - leave the nicas off! Later, in my twelfth book about the UK prison shambles, I ask whether we should have Freeview TV, emails, and in-cell phones? Have prisoners' human rights gone too far? However, it's not all glamour! On the 'ones' (ground floor), I heard it was a rat and cockroach infested cesspit. Thank you, God, for sticking me on the 'twos' - out of reach of the vermin (non-noncy prisoners). Apparently, if you got up for a midnight piss downstairs, you'd see the cockroaches scuttle into the walls - whilst the rats jumped out of your McVitie's chocolate digestives, headed for the crack in the door, and then returned for a drink out of the bog. Hardly the Bellagio in Las Vegas, is it? Every con assures me that this is identical in every single CAT-B local/remand in the UK. For me, it was a free, shitty Travel Lodge to get my books done. I gave it no more importance. Don't think I haven't slummed it before! I stayed in a caravan in Grimsby – GRIM is in the title!

I would have rung the current Mrs B, but she was already on a 747 to Barbados to celebrate her temporary freedom from my tallywacker - having already put the house on Zoopla! I don't blame her. If I'm going down and getting banged up - what's good for the goose is good for the gander, hey? Smart gal!

Chapter 12

Barter, Banter, and Coping Strategies

One of the hardest things for me is 'banter' - when I'm not on-air - because my gob has been known to piss off the dopey, unwell, unstable, and medicated looney tunes. The consequences of getting on the tits of someone on a radio show is 99% radio gold - great entertainment - but a 1% chance they might boohoo to the police like a big baby and get you arrested. The risk in jail is being slashed with shank (= prison blade!).

Getting weapons into a prison is now easy, and you HAVE to be constantly on your guard. Homemade weapons - created from razor blades and often stuck on toothbrushes - can be deadly. In private jails, gangster types won't leave their pad without a shank (= makeshift knife). You don't need a blade to cause life changing injuries in the hoosegow!!! There are more simple risks, that can be devastating at best - or terminal at worst. One of the 'old tricks' in prison is to 'kettle' someone. That's not to whack them in the mush with a Russell Hobbs finest, but to boil sugar in the kettle and then throw it over the victim, causing life changing injuries. If you can boil bleach, then this is a hundred times more deadly as a weapon! You can imagine the consequences - as all of this stuff is widely available to every prisoner. So simple, cheap, and impossible to avoid. Every night at tea, we would get a breakfast pack - including five sugars. This is a real risk. You're given a new kettle at induction. What can you do? There's no way of avoiding prisoners saving up their sugars for such a premeditated attack. You can't allow yourself to become consumed by paranoia, but these are real daily concerns of inmates, that happen far more often than you'd think. You don't want to be on the wrong end of a lunatic con - with nothing to lose and a lot of scores to settle. Equally, a loo brush handle can be filed down to be a very deadly weapon. You don't need an AK-47 to cause serious harm - just look around your house! I asked a lot of lads and staff about violence and 'kettle' assaults, and 99.9% of the time it's gang, drugs, or debt-related. It's almost never random, which is somewhat comforting. Debt isn't necessarily thousands of pounds in credit card bills - far from it. In fact, it can be as stupid as 'you owe me a vape' - and weeks later, it escalates out of control. I've never felt fear in jail. However, I'm very aware the place is full of unhinged lunatics who can kick off at any point. You don't want to be in the crossfire. Trouble is never far away - even if it's absolutely nothing to do with you. Many before me have paid the price for a bozo's dysfunction or meltdown. Keeping counsel and staying mostly out of the way is critical. This is not the place for me to do the act and court any attention.

We never stop learning. Seeing the amber light, before it goes to red, is a skill that takes a lifetime to master. In the slammer the consequences of 'crossing the line' can be <u>fatal</u>. I'll pass! It's simply not worth the risk. When low intelligence meets addiction - or strong, even psychotic medication (with a dash of recklessness) - the outcome can be catastrophic. So, I told myself - from second one of 'you're guilty' - that my banter days were over with everyone, except for those I loved and trusted on the phone, in the privacy of my own port-a-loo-sized mansion. DONE. I did not want to get into a 'he said...' situation with anyone - INCLUDING STAFF/OFFICERS. I would become a smiling, aloof enigma as self-protection.

This wasn't paranoia, by the way! I remember reading on the wall - the most terrifying sign ever! It said: 'Any perceived racism will result in formal disciplinary procedure.' Excuse me? PERCEIVED? Fack me, this is worse than the hearsay vomit of evidence I sat and listened to in the Clown for five weeks. The word 'perceived' makes me quiver with fear. It's so open to numpty interpretation and shenanigans - from people who want to play the victim, manipulate the truth, and seek reprisal to aid their own vendetta. Sounds familiar, right? Look, it would be disingenuous of me to claim that this hideous stitch-up hasn't changed me. It has! It has made me <u>VERY</u> cynical about almost everything - outside of my love-packed world. Remember, I was sent down for '<u>perceived</u>' threat of violence, that <u>DIDN'T</u> HAPPEN, from people who <u>didn't</u> exist. It's all virtue-signalling - huge, hairy, dangly bollocks. My 'perceived' influence could have potentially incited the invisible man to commit a fictional crime on my behalf... that wasn't even alleged. Pfft. What a crock of shite! Now I'm in the slammer - endorsing the exact same culture. So, after all of my court nincompoopery over words, I'm now in the clink where 'perceived' actions or words could land me in segregation for a week! You want to hear half of the potty mouthed screws – not to mention their managers! It's a culture of fake comfort, pointless protestations, and platitudes, to delude you into the belief that you're safe and someone cares...... whilst surrounded by murderers, kiddie fiddlers, and granny stabbers. Infantilised dopery. It's all open to huge manipulation which is TERRIFYING!

If you get yourself into debt in jail, you are technically screwed – it will catch up with you, so one of the best bits of advice I was given in the beginning was do not borrow or take kindness off anyone. This is a prison, and these people are pros at luring you in. They can spot a naïve newbie a thousand miles away. They'd see me coming like a fat lass at an all you can eat buffet! 'New Meat' in any environment is always fun for the old-timers - who want to make a bob or two. It's good advice, though, not to trust kindness – initially. There are <u>some</u> genuinely kind souls who only want to help, and make your time behind bars a little easier through their unbelievable kindness. These angels (who you'll meet later) are few and far between - but lift your heart beyond comprehension. Never let a few rotten eggs ruin the scramble to survive.

My timing for this stretch couldn't have been better for me - and worse for the MOJ! HMP is on life support and on the verge of 'harry carry' cardiac arrest. These daft twats had inadvertently handed me the exclusive of a lifetime - smack in the middle of the country's catastrophic penitentiary collapse. The Lord works in mysterious ways, hey? Prisons were officially full, according to the BBC - and they never lie! But there will always be plenty of room for me! Despite the clink chaos and barely a week of being gagged and banged up, the most amazing thing for any prisoner happened – a visit! Proper <u>REAL</u> incredible humans – to hug!!! Two Bobby Dazzlers would now also be sent to jail….

Getting a visit is another bureaucratic ball-ache - one that I'm sure makes it impossible for 'special' inmates to even be arsed to engage with. I get it's a prison, but (identical to the phones), you need your guest's full name, date of birth, full address, and email - which must all be corroborated by two forms of ID when they arrive. If <u>ANY</u> of this is wrong, they will not be allowed in! Honestly, half of these guys can't walk in a straight line or find their gentlemen's area without a satnav - let alone work out the nuance of a VO (visiting order). Once you have all of this info, you fill in a form - and it's put on the 'system' by night staff… as and when they can be arsed. It's then signed and shoved back through your cat flap to arrange a visit. Exasperation doesn't cover it. Again though - what if you don't have the number of the person you want to visit? Or don't have any phone credit to find out their details? What if you can't read or write? Many cannot. To people like me, who are determined to get stuff done - it's annoying. But imagine if you're a smackhead who's lost the will to live - or a foreign national who doesn't speak the language? No one on the outside can book a visit until you've done this. Exasperating!!! I was hot to trot and did it straight away - it was my absolute priority. I put everyone on the list, including the milkman and my gynaecologist (just in case). Again, despite all the woke BS and do-gooding signs about 'we're here to help' - staff are so pissed off with their box-ticking lives and answering dumb-ass questions all day, they sprint to the other end of the wing to avoid you if you cry like a baby, 'Miss! Miss! Miss!' How is there any time to do this - when you're behind the door 23 hours a day. Impossible! Again, prisoners are far more helpful than any screw! I would not have survived without the kindness, advice, guidance, tips, and generosity of the few good men who genuinely care – even at this early stage. What staggers me about officer training - which takes ten weeks max to complete - is that they do not spend a second on PSI (= prison law) - the rule book! Unbelievable. How can you be the referee if you don't know the rules?

Curiously, as time has gone on, I've noticed a fury and resentment from staff when you quote the rules or appear to know your entitlements. Undermining a screw never ends well! I guess no one likes a smart arse - and they've got the keys. Anyway, I did it - VO (Visiting Orders) sorted for Mum and Dad. But then you have to fill in ANOTHER paper form to request your preference of top three dates/times for visits - which is about as much use as a hard-on at the Celibate Christmas party. You're back in limbo, awaiting a civil serpant to pull their finger out of their anus erectus. After six days, this process was complete, and I could have my first of two visits a month. You get a third visit in three months - if you were well behaved and became 'enhanced.' If you're in private jails, you get four visits. Makes absolutely no sense and is totally inconsistent. Rule one of HMP governance is: you cannot presume what happened last month will happen this month - or even tomorrow. They make it up as they go along, with total impunity. They move all the goalposts without any prior warning - and you cannot argue. Blind compliance!

I will concede - HMP are faultless in timekeeping. You can set your watch by 'moves' and bang-up. As I was politely warned, a few days into my social experiment behind bars, the 'call bell' is not a 'call bell' - it's an 'emergency bell.' My reply of, "But it says, 'call bell' on it," was not well received. "Listen, dickhead, this is prison - not the Ritz. Don't press the bell!" Officer Big Bollocks (as charming as he appeared) wasn't joking. Smile. Ignore. Store for book. Revel in the fact you're not them. Move on. The mental illness and irrational tyrant instability amongst some staff is staggering. I wonder if they've ever felt excitement - or true love?

Finally, I had the pure joy of calling home to confirm I would see my parents Saturday at 2pm! It was like winning the lottery.

Even now, <u>everything</u> builds towards visits for me. I get through every day to 7pm to make my calls - but the entire week leads to my real life, the only thing that matters: in the company of sane and gorgeous human beings, who travel at great cost and inconvenience to see me. Visits - for many, especially lifers - are just too painful. Most prisoners, it turns out, choose not to see anyone. For me, it was an early Christmas. Lest we forget, it's absolutely humiliating for people to be dragged through security, and the indignity of even coming to a Scumbag Centre for the depraved.

The University of Slammersville's soundtrack is that of legend. HMP particularly thrives on hierarchy and regiment - there's no messing around or shenanigans. Private prisons couldn't care less. Inhabitants - prisoners - are classed as 'residents,' not murderers or rapists. Residents? I ask you?! This sickens me, to be honest. This woke bullshitery is only surface-deep. Trust me - when a box-ticking, eighteen-year-old, big-boned, tongue-pierced, peculiar-looking lump screams 'Roll Check!" like a hyena - despite her lip gloss and eyeliner, whilst smoking her vape, with a tiger tattoo on her arm (the size of Gemma Collins' gunt) - I can assure you: she's not messing about. It's prison. They mean business. Get behind your door - or ten men in black will be called to twist you up (that's a real thing), and help you do so! This is not a request – it's a demand known as a direct order. Their stench of Lynx Africa will knock you out - long before their overwhelming dull personalities and PAVA spray demand your attention. No ADHD diagnosis or fits of 'anxiety' will count a jot, trust me. You're going behind that door, so get over your Aspergers! This is prison not Oprah!

I wouldn't do this job for all the tea in China - or all the chocolate and snacks in James Corden's pantry. Good Lord, I'd rather be on the dole than do this precarious job. So why do they do it? I think inadequacy, insecurity, men's issues, and a power trip would explain it for a lot of the whippersnapper screws coming through the turnstile of juveniles - the size of blimps - in their droves. Many tell me it was the only job they could get - not exactly a raving endorsement. The days of ex-military and police holding court and keeping order have long gone. They desperately need them back! Now they've got excessive numbers of three-foot-five (wide) women — as they claim it 'de-escalates situations and avoids conflict.' That may be true... but they're facking useless when it all kicks off!

Some officers LOVE to bang and clatter their way through the labyrinths of corridors and doorways. It's all theatre. Totally unnecessary. Pure willy waggling. These doors can be locked as quietly as any other door. I invested in a pack of £1 ear plugs off the canteen. <u>BEST</u> investment I've made - since the bacon factory in Israel and holiday homes in Ukraine. I'm three sheets to the wind when I insert those shushy-shushy inflatables. Can't hear a dicky bird! The racket is all panto - designed to put you in your place. Good screws don't play these silly, childish games. If you're remotely anxious, this can be a very effective way of creating an air of discomfort and paranoia. I've already worked out the kangas with a lot of years under their belt are the toppers. The other doozies - I avoid. I trained myself, over time, to zone all of this white noise out. It's like living under Heathrow Runway 27 Left. Eventually, you don't see, hear, or notice these noisy attention-seekers anymore. I'm not kidding - screws are like Just Stop Oil protestors: only to be ignored and of zero interest to me! You might think 'he's making this up, to pretend he didn't care' – well I don't. I am always ahead of the game. They won't ever tell me what to do - or catch me out. You cannot let their 'stunts' chip away at your soul or confidence. Perspective - and one hundred percent contempt for their insanity - is the only way to survive. Visits are my Achilles' heel, as they are for most family men. Kangas can conveniently 'forget' to unlock you for visits. I saw it happen many times - and it's a guaranteed way of getting the unstable and desperate to kick off.

Everything in jail is a paper trail of excuses. If that piece of paper - saying you have a visit or appointment at any stage - doesn't reach the right box-ticker, your door simply won't be unlocked. Press the 'call bell' at your peril - half an hour later, you might get a screw to open your flap. I was neurotic about not keeping my guests waiting - as EVERY second counted. I prayed they'd get me at 1.30pm - in plenty of time for a 2pm visit. I couldn't help but feel blessed and different, as most men were utterly defeated and in no mood to get out of bed - let alone have a slammer soirée. It still hadn't registered that this was proper prison - and not a Louis Theroux documentary. Long may my delusion last!!! Most men (especially in VP) have no hope of ever getting back to normal life – let alone a happy one. In many cases, there's huge shame and family had (rightly) given up and headed for zee hills. Once again, I'm in my own little world. A screw unlocked at 1.35pm. Plenty of time. I waited by the back door - identical to the chapel. I stood there and chatted with a 22-year-old lad! He too was upbeat. He explained why a lot of VPs - and the very worst offenders - keep a very low-profile. Bad lads - will pay big money to put a hit on a 'VP.' There's a lot of kudos for belting a nonce – it's an unspoken reality. The entire structure and pecking order are built on your crime, intelligence, popularity, general confidence, and personality. Being a sex offender, five foot tall, and nine stone, will leave you unbelievably vulnerable! No wonder they're too ashamed to show their face. A nonce will NEVER do that. They'll forever look over their shoulder - and rightly so. I'd noticed the truly bonkers, darkest, and creepiest simply come nowhere near you. What a relief! If you're a high-profile paedo, you're not going to discuss it in this dangerous environment. They wanna be 100% persona non grata. HOWEVER - it's 2020+, and there's a thing called the internet! The cat is out of the bag. The enormous Pandora's box is wide open - legs spread like an Amsterdam call girl. Bad lads won't kick the shit out of you - they'll pay a smackhead with drugs to do it. Smart, hey.

As I know all too well - you cannot escape your past or present. Little did I know the jail was flooded with illegal smartphones. Like drugs, the system has virtually given up trying to stop them. Who needs an iPhone anyway? You just call up your Mrs from the pad, give her the name plastered on their door - twenty seconds later, Mr Google spills the beans.

Chapter 13

Mum and Dad were Prisoners!

The day of Her Majesty's funeral was non-stop doom and gloom - courtesy of glory-seeking journalists, many of whom proudly worked alongside BBC paedo heroes like Huw Edwards. Ouch! Now, do you catch my drift about the nonce factory? What a difference a year can make, hey? History will be my vindication - the truth WILL set me free. All I could think about was seeing the two most important heroes in my life - who were about to enter the toxic world of prison to see their son. I had to put their minds at rest... but how unedifying! All a mother wants to do is see the white of your eyes, but let's face it, they'd prefer to do it in the Palladium than Belmarsh! All a dad wants to do is high five you - and pretend he's cool and couldn't care less. I was having none of that nonsense, I wanted the biggest hug ever. For the first time in my 42 years on this mortal coil - I needed my folks more than ever - just to prove that 'I'M OK!'

As the hours passed, I suddenly had a hideous guilt that I was putting my parents in prison. I became increasingly uncomfortable with the reality of this environment, but I was shackled to my 'new normal.' My bravery and refusal to be mentally incarcerated was irrelevant. They would now have to live this hideousness - and be put through the indignity and security charade of this shithouse, designed for dads who shove coke in their baby's nappies to make a few quid. That happens regularly, by the way - this place ain't a bed of roses. My conviction would now impact them - through no fault of their own. They did not deserve this. Everything was beyond their control – <u>EVERY</u> parent's worst nightmare. Never underestimate the punishment on those around the condemned. These are the unavoidable devastating consequences of prison. Those that love you - are sentenced too. How will I ever make this right? You can't. Just like buying back memories – it's impossible. But, like a terrible injury, cancer, or tragedy – time passes, and you can get through it <u>TOGETHER</u>. That's what true family and friends are for. It's a time to hunker down - knowing there's a huge light and love at the end of the 2-year, 9-months-long tunnel!

Nothing can buy back time in a hostage situation - or make right the hurt and distress of coming into these Asylums for Arseholes. My job was to go the other way - turn this around, and make sure this kidnapping would become content to profit from in the future. I would own this hostage situation. One of the worries you have - having looked forward to this powerful reunion for days - is that something may have gone wrong at security, and they'll be sent home. You'll be sat there like a prick - by yourself - knowing everyone is looking at you, thinking you didn't have anyone who loved you enough to turn up. It would be more humiliating than going on *Celebrity First Dates* - and Katie Price walks through the door. Excruciating! If you forget your ID, you ain't coming in - without exception. I've regularly seen it happen to others - it's so depressing and heart-wrenching. I can't imagine the pure frustration and heartache of knowing there is a wall in between the insanity of this sanctuary for sickos - and your loved ones. Equally, being inappropriately dressed gets you kicked out of the Big Bro House too. This is not a bingo hall, for very good reasons: no cleavage, no legs or shorts, and certainly no revealing underwear. I found this a relief with my mother coming in - I asked her to wear a burka, 'just in case.' You can't be too careful.

We were walked across to the visiting hall, which had a cold and clinical doctor's waiting-room atmosphere. You are led in, scanned, pointlessly searched - and then you're taken to your numbered table, with a band on your arm in various colours, to identify you clearly as a political prisoner - not a granny-fanny offender. Mine was brown – the colour to symbolise the shitstorm they'd created! The days of 'school' tables have gone. Don't believe what they show on Corrie and Eastenders - in darkened rooms. Obviously, this ain't the Garrick Club, but who cares, you're with your loved ones in a very relaxed and comfortable atmosphere! You sit and wait - amongst dreadful prisoner art on the walls - befitting a special needs centre. You're praying that your people have got through the hour-long security process, where they x-ray your toes and stick a finger up your anus-erectus, 'just in case...' My old dad asked for two fingers - for a second opinion. Smart chap. After about five minutes, my mum ran through the door like a Labrador puppy - not dissimilar to the reaction I get from Doddy when the doorbell goes. It was electrifying! For all of the lows of the evil system, the pure love and joy received through the presence of my parents was worth a million dollars and far above any sense of belonging I'd ever felt before. Maybe this was a huge wake-up call for all of us? As our eyes met and our hands embraced, all of the previous week's toxic, evil, wicked, and disgusting events were whisked away. It was like a Criss Angel Vegas illusion - Piff Paff Pouf! A magical cloak of protection engulfed me. The overwhelming love made all the bags of BBC, police, and corrupt court bollocks disappear - in a heartbeat. It was almost as if - instantly, within one second - my batteries were taken from near empty to full capacity. I've never had that intense boost before or since. In recent years, I've been on stage in front of a thousand-plus people to a standing ovation - and yet, the feeling of that reunion and embrace outweighs any sell-out gig. It's Red Bull for the heart and soul.

I then did something I'd never done before in thirty years - I hugged my dad. I kissed my dad on the cheek, and I told him that I loved him. It was one of the most beautiful and most memorable moments of my life. I cannot tell you the comfort it gave me to tell my father - and hero - that I loved him... and I do! Fellas 'up North' don't do this sort of sloppy, soft, and wet wipe numptiness - but I HAD TO! I'm so glad I did... and do, every time. I've told my mum, sister, and almost every punter I've ever met that I love them too. In different ways, on different scales - I genuinely DO love them, and there's nothing they can do about it. Now was the time to sing it from the rooftops! Manly men from pit estates don't tend to show too much emotion, but it's my rules now! Prison is one thing - BUT all I truly care about is getting through this with my folks fit and well. So, this was one of the most amazing days of my life. My mamma and pop were back with me and boy did we have a good time! After the initial tears of relief and overwhelming joy, we could have been swigging vodka and diets on my posh Ladyboy sofa at Alex's Acres - in my back passage snug. What prison teaches you is that this is ALL a temporary artifice and façade - it doesn't matter. A lad once said to me, 'The difference between cons and screws is that the screws haven't been caught yet!' I did smile. That profound insight couldn't have been more true.

This visit was about confirming to my folks that these bastards would never grind me down - and that this test of my endurance and patience would not break me. Seven days into my hostage situation, I felt loved, cherished, needed, supported, and adored. I wonder if my assassins were blessed with these gifts? Maybe the motive of the jealous trolls was to take away my blessings - because they'd never had them. I had hope and faith, as my loved ones wanted me back. What more can a human being ask for? We sat and processed the last two years. The last two weeks, in contrast, summed up the ridiculousness. We couldn't help but reminisce about my 24 months of YouTube insanity! From selling out venues and getting standing ovations - from Southampton to Glasgow - to landing in the slammer for almost three years... what a story! It could only happen to me, that's for sure.

My darling mum said, "We're so proud of you" - those golden (but crushing) words. I begged them not to worry. I repeated a thousand times that as long as they stayed well – I'd be fine. It finally sunk in. It was a deal sealed on a comedy handshake. This was now a team effort. When you're under attack, all you need is unity and an endgame. Light always extinguishes darkness. They'd got my back - and I'll always have theirs. How remarkable is that? I'm a lucky boy. At my lowest ebb, I counted my infinite blessings.

Visits are designed to be a relaxed affair. Dad, like me, noticed the shitty prisoner art on the wall - similar to being in a cringe primary school. It was for sale at £200 for a tin of dropped paint! It's more Pollock than Banksy. I'm sure some lefty gallery will stick it up to vindicate a child rapist... Pfft! Thank God I wasn't reviewing this restaurant - it wouldn't be five stars, that's for sure! You get coffees, sandwiches, chocolates, cakes, and most other dead carbs. It's designed to perpetuate the myth that it's all cute, cuddly, and friendly for 'family ties' – the priority of modern HMP. I hardly think two hours every two weeks is the perfect way to keep bonds with loved ones…...or even 18p a minute to call a mobile during the day. All woke window-dressing. Officers mince around, ready to pounce if a whippersnapper's missus pulls £1,000 worth of ket out of her crack! (No, really - they do!) This visit was, thankfully, uneventful.

I looked into Dad's eyes. The age of my father especially concerned me. It played heavy on my heart. At seventy-eight he's no spring chicken and he had lived life 100%. Travel, food, and drink are my folks' priority after retirement. God bless them! I encourage them to live life as if it will end tomorrow. They've had the best life possible and adore their simple pleasures of time, dinners, trips, friends, and holidays - all with the ones they love. The pain that I've inflicted on them is totally unimaginable, but it could be a <u>lot</u> worse! I think of my dear best friend Matt who died of a brain tumour at thirty. How on earth his parents coped with this tragedy is beyond my comprehension. Surely, we can't compare? Time is an illusion. Look, a week had already passed – a hundred and thirty-one weeks to go! We just have to get there TOGETHER. If it weren't so malicious - it would be exciting! My dear mate James had a profound thought - that this was akin to a two-year-nine-month cruise contract around the world. You're captive, with a lot of people you don't know or like - but they are giving you the time, opportunity, and experience to see another world, which I can profit from later. If I used my time wisely, I could document this 'opportunity' to expose another fundamentally flawed institutional monolith. This was a game-changer in terms of my psychology. What optimism. What's the difference between working on ships, oil rigs, or anywhere abroad for years (which so many people do), away from your family and friends? Mentally, this was empowering - and it kept it all in context. <u>PERSPECTIVE</u>: if you can keep that, you will win!

I knew that my life would not be behind the door for long - CAT-C was imminent. Then I could do my bird in a 'soft' jail. If five arrests and three raids don't scare you into silence and push you over the edge, nothing will. I remained resolute and 100% resilient, knowing that my Human Rights Act Article 10 was stolen - for now - but it will resume and return. Seeing Mum and Dad was just what the doctor ordered! Had my critics considered father time? They cannot silence me forever! They cannot prevent me returning to my JOB as a gobshite.........I mean journalist – even the judge made that clear. I'll have to wear this free speech conviction as a badge of honour – not shame! I'll own it, not sweep it under the carpet. I'll sing from the rooftops (until the cons come home to roost)! I AM A CONVICTED TALKER!!! Stick that in your pipe and smoke it! All of this clarity came in just two hours of chit chat with my folks.

Love and unrelenting ambition would get me through! I looked into the eyes of my parents. They know that I have never told a single lie - ever. I wasn't even accused of doing so. It was, indeed, the truth that landed me behind bars. What anyone else thinks is completely, utterly, entirely, and totally irrelevant! Me and Team AB know the truth. Through history, this is an age-old story: they malign you; they try to kill you - painting you as mad - before the whole thing goes full circle, prior to a second coming. Ask Trump, Tommy, Jesus, Farage, or Katie. I'm in good company!

The time flew by in what felt like two minutes, not two hours. The bell rang, and I thought it was a boxing match half-time for entertainment. That was it, sadly - done. My final words of counselling were to remember that we saw each other almost daily for forty-plus years when I wasn't working away, yet weeks passed when I was. This is no different! Most families don't get to see each other for weeks or months – if at all. Some are lucky to get a Christmas card. It's all about keeping this in proportion and perspective. Our love was boundless - and for that, we HAD to be grateful. I was now doing a proper job for the first time in my life: writing books ahead of my relaunch and the biggest tour of my life in 2025. That was that. Platitudes will get us through! I begged them to live their lives, enjoy Doddy - who they obviously loved way more than me anyway. Who wouldn't?! She's much more fun and cuddlier, and she has a far more impressive tickling-stick waggy tail than I do. She had now become the heartbeat of my entire family. A little bit of me was there with them when she was in the room - stealing the limelight and pulling focus from my unfortunate absence. I don't need to say how much I miss her; that's stating the bleeding obvious. The kids and animals always stick in your craw more than adults. The memories you're missing always feel a lot more precious. The hardest thing for me was the thought that my little cockapoo didn't know why her daddy had left her. I was on loudspeaker nightly, so she could enjoy my dulcet tones. I just prayed that the fun, strokes, and love from everyone else would distract her.

What all of this confirms is that it's horrendously cruel for those around me. I take full responsibility for this - and nothing else. The price of notoriety, hey? Mum and Dad stood up, and we ended this 'audience with' exactly the same way it began: all hugs, kisses, and 'I love yous.' I truly felt like the luckiest man on earth. I only had two visits per month - for now. I had a lot of people I wanted to see, but I felt in my heart my folks had earned the right to be my only priority - for now. You can have three adults, plus kids, so I'd use the plus one to see everyone else, one by one. Should prisoners have to make this choice? If 'family ties' are the main priority, why can't we have two visits a week and forgo the luxuries of percolator coffee, tins of corned beef, pedicures, and moisturising cream? The answer is simple. The stuff on the canteen keeps the arseholes - who prioritise 'stuff' over human hugs - quiet and compliant. What a depressing realisation. This system has no compassion, empathy, or common sense, as you'll discover. I left buoyant but broken-hearted for them. It could never be harder than those two hours. From now on, it's time for some stiff upper lip bulldog spirit. We've got this - and there's nothing anyone can do about it!

Chapter 14

The Worst Feeling in Prison = 4pm Saturday

I can categorically confirm that the worst feeling in the slammer (and the world) is not Friday night bang-up, communal showers, dealing with dickhead screws, or the potential threat from whack jobs stabbing you in the ball sack - but the walk of shame back to the wing after visits, knowing how they'd be feeling. The worst moment of my life was leaving the folks after the first visit. OK, for me - I know some reading this will say, "Who do you think you are? We don't have families. You're lucky to get a visit." Well, it's my book - so piss off! And NO, I don't give refunds. Thanks for the 99p in the Pound Shop! If the notion of having love in your heart offends you, this isn't going to be the book for you - sorry about your luck! I'm talking about those tug-on-your-heartstrings moments, like waving off your kid to uni, or saying goodbye (for what feels like forever) at the airport to your Aunty Fanny with a dislocated rectum - who you'll never see again. If your intention was to stab me in the heart - bullseye!!! Nothing during sentencing had 1% of this emotional toil.

So, where was I? Yes - the walk of shame. It's not so bad now, as this calms down and normalises, but for the first three months (at least) of any prison journey, you'll struggle to process the horrific inhumanity of being torn apart - by order of HMP - after visits. Your kidnapping becomes very real as they walk away. This is ludicrous. Barbaric. And for the most vulnerable men, the most unbearable and stressful time - exactly when you need a guiding hand the most. Lest we forget, self-harm and suicide is a major issue in prison, killing hundreds a year. NOTHING will be worse than your first few weeks in a new jail. It's like your first day at school - but a thousand times worse. Your teachers aren't trained (other than to lock doors), don't care, and your fellow students are on crack or off their tits. Fight or flight kicks in as the body cannot cope with powerlessness and the unknown at the same time. By the way, kids who misbehave are put on basic - with just one visit per month. I simply don't see how visits correlate with behaviour. Surely the worst-behaved need more visits to convince them to snap out of it? Visits are used as a carrot. If you screw up - literally - they become the stick. Once the hall is cleared, everyone normally stands and leaves together. But of course, I was an HMP Lincoln VIP - so we left first. We were then put into a holding pen, like sheep being herded on a farm, 'for our own protection' - away from the 'normal'/main non-perverts to prevent argy-bargies. I asked the chap next to me, who looked a cross between Rylan and Russell Brand, "Did you have a good one?" He said, "It's my first visit in a year. It was shit. Not facking doing that again." Ouch. Not exactly the Nolans is it? Maybe it is! I wanted to be silent, but curiosity killed the cat. Another fella looked like every movie con from the sixties. He was six foot tall (and wide), tattooed head to toe - including his neck and face. "You're that chap off the telly, aren't you?" he said to me. "Oh God," I said silently to myself. How the fack do I even answer that? This would happen A LOT over the next twelve months. I said, "Yes mate. Do you mean *Crimewatch*?" He laughed. "What did you do though?" Here we go: "My KC's still not sure, but apparently hurty words causing crocodile tears is the new terrorism!" he laughed. "It's bullshit. I can't work it out." I'm fair game for this question, but I've never found the 'perfect' answer to explain the unexplainable. Then he said, "They facked you, big time - you've pissed someone important off!" I wonder who that 'someone' is - who really pushed this? How do you rationalise this to a layperson... or indeed an armed robber... let alone my own brain?

My advice to anyone who pleads not guilty - because they 100% believe in their innocence - is to say as much as you can publicly pre-charge, and say NOTHING to anyone in the system. All they want is a glitch in the matrix to leg you over. Don't fall for it. The whole court system and legal profession thrives on pressure, intimidation, and power... all so they can do a dodgy back-room deal upstairs when you're not looking. Even after jail, it continues. Turns out, once you're released, HMP and probation are identical. It's called MAPPA - Multi-Agency Public Protection Arrangement - i.e. all the backstabbers from the Police, the Prison Service, and the National Probation Service working in cahoots in a mafia of prejudiced establishment mobsters, entirely designed to control you. Being polite, sitting quietly, and 'knowing your place' will get you nowhere. Thank God I told my punters everything! There's no question it saved my reputation, career, and mental health throughout the trial - by being so transparent through my court reports. 'Open court' (that is to say every word can be reported for ever), is the only good thing about our broken corrupt system. In summary, the last people you should <u>ever</u> trust are the corrupt police, prison service, or probation! <u>NO COMMENT</u>!!! They write down, manipulate, and distort everything! Sadly, lawyers will always have one single agenda (with few exceptions) – to make money and drag it out as long as possible. This tattooed-faced genius in visits crystallised everything in a heartbeat - and brought me great comfort without even knowing it! It's all nonsense and should be treated as such. This is just a shushy game. The line that every fellow co-star would say repeatedly is, '<u>you'll never beat the system</u>.' What they mean is - when you critically embarrass the BBC as their number one whistle-blower for over ten years, causing irreparable damage... Then go on to expose the police as liars, paedo protectors, bullies, and an incompetent, vile mafia (with video to prove it).... And then take on the courts by yourself - it's never going to end well. What a sad reflection on our United Kingdom. We mock Russia and North Korea – why? I can't see any difference! At least China brag about their dystopian shushy dictatorship.

This 'unique' man was one of HMP's top punters, who - like many - had anger issues and didn't tolerate rudeness from screws. He'd been behind bars for nearly two decades. He was a pro and had seen it all! "What's your name mate" I hastened to ask. "They call me Handy Andy" ....in for a penny, "Why do they call you Handy Andy?" I quivered. "Because when the screws piss me off, I get handy and five of the leary twats have ended up in hospital for pissing me off. I'm on VP for their protection not mine. Oh - and it gets me a single cell because I'm very high risk." WOW. How do I even begin to digest what I was being told. Firstly, lifers have nothing to lose. If you know you're almost certainly not getting out, your scorecard and reviews on HMP Tripadvisor are totally irrelevant. If you do get out, 'life' really means you're on zero-tolerance licence conditions for the rest of your life. Prison has a system to totally infantilise prisoners - like children - by using a positive and negative score system. If you 'do something nice,' you get a 'positive,' and this (allegedly) helps you get promotion to a better jail. All childish foolishness. A positive for taking the rubbish out will not get me to CAT-D, trust me! It's like giving a sticker to a retarded kid for putting his socks on. So silly. It's Big Brother noting your every move and behaviour - with the intention, more importantly, to list your negative behaviour, known as 'IPF warnings.' This is one step down from a proper adjudication or nicking, which takes place in front of a Governor. Remember: the people commenting aren't psychologists, or even professionals with experience... yet their words carry great weight. At first, I found it terrifying that I might get 'a negative' for offending a member of staff. However, I quickly realised that, like so much of the legal, court, and prison game - it's all window dressing. It makes absolutely no difference whatsoever. They will do what they want to do - exactly when they want to do it. Nothing you do will ever change that. They'll pick and choose what they want to hear.

NOMIS (your file) is basically the Neighbourhood Watch of the prison service - well, more of a snooper's charter. It's all cloak and dagger - but like anything, over time you find officers and staff who'll 'check' it for you and tip you off if a backstabbing Judas is trying to cause trouble and stick crap on your chitty. If you're on a life sentence, you're not going to care that some non-binary twelve-year-old work experience officer found your tone aggressive - or disrespectful. Sadly, it's aimed at the school-kid mentality, which packs these disposal units with doofuses and dickwads, day in and day out. I guess this game's not designed for the likes of me. You're meant to follow like sheep... just like most did during Covid.

I aimed to avoid all moronic fart-heads who wanted to play these mind games. My only interest was finding the few 'good' family men - the sort I'd be on holiday with - knowing they would see the wood for the trees, and hopefully link a sentence without littering it with 'like' every three words. After our chat, we were walked back to VP and collected our food: two BBQ chicken sandwiches with the obligatory Walkers crisps. Good Lord, I can't afford them on civvy street! No credit crunch here then. I won't eat them because of that lefty prick Lineker. For some reason, every bag tastes of arrogance and hypocrisy to me. Now he's given up his £1M from the BBC rape-tax wage, I might find the 'Beef Curtains' flavour slightly less distasteful. At 4.30pm, the door was locked until tomorrow's room service: toast and jam. It was my second Christian service in the morning. For me, even after one week, my survival strategy was now about dates in the diary. As long as there was something to aim for and look forward to, I was as happy as Larry. Who is Larry, BTW? Surely not the fella in G-27 who shagged his sister's llama at the kids' farm and set up an OnlyFans page - FarmyardFanatics?

I now had the warm, cosy afterglow of my parents' visit. I'd explained to them that I should be on the move within days - though I'd only find out that morning, for 'security reasons.' I just had to be patient. I went to great lengths to explicitly describe as much as I could to my beloveds. Knowledge is power in these confusing circumstances. Ironically, CAT-Bs are now the bottleneck of the prison service. They are truly the dumping ground of HMP - yet they have the worst conditions, the most violent and volatile men, and the least, most pressured resources. It's a cesspit of sinners - from which I couldn't wait to leave! Moments later, a gift came from the Gods. The door cracked and Officer Shifferbrains said, "Mail Belfield, you're a popular boy!" I was given a pile of thirty letters with self-addressed envelopes. Nick's message to my punters was being processed. This was the best day ever!

At six o'clock sharp, my first call was to - my Aunty Dot - when phone calls became half price. She too was under house arrest due to her MS, whilst I was enslaved by Boris' dictatorship. I told her that Mum and Dad had been, and we were all OK. She replied, "I've just read *The Guardian*. They've done a three-page hatchet job of you." I wanted to say, 'Take that lefty, worthless, on-its-arse, biased, agenda-driven crap - and get your carer to wipe your arse with it!' Instead, I couldn't resist: "Thank you God it's in *The Guardian* - at least no one will read it" ...Which they didn't. *The Times* and *The Guardian* are two peas in a stinking pod of rags that wanted to dig the knife deep. I wonder who was working them from behind? Who's funding this very specific agenda and storm in a teacup? Three pages – Oy Vey! They appear to be influenced editorially by some most peculiar sources - almost as if they know their days are numbered and want to kill off their loudest critic and biggest YouTube competition. *The Guardian* admits it's not profitable and is unsustainable in print. Both of these propaganda promoters are more redundant than Phillip Schofield's accountant. They have a tiny audience but act as the mouthpiece - and apparent gatekeeper - for powerful dark forces, the establishment, and their affiliates. All newspapers are screwed - even Murdoch admitted *The Sun* isn't even worth £1. My business online is the future for all mainstream monoliths. So who cares what these toilet rolls think?

Days later, Anna Brees sent me a copy of the article in full - which I refused to read. Straight down the toilet for that. Anna had been a good friend during lockdown. She was aghast at the diarrhoea and creative licence. They'd already gone with the 'he's in jail and dead — we can say what we like.' Shocking. She's a former ITV and BBC journo who, like me, went rogue during Covid - in defence of the millions of kids, teens, families, and people whose lives and businesses were destroyed by Boris' bullshit and medically incorrect guidance. She bravely spoke to doctors - yes, qualified doctors - about the risks of the jabs, and was quickly banished from YouTube. She was mocked by the lefty sheep, who've all been collectively and brazenly bought by the deep state. Along with MP Andrew Bridgen - another hero of the masses - she lost everything through THE TRUTH! Neither told a lie. Neither were wrong. Both were ridiculed and wiped out. Sickening. They were spot on and totally ahead of the game. They deserve an apology, big time. So why were the MSM so viciously protective of the government during this period? Could it be the BILLIONS Boris spent on advertising for 'public service adverts' - the lifeline that kept them afloat, ICU-style, while being given their last media rites? Shameful conspiracy. Who's the covidiots now? The truth always outs in the end.

We later proved *The Guardian* article was fed by a top BBC journalist who had a very clear axe to grind and a vested interest. This person - fack it - this spineless, closeted, unhinged, and EVIL weasel wanted the final nail in my coffin and hoped this was the way to do it. <u>FAIL.</u> This duplicitous snake loves to point fingers at others, forgetting several point back at them at the same time! There were so many factual errors, lies, and convenient untruths that the person who fed this laughable guff more or less signed it at the bottom. Why are these people still <u>SO</u> consumed? What are they scared of me saying? I'm in jail, gone, bye bye – what more was there to say? Well, according to that diarrhoea rag for woke, bonkers lefties and platitude-pissing purveyors - there were pages of intended career assassination. Working as the Dignitas for the BBC and police, their goal was to convince the public I was a monster on a level never seen before. First *Newsnight* - and now this. Even Wayne Couzens didn't get this level of vindictive and vitriolic spite. There was 10% truth and 90% intentional fantasy in that colostomy-bag triple-page windy pops. It was rumour, guesswork, and the incendiary imagination of that hideously vile, disgusting, Beeb-funded Judas and creep who helped script it. What a breed. Even the BBC's paedo statue on Broadcasting House covered its eyes in shame... Not because of the naked boy with his cock out beneath her... Or the fact its stonemason, Eric Gill, was a convicted paedo who raped his two daughters and the family dog... No, no - This was an unadulterated and shameless smear campaign, published at a point I couldn't defend myself. Classy, hey? What trusted journalism we have. Go 'verify' that, you pigs.

Like all gutter press, I treat it with absolute contempt. It wouldn't be the last article written, I'm sure. To call it 'tomorrow's chip paper' was a compliment. I wouldn't put my pollock and scraps anywhere near it. But curiously, like all the other sabotage by the old-school media (on life support), it made no difference to me - BUT it did devastate my loved ones and defenders. Dorothy, like so many who saw the TV and print coverage, was outraged on my behalf. It was such an absolute liberty - an audacious fabrication of reality. My reaction is always the same: complete nonchalance and apathy, knowing my time will come... And knowing that all publicity is good publicity (unless you're a paedo). Would these scum sucking pondlife say it to my face? Nar - they're too busy on the dark web in the spare room, while their butch wives iron their gimp costume. Again, it's all a game - played by some very sick, obsessed, possessed saddos who have a lot to hide and a lot to lose. I'm steadfast!!! Don't forget: my house was raided three times, and they found nothing. Not a single piece of evidence - let alone anything incriminating or even embarrassing. I was told categorically that the evil Notts Corrupt Police (NCP) couldn't find a shred of anything to besmirch my character... That's why they were sent back again. And again. I'd love the police to search the medicated mental's filth riddled daily online history! Time will tell - and I'm 100% confident that KARMA will kick these backside backstabbers in their ass like a rent boy swiping his credit card between their butt cheeks in Soho! Just wait. Despite my bravado and ability to see this for what it is (and, most importantly, instantly disregard it), I did have to explain how it works to elderly family who simply couldn't process the unprecedented and vitriolic venom. For them, it was heartbreaking. They lived all this with me - and they know the real me. What ultimately had I done? Aunty Dot summed it up in one: "You opened your big gob, didn't you?" I replied, "Yes love - and like in China, that's now an imprisonable offence in 2022." She laughed. I was only the first of many citizens being locked up for words - while paedos remained free to rape our kids. Why do judges have such sympathy with nonces? I'm asking for a friend. I left the call with a reality check: "You know me, my heart, and who I am - they can go and fack themselves with a cactus!" She laughed every time. "One word, Doll - jealousy. Root of all evil." Like the Phoenix, I'll be back. My embers are burning bright!

Over time, you do become totally desensitised to this type of gloating word mucus, criticism, and media bummocks. It's the opposite of #bekind - it's bullying, and flies in the face of mental health and all the guff lefties spunk. It parallels <u>exactly</u> what they accused me of. The very people who have LGBTQ+69s flags on their profiles with 'Love not Hate' are the first to expose themselves as the putrid, twisted enemas that they are. Three pages tells me there's funny business, shenanigans, and dark forces at work - and clickbait to be had. We all know people who buy *The Guardian* are too busy sellotaping themselves to the M25 to read this comic. They only have it delivered so the post boy tells the neighbours. I take it as a huge compliment. You have to see it for what it is. If Boy George can end up in panto after his criminal record - not *Karma Chameleon*, but the radiator incident with the rent boy - then...

Look - if you dance with the devil of public attention, it can bite you in the ass. Ask Barrymore, who almost drowned under the negative press - as did John Leslie, based on pure vitriol and no wrongdoing. The media choreographed and profited from their unjust demise. Tickle the tits of fame, and the minge of media will eventually leave a nasty taste in your mouth. They build you up to tear you down. The profit's in your demise - not your success. What's good for the goose is worth a gander, right?

Ultimately, though, the public will decide. That's one thing I've never doubted. Unlike Tate and Brand, my 'crime' isn't sexual – that's far harder to overcome. Although the smart people can see through the transparent media vilification and horseshit, it's very tough in this climate to fight back mainstream - in theatres, etc. They, of course, don't need MSM - they're much bigger than that. We shall see. I don't think most people believe a word of the press nowadays. Have you noticed Piers and Clarkson are far less trappy, chopsy, and controversial since my temporary eviction from the airwaves? Coincidence? Anyone who thinks showbiz is all First-Class flights, 5* hotels, and press nights is delusional - and never had any success. The price you pay for our passion and <u>integrity</u> is enormous on all of those around you. In hindsight, I should have been more honest with the silver-tops about how vicious the loons were - and how determined the state was to teach me a lesson and 'close me down.' I did keep most of the online cancer from them. Regrets? I have a few...Telling the TRUTH isn't one of them. But buttering my parsnips and playing down the extent of my ejaculation from public life - that was a faux pas!

Chapter 15

Off to HMS Stockings

A new week began, so I was up about 7.30am to watch Nana Manshushy spewing the BBC box-ticking propaganda - and articles on lady garden leakage and potholes. It was set to be just another uneventful day at HMP, as most are. I was planning the delights of *This Morning* and waiting for *Loose Women*, but it wasn't to be. The legendary unlock came at 8.30am, with yet another officer I hadn't seen before - stood with a pile of bags. This only means one thing...

"You're being shipped out, stud," he said, as his friendly eyes looked at the other. Stud? For the mother of God - are all these Neanderthals fruity? I suppose eyeliner was a giveaway. It's like any man who says 'drinkypoos' or 'footy' - you've got to be suspicious! Anywho... "Where am I going?" I cautiously asked, dreading it could be the segregation block at Belmarsh next to Assange. It wasn't. In fact, when he said "HMP Stocken" - I was none the wiser. I rang my PA, Big Boned Jean, and asked her to do her best Miss Marple. I quipped, "I don't want you to stalk the prison - but find out as much as you can." The biggest frustration with prison is that people can't phone you back - so you have to call back, praying that your 10p for three minutes wasn't wasted. I truly hadn't got a lot to pack – one big bag of books, paper, undercrackers, and a few leftover biscuits. BBJ told me that HMP Stocken was best known for having Johnny Vaughan's presence years ago. Hardly the Great Train Robbers, was it? This was a 'security' CAT-C 'training' prison. The addition of those two words was very important. This wasn't an ordinary CAT-C category jail. It certainly wasn't a 'resettlement' slammer for people with under three years left - who'd quickly be heading home via open jail. This choice of pokey was revealing - even as a nick novice!

About 11am, they came to escort me to reception - to take me to this twelve-hundred-bed Pontins for Pricks. I did smile. A 'retraining' prison - to what? It's a lot too late for that! I'd make a terrible urologist! Anyway, those blue gloves wouldn't fit with my extra right-hand finger. Any con will tell you: the unknown is the most terrifying thing about the slammer. You can never trust them - or believe where you're going. BUT I knew this had to be an upgrade. CAT-B locals are intentional shitholes. Most are now at twice capacity - with nearly all single cells turned into doubles and fit to bursting. Please God, let HMP Stocken have a little more decorum. The most revealing word about this CAT-C is that it's a 'security' slammer - offering far greater wriggle room for surveillance, monitoring, and forensic observation to keep tabs on you. Especially when it comes to letters and phone calls. Sixty percent of staff at this hoosegow work for security - which is totally unique. This was no coincidence. I couldn't care less. I'm shameless. Regardless of the category, they're basically waste disposal facilities for wrong'uns. The government now wants the public to believe the 'new' HMP is all about rehabilitation - in pretend Mickey Mouse private prisons.

Doing 'time' used to be about punishment, now it's about making you into a better, re-born human. All bollocks – all I needed in my head was the hope of progress. I knew they couldn't do anything for me, so I was woefully aware that everything would be about long grass - a complete waste of time. It was all about dragging everything out to keep me gagged, contained, and persona non grata. Officer 'I think so' walked me in reverse through the rat-infested corridors that I arrived through ten days earlier. I wasn't sorry to be leaving, but I couldn't help but think, 'It's not as bad as I thought.' I promise you - that is true. That's not me being brave or coy, but it wasn't. There's no punishment other than the perverts, creeps, and imbeciles you're forced to live with. I'm sure it's the same on the rigs - or at the BBC Christmas party. Listen - a week before HMP Lincoln, I had a suite at my beloved St Pancras Hotel. I know comfort and luxury. But as hideous and primitive as HMP Lincs is - how bad could it be, with Freeview, a sink, toilet, shopping delivered to your door, and a phone to call my people? It's unedifying - but far from torture. I'm proud that I took this approach. It fared me well - long may it last! If you fight the inevitable, you'll be knocking on wood by teatime. Even the food wasn't hideous. I expected worse. Why should prisoners eat like kings? Shouldn't prison be a deterrent - not a drop-in centre or a lock-up for losers during cold winter nights? I guess I'm just a guy whose pint is half full.

I walked into reception and had another quick search – another waste of time. The same Freddie Mercury fella was on. He couldn't be bothered to x-ray my toes or examine my sphincter – he knew I was far too boring to have illicit drugs, or an SD card secreted up my bell end. Yep! Your man sausage is a great storage facility apparently, if you're too cowardly to 'bank' a clingfilmed package up your arris! Not for me. I won't even use a loofah in the shower, let alone a turkey baster in the back passage. I thanked him for his genuine compassion and courtesy. He said, "No one's ever said that before." Not surprising, but sad. I promised myself that I wouldn't let this hideous situation change who I am. I would try and treat those how they treated me - every single time.

I sat in a little room waiting for the 'bus' = prison van. It was all very normal and relaxed. You might think it's all formal and 'high security' - backs against the wall. Far from it. Quite the opposite. It's just routine to them. Anyone who's a real threat in transit is stripped naked, dressed in a bright orange onesie, and cuffed to the floor of the van - with four officers for every limb. These men will be in AA or CAT-As (like the inner prison at Belmarsh) - they're not even here... let alone a CAT-C. They know who's a risk and who's not. The reality about security in a prison, to me, was simple: only a moron would try and escape. Where would you run to? It's totally pointless. Someone as slovenly and 'high-profile' as me ain't a risk! Still no cuffs, of course, as I was shown to the charabanc. Luckily, I was once again in 1A - The Rosa Parks Suite. How lovely. My co-travellers were 20-ish arseholes: angry, frustrated, and behaving like spoilt brats. I'd have slapped them around the gob with a Vileda mop if I were the driver. They needed a slap around the arse. You get a driver and stewardess for refreshments. Ironically, our trolly dolly was far better dressed than those Pan Am slappers in the nineties. The girls that sit on the bus with you are clearly pros at pacifying volatile and impatient dopes. They get an A* for 'Eye Spy,' food, and beverages - lag logistics. They're like low-rent Ryanair rejects who didn't quite have the finesse to serve cashews. Instead, they've got a multi-pack of Walkers to shut them up - and an egg mayo sandwich to pacify them.

As we'll discover more and more, there seems to be a big correlation between ADHD and the majority of prisoners. 'Attention Deficit Hyper-Activity Disorder' (yep, catchy) used to be known, in my day, as a 'big pain in the arse.' I'm not kidding - it's just (mainly) lads who haven't been told no, or taught manners. It's a great ruse to behave like a prat. I HATE these rude bastards more than any nonce. At least paedos are too ashamed to speak! These whirling dervishes won't shut the fack up! Such rudeness, no self-awareness, and often zero class. The pills they're given basically calm them down and keep them pacified - and a bit less annoying. I'm known for being dismissive of a lot of these millennial conditions, as I believe they cover up the main cause and simply sedate twats to put a sock in it. With over seven million Brits on anti-depressants, you have to ask the same question - why? Are they medically depressed, or do they just need to pull their socks up and get on with it - like we did in the good old days when we were at war with Germany and died of syphilis? I truly find it outrageous that doctors give out these highly affecting drugs like Smarties - to placate often sad and frustrated people who don't need drugs. They need happiness, boundaries, and/or help. Of course, some people need pills to regulate their moods - but please, seven million? That's 10%+ of the adult population! Ridiculous. I clearly don't need to be in a meat wagon like a caged rabid monkey - but frankly, a lot of these lads do. They can't stand still for twenty seconds without their knees jerking like a noncy journalist having his WhatsApp messages checked by the police.

I looked at the twenty-five-year-old woman who was with us onboard as an escort (escort on board, not expensive lady of horizontal refreshment). She had those adorable painted-on eyebrows - perfect for Halloween. Hanky panky with her must be like shagging two caterpillars on a corpse. She sat at her desk to the left. My cubicle was tidy, and I had a fab view through the window. The drive from HMP Lincoln to HMP Stocken was less than an hour - and took in some gorgeous British countryside. I loved it......other than the dickheads whining like babies for more wine gums, up my rear! It was bizarre to think I may not see roads, cars, petrol stations, McDonald's, or even a road sign again - for the best part of another three years. The shitheads behind never stopped chuntering, 'Are we there yet?' Give me strength. I pondered: what would I do for nearly three years? I point-blank refuse to 'retrain' - that ain't happening. You can't teach an old dog new tricks at my vintage. Obviously, I didn't need - or want - educating (brainwashing), nor did I want or need a job. But trust me, the eleven hours a day you can be 'free' are best spent distracted - to avoid madness or cabin fever......oh, and conversations with fart heads like those sat in cattle class behind. Like Danny in 3B, who by Oakham had made his knuckles bleed punching the door... the loony bin is only days away if you're not careful. Eventually, after the three hundred roundabouts on the 'not fit for purpose' A1, we arrived at Stretton - in the middle of nowhere. HMP Stocken is completely isolated near Rutland Water, a glorious place to visit - as we did over thirty years ago as a family. I was happy, as this clink was an hour away from Notts, which was perfect for visits - my biggest (and only) priority. Despite prison law being explicit that you have to be within 120 miles of home, that's all gone out of the window since overcrowding. Some poor bastards sent to Rutland were from Scotland, Wales, the South Coast, and the Northwest - making visits all but impossible for these lads. Which is unlawful and unforgivable. It's barbaric and cruel - not to mention completely contradictory to every family ties policy in the nick that they bang on and on about. Box-tickers at HMP don't care. They're heartless and cynical. BTW, if you refuse to go - no matter where in England - they reserve the right to 'bend you up' - removed by the mufties via force. I think it's better to use your own two feet and not be carried like a coffin, don't you? Imagine having family and friends - but not being able to see them because of MOJ logistics. Inconceivable! Trust me, for all the human rights crap - you leave them at the reception door the second you become a political prisoner.

The bus meandered through the most glorious countryside, passing adorable houses like picture-postcard village palaces - some with thatched roofs - as we cruised into port. We turned right into what would now be known, from this moment on, as HMS Stockings - the cruise ship for plonkers who can't afford P&O. In that moment, I had my purpose. I was now commissioned to write HMP exposé epistles. What really goes on in these holiday camps for cons? I would meticulously document my every move - simply to keep me awake, alive, and creative. This old tug of a Titanic travesty would become my home - and my job. Did no one think that this was my only option? Isn't it obvious that a journalist with time on his hands will just write? What an own goal. What nob jockeys! Held captive for now - but one day, this tatty old vessel will dock, and freedom will resume.

We pulled up to the 'airlock' security gate. Same as all prisons, this is a tiny space where the van pulls in between two impassable doors - one before and one after. This is the space where the paperwork is handed over (including each prisoner's warrant), and the van is checked 360° to ensure everyone is onboard - and that no one is on top, underneath, or inside who shouldn't be... unless you're clinging to the undercarriage of a bread van at HMP Wandsworth. Don't ask - these things can happen! BTW, I dream of the day I can cling to an undercarriage once again. Memories, Mrs B! Happy days.

Next, we're taken to reception for the same palaver I went through less than two weeks ago at HMP Lincoln. Yep, there's no efficiency. <u>EVERYTHING</u> has to be repeated <u>again</u>! They'd list my items for a third time. One by one, you're called, unlocked, and then you make your way inside to be processed and taken to induction. I have to say, the staff were more than spirited - amazingly polite and unbelievably patient with us - considering the ill-tempered gobshites in the back, two of whom pissed into a mobile slash bag, as they couldn't possibly 'hold it' for 56 minutes... just like your average nursing home silver-top bus trip to Skeggy! These staff are salt of the earth, for sure - they'd heard it all before. The Queen's English is replaced by 'fag ash Lil' screaming to Gladys and Fanny over the fence. Think Angela Rayner - that's your average lady(ish) type screw! What they lack in femininity, they make up for in mascara and hairspray. I get the feeling these trollops have had more pricks than a second-hand dartboard. They've definitely flattened some grass! 'Fish wives' might be a little insulting... but it nevertheless paints a completely accurate picture! These old-school female(ish) kangas are definitely more intimidating (and big boned) than their male colleagues, who appear to be channelling more Ant and Dec than Giant Haystacks! I'm not casting aspersions, but a lot seem light on their feet - regardless of the wedding ring. I guess the truncheon and cuffs all feel a bit Village People to me. Sitting silently and observing prisoner and officer conversations has become one of my favourite pastimes - something Peter Kay could turn into a modern-day *Porridge* to rival *Gogglebox* within an inch of its life. You couldn't make up half of this incomprehensible and totally inappropriate guff these people spout. Again, I wouldn't get three words into these convos before a hit squad would whisk me off to a CAT-A, yet these neanderthals have carte blanche to spew any filth.

Reception was slightly more relaxed than HMP Lincoln. Word had clearly spread about my arrival - impounding their second most famous inmate since *The Big Breakfast* mush mouth. I wonder if Denise Van Outen visited? She had tremendous lallies in *Chicago*, if I recall correctly. A visit from her would get chins - and inner thighs - wagging big time in the pokey. I waited in a side room alone, and that was when I met my first prisoner - and boy, was he a legend! Jock was a very Scottish former army hero who had spent the best part of two decades incarcerated. "Canteen?" he said, in his charming Celtic tones. This is the six-page HMP Stocken shopping list - everything from ground pepper to pitta breads. I stupidly said, "No thank you." Jock boomed, "You won't get it again for a week mate, I'd get something if I were you." Honestly, tins of tuna back then were the least of my worries - now it's the highlight of my week! I wanted every penny for my phone calls, so it was a 'no' from me. "OK, pal," he said. A few minutes later he said: "What kit do you need?" "Kit?" Honestly, I thought it was secret code for heroin. "Sorry, Jock…" He said, "Your first time, isn't it?" "And hopefully my last, big man," I replied, earning a titter. WOW! Humanity - a man with a brain - I was truly elated. "Do you need any clothes, Alex?" he translated. I'd left everything at Lincoln, as I was told. BIG mistake. Never trust anyone! Take everything with you!!! Just in case there isn't a knight in shining armour like Jock to help out. I said, "Oh yes please, everything mate – I'm naked under here!" Ten minutes later, Jock came back with a big black bag full of new pants, socks, T-shirts, shorts, trousers - and even a coat! Jock said, "Here you go, big man. Welcome to 'Sticky' Stocken." I asked, "What does that mean?" He said, "Since Covid, this place is known as 'Sticky Stocken.' Once you're here, you're facked!" Not the greatest endorsement I've ever heard! It doesn't bode well for my 'progress' to CAT-D and getting home by Christmas, now does it?

Little did I know Jock would be on my wing - and become a dear pal before a huge tragedy just six months later. I would end up playing at Jock's funeral. Prison life was set to be an emotional rollercoaster - both inside and out.

The next cab off the rank was a big-boned, jolly lady called Connie Lingus. This woman was given the impossible task of being my POM - 'Prison Offender Manager' - from what was to become my nemesis: OMU - 'Offender Manager Unit.' They're prison probation. It would be her decision as to when I was ready for 'progression' to an open prison. This bubbly lady would decide when I was 'rehabilitated.' She would dictate when I was 'no risk to society' and could effectively go home... even though probation didn't think I should be here in the first place. I'm not soft. Obviously, this palatial pelican face would be entirely worked from behind by the dark forces. She was just the unfortunate gatekeeper to keep me quiet and detained at HMP. She was the bullet in the establishment's gun. As an investigative journalist of twenty-five years, my only question was: 'What are your qualifications?' It certainly wasn't in hair, make-up, or fashion! Now wasn't the time for my grilling - I'd save that for her first sabotage. This ain't paranoia - it's inevitable. She is part of the department regarded as the most despicable, discredited, failing, broken, duplicitous, incompetent, malicious, vindictive, and vile saboteurs at HMP. OMU are every prisoner's kryptonite - universally despised by prisoners and officers alike. Their arrogance is equalled by their power - which is breathtaking! Connie, though, was regarded as the best OMU at HMS Stockings. She was older (thank God), direct, smart, and - from what I could see - appeared sincere. My biggest mistake at HMP was believing they would know what they were doing. They certainly do not. You think it's conspiracy - but it's almost always a cock-up! I would endure breathtaking incompetence and corruption that makes the evil BBC and corrupt Police look like a Disney film."

Connie Lingus was gracious and courteous. I asked her to explain the procedure. Basically, when you go to prison, you're in no man's land for three months - regardless of your crime. For ninety days, you're monitored and cannot progress until this profiling of every part of your behaviour is documented and analysed by the distorted box-tickers and security. That would take me to just after Christmas before I'd have any privileges - and qualify as 'enhanced.' Of course, in reality, the screws know within days whether you're a pain in the arse or not – it's just more bureaucratic bollocks to buy time, which appears to be the only ambition of HMP. So, Connie advised me to keep my head down, get a job, and talk to her in three months. She then said, "All being well, it shouldn't be too long before you can progress to CAT-D." That's that. The official 'risk' document - called 'OASYS' - would be sorted by then to decide my progress. This sixty-page document collates your crime, lifestyle, and past, and comes up with a risk score. It can't be tampered with - I was assured. This would be very revealing. There was NOTHING else I or Connie Lingus could do. For me - a man of previous great impatience and relentless ambition - this would not be easy. But I accepted this was my new reality and got on with working hard at doing nothing. Of course, I wasn't worried about getting into fights or trouble - I always knew my issues would only be with imbeciles in box-ticking central. I said my goodbyes to Connie and Jock and was blown away by their civility. There are always a few gems in jail - you just have to find them!

After an hour or so, I was walked to Induction - or F Wing - right at the centre of the slammer. This felt completely different to HMP Lincoln, which I prayed it would. Look, prison is prison - let me give away the punchline to the book. You've already paid for it, so it makes no odds to me. Prison = the removal of freedom. This is the only punishment. Oh, and you're gagged. Anything else is virtually irrelevant. The pure reality check of jail is losing the four F's: Freedom, Family, Friends - and FREE speech! It is shocking - but for me, I'd done abandonment and isolation my entire life, with gigs in Kenya, Spain, Germany, and even South Wales. You can be one mile or one million miles away from home and still feel alone. Entertainers live on their nerves and master dealing with this discombobulation. If you can't see your loved ones, it makes no difference whether you're in Newark or New York. Longing, pining, and missing your sweethearts and beloveds is a toil that so many of us have to deal with - it's not exclusive to the department store for douchebags. From peripatetic builders on the road to cabin crew, all of us have 'that' pang of abandonment when working away. I switched it around to what I could do - not what I couldn't. I had learnt to (try to) manage this animal instinct of loneliness and stay focused on the fact that IT WILL END. And in between, I've got my visits - when HMS Stockings hits port. Easier said than done, of course. If I had a bad day, I owned it. If I felt pissed off, betrayed, or deserted - I'd earned the right to feel that way, so I embraced it. This way, it passes much quicker, and you can re-find your equilibrium. Stocken was an older prison, with new wings added. An officer - who looked identical to 'The Pub Landlord' (and spoke like him too) - said, "You need to get on Newton Wing. It's perfect for you, just keep your head down and you'll be moved." Ten days into my captivity, I couldn't help but check: "Is it for nonces?" - as so many had insinuated. He looked at me with a smile. "No, believe it or not, we don't have VPs here - we're a training prison for people who can be rehabilitated." Ouch. Wow. I have to admit, a weight was lifted knowing there weren't any paedos scuttling through the corridors or cluttering up the chapel. I'd had enough of that sort of thing at Broadcasting House!

The screw moved his palatial beer belly out of the way and banged on the induction door at volume; this racket would become my #1 annoyance behind bars. Nothing in jail is done with subtlety. Getting in and out of anywhere is the obvious elephant in the room for lags. Why can't they have a facking Ring doorbell like everyone else? Kicking ten shades of shit out of the glass won't get you in any quicker. The door to the wing opened, and several men of a certain age were sat on seats. "Alo," I said tentatively. "How are you?" they responded. 'Good Lord' I thought 'surely this isn't prison?' I later learned that one of these was called Alf - Alfredo, an Italian-born airline captain. Then there was Brian - a family man who ran a garage from Mansfield - and Julian, who worked in the Bistro. Little did I know we would spend hour after hour walking and talking together over the coming months. I would be indebted for their solidarity. To the right and left of me were the two spurs of the wing. I went into the office on the right, where a strange man in his thirties said, "Are you Belfield?" I replied, "Unfortunately, sir - you can't have everything." He smiled. "You're in nineteen on the twos." The 'twos' (etc.) refer to the floor level. F Wing only had two floors, so 'twos' worked for me - as I'd been told in Lincoln that 'all' prisons are riddled with rats. So being above ground level is a huge advantage if you don't want to be surrounded by vermin... (fill in your own punchline). Who knew my life would go from my country park dream home to avoiding the ground floor - because of rodents creeping around like media lefties in a dodgy gay Soho sauna.

Induction is the smallest of all wings and therefore the best. Why? Smaller the wing = fewer men = less noise and less chance of twats! I walked up the stairs and passed two men in their fifties who looked like every drama criminal - as wide as tall, built like a brick shithouse, and covered in old-school tats. I'm not talking about the mincy 'Beckham Sleeve' - I'm talking about a series of pictures that described their life story, from births to 'RIP' tributes - just like my old grandad used to have. Both said 'hi' and ended up being two of the nicest men in the slammer, who always had my back. With no nonces at Stocken, it made induction a <u>LOT</u> easier — this is <u>not</u> the case in mixed prisons. These men are salt of the earth and proudly honourable. 'On the out' - I'd probably be too intimidated to talk to them. My first huge lesson was about books and their cover! I learned so much - including that looks mean nothing. We're all the same…. it's just that in here you need to be pickier and choosier! F19 was my new home, and I have to admit it was <u>MUCH</u> better than I'd <u>ever</u> imagined. It wasn't dirty and had everything I needed - including a phone, my priority - so I picked it up, and it worked. Phew! The relief was palpable. Now I could cope with anything. Most importantly, I was alone in a single pad. What a relief!

The only efficient thing that HMP does well is copy over your numbers and visitors from slammer to slammer. I now had the maximum twenty numbers - but, to the fury of the box-tickers, I'd found a way to speak to five new people every week in rotation, simply by filing new 'apps' every three days. I'd get them to delete one - then add a new one on. They have to call up to make sure it is the person you say it is - this is for all cons, for 'public protection.' They were having none of it! They were incandescent with rage at me making them do their job - and with any civil serpent, this is a sure way of ruffling feathers. They were powerless, as there are no rules about number changes - no one had ever done it before. I intentionally caused them a ton of work - the only revenge you have over lazy, institutionalised, brainwashed, and braindead lefty government box-tickers - to my huge hilarity and satisfaction. For now, I was over the moon. Within ten days, I was in a single pad, everything worked, it was newly decorated, with a decent view, and (so far) I'd mostly met decent older guys who could link a sentence and weren't off their tits on spice... we were more 'Old Spice!'

The single pad thing has been my biggest blessing in custody - by a mile. Almost immediately, 'Safer Custody' decided that I am 'High Risk Cell Share,' which removed any possibility of ever being padded up with a prick, pillock, or prat - for my own protection, and to cover their hairy white ass as a duty of care. I'll be honest - THANK GOD - I know this is the only reason I've coped so splendidly. Because of my profile and public notoriety, HMP couldn't risk putting me in with someone else - in case they injured me on behalf of 'other people,' known as 'a hit.' Ermmm... This happens all the time, for a box of vapes here or a fiver there! You can't be too careful. Only lifers and medically vulnerable (incontinent etc) are guaranteed a single pad, so I was 'lucky'!!!

I only had one bag of tat, but it was now my life. I'd got a few pictures and paper, but no bedding or towels etc. "Go and speak to Jarvis," Officer Tess Tickle said. Jarvis had a unique character - in his fifties, and he'd seen it all. His schtick was 'the grumpy old man,' and he always answered 'no' to everyone and everything. It took me a minute to find his rhythm, as he had a glint in his eye. Once you got his 'act,' he had a heart of gold and was very generous. He was F Wing's laundry man - a crucial ally to have, second only to the servery. The bribery of a box of caps will always push you to the front of the queue in these critical departments. Officers have nothing to do with either - it's all 'managed' by cons.

So, with Jock and Jarvis onside, it was a great start - they could basically sort out anything, as they were the 'no messing' patriarchs of the wing. Prison is all about who you know. If the wing gaffers don't like you - you're effectively facked. Jarvis sorted me out a new duvet (still in the bag), sheets, plus two new pillows and towels. Prison is not an aparthotel, but pads are usually cleaned before you use them. I got lucky - there's no doubting that. My prison experience would now begin. No time for boohooing or questioning the jury's decision. I just had to get on with it. F Wing had recently been re-decorated, so I was shocked how nice it was. Unlike Lincoln, I had a 'real' porcelain toilet with a toilet seat and a sink with taps. Nope! I can't believe I've just written that either. This is now unheard of in jails, because lunatics can easily rip them off the walls and smash them up - using them as weapons to harm themselves and others. They now have buttons for flush and water, etc., fitted in the walls to avoid these costly and damaging inconveniences. All of this was such a revelation to me - you never think of such stuff until you're at ground zero of Twatdom. Everything is imbecile-protected in the nick. It's like baby gates and child locks for rampaging dickwads. Things that you never think of - like 'taps' - have never crossed your mind until they're missing. Imagine what a weapon that could be if ripped out of the wall and swung in a sock! Pool balls are another weapon that have caused a few bruises over the years!

The other lightbulb moment of living in the 'Maison De Moron' was that all of my mail was photocopied. It is 'de rigueur' for all prisoners at Stocken, as druggies sent letters in that were dipped in water with diluted drugs. Once dried, they'd be posted to the prison to be smoked or sold for huge profit. SPICE is the most common drug in prison - with a mixture of everything from rat poison to ground pepper mixed in for a cheap, quick high. Basically, any old shit that might get these dopes off their tits will be used by some lost soul. It can be a killer. The effort lads will go to in order to get their fix is incredible - you can see the desperation and infatuation on their faces. No one from HMP helps to stop their addiction. They're too busy running wellbeing courses to worry about smackheads. If you're caught, you're banished behind your door - with often fatal consequences. It wasn't a huge problem at Stocken, because of security - but lads having a fit would get 'code blues' (not breathing) on an hourly basis!!! It's terrifying. As I write, a prison in Wales has had ten deaths in six months from this type of insane, toxic, gruesome 'high.' The belief is, no matter what lengths 'they' go to, to wipe out drugs – it will never happen - so why bother? It's a total lost cause. I suppose it's now just a case of firefighting. I've gained an unedifying insight into this world - one I never thought I'd witness, even in my worst nightmares. You can never second-guess who is or isn't involved. Spice heads generally don't get violent - they're virtually comatosed. They often fall unconscious and choke to death on their own sick, or they frequently fall asleep standing up - that's why they call it the zombie drug! I have the same reaction listening to Vernon Kay on Radio 2. It's so profitable, even solicitors have gone to jail for sending drugs in via sealed 'Rule 39' - prison law mail that can't be opened or read. It's 100% cat and mouse for the post room. You don't read this on the glossy HMP website now, do you? What I've learned is that you can avoid that entire world - should you choose.

I've never, to this date, been offered anything - ever. I guess gingers aren't welcome in the crack club. The terminal effects of SPICE and other widely available brain corruptors are shocking. I guess we all make life choices - I'm lucky it's a world I have no interest in getting involved with.

So, why is it so prevalent? MONEY! It's big business! An A4 sheet of SPICE is £800 on the wing as it's so hard to get. That's not the case at private jails - where a sheet of spice is a tenth of the price. It only costs the dealer £50, so even Lord Sugar would be impressed by that profit margin. How does it get in when everything is photocopied? It's now almost always through corrupt staff. Visits is another place - but at Stocken, it's virtually impossible, as Security are so switched on here that you can't fart in the wrong direction without getting searched and chucked out. The luxuries of emails and phones in the cells have made nefarious operations much easier for cons to arrange since Covid. The only other way is drones - although with Stocken being so remote, it was too risky for crims to fly them in. Twelve people at HMP Five Wells CAT-C have been charged over drug drone drops in the last year. It's very lucrative for both sides.

Curiously BTW, HMP Stocken allowed cards to be received, but not letters without photocopying. I still can't understand the difference... thick or thin paper is still paper, right? Hey ho. I guess you can't smoke a card - nothing gets past me! As you'll see, so many of these rules just don't make sense, and are almost never consistent from jail to jail. Over the coming weeks, I would fill the entire wall with beautiful photos and cards from my angels - who have 100% kept me alive and focused since day one. Those early days were bleak, but Network Nick once again let the punters know where I'd moved - and the letters started flooding in again. Because of my popularity, I would become the enemy of OMU and the post room within days. It was war by the end of the first week, as my bulging male sack (typo) left them boohooing like a tantrumming toddler - everything had to be checked and copied. Between my common law assistant, Big Boned Jean, and my technical genius and friend, Network Nick, they have kept my candle flickering bright throughout. I've spoken to them both <u>every</u> single day. Nick has kept the VoR family updated and in contact - which has single-handedly kept me busy, focused, and <u>ALIVE</u> (in body, heart, and soul) - with emails and letters every single day. BBJ would soon become my manuscript mule, getting these books in and out week by week. I'd later become dear friends with Dame Jan, Nick's partner - who had to decipher my handwritten scribbles to transcribe the books. What a team. I'm a VERY lucky lad. You <u>CANNOT</u> survive the slammer alone. Along with my two producers, James and Hayden - they were collectively my eyes and ears, and chief motivators from day one.

The beds on HMS Stockings were far less durable than the 'old school' metal beds in HMP Lincoln. The criss-cross metal warps over time - like so many of the eejits who lay on them - and therefore the mattress would mould to the shape of your back in these CAT-Bs. Stocken replaced them with entirely wooden 'IKEA'-style, screw-together (easily replaceable) six-foot troughs - which cannot be used as weapons, unlike the metal-framed and dangerous scaffolding at knuckle-draggers' jail, where they seemingly couldn't care less. Unfortunately, the geniuses at HMP didn't realise that you could lift the top off these jigsaw beds by unscrewing it with a corned beef tin key - making the base a PERFECT den to hide hooch or contraband! Obviously, the mattress (which is about two inches thick max) is not going to adjust 'ergonomically' to your back issues and in no way compares to my £3,000 Tempur mattress at Alex's Acres. This mattress is more a less a yoga mat! I needed a plan fast! The pillows are like bricks – even a Rhino would struggle to find any comfort or relaxation in these breeze blocks. The blue HMP pillow made a marvellous draught excluder though. I'm not limp under the cap, and of course, I wasn't going to bring this up with the screws - they'd have loved that! So, I needed to be inventive - as ALL prisoners become, by necessity. I popped back to Jarvis and politely asked if he'd got any clean but old/used jumpers, etc., that he didn't want. After a lot of theatrical huffing and puffing, he found me a few and was delighted to give them to me. He said, "You're not flogging them at a car boot, are you?" I said, "No! I'm going to use them as a makeshift ladder to climb the fence!" I stuck six old jumpers under the mattress - and BOOM! It made a world of difference, and my makeshift Dreams mattress boudoir was complete.

I still laugh at the insanity of 'what a difference two weeks' makes. I know I'm privileged, and I always invested in my bed, shoes, and couch at home – the three things you spend most of your life in or on. Clearly, my preconceptions of life's priorities were out the window now. All I could do was make the very best of this shitstorm - learning like I've never learned before - to stay ten steps ahead of the broken system around me and maintain some sanity. My cell was a place of solace and a sanctuary of calm. I knew I couldn't remain on induction indefinitely - the clue is in the title - so I was always prepared for the next removals van to a permanent wing. But for now, I felt settled and safe. I had everything I needed, thanks to these kind angels, and I was under no threat whatsoever.

Secretly, this wing was ideal - it was more gammon-packed than fart-head-filled with Taylor Swift fans. I think, behind the scenes, conversations were happening about what they were going to do with me. This anomaly wouldn't fit in anywhere - so now what? They're still clueless. I was already a BIG thorn in their side, and I wasn't about to make their lives easy either! I'm not sure 'they' thought I'd survive this long!

There are no rules in the Sheraton of Shithouses. Talking to some of the lads on the wing can be very dangerous, as their advice is only based on their experience. Clearly, there aren't going to be many forty-two-year-old entertainers with twenty-five years' experience in showbusiness who are non-violent or non-noncy. You have to be VERY careful believing everything you're told. Little did I know that this wing was the crème de la crème of this Theme Park for Twits, Twats, and Tossers. The only place better was the 'enhanced' Newton block, as I'd already been tipped off - but that was impossible for now. So, I'll hunker down. At 4.45pm, it was time for dinner, so I took my plate to the servery. There was a very nice lad called Cliff who worked there. He could see I was wet behind the ears and was incredibly kind - right up until the final day I left. It's amazing to me how you can immediately feel empathy and compassion, even in jail. It happens! Who knew that within seconds I'd find people who cared! I chatted a lot to two old timers called Alfredo and Brian – both sixty plus, who were very chatty, friendly, helpful, and a hoot to be around. No negativity at all. It was obvious these would be 'my' people. With no nonces at Stocken whatsoever, it was a far more relaxed atmosphere, as even though there were lifers for murder and drug dealers, there were no rapists or kiddie fiddlers to worry about. A huge weight off all criminal's shoulders!

Unlike CAT-Bs, where you're escorted everywhere, here, you can move around this prison completely alone, so it felt like being back at school. In fact, there is an argument that CAT-C prison is indeed a borstal for toerags......elevated to Butlins when you qualify for the heady heights of enhanced. No one is equal in jail! If your face fits, you'll fly and be protected. If not, you'll be left to sink with no safety net. My new neighbours initially appeared intimidating, but were nice guys once you got past the lazy eye, rotten yellow teeth, and self-inflicted cuts up their arms. The tear tattoo under the eye means they've killed someone - so I'm told. Don't ask! I was riveted by their life, lived experience, and knowledge. They became very helpful colleagues on this HMP exposé mission. Curiously, the police, MOJ, and HMP did not have many fans with any of my co-stars. The system appears more flawed and corrupt than the Post Office legal department or Boris Johnson's moral compass. Rotten to the core!

Word had spread as to who I was and what I'd done... or not done.
Your name is on your door, so you can't exactly pretend to be an 'Extinction Rebellion' lefty when you're me! The days of prison anonymity are long gone. The bad lads aren't daft - and quickly,

one by one, they'd come up to me and ask all kinds of inappropriate questions. My policy with everyone has always been complete transparency - shameless honesty. I have no embarrassment, so if they asked nicely, I'd answer any questions. Dave from Mansfield (three doors away) was a big-time drugs guy. He'd done a long stretch and been around the houses. He was fascinated by my sentence. He said, "They've completely facked you over, right?" I said, "I did have an idea, but this was a unique case." He then gave the killer line. He said, "You do realise that if you'd have beat up four people and seriously injured them, you wouldn't have got five and a half years for a first offence?" Again, what can I say? Two years later, during the 2024 summer riots, a Muslim lad beat up four white Union flag flyers (and smashed the teeth of two before flooring them) and got two and a half years. Chilling proof of the disproportion and two-tier justice of our once Great Britain. Dave continued, "Listen, if you need anything, you let me know, Alex." How kind. This story has been repeated throughout my introductions everywhere I've been. The compassion by proper cons is beyond heartwarming. It's almost as if there's an honour and a code - that 'you get what you deserve.' But when you've been shafted, it offers you a level of protection and genuine sympathy from your comrades. It's quite inspiring.

I promise you, on my entire family's lives, that I have not met one prisoner who believes this is anything other than a political stunt - and totally ridiculous. It doesn't help my exit to freedom, but it does give me a sense of reassurance that my family, friends, and fans aren't delusional and off on one simply to spare my blushes. I did feel comforted by this. Recently, I have seen lads come in who have been given a very different 'welcome.' These guys are quickly moved off the wing and usually removed from the prison for their own safety – due to crimes involving vulnerable people, women, or children. You can run, but you can't hide in jail! The food at HMS Stockings seemed a thousand times better than Lincoln - if you get in quick. Induction is notoriously tricky if you're last in the queue! I had the chicken salad twice a week, which was presented in a large chip shop takeaway box. I was impressed - it came with wedges and peas. Not too shabby for a pauper's pokey. My pit estate upbringing taught me: if you have low expectations, you go through life uplifted by mediocrity and less disappointment. I'm glad I'm an optimist. Prison is not the venue for righteous, arrogant, and entitled prima donnas! One sniff of that and you'll be given a VERY difficult uncomfortable and solitary stretch!

My big question was 'how do I get a job?' and the answer came back which answered every single question at Stocken. 'Fill in an app.' Dear God, it was infuriating. No one will answer a single question to your face. It's a tactic to frustrate and dehumanise. You cannot find anyone who does any job, and you are deliberately delayed and pissed about from arsehole to breakfast time to get anywhere. Naturally, most imbeciles and lazy bastards just give up - which makes the bureaucrats' job a lot easier. Greta Thunberg would be spitting feathers at all of this four-by-A4-sheet 'apps!' So much time wasted - on thousands of trees' worth of paper - every single day. It would take five days at least for a reply, so weeks and months can easily fly by. Every department hide behind doors like the weasels they are. No one is brave enough to speak face-to-face. To get a job you have to send an app to 'Activities' – why not call it 'jobs?' This is the same with every other department -given stupid, bloody, 'woke' names that no one explains. Again, a newbie has to be psychic to work all of this out. I wrote immediately stating, 'I want to work. Please tell me what I'm eligible for.' The answer, because of my (lack of) a proper crime, was literally anything. Security determines your risk. Clearly, a stabber shouldn't be in the kitchen, and a prolific shoplifter shouldn't work in the DHL canteen. Yep, a private business – DHL - is based at HMP Stocken, running the shop for huge profit, using desperate lads to work their arses off all day for £40 a week (a fortune behind bars). So, I awaited a list of opportunities on the Happy Ship Stockings. Nothing teaches patience like jail. Until you accept this infuriating reality, life is misery. You have to let go of any sense of efficiency or professionalism and put yourself first. My pad became more and more important as my safe space - mine, like a puppy in its first training cage! Stick a towel over me, say 'nan-night,' and I'm away with the fairies...

Chapter 16

Five Months on F Wing

I woke up at 7.30am to silence - this was my biggest surprise about jail. The one thing the lads pride themselves on is getting a good night's sleep. Any wet wipe who gets in the way of that will regret it! The bad lads don't mess around with their kip. I'd heard horror stories about banging doors and blaring sound systems. It's true that on some of the younger and more 'ghetto' wings there's music - but rarely overnight, and certainly not before 8am. HMP Stocken was surprisingly civilised and sleepy, especially compared to a Sickdiq Crapital slammer. For me, the worst annoyance was the odd imbecile who should be in an asylum, not prison. On every wing, there's always one moron who ruins it - or tries to - for everyone else, often unintentionally. Normally, they end up getting a kick-in (in the privacy of their pad where there are no cameras), but we'll draw a discreet veil over that. On F Wing, there was a lad called Pyro Pete who was severely autistic and in prison for arson. He'd tried to set his pad on fire in a hostel, and in doing so was basically found guilty of the 'attempted' murder of the other thirty people living there. He meant well but was a danger to himself. Why shouldn't you light a disposable BBQ in your own one-bedroom flat? Good question, Pete! He was one of the most vulnerable people I've met. Anyone could see from a thousand miles away that Pyro Pete is ill, not a criminal. He's clearly Asperger's - a big baby in a man's body, with high intelligence but a total inability to communicate like an adult or discern any risk to himself or others.

Sadly, prison is littered with these social anomalies who need a madhouse - a haven for crazies - not an HMP heartless lock-up centre for serious criminals like me! There's no one to help these social derelicts at all. It's heartbreaking to see them flounder, pushed from wing to wing, from jail to jail. Pyro Pete always had a smile on his face - he was in a world of his own. He was Monday-morning mad, and I rather envied his crackpot hallucination of reality. He was, at worst, a bloody nuisance - but in truth, he needed very specialised care. He clearly had one of those exhausting ADHD conditions where he needed entertaining 24/7 -like a sheepdog on acid. It was basically like managing a toddler. The system has no resources, or staff, capable of dealing with such a complicated character. In fact, officers don't get training for ANY neurodiverse, ill, or disabled prisoner - which is a scandal. You'd be amazed at the effect one OTT dickhead can have on 120 other men. Off his head- but his infantilised joy was often highly entertaining. Men taunted and teased him for kicks. It was cruel. If he got bored, he'd decorate his pad from top to bottom in toilet paper. Who knew that toothpaste is a brilliant glue substitute?! Pyro Pete didn't eat anything healthy. So, in true nick style, I'd swap my crappy crisps, biscuits, and cheap chocolates for fruit, extra cereal, and milk for my coffee. Milk is like champagne in jail - with just 189 ml given per day, I'd have that in one latté. There's always someone willing to swap. Excellent teamwork.

On the other side of the wing, there was 'Praise the Lord' man. He'd been in a terrible car accident, was severely disabled, and needed a stick to hobble down the corridors, chanting his catchphrase. He would relentlessly scream 'Praise the Lord!' every two minutes at the top of his voice when he was off on one. He was a devout Catholic. It sounds almost cute and became hugely entertaining for men around the prison who didn't live with him - but when you're surrounded by it all day long, it's absolutely facking annoying! Again, he needs help - not the baiting and mocking of cruel cons begging him to scream his renowned shriek like a freak at Barnum's circus, as they ran past him on the way to the gym. These are just two examples of thousands of men who don't need to be incarcerated in prison; they need to be in a facility for their 'condition.' Sadly, over my months amongst the (great) unwashed, under-educated, and un-free, I met endless men who ended up in prison through no fault of their own - BUT will never get out because of illness. Why can't the system filter these people out, with their bulging departments of psychology and mental 'elf crap? Despite the endless claims about 'progress' and helping such victims back into society, I have ZERO faith that they'll ever be free. It also felt like no one was fighting for them. I felt great sadness for Pyro Pete. His complex needs were WAY above the pay grade of any officer - and all medical professionals in prison healthcare. Screws would get agitated and sometimes furious, locking him behind the door just for peace and quiet. Trust me, if they could spell 'naughty step,' they'd write it over a trap door. There but for the grace of God... As for 'Praise the Lord,' I did a service once in the chapel - not a dicky bird. You couldn't make it up! Total silence in the house of God, yet at 3am he's on his knees, ramming the fear of God into his neighbour's porthole and cat flaps! These 'characters' are everywhere. Lost and hopeless. When I joke that prison is a human dustbin... well, you take my point - it is. Depressing.

The officers on F Wing were equally very strange. You could start a conference with their special needs! They concerned me greatly. There's something about the breed of induction staff. They all seemed to have a screw loose! There were two incredibly peculiar oddballs that unnerved me massively. One officer, let's call him 'Mr Scrufkant' (I don't need another defamation claim), was nothing short of a thug and a bully! He'd recently been suspended for his behaviour, but shoved back into the most volatile and unsettled wing in the jail. A mega FAIL! This man intrigued me - he had greasy hair, a noncy vibe, and the malice of Wayne Couzens. By far the worst-behaved inmate on HMS Stockings, this government representative was exactly the kind of basket case who should never be allowed a set of keys. Beyond loud, he subscribed to the old belief: 'All prisoners are scum, so I'll take my miserable life out on them.' I have no idea whether he was an alcoholic, kiddie fiddler, or druggy, but he came in looking like he'd done New Year's Eve with Amy Winehouse on a daily basis - everyone knew; it was so obvious. His language was obscene, his aggression totally disproportionate, and his entire body language provoked even the stupidest to spark a scrap. Of all the imbeciles I've encountered wearing a shirt and tie, desperately trying to look powerful, this pilchard was the most retarded and totally fallacious. This unshaven Pound Land Cop couldn't wait for trouble! The second there was an emergency alarm sounded; he'd be the first to run to give a kicking to some 'three sheets to the wind' lag. He is odious on every human level. Sadly, he was one of many I've encountered who should never be responsible for people's safety - which, ironically, is the only job of an officer. I avoided this bully like the plague but never missed a trick. Utterly vile.

A big problem with HMP is the age of recruits. Sadly, millennials - and especially Gen X/Z - don't understand boundaries. This is causing a lot of 'HR' and corruption issues at HMP. Officers are in charge, and not your friend. Unfortunately, their insecurities, lack of class and experience - not to mention their socially deficient and medicated lives - lead to many boundaries being crossed. The office for F Wing was in the middle of the two spurs (left and right, with the yard in the middle). It was an Aladdin's Cave of everything I needed - not drugs, vapes or hooch - just paper, pens, deodorant, razors, shaving cream, hair gel... basically, Boots the Cash Chemists! I couldn't believe the bits and bobs they had. People think you live like Norman Stanley Fletcher, but half the lads walk around looking like they're auditioning for Calvin Klein. It's extraordinary the effort they go to... just to impress themselves!

Paper was my number one priority, as it would be my sanity and saviour during those long winter nights. It would also allow me to finally tell my story. I believed the truth would always set me free - and now, I'd been blessed with the time to write my epistles. By now, word had gone viral on the tippy-tappy that I was at HMS Stockings - the less-than-glamorous cruise ship with brown palm trees and concrete deck chairs. Katie Hopkins had kindly given out my address so that people could write to me, and the tsunami of love was about to hit this shithole like the Titanic hit the deck. Horsefaced Hopo was great at rallying the troops - I'll be forever indebted. I'm not embarrassed to say this saved my life. The people who write hundreds of letters every month are my angels, and have been ever since. I would not have survived without this hope, faith, and stimulation. Their optimism was my drug of choice. The question was: how quickly would HMP filter my oxygen of love from the gatehouse to my palatial matchbox cubicle? Little did I know they were planning to sabotage my mail and bait me to kick off. EMAILAPRISONER became another breath of fresh air on a daily basis. This scandalously expensive - 80p an email - rip-off is a brilliant lifeline. Still cheaper than a stamp. At least Dick Turpin wore a mask! These had to be printed off, but piles would arrive daily. The nasty numpties in the mail room made sure replies took weeks, as once again, it all had to be done manually – totally missing the point of an email. I began spending five-plus hours a day writing, whilst Pleasuring His Majesty as a political prisoner. I love it. These word-hugs kept my mind alive, my heart full, and my soul inspired to get through the next day... and the next... until eventually, it would (hopefully) end.

Sadly though, the palpable resentment it created within management was breath-taking! I was told recently (in writing) that I had more mail than the entire 1,200-bed prison combined, and required my own mailbox in security - plus an officer to act as my PA. They claimed they read every letter - impossible. They do have to photocopy them, though. Hours and hours of relentless work, all in the hope of catching me out - which they never did. I was assigned an OSG, which stands for 'Openly Stupid and Gormless' - a low-ranking, non-operational officer akin to a PCSO pretend cuntstable - tasked with noting anything of interest that could stitch me up. Millions of words written and read......the square root of fack all was found! BUT, huge sacks of 'intel' was put on my file, detailing all of my opinions - with them knowing I am 'proud and prejudiced' - as stated in my autobiography. I wrote four A5 pages per reply. This is sanctioned under PPU (Public Protection Unit) within my entitlement. The goons tried to catch me out - and failed miserably. Good luck with that! To receive this daily love-bomb was just sensational. Again, the whole objective of this witch hunt was to isolate and break me. They did NOT want me to get any encouragement - they wanted to remove me from society and punish my family and me to the point I'd be swinging from the wing chandelier. However, little did they know I would feel more love in the first month behind bars than I'd felt in my entire life. What a blessing. The box-tickers have never forgiven me for my shameless audacity to not give up - and not give in.

The lads became a huge saviour to my wellbeing on the wing. I never thought I'd say this. I still can't believe it's true. The playground - as I call it – 'the yard,' was pretty big, and despite it being the end of September 2022, it was still unseasonably warm (I'm a big fan of global warming). This meant that during 'SOC' (social time), I could go round in circles - a bit like my career at the BBC - in a big Ferris wheel of chat with a few rare and interesting people. There was an Italian man, in his early seventies, who looked very different and clearly didn't fit in. Touché. I was intrigued at first. He was intimidating - so self-assured, tall, and well-spoken. Alfredo was a 747 captain and was probably the smartest and most fascinating guy I've ever met behind bars. This was truly a wake-up call for me - totally unexpected! It taught me a good lesson: despite most cons being annoying whippersnappers who are social rejects, you WILL meet the odd, rare diamond who teaches you something and imparts endless knowledge and wisdom. It's true that 90% of prisoners are just thick arseholes - the underbelly of society - who are of zero interest to me and spend their lives on the Ferris wheel of HMP. Each to their own! The sanitary bin of life can attract some salt-of-the-earth, decent, kind, well-meaning folk who blow your mind with compassion. Alf was one of them.

With seven years to serve - and ten-plus already under his belt - I couldn't help but wonder if he'd ever see 'daylight' again. I pray he will. Older people (or disabled folk) in the slammer never seems right to me - other than scum paedos, for whom we can all agree it's only right to throw away the key or pay for a one-way ticket to Dignitas. Surely, they could have an 'old con cockery' for OAPs? Despite being 'criminals,' they're clearly no physical risk - though they still need punishing. Most disabled prisoners get helpers called 'buddies' - paid prisoners who assist them and act as their effective carers. BUT that doesn't help them get into bed at 10pm..... or get out again to use the loo - when they're locked behind the door. Illness in prison terrifies me. You're so vulnerable and alone. Again – NO ONE CARES! It almost seems inhumane to mix these senior silver-tops alongside eighteen-year-old twats who just need a slap! Bullying is rife in jail - it's every man for himself. This isn't a fair battle.

Al was far from weak or feeble – a powerhouse of a man and fit as a trout! He was ebullient and kept a smile on his face despite his incongruous predicament – I feel his pain. He loved Italy (where he is from and has a home) as well as travel and cooking – three of my passions too. I'd taught an Italian choir for the Catholic Church for years, so I knew his 'strong' personality was a characteristic of 'men being men' - no nonsense with the Italians. Although, now it's viewed as a hate crime in mincy Broken Woke Britain. Ask Gio from *Strictly* or Gino D'Acampo how being a man's man has gone for them in our pitiful cancel culture UK! Hurty words can end careers these days... or land you in the slammer. It's woeful how pathetic we've become. People need to man up - and grow up. Alf loved the news and was old-school in his thinking, so we immediately clicked. We both went to the gym every day, so that kept us fit and focussed. Trust me, he could take on any prison goon a third of his age. He could see I was out of my depth, and despite his 'no messing' exterior, he was incredibly kind and generous. He was a huge beacon of hope and support. We immediately bonded. BOND – something very rare in jail! We walked miles together. He epitomised keeping perspective. He had been all over the country, in endless jails for many years, and knew all the rules and pitfalls. He has NOTHING but palpable contempt for the system - especially probation, who are notoriously useless and conniving. Alf got me a remote - gold dust in jail! Sounds like nothing, but it's a game-changer when you're a lazy bastard who gets bored within seconds of most TV guff and mutes all adverts by default. I was like a sponge, learning about the 'process' back to freedom from Alf. He was the oracle. Sadly, thanks to the 'unique' severity and 'public risk' of my case, none of the rules applied - and clearly still don't. However, it was great to learn what SHOULD have happened, if my case hadn't been so utterly corrupt and manipulated by the evil cabal of shysters within the judiciary.

So, this was my new life. It wouldn't change any time soon, and if the box-tickers had their way, they'd make it as tortuous and extensive as possible. I'd need interminable energy and tenacity to survive this subjugated, shushy sentence and sham. I simply embraced my blessings, pulled up my socks, and got on with it -

taking comfort in my prison pals and my mail bag, which were collectively keeping me alive.

By Friday, a knock came on the pad door, and a nice bonny lass from 'Activities' offered me a job in 'VT Catering' to start on Monday. It was £15 a week! Blimey - I'd finally made it bigtime! I'm almost on West End Twirly Hoofer wages! Basically, the purpose of HMP Stocken was to teach lads with no discipline (or life skills) how to get out of bed and turn up for work. Various options were available, of course - some jobs were much better than others. The lowest of the low is 'Tea Packing' on HMS Stockings - literally putting two teabags, three sugars, and a biscuit in a bag for each of the lads at breakfast. This job is deemed more pointless and lowly paid than a probation officer. Ouch! You do hundreds of breakfast packs a day. That was £12 a week, and known as the Noddy Shop. The best job is in the gardens, but you needed top security clearance. That was impossible until the new year. Oh - and it was too cold for me to be cutting grass and trimming my bush in October! The highest-paid job was with DHL, who do the canteen for various prisons. You get £40 a week to make them thousands. It was a modern-day sweatshop, and my idea of a nightmare - a load of goons in a factory counting cans of energy drinks and vapes into a basket. For men with no money sent in from home, this was the dream of the slammer - at three times the HMP going rate. There were several practical workshops like car repairs and plumbing (zero interest to me – don't get my hands dirty) - so VT Catering was gold for the winter! VT = Vocational Training (not Voluntary Transgender!) – I haven't got enough to chop off anyway! This course was the dream gig at the 'Marriott for Morons,' as it offered free food twice a day. I got very lucky and was the envy of the 1,185 other men who didn't have this gig. You get a worthless piece of paper at the end of the course - and I can assure you, working in a Beefeater wasn't my vocation. BUT, if it passes four hours and gets me fed, I'm well up for it! The prison gets paid a fortune to deliver these useless qualifications - which aren't worth the paper they're written on. Ofsted judge the prison's success on how many doofuses they can give these worthless pieces of paper to. All box-ticking horseshit. This way, HMP can claim it's teaching numbskulls how to 'cope with life.' Bollocks!!! This workshop kitchen had only fifteen lads max, so it was highly prized as a 'job' for the 1% club. You get to eat what you cook - priceless in the slammer. Better still, it supplied cakes for the staff bistro, as well as soups, curries, pies, etc. - with leftovers as an added bonus perk.

Unlike DHL, which employed hundreds, this was relaxed and more personal. Again, because of carving knives etc, I needed top level security clearance - so there's a compliment there somewhere! This was HMP's first backhanded compliment and admission I was NO RISK! You had to have Level One English and Maths to be considered, so again, the most stupid and disadvantaged are ruled out and totally unable to get the best gigs, even though cooking is a creative talent. I went and told the lads that I'd got this job, and I could see the palpable fury -

jealousy, even. This was the first 'Who does he think he is?' moment! I had no idea how this pecking order stuff was so important. 'I've been on the waiting list for three years!' Ouch. We all know that in life, there is no waiting list. Cons do take their jobs seriously. You cannot miss work; they'll kick you out of bed if necessary. If you refuse to go it's a nicking, three adjudications and you're put on losses, moved to basic (one visit a month and no TV) and you're behind the door. This is discipline with consequences - like REAL LIFE. What this did tell me was that there was no conspiracy in this slammer, so far. If they'd wanted to, they could've given me a 'wing cleaner' job and played with me like a blind kitten. The pay is identical on the wing, but you're totally cocooned - and you'll go stir-crazy very quickly. A job off the wing allows you to live an almost 'normal' life. What would you do for the other 23.5 hours a day if you're a wing cleaner? No wonder half of them end up potty and addicted to pot and QVC! I knew, if I was going to survive, I had to keep busy and get off the wing IMMEDIATELY! This wasn't exactly selling out the North Pier with a standing ovation in Blackpool - but within three days, I'd got a cushy job, my own pad (alone), and met some 'top' people. As jail goes, this is pretty cushty... yet still totally pointless.

The next cab off the rank was the chapel - I had to get 'on the list.' For obvious reasons, despite this being CAT-C, the prison was still pretty strict on movements (your freedom to leave the wing). It more or less operated as a CAT-B due to staff shortages and the lingering 'Covid regime' - a year after the

Covid nonsense had ended. All just an excuse to bang up men who didn't work, for twenty-two hours a day. I wonder if they thought I'd refuse to work - and that this could be their proverbial stick to bang me up and drive me crazy? Little did they know that I couldn't wait to get my £1.50 per session and spend the winter icing fairy cakes. A lack of compliance would have given the suits a LOT more control. I was 100% compliant, thereby giving them no leverage to control or discipline me whatsoever. They quickly worked out that I was no bother or risk - so let me 'off' (out) to go to the chapel and library whenever I wanted. For all the rules and regulations, once the screws know and like you, you can get anywhere - if you're canny. Let's face it: with all the smackheads and violent lunatics, some daft showbiz twat who wants to pop off to finger his organ in the chapel is the least of their concerns!

Stocken is a huge campus. It's almost a mile from visits to the Newton wing. Fab for my steps and inner thighs. Containment is the best way to secure prisoners. In fairness, HMP Stocken had mastered this with enclosed corridors outside. I loved it - it kept us dry in the bleak mid-winter. However, be under no delusions: we're all caged animals. Only a very few would qualify to go beyond the entrapment fence or outside certain boundaries. As the estate is collapsing, all CAT-Cs are upping security to CAT-B levels - to the fury of the long-timers. Stocken is crammed with lifers, as it's not a resettlement (last three years) pokey like HMP Five Wells or HMP Fosse Way down the road. This is all about monitoring, observation, and stalking my every move. You cannot have twelve hundred criminal men mincing around the jail 'borrowing,' buying, or selling 'items of interest' willy nilly. Separating people wing by wing is paramount to security. The smaller the numbers, the easier it is to manage the herd - that's why new jails are built in houseblocks, splitting men into a maximum of sixty per floor, as opposed to up to 350 on old-style wings. There's one rule for one, and one rule for others. We are not all born equal in jail. It's one BIG gentleman's club with a blatant pecking order - based exclusively on violence. I clearly was not deemed of any risk.... other than when I open my gob on-air over the fence! This was a relief, helpful, and very fortuitous in terms of jobs and lifestyle.

On Sunday, I went to the chapel, which was to become my spiritual home - a place of total comfort, safety, and relaxation for the next year. I was greeted at the door by Tim, the Vicar. He was a very tall and imposing man, who welcomed all with a big smile. He ran the chapel with a rod of iron and tolerated no nonsense from cunning cons using God for nefarious, dodgy dealings. Incontinence appears to be a major issue in prison prayer palaces! No cameras and no judgement leads to a car boot sale by the urinal - Tim was having none of it. I took my pew and enjoyed his sermon. Again, I find a lot of the scriptures confusing and contradictory; however, the sense of calm is more than compensation for ninety minutes of investment. He radiates optimism. He is a great communicator.

Most impressive is the band: Tim played guitar, there's a drummer, a remarkable bass player, and an adorable lady on the piano who looks and acts sixty - but is, in fact, eighty! This lady is called Anne, and she is the heartbeat of the chapel. She has inspiring and kind words, a huge smile, and a warmth like few I've ever met anywhere in life - let alone in the big house. Truly remarkable. Her energy is astonishing. She appeared the most genuine soul on earth, with time for everyone. She is adored by the men - a bundle of love and hope that, for many, is their inspiration to fight the broken, vile, and disgusting system. She has volunteered at the chapel for over twenty years - every single week! I couldn't resist chatting afterwards and shared my passion for the piano with her. She'd been playing for decades and was wonderful to watch. I said, "You're fantastic. What a joyful noise the band are!" I wasn't being sarcastic. It was unbelievably uplifting and professional. The kindness in this lady's voice and body language gave me faith that I could survive this nightmare - and even come out stronger, simply based on her and Tim's sincerity. I felt human again around this octogenarian delight. She'd mastered the art of making all men feel 'normal' and loved - what a gift!!! I will never forget the beacon of light that Tim, Anne, and the team would offer over the next year. The misconception that jails are entirely evil and toxic was dispelled in one handshake of these two heroes' hands. The Lord works in mysterious ways. He had sent angels to motivate me and give me something to look forward to.

I parted by saying, "If you ever need cover, just shout!" Anne so kindly said, "I would love that." She asked me to play for her, as Tim cautiously listened on from afar. She was so kind and gracious. Everyone thinks they can play, of course - most don't know the difference between a C and G string! This had been my number-one passion since I was four years old. She was over the moon. Totally selfless and unbelievably encouraging. "You're brilliant" she said. I think she's so kind that if I'd have played like Les Dawson, she'd have applauded. I've never met a person more full of undoubting enthusiasm. She truly is the most encouraging and inspiring lady I've met since my old gran - back when I first started tinkling the old ivories in 1984. She said, "I'm off next week - would you help the band?" I couldn't believe my luck. It was meant to be. "We practice on a Wednesday; would you be willing to join us?" Wow. Would I be willing? I'd be delighted! Blimey - I hadn't even been in my new 'forever slammer' for a week, and I'd already been reunited with my beloved piano and met people I truly respected and really liked. Sanity was back on the end of my fingers! You have no idea the happiness, joy, and therapy those keys give me - they have done for my entire life! When I'm at my lowest ebb, especially after a bereavement, the piano lifts my heart and soul within seconds, and grief disappears through the old Joanna instantly. It's as if the negativity just disappears via the genius of the ebony and ivory plinkety planks. This was a dream - to be given such a blessing on day one. I couldn't wait for Wednesday to bring music back into my life. I'm still uncertain about 'God' and his plans for our lives, but I can assure you - the people he attracts have been a lifesaver for me.

My next home would be the library, so I quickly got to know two kind ladies - Helen and Marie-Ann - who ran it old-school. For five months, whilst writing my autobiography, they allowed me to sit there for hours, wrapped in the warmth and comfort of books, through the dark winter of '22. It had a very primary school vibe - far from threatening or anything nick-related. It was relatively small and only had twenty men in at a time. Mostly, it was empty - and felt as safe as humanly possible in a hostage centre for halfwits and has-beens. As is always the case in life, the library is not a democracy. They wisely picked and chose who could and couldn't come in. They suffered no fools and accepted no nonsense. I was so grateful for the heavenly peace and quiet. I sensed they 'got' me in the first second - instinct in the clink is priceless. A chapel of books indeed. If it got no better than this, I'd be absolutely fine - I just knew it. My guardian angels had been found just seconds away - in the chapel and book centre. Collectively, these two homes of good books were my sanity saver. It may surprise you to know that I haven't read one word from the library - EVER. I've been too busy writing my own epistles. I haven't had a second! The key to surviving the slammer is being proactive - survival of the fittest and king of the jungle. No one will help you. You can only help yourself - you have to fight for what you want, as you're just a number in a system of twelve hundred other men who all blur into one. No one will find you - you have to get noticed and be seen. For me, my only priority was to remain busy, distracted, and as happy and focused as possible - despite the gruesome circumstances I'd been dealt. I would - and could - not let this foolishness beat me. I'd got too much to do in thirty months' time, when this shitty cruise ship contract ends. I'd made a great start. At no point did I feel scared or even out of my comfort zone - which is extraordinary. I was either invisible or curious to cons - but no threat on either side whatsoever. I was shocked by the relative 'luxury' and comfort we were given. I never expected to be handed a kettle and a budget for Nescafé Gold. It's a bewildering place of contradictions... serving absolutely no purpose.

One of the strange gifts I've received whilst in 'The Custody of Cockwombles' is daily prayers from godly angels. From Anne to my own KC, and hundreds of VoR diamonds, I would be donated prayers daily and be in their thoughts. This is powerful. I don't fully understand it, but I am hugely grateful. Any donations of positivity help big time - what bigger compliment is there? What harm could it do? It was disseminated from above with the best of wishes and top intentions. The biggest thrill, though, was being invited into the chapel band for the first rehearsal. Music is my form of prayer - and a music score is truly my Bible. Despite the generosity of Anne's offer to play for the men, I did not want to appear pushy or put anyone's nose out of joint by 'taking over.' I was very aware of not upstaging or pissing off the band - least of all Anne, who is a diamond and had earned her place behind the Altar of Steinway! She was such a beacon of joy, and the last thing I wanted to do was upset her or make her feel redundant. She is the most loyal and dedicated person I've ever met at HMP - ever. She needs an MBE (at least) for her dedication to the chapel, which she attends (no expenses) three times a week. I like the sound of Dame Anne - very befitting.

From that day on, I was in the band and shared the old Joanna with Anne - 50/50. The kindest thing anyone has done for me EVER! Tim, Dan, and Pete couldn't have been more welcoming. They're all exceptional talents - and hugely compassionate souls. Dan on bass had been in jail for years, as had Pete on drums - twenty-seven long years. I do not know how these men function... especially with such grace. I was made up. They couldn't have been more welcoming - and despite their lengthy incarceration, they were boundless in energy and positivity. I'm back in showbiz, boys! The Lord works in very mysterious ways!

Chapter 17

Food, Glorious-ish Food

Food became my #1 pastime for my first three months on HMS Stockings. VT Catering was located at the very top of the prison, in the workshop compound, along with DHL and 'industries.' I was given 'work shoes' - clumpy, heavy, steel-toe-capped brown shoes, perfect for a vegan, *Guardian*-reading, quiche-eating eco-warrior... or ladies with beards who are considering the snip snip. This wasn't a fashion parade, so 'butch boots' it is! It was take it, or leave it. 'Elf and safety' and 'mental 'elf' are big buzzwords in the slammer.

At precisely 8am on Monday morning, the door opened to the second - so I trudged up from F wing to 'work.' For the love of God - how did it come to this? The noise in the Twat Tunnels by peacocking tosspots was deafening. The endless chest-pounding alpha males made me want to puke with their butch shenanigans. For the first time, I missed the West End Twirlies - they're too busy painting their toenails and Googling drag shows to worry about being manly! It was like a boxing match in Vegas, every morning. Who has the energy? Turns out, nearly everyone has ADHD - or at least verbal diarrhoea! Makes my teeth itch! To think - two weeks ago I'd wake up with a croissant, pot of cha, and Aled Jones on *Classic FM*... Now I've got heckling hyenas sniffing their fingers, fisting each other, and mysteriously giving man-hugs (shoulders only), resulting in tiny packets being swapped and bromantic fantasies fulfilled.

I went to the door of 'Workshop Five' and I was greeted by Stella Virgin - a stalwart of HMP Stocken. A lady after my own heart, you don't mess! She'd seen it all - and was suspicious of everyone, including me! I do like a challenge. She then uttered the sweetest words I'd heard in weeks: "Go put your whites on." Oh, Gordon Ramsay - eat your heart out! Mary Berry on a Penny Farthing, this might be the sexiest order of my life! I bet I could make my donuts look like Fanny's! (Sixties joke — Google it; Johnnie would be proud). Well, well, well... what kind of pointless prison service is this? Surely this isn't their much-promoted 'rehabilitation?" I was very grateful for the opportunity - but what a total waste of f'in time this was going to be...

It was a mixed bag of lads in catering. One of the mentors was a man called Julian - a family man in his early fifties, who'd been done for fraud on a first offence and sentenced to seven long years. He had nine months left after being banged up during lockdown - serving three and a half years behind the door for a Ponzi scheme. He'd had a great career before it all came crashing down. This had destroyed everything - including his self-respect. This was my first red flag: that 'justice' was not about prison - it was about humiliating you and stripping you of everything. We became good pals over the next few months, as he lived on F Wing, on 'the ones' - the other side of induction. He's a very friendly man, who I was paired with for a cooking competition on day one - which was visited by lots of top brass. This never happened again. Coincidence? Serendipity? File under 'It could only happen to me!'

238

Only I could be part of a one-off competition - with the Govs all wandering around on day one to sample our goat's cheese and ham tart. Julian created it from a stack of random ingredients in a *Ready Steady Cook* style. I had to laugh at myself, looking down on this ludicrous situation. Julian was the server in the Bistro Café for staff, and a very talented cook - having devoted his three years to perfecting baking and curries. Not sure how this embellishes his life or qualifies as 'rehabilitation' - but there you go. Like me, he was a family man. Not dissimilar to myself, locking him up achieved <u>NOTHING</u> - other than torturing his family. Total waste of public money, which resulted in him losing everything, destroying his marriage, punishing his kids, and him leaving jail on benefits. <u>YAY</u>! What a success HMP!

I couldn't believe my luck! The kitchens had a pantry full of everything! I love cooking - but hate clearing up. Since the rise of the 'Voice of Reason,' I hadn't done any cooking, as I couldn't be arsed. Uber Eats was a lot easier on my Fairy Liquid hands! I'd rather hire a boy called Sue (chef) than toss a salad or shank a ham! Now, twice a day, I'd be cooking at the taxpayer's expense of £48k a year. No more modelling marigolds for me! Alas, we won the competition due to Jule's culinary genius - and we got £5 credit on our accounts each. I was cock-a-hoop – that was fifty, three-minute calls! £5 is worth £50 in the slammer. Again, someone was smiling down on me – pure fluke and nothing to do with me. Never take credit for another man's work! I was told that at a swinger's club when I handed back my set of jump leads! Stella Virgin was very strict about 'no eating until the end.' Forty-five minutes before we cleaned down, we all sat and ate our produce of the day. Julian's pastry - hand/homemade - was delicious, fine, and crispy. No soggy bottoms in sight! Nigella would pout with approval. I quickly realised why VT Catering was the envy of the slammer - we got fresh-cooked food, including eggs, cheese, and bacon, daily on demand. It was the stuff of dreams for those without money, and even for enhanced prisoners on Newton. It didn't pass me by that I'd gone from being a Michelin Star restaurant food critic for fifteen years to a master baker in the clink. Funny old world, hey? As I walked home from work that night at 4.45pm, I couldn't help but wonder - what is the point of prison? This can't be it, surely? When will it start? It never did. How is this punishment or rehabilitation? These are the only two functions HMP is supposed to serve. Of course... it is not. For now, I'll revel in a day one first prize.

At exactly 6pm, I rang my Aunty Dorothy for our nightly catch-up, and she was thrilled! She'd been a home economics teacher for thirty years, so this gave her great satisfaction. Everyone found it utterly comical that my torture in prison - designed to push me over the edge - was a cooking course run by Jamie Oliver's grandma, Stella Virgin. What a battle-axe. One look from her and armed robbers would clench. Hands like shovels, making that pastry - you wouldn't want a smack in the gob, I can tell you that! As for Stocken's servery - with five choices per meal - I was left shocked by some of the options: salmon quiche, prawn cocktail sandwiches, breaded chicken, fresh pollock with cheese, and the 'delicious' Sunday lunch of gammon, which consists of two slices of Asda-quality ham: totally inedible and indigestible, wafer-thin salted plastic. Swerve that if I were you! Lunch included soup and two sandwiches - BBQ chicken, egg mayo, and vegan grated cheese with fresh tomato - typically served with a yogurt, Walker's crisps, and a piece of fruit. How could you possibly mock? They claim that we're fed on less than £3 per day. If that's true, then the general public should be screaming at their local supermarkets over the mark-ups! For me, though, all of my nutritional woes were over whilst in this job. For the next three months, I'd be fed like a king! However, the problem with cooking is that it doesn't take three hours to prepare, cook, and clean up after a dish. I'd need a distraction... Ahhh - I could be paid to do VT Catering for an hour, and then spend two hours writing in Stella's lovely warm office, on a nice office chair. Genius!!! Almost two years later, during a subject access request to the MOJ, I found out this was when I first pissed off the box-tickers upstairs - big time. Right then, I was blissfully unaware of their snooping and fury - but they were already clutching their pearls and hiding behind their mantilla. They were scheming to stop me doing ANYTHING that involved a pen. This weapon was more feared than a machete - by my assassins.

Another surprise at HMP is that you get dry cleaning - well, a laundry man who washes, dries, and folds your clothes once a week, for free. My cleaner, Formaldehyde, is £40 an hour in Notts! I genuinely couldn't believe this. I can't even get the current Mrs B to peel her own drawers off the bathroom floor - let alone Ajax the gusset of my Calvins! Now I had room service - Jarvis - to vanish any unsightly spillages on my smalls and return them pristine the same day. You pop your 'sprout sack' laundry bag - full of mucky and filthy undergarments (corsets to man-bras) - outside his door, and before you can say Kim and Aggy, your girdles, socks, undercrackers, and britches are spotless and returned to your pad before you can say piff paff pouf! Bloody hell - blow my bloomers (literally). I, of course, am house proud. I like my pillows and towels done twice a week, so I got Jarvis to do my ablutions twice weekly for a vape. You get three in a pack for £3 - so I thought this was a bargain. A pair of socks in St Pancras costs £2.50 to freshen up! I couldn't believe my luck. Jarvis was so proud of his job - and more than willing to lend a hand!

On Saturday at 9am, I had my first visit in a 'relaxed' room - with more shitty drawings, ones that looked like they came from a local nursery. Little did I know, it was the Level 2 Art course on the happy ship Stockings that had created these unsightly monstrosities. I've seen better 'art' from the elephants at Twycross after a huge trunk sneeze. We all had to go dressed in prison jeans and a short-sleeved shirt - to humiliate us in front of our loved ones and dehumanise us further. It makes no sense, and no one could tell me why. The fact I was showing my peaky ginger arms was a big enough fall from grace for me. Other CAT-Cs don't do this – just here. Mum and Dad came with BBJ – Big Boned Jean, my common-law personal assistant – and being studious, they were in by 9.10am, at the front of the queue. We had coffees and butties, and had a lovely time chatting. Then a gentleman of colour came over to shake my hand and said, "Keep going, Alex - we're rooting for you." How kind! Then, as last orders were called at the café, another VoR stunner came over - virtually in tears - saying how sorry she was. She was the grandma of Elliot and his cousin Ben, both of whom were at the prison and seated at separate tables for the visit, because 'them's the rules!' Ridiculous. You'd be amazed how many brothers, fathers, sons, and cousins there are in the slammer. I don't know whether it's #fate... or tragic.

I was blown away by their kindness. Shortly after the bell rang (yep, proper 'Round 2' boxing bell), our two hours of soul food and emotional ecstasy was over. My three troopers left, and I smelt a rat. I could see security poking around like a cocker spaniel sniffing a tramp's knackers. "Wait there Belfield!" I knew what was coming. Randomly, one man gets stripped searched every visit. Normally, it's a stereotype that you'd never get away with in real life. Usually, it's a gentleman of colour with dreamy eyes, braided hair, and jeans below his buttocks. Today it was me – revenge for my affirmation in front of the whole visits hall. Remember, I'd done NOTHING wrong. So, like when Nottingham Police illegally raided my home without a warrant and then strip searched me, these bunch of closeted anal beads wanted to, once again, bring me down a peg or two, by having a look at my half an inch and a dozen wrinkles. This job is only allocated to the creepy or demented. Only an unhinged pervert would want a job to look at other men's cock 'n' balls for a career! Sickos. I bet they know all about being 'Pegged!' (google it!). What they didn't know was that I'd got a Julian Clary routine for the LIVE show - about the police pilchard scrotum sniffers who pulled the same stunt. Three cuntstable Anusols took a peek that day....I was clenched and ready to go for today's bell end botherers. BTW, in a proper prison, they stick you through the scanner - and all of this noncy cock nonsense and gloating is banned.

I followed Officer Pecker and his two-stripe, Shuffolo, to a tiny room - where they had me do a striptease for the obvious provocation of a kick-off, or the titters in the staff room on Monday morning... confirming I had a minuscule schlong. I could not resist. My favourite lines included:

1) 'Hey Gov. How much do they pay you to look at another man's penis!'

2) 'Sir. Do you ever get aroused doing this? I got aroused watching countdown last night – 7 letters.'

3) 'Chief. When you get home to your wife and boyfriend, do you ever roll play that they're a pervert asking you to get your nob out?'

4) 'Boss. Don't you think for a micro penis it's above average?'

5) 'Can I apologise if at any point I get excited. It's the rubber gloves that turn me on, not two old fat men.'

They were seething but speechless. Their cheeks were bright red - like beetroot. Like the goons at NCP (Notts Corrupt Police), they have no button for ridicule and contempt - my two default positions with such imbeciles. They couldn't get out quick enough. They were speechless. I was never asked to do a strip search again. BTW, they don't actually get to see your penis. It's meant to be discrete - you're meant to turn around, with your back to them. When they say 'shake it' - they mean your pants... not your gentleman's parts...Which, naturally, I couldn't resist rising to the occasion. You know you've got a VERY creepy officer when he asks you for a strip search after a 'purple' visit - that's via the computer, where you don't actually go near anyone. Trust me - it happens! I wouldn't let these men babysit your kids, if I were you. This officer is a prolific cyclist. I'm told he always slows down outside primary schools so that his GoPro doesn't blur... should there be any speeding motorists. How peculiar, hey?

BTW, the prison parlance for shoving drugs up your arse is 'banking.' Yep, I can confirm these two found fack all, but I did make them look a pair of bankers!

Chapter 18

Time to Explain – Headline News

On the second Saturday onboard HMS Stockings, I got a lot of curious nods and stares. Oy vey, here we go. I'm pretty long in the tooth - and I knew shenanigans were afoot! When you've been in the business - we call it show - as long as I have, you know when someone knows who you are. I don't know how, but you can tell. I did my usual gobshiting with Alf and Brian, putting the world to rights around the playground for numpties and cuckoo clocks. One of the brilliant things about HMP Stocken, being in the countryside of Leicestershire, is that the airspace is used by the UK and US military to fly by and practice. We saw everything - from the Red Arrows to the Eurofighter and US jets - endlessly passing by (often in glorious formation) from the Lincolnshire coast and local airbases, showing off and proudly showing off with their overhead ballet. I loved it! I've been obsessed with planes since being a little boy. Watching them - with a 747 pilot in a nick - is surreal. On a sunny day, I would often look up at the trails and fantasise about my next flight to Barbs, Vegas, Majorca... or even brilliant Barcelona. Little did I realise those trails were the government's attempt to turn down the temperature of the sun. Who knew?! I promised myself that my comeback would enable me to enjoy the luxuries of travel even more than before. This, after all, is my biggest passion. Looking up at the planes inspired me more than words. They are the definition of freedom - and the joy, fun, and experience that comes with it. For the first time in years, I was weirdly excited.

There's real lift and longing here - an emotional jet stream. You have no idea what blessings you have until they're taken away. I guess I'd taken a lot for granted - working relentlessly for nearly three decades. When you work for yourself, saying 'no' is almost impossible. This was a brilliant wake-up call. I'd often look at passing pigeons, wondering how they bizarrely had more freedom - and a better life - than me. Who's the vermin and pest now?

Anywho, on our six-hundredth lap of F Wing Yard, a fella called Doug came out and said, "You're all over The Sun today." I replied, "Oh marvellous - not again! All publicity is good publicity, mate." As a man who's written two-page spreads for *The Mail*, *MoS*, *Mirror*, *People*, *Express*, and - indeed - today's chip paper saboteur, *The Sun*, I totally understand the game. If I'm two pages, the editor must believe I have value and clickbait appeal. There's another backhander! No matter the guff, litany of lies, or hatchet job contained within - a Saturday spread stinks of troll and clickbait, if you ask me. Thankfully, most *Sun* readers only look at the pictures - and then make the rest up for themselves. To think that *The Sun* - which I'd worked for under Dan Wootton and Andy Halls for over ten years - had stabbed me in the front was absolutely not astonishing. Like so many of their 'exclusives,' you don't have to dig very deep to find the screaming holes and Grand Canyon-scale whoppers in the text. It's always been bluster in a rag - described by its own boss as worthless as a business in these disastrous times for print. Their game is to fill column-inches at any cost. When I went onto the wing the paper was open on the lunch table, with ten lads sat around with my ugly mug (shot) looking up at me. This was my first major test in the slammer.

What can you possibly say? Jail is like *Loose Women* - a load of gossips, gobshites, and nosey parkers, desperate for anything to talk about. I'm the most exciting thing that had happened to HMP Stocken since Gary Glitter applied to do the babysitting course in Education. There's a lot of hours to fill in the pokey - and their world is very small. Any drama will get chins wagging. I have never, in my life, encountered men who can be arsed with such endless minutiae, inane shite, and repeat nonsense as in prison. The repetitive dullness, for most men, was mind-numbing - so I was like a walking *Butlins*. Think about it, what else is there? Most have nothing and no one. This is their entire world! It was Saturday lunch, and I went to get my plate out of my pad. Bacon, sausage, two hash browns, beans, egg, and toast! How's that for weekend scran? As I walked past, I said, "Christ, I must be famous to fill two pages, most men only have five inches." A couple of the smart ones laughed. Cocky (so to speak) but it paid off. You cannot reverse out of an HMP cul-de-sac. If you show fear – you're finished! You have to walk into the flames, or you'll be walked all over. When I got back from the servery, I was astonished (but not surprised) to see it was one of the 'NOT GUILTY' BBC women who had sold her story. I actually laughed out loud. I couldn't resist reading about myself – who wouldn't. For the first and last time, I sat down at the twenty-seater table on a seat that resembled a 12" record on a stick - and I opened myself up to any brave critics!

In fairness, *The Sun* went to great lengths to make it clear that I was vindicated after the preposterous lie that I'd sent 'thousands of emails.' This was an instantly disposable, pre-planned pile of horseshit. I had never sent this woman ONE direct email - EVER - let alone thousands. In fact, all the prosecution could vomit was about twenty emails 'sent to all' over ten years, regarding BBC FOI and programming matters. NOT GUILTY! This woman (who no longer works for the BBC) wasn't believed by the jury. The Sun's final line was 'Belfield was found not guilty.' Absolutely extraordinary! I've never heard of such journalistic insanity before. Talk to a 'guilty' victim, of course - discuss 'stalking WITHOUT fear, alarm, or distress' for a laugh. But someone who was disbelieved and still given column-inches to repeat their fantasy and word vomit? Hysterical! No one could believe the foolishness. Laughably, she blamed the BBC! She wasn't even angry at me - she demanded an internal investigation. Told ya - BBC is the king of self-flagellation. They always turn on themselves and eat themselves alive in the end. The irony that this person was calling for a BBC investigation on behalf of the four disbelieved/not guilty BBC women was, to me, comedy gold. Read the room! The jury believed I was, in fact, the victim - not them! Remember, in open court, they admitted calling me names and plotting behind my back. The lads devoured the ludicrous accusations one by one - while I had absolutely no right of reply in the newspaper. They laughed, guffawed, and mocked this clearly pre-scripted dopery by the author. Jock sat beside me. He is such a class act and gentleman. I could see him becoming twitchy - but he'd got my back, whilst remaining quiet, to see how I handled the baying cons. I said, "Ask me anything!" One smart arse shouted, "Why did you do it?" I replied, "I didn't 'do it' - I was found not guilty. Can't you read?" Everyone laughed. BOOM! That was exactly how to handle it - fearless. You can't show weakness.

In court, this person told a ten-minute story under oath - about how I followed her from her house to a bus stop. She kept walking into the park and sped up until she was nearly running. She finally ran out of breath, in hysterics (with tears in her eyes), and turned around to tell the jury, "But it wasn't him. It was someone walking their dog." How do you deal with this level of fantasy? Total laughingstock in the public gallery. I told them that story - and they were gobsmacked. Jock said, "Yes, she said that story in there." How can you follow someone, when they admitted you have no idea where they lived – for which you were found <u>not guilty</u>?" Thank God for our British Press! Where would we be without *The Sun* - valued at £1 by its owner - hey? I'm grateful to Murdoch; he bought my home with ten years of stories. They forgot to mention they paid me tens of thousands, over a decade, for my journalism - for which I'm totally guilty, Your Honour... mostly exposing THE BBC! File under 'hunter turned gamekeeper.' So funny when you stand back and see the wood for the trees.

Once again, this 'out-of-body experience' was hysterical - not dissimilar to verified Vicky on naughty *Newsnight*. This shameless, tatty journalism - based on total hearsay - backfired again! This campaign (entirely choreographed), even post-conviction, left people scratching their heads - confused and cynical. They want their readers to believe and have sympathy for something a jury unanimously disbelieved. Crackers! I hope they enjoyed their 'moment in the sun' - and their tawdry bauble of a 'sell your soul' payment for 'five minutes of fame.' Some people will do anything for attention, it seems. What a legacy that they used me for their continued glory.

What was remarkable, was how quickly the lads could see through the razzle-dazzle and simply dismiss it as 'not guilty' – therefore, NOT a story. Fortunately for me, every time another one of those dopey, boohoo, attention-seeking, victim-playing, political takedowns was published - it only added to the stitch-up conclusion from my people and the public, who couldn't make head nor tail of the entire cockamamie heist. Even my biggest critics (and enemies) could see this was absolutely bonkers. In what other scenario would a 'not guilty' loser - criminally - be given a platform to repeat their lies, that my KC annihilated, and still believe they had a moral or legal right to repeat and fabricate in the press? Others have questioned why so many of my devastated 'victims' are so keen on so much relentless association and attention - on the back of my demise? Well, one word 'BBC!' I do wonder which powerful journalist was pulling the strings at the Beeb to continue these ludicrous tales of exaggerated, manufactured, and created brown smear bullshit? Just like the three-page advert in *The Guardian* Andrex paper a week or so ago - it's a circus! Regardless, this 'not guilty' lunacy cemented my credibility on HMS Stockings. It also gave me a sense of celebrity, which - as it turns out - is no bad thing. It told all the bad lads everything they wanted and needed to know about my unique and bewildering situation. This own goal projected me into martyr status - a <u>very</u> bad idea when you're trying to actively destroy someone. Giving your 'attacker' reflected sympathy is surely an own goal?

As we were banged up for lunch at twelve noon, I called my sister - to protect Mum and Dad from this guff. She said, "Don't worry - they wouldn't allow that toilet roll in the house after Hillsborough." Isn't it funny how you can't edit people's memories and true feelings? It's been decades since *The Sun* blamed Liverpool for that tragedy - thirty years later, people have not forgotten. This public awareness gives me massive faith. The public are so loyal, clever, and smart. They won't be brainwashed by dinosaur hacks looking for cheap clicks. The good news is that they can't make you like something - and equally, they can't make you <u>NOT</u> like someone. Genius! Isn't it fascinating to watch the demise of the BBC, mainstream media, and all the government-funded totalitarian enforcers since Covid? These sanctimonious and supercilious pricks are redundant - and totally discredited! They are a breed of disgusting souls, with almost no humanity, who believe they can pull the wool over the public's eyes. FAIL! As always, I called my

PA, Big-Boned Jean - and she answered the phone laughing: "Alo Alex, have you seen the comedy in *The Sun*? Trial by media overrides a judge and jury, does it? I've had thirty texts from people pissing themselves." This kind of reaction keeps you alive in spirit - during times of massive sabotage and attack. The entire game of this shoddy, gutter-paper filler is to whip up a storm, bully, and intimidate. Since phone hacking - and we <u>all</u> know who turned a blind eye to that - it's over! The huge lesson I learned over the nine months of relentless headlines is that it's all worthless. It doesn't change anything. IT'S <u>NOT</u> REAL. It is purely done for copy - to fill airtime or column-inches for attention, vanity, and ego-wank for the editor. It's panto at best - *Coronation Street* kitchen-sink drama or over-the-fence dopey gossip at worst. Tittle-tattle for people with no lives. As Network Nick, my tech genius, quite rightly pointed out: "Two pages on a Saturday must mean you're someone. They'd saved that up all week! If you were a nobody, it would've been a filler column-inch on a desperate Tuesday." Poetry, right? Like all storms, it quickly blows over - and no one stable and sane gives two shiny shites. One thing is to be remembered from all this: NEVER believe a word you hear or see on the news. It's all ONE BIG GAME to tickle the tits of their tawdry agenda.

Then, as if by magic, at 1pm - just sixty minutes after the door was locked for lunch, for roll-check (i.e. head count) to take place - a very nice female officer said, "Alex, can I come in?" through the spyhole, the two-inch observation panel in the door. It was like being back in Amsterdam in the 1990s. 'Oh God' I thought what now? Click clunk. A butch screw - who put me in mind of Pat Butcher's more masculine twin - said, "Fack me, you're popular. Why are all these people writing to you?" I laughed. "Oh, it's only the Inland Revenue," I replied. She slapped about fifty letters from my angels on the desk. Perfect timing. "Have you seen yourself on the TV?" she enquired. I said, "Yes, love. I've been on three series of *Crimewatch*." She tittered and pootled off - not a moment too soon. Even now, I won't reply sensibly to such questions. There is no right answer. In the click of a finger and the blink of a sphincter, a soul-lifter had arrived - delivering a tsunami of love, counter-balancing the two pages of *Sun* word guff by a mile! WOW! From the puke-inducing venom of the tabloids to a pile of hope in just one hour - I was whizzing my tits off and, once again, felt safe, protected, reassured, and loved. Impeccable timing, I have to say.

From that day on, some eight days into my cruise contract on HMS Stockings, I NEVER had a single day, hour, or minute, without one of my VoR angels to reply to. Someone gorgeous and delicious was always by my side to talk to - filling my heart with pride, 24/7, for the entire thirty-plus months. I truly am the luckiest man in the world! These letters and emails saved my life, soul, and sanity. Prison is EASY in CAT-C. It's a world away from CAT-Bs - like barbaric bang-up Lincoln. Piece of piss. Luxuries, TV - oh, by the way, we had ninety-plus TV channels to watch at Stocken. There's relatively no violence, a job, a chapel, and a library - but there are still 24 hours in a day to survive in the wilderness of isolation. Every day was taken up in the company of some of the biggest-hearted, kindest, and most thoughtful family of fans a gobshite like me could ask for. This was my blessing. Idle hands in the slammer lead to big trouble - and crackers cons. I've been run off my feet and kept 100% grounded and focused in the glory of my angels' unwavering support.

My BT white phone had nine preset numbers. #1 was the folks. I pressed it, put in my seven-digit unique access code - and the proverbial pre-recorded message wittered on - that the phone call 'might' be listened to, entitling them to be nosey bastards in the hope my 'mask would fall' and the 'real stalky Belfield' would appear. They do catch a lot of men out this way. Akin to Big Brother (irony) - eventually, the 'real' you comes out. The phone is a telescope exposing your true character. Which poor twat was tasked with listening to my <u>ninety hours</u> of phone calls a month? Oy Vey! God bless their ears. More waffle than a breakfast diner in New York! I wouldn't wish that job on my worst enema! Imagine me wittering on three hours a day about absolute rollocks - and then some poor cow has to 'check' hundreds of Belfield letters. I bet there are droves of 'Public Protection' operatives currently flooding the Betty Ford Clinic. They were poised for the magic moment... but it never came - a bit like my trial. It was like a week's phone-ins every night. However, they were on a mad tear to find ANYTHING to cause trouble. Same script as the corrupt and clueless Notts Police cuntstables!

"Alo, love," I said to Mum. "You won't believe what's just happened - I've just had fifty-odd cards and letters delivered. Aren't people kind?" It might not mean much now, but for me to give my two legends some positivity and hope - it was worth a million dollars. It lifted us all. Remember, it was £3 a go with a SAE! To make matters worse for HMP, I told Mum, "Ere, once I've read them, I'll send them to you." This made upstairs - and the head of 'Communication Unit Nitwit Testing' - even more furious. Not only did they have to check and read the letters on their way in, but also on the way out (in case of additions). And that's after photocopying them all and checking my two A4 replies! The twisted, tongue-pierced, dungaree-wearing, Sue Perkins type must have gone crackers. Delicious karma - there's no prison law to prevent volume, so they had no choice but to do it. It makes me smile just writing this! They started it! I didn't want to be here - I'm a hostage with a whopping backpack of pissed-off punters who are entitled to their free speech... as am I - even in prison. I don't think they considered this glitch in the matrix. The public are never wrong!

I now had an entire fifteen-foot notice board full of love and hope - the entire length of the wall. To this day, it is my 100% focus whenever I get a glimpse of feeling lost, alone, or forgotten - the biggest fear of all globally discussed gobshites. It truly was a literal comfort blanket above my head. Oh yes - you can buy five hundred drawing pins for £1 on the canteen. They've thought of everything! Bravo!

It took me almost three weeks to get to the bottom of my pile of letters - by which point, another hundred had arrived! I wrote every reply by hand, and each letter was personal. I didn't rush. I read every single word, drank in every inspirational encouragement, and replied carefully. It was my honour and pleasure. I've never taken the incredible effort from my punters for granted. I mostly write at least three letters in the morning and five in the afternoon - in between writing the book - religiously, every single day. This never changed.

Chapter 19

An Asylum Not Prison

To this day, I believe 90% of the prison estate is an asylum and drugs den - designed to hold men captive who will never change and actually need huge psychiatric help. HMS Stocken was relatively well-run, although facing huge staffing issues. Due to Stocken's remote location and lack of public transport, recruiting local staff proved impossible, leaving everyone reliant on driving in. The regular staff endure a relentless and near-impossible task of keeping the place ticking over, all while earning poor wages for high-risk, ten-to-twelve-hour shifts - locked in with nutters and bread bins. Induction is the most unhinged - it's a conveyor belt of men being farmed off to 'appropriate' wings depending on their age, crime, and character. Security also has a say in where people go, due to gangs, drugs, etc. There are specific communes for 'drug recovery,' which appear to be the best place to get any drug you require - ironically. I clearly didn't fit into any category. For several weeks, they left me on F Wing, but one day I was called to the office as I had to be moved for another newbie to be processed. I expected it, and frankly, I'd been lucky to last this long.

There was an appalling old battle-axe on F Wing, who I avoided like the plague, called Miss Detestor - an obnoxious old bag who thrived on banging doors, being rude to the weak, yet nearly always flirting with the wing lifers and six-pack studs. Sadly, none of these desperate murderers would give her a portion if she were the last lady part in the nick. It was rumoured her undercarriage resembled a dropped kebab covered in mint yoghurt sauce! She couldn't be a day under sixty (stone), and she was clearly the most institutionalised of all patients in the nut house. Vile - a typical bully who preyed on the socially deficient and verbally retarded. One day, she stopped me at the door to the library. "Where you going?" it screamed. I said, "Where am I going, Miss?" Ouch. "YES! Where you going?" it spewed. "Sorry, Miss. Where am I going?" I replied. "You know what I mean," it cackled. I said, "Oh yes, but I don't want to misunderstand you - in case you're rude and aggressive to me, Miss. I'm very shy." Without saying a word, it opened the door and never spoke to me again - EVER. BINGO! If they smell weakness, these five-foot Hitlers, with faces like Bernard Manning's ball bag, will never leave you alone. Fight fire with fire! Humiliate them into embarrassment to leave you alone. I'm not as wet behind the ears as I look. The rookie is learning fast!

I never faced any bullying at all from prisoners in jail, but certain cretin officers couldn't resist trying their passive-aggressive luck from time to time - simply because they wanted a good story for the officer's mess, vape, and drug-dealing den. You have to stick up for yourself, but I knew this after fifteen years at the 'Bully and Bollocks Castration!' Weakness will not fare you well at all in jail (or life). Confidence is king - and that I don't lack, thankfully. Cockiness is different - that'll get your face smashed in. I couldn't risk that with my matinee idol looks! One thing the officers don't like is to be made to look stupid... especially in front of the men. My wit, sharp mind, and acid tongue was a very powerful defence mechanism to fend of fack wits like Miss Detestor! I used it wisely and sparingly - as we know, civil serpents will lie, cheat, and exaggerate anything to reap revenge before you can say 'stalker!' My reputation (wisely) left most keeping their distance. Strength is not just physical in the slammer! Anyway, later, this dear-hearted cross between Hyacinth Bucket and Harold Shipman was in the office. I immediately said, "It's OK, I'll come back later." She knew… "No, no - can I help you?" WOW. Turn up for the books! "Yes Miss" I graciously replied, "I hear they want me off the wing." She smiled. "Do they? I wonder why." "Exactly my question, Miss. Anyway, could you ask Safer Custody to see me before I'm moved - as a matter of urgency?" I politely begged, using my fake 'I'm being nice to you but don't mean it, as you're a tosspot' voice. "Why do you need them, Alex?" she replied, in her fakest 'I want gossip' voice. "Oh Miss, far too personal for you - I couldn't possibly burden you. You're too busy and important. Let's just say I'm under threat - so make a note that I told you," I replied, before speedily exiting the office, giving her no chance for an add-on question. It's an old trick I learned in PMQs. Last thing I'm doing is an Oprah-style boohoo chat with that one. She makes my teeth itch. The killer phrase is 'under threat' (which I wasn't). However, even this haemorrhoid on the HMP buttock wouldn't risk not putting it on the record - in case anything happened.

Before I knew it, SO (Senior Officer) Dan Gleeballs came to my pad. This guy was second in command and had always been affable – he asked, "Can I help, Alex?" I said, "Yes, Sir. I know I'm in prison, but I hear I'm being moved. As you know, I appear to be in the news more than the Prime Minister, so I need to be protected from lunatics who won't understand my situation. I've fitted in very well on here - no issues whatsoever - so basically, may I request to stay on the other side? I get lots of threats from men on other wings who are hard of thinking! Some even accuse me of being a stalker - that's outrageous, Sir." I entertain myself sometimes. Now you see - he'll have to cover his back, like Spanner Face covered hers. (I call her Spanner Face, as when I look at her, my nuts tighten).

On the other side of F Wing, I had my mates: Julian, Alf, and Brian. I asked to move over there and confirmed, "You'll get no bother from me." I repeated, "Please can you make a note of this conversation on my NOMIS record for Safer Custody - in case anything goes wrong?" Now he's responsible for my safety. Very important. "Of course," he said, as he pottered off scratching his head and nuts. I'm certain he understood at least 35% of what I was saying. My old BBC training of 'cover your arse', where these snakes and weasels are concerned, has never been more useful. Jail can be a dangerous place - so you have to make sure that they know your situation (and profile, in my case). Then you have to force them to write down, what could later be useful, or protect you from certain situations. Purely strategic. Listen, total transparency, officers will lie to your face as do all civil serpants. They'll get a kick from catching you out, and trust me - once you're out of your pad, it's <u>WAY</u> too late to go back or argue your case. You've become someone else's problem. It's <u>NOW</u> or never in jail. You simply must get everything in writing to force them to do the right thing. He doesn't need a 'duty of care' issue on his watch - not worth the stress or risk. Ultimately, he can override any officer.

So, the Senior Officer came back shortly after and said, "I've spoken to Safer Custody, and they agree you can move over to the other side of induction." This was a HUGE relief for me. I was genuinely concerned about being intentionally screwed over and sent to L, K, or M Wing - which, frankly, are ghettos, lunatic asylums, and drugs dens for the bewildered, brainless, and unspeakably broken. For now, I was safe - and Gleeballs' arse was cautiously covered!

Curiously, the 'best' wing for lifestyle in HMP Stocken was the official DRU - Drugs Rehabilitation Unit. 'I' Wing is where they are given the most freedom, benefits, and luxuries for their 'mental health', and to bribe and blackmail them into sobriety. This caused huge fury throughout the jail - that being a drug addict got you out of your cell ALL day for 'wellbeing', whilst the rest of us law-abiding, clean cherubs were either at work or banged up on the 'AMBER' regime. If you didn't work, you'd basically be banged up twenty-three hours a day (identical to a CAT-B) - but NOT on 'I' Wing for crackheads and crackpots. Of course, wing 'workers' - who, despite only having to clean the wing for an hour max daily, or empty the odd bin twice a day - would be out all day, every day. So, you could argue that being a cleaner as an addict on the drugs wing was the most highly acclaimed and profitable promotion in the entire slammer. INSANITY! This, sadly, sums up everything that is wrong about the Prison Service and UK society in 2020+. If you don't tick a box, you ain't coming in! Victims profit, whilst good, hard-working, sane, and sober souls are overlooked. Don't get me started on the 'kick off and get rewarded' culture. If you're a self-harmer - a massive problem in jail - it's a surefire way of getting an Xbox to keep you on the straight and narrow. Equally, 'emergency vapes' are on hand for the 'I'll top myself' brigade -another post-COVID bullshit boohoo weapon used by mentals to play the victim and blackmail the system into free gifts and pretend cigarette dummies... for dummies! Heartless? This is prison, not Pontins!

Within an hour, I'd got some bags and moved to F97 on the left spur. My pad was clean, newly painted, with a lovely view of the grass and trees outside - and, remarkably, no fences. The view does make a difference. I later went to great lengths to get pads with no view of the slammer, whilst facing the sunlight - and, if possible, at the end of the spur away from the douchebags. If you ever find yourself in this predicament, these small blessings make a BIG difference and are worth fighting for! Regardless, my head is always over the fence - I'm only hostage in body, not mind or soul. Annoyingly, next door was a young Scouser who appeared to have a rather large PA system that could fill Wembley... we'd have to kick that into touch - sharpish! I did. Maybe I'm a little more intimidating than my critics confess. To the right of me was a very quiet man from Mansfield, who was never a bother. We both got lucky, I guess. We never had a conversation. Some you win...

My first job is always to wipe down my chair and desk with disinfectant, along with the bed. I have to admit, it was almost spotless. With it having been decorated during lockdown, it was, quite frankly, as good as it was ever going to get. There was a big brown metal pipe along the end of the room - unlike Newton Wing, which has underfloor heating. This currently redundant pipe would become my best friend over the coming long and cold winter months. I'd heard horror stories about freezing Victorian jails. I'd rather be dead than freezing - seriously. No heating is a surefire way to get me on the roof! My cell was configured with my TV near the window, my door behind, and my bed to the left - which is perfect, as I'd never see the locked door in any position. I'm smart, right? The entire right-hand wall was a plasterboard for pics. I was desperately awaiting a pack of photos from my sister (care of FreePrints), which were allowed to be given to all prisoners - but for now, I had about ten pics that I'd brought with me to keep my love muscle going. Pictures went at eye level (deliberately), and then the hundreds of gorgeous cards that had so far been sent in from my angel punters were put all around them - covering three metres of hope. As new cards came in, I would swap them around.

So, I was settled in, this would be my home through Halloween, Bonfire Night, Christmas, and New Year's Eve – my favourite family events of the year. I loved that pad as much as my own home; it was <u>my</u> oasis of calm and new permanent sanctuary. You'd be amazed how safe and secure you feel in it. You naturally get your own key - you can't be too careful these days, with criminals and so many bent screws roaming the wings. Nobody came in unless invited. I could count on one hand those I'd trust to penetrate my inner slammer sanctum.

F wing was pretty sleepy. No whipper-snappers clattering around, but it was clear that there were some deeply unwell people. One night, in my first week, around 6pm, there was an almighty racket across the wing. It was the first time I'd seen it happen. A newly arrived, creepy-looking chap in his forties - dark and menacing, with long hair and a disturbingly familiar Savile-like aura - had just been locked up when he exploded into a fit of rage, screaming and hammering furiously on his cell door. Next, he grabbed his metal chair - still fitted with the banned wooden seat - and used it to obliterate the observation glass in the door, tear the sink clean off the wall, and reduce the toilet to pieces. <u>This</u> is the real risk of prison – the odd whack job who can turn on a sixpence. You cannot demolish the modern sinks and toilets - he got lucky on this old-school crapper wing, which I personally appreciated. Next, he found the energy to destroy his bed. He'd flat-packed that before the screws had stopped playing pat-a-cake in the office! The TV didn't fare very well either.

Seeing this level of violence, from zero to sixty, is unnerving - it makes no sense. You cannot rationalise this level of insanity or fit of rage, for seemingly no reason and completely out of the blue. Look, you are not going to break out of your pad under any circumstances - it's literally <u>IMPOSSIBLE</u>! All you've done is destroy any hope of trust or progress for years, shown yourself as high-risk, and physically hurt yourself in the process. You've basically outed yourself as a violent lunatic who's off his head. I guess you must be at your lowest ebb. When this happens, the kangas don't panic - as he is contained. He's only a risk to himself. Sadly, no one flinches. There's certainly no rush from the screws, as they would NEVER open that door until at least six to ten officers were present - AFTER he'd calmed down! Why go in when he's at his most crazy? Would you? The SO (top Gov) attended and eventually pressed their tiny red alarm button on the top of all radios - and within seconds, all available officers attended. By now, he was bleeding, having ripped his hands to shreds on the porcelain bog and sink. Officers have a duty of care to protect him from himself, but also to protect themselves from him. TRICKY! There was no way that door was ever going to be opened until he'd burned himself out. Twenty minutes later, a group of officers - what is the name for a collective of screws? A goon of Kangas maybe? Anyway, they escorted him to the block, dripping wet. Now he'd have total segregation, with concrete furniture that is 100% tantrum-proof. Unbelievably, a week later - before his pad had even been repaired, gutted, and replaced - he was returned to induction, to the amazement and total dismay of officers... not to mention prisoners! Not surprisingly, three days later, he destroyed the next pad -identical to the last. This happens regularly, on every wing, in every prison. He needs a mental hospital - not 'rehab' for nobheads.

One of the weird things about officers is that they're as trappy as their punters. They love to gossip, and I can assure you they have absolutely zero discretion. They didn't have time for GDPR and Data Protection training during their ten weeks of practice prison - staged in a wacky warehouse. The Gov had sent him back, as he'd had a 'mental health incident' and been prescribed a second chance. Jesus. Give me strength! Can you imagine if I did that? I'd be sectioned under the Mental Health Act and never seen again! I'd be wheeled straight off to the funny farm and sedated within an inch of my life - and then shanghaied to Belmarsh AA to double-pad with The Yorkshire Ripper! The double standards are outrageous. Anyway, no surprise - two days after he destroyed another cell, he was shipped to a more secure CAT-B, where he should have been from day one. Far too many unstable, broken, and crazy macaroons are being sent to CAT-Cs, who - prior to overcrowding and COVID - would never have been allowed out of a CAT-B. They're turning more blind eyes than Stevie Wonder. Lives are being lost - and will continue to be lost - over this catastrophic policy by the MOJ to downgrade dangerous men for 'logistical' reasons. I'm sure back at HMP Leicester, he would continue his re-development of every cell in His Majesty's Penitentiary for plonkers, pricks, and divvies - but at least it's not at HMP Stocken.

I did find this unnerving. Being around such unhinged aggression is beyond alarming. Although I'd not yet seen a fight at HMP, I'm aware this is an extremely dangerous place, full of men on the edge who are waiting to kick off. This level of violent red mist is disturbing - leaving you always on edge. I never lose sight of that. Do I walk round in fear? No. But I'm not stupid - this place can kick off at any point... just like Mansfield on a Saturday night! The difference is, Mansfield has qualified security outside every pub, whereas HMP appears to have former air stewardesses with a set of keys. At best, you've got a few good old officers to help you -however, honestly, before the cavalry arrives, you'll already be facked. Trust me, it would be way too late if this loon erupted. As for needing an ambulance, by the time they arrive, you'll be long gone. It's at least twenty minutes to get through security and to your pad. Not worth focusing and fixating on, but it never leaves the back of your mind that you're doomed if it goes wrong. 'There by the grace of God,' they say in the chapel. They also say, 'Oh Lord, take me now!' What will be, will be - sadly. These prayers are needed from my gorgeous punters! That's for sure!

My first night next to DJ Soft Sod the Scouser began with some drum and bass out-talking my TV - I was miffed! I put up with it for an hour, then I'd had enough. I pressed my cell bell for the Night Porter, who eventually arrived and shouted, "Yes!" through the open flap. Oh dear. This wasn't the Dorchester-style service I'd hoped for. I said, "Sorry, Sir, can you ask DJ Fat Boy Dim to turn down his 10,000-watt PA, please?" He replied, "Wow, is that you - Alex? God, I wondered where you were. I'm a huge fan! Anything you want, I'd love to help you - are you OK?" I couldn't believe it! From sellout shows, standing ovations, and millions of hits a day, to a prison guard showering praise through the two-inch wide cat flap, whilst I'm requesting DJ Tea Spoony swops dance anthems for some Fleetwood Mac! Boy, what a Netflix special…...NAH, no one would believe it! He had a word with Clay Balls next door - and silence. Phew! Never heard a peep ever again. This guy wasn't my only secret ally. There was a very nice lady who worked on the wing called Lesley. She worked as a box-ticker, helping homeless men get a basic account, driving licence, and TENT for when they're forcibly evicted. I always laughed at how they give a microwave meal to homeless lads when they left. Good luck warming that up on a wood fire behind the Co-op! Unlike 99.9% of this breed on HMS Stockings, Lesley had incredible compassion and was one of the kindest people I'd met. She was consumed by frustration at the pointless, broken, and completely hopeless prison service. "My hairdresser was asking about you yesterday, Alex," she said. "Oh," I replied. "What I could do with a short back and sides and a blow from the front is no one's business!" She laughed. "Are you OK?" she asked from the heart. She was worried. "I'm fine, love. You can't boohoo and cry over spilt milk. It will end," I crowed. "Well, you shouldn't be in here. We haven't got room for people like you. There are proper criminals that need your pad." How kind.

These words of encouragement meant the world. No matter how unusual and unique my situation, people like this kept me going, as they're so clear about who I am and how this stitch-up happened. No one had fallen for this malicious takedown... other than those invested. Unlike the Celia Imries with folders under their arms, these sweethearts had my back and became my eyes and ears - essential in such a cesspit of sin. Lesley could see the wood for the trees. Months later, she gave up and resigned. "Alex, they don't want to help, they just pretend to care so the stats look good." She told me. Damning but entirely true. She's a great loss to the estate. So many brilliant people give up because of the sickening hypocrisy and relentless vacuous virtue signalling of this atrocity - that can't work out if it's social services or a North Korean dictatorship.

I'm proud to say that my life from October 2022 until New Year's Eve had found its rhythm: cooking, library, writing, chapel, and walking. I guess, by prison standards, this was a uniquely healthy mix. I'd also found great rapport with Alf and Brian, who had become my confidantes and levellers. It may surprise you, but every single day we laugh-out-loud – A LOT! I was warned early on that 'no one is your friend in jail,' which is completely sanguine advice. However, despite not picking out curtains, I met a handful of prisoners whom I regard as very nice people - people I trusted, respected, and learned so much from. We won't be swapping a kidney, but I would like to see them again to thank them for their solidarity in this completely alien world. The Big Brother Shithouse is a pressure cooker. It's intense. It's identical to those holiday friendships - 'we'll keep in touch.' You mean it at the time. You have to pick wisely and bite your tongue. Idle gossip and loose lips won't only sink ships like HMS Stockings, but it could land you fatally injured…...or worse! I've never made that mistake. You know what they say, 'snitches get stitches!' My career relies on my looks...I ain't risking an incident with a shank (= prison homemade weapon) across my mush!

At unlock, I would get myself ready to go downstairs and have a walk with the lads. Because I was 'working' full-time (master baking and doing something impressive with a large courgette and two plum tomatoes), we got out from 6–7pm as well - whilst most were banged up from 5pm. The late session would often be a chance to meet other lads. Their stories were mind-blowing. In the mornings, I'd normally meet Airport Alf and Mansfield Brian to discuss the news, put the world to rights, and chat about prison life over a coffee. Brian and I had come in days apart. He was in his sixties and no more familiar or suited to the clink than me. He'd been found guilty of importing fags and was sent down as part of a 'gang.' Brian was struggling. Despite his two decades on me, he'd had his family torn apart and didn't cope well with the indignity and embarrassment. He'd only got four years. Alf had already done over a decade. Sometimes it's hard to moan, considering the stretch a lot of our co-stars are enduring.

The difference in crime and length of sentence creates a huge dilemma between inmates - and a palpable friction. I 'only' had two years nine months to serve, and Brian had even less. We were still processing how we'd serve this time, but imagine if you'd already served five, ten, or even fifteen years yourself - and had no guarantee of release. We must have been more irritating and annoying than Susan Calman trying to do a piece to camera on that dreadful Channel 5 cruise ship show. We must be like the annoying toddler, asking too many questions and getting on everyone's tits with our 'imminent' release - which was, of course, a lifetime to us. Equally, imagine being seventy-plus with another ten to serve. How would you keep the faith? It's all relative. I do feel bad for Alf. He graciously indulged Brian and me for weeks about the pitfalls of OMU (Offender Management Unit), parole (thank God I don't have that - or I'd never get out), and progressing to open prison - CAT-D... the dream for all cons with less than three years to go. Alf could answer any question and was happy to do so. Would I ever get a tag or open jail, with being so high-profile and the pariah of HMP? We'd walk and talk for hours, elucidating on any old shite that crossed our minds. We'd pop in for a coffee, watch a bit of Rick Stein, and then do more steps in the fresh air. You'd be amazed how many men never leave their pads - let alone go outside and exercise. I guess that's what being 'institutionalised' means. They never left the wing. "Why bother?" they tell me. Terrifying and pitiful - but I see their point, if you're a lifer. We loved it, and it all felt very normal. Alf kept everything in perspective and made sure I saw the insanity of this unfathomable witch hunt. This was vital for me, keeping my feet on the ground.

Alf was the man to teach me the biggest revelation in prison - how to 'properly' make a bed. I have John Lewis fitted sheets at home and I'd never thought about such whimsy. This was just a normal flat sheet that would be on the floor by 3am on a bad night, if you're tossing and turning... sometimes turning, occasionally trying to get back off to sleep! You basically tie the top corners together in a firm knot, then do the same with the bottom corners. This shortens the sheet's footprint and creates tension across the surface - so that it's as rigid as Ann Widdicombe's lady parts by the time you stick your duvet on top. Who knew? A prison miracle! Folding under the duvet leaves your sheet as limp as a priest in a nunnery - it simply won't do! You live and learn. I'd waited forty-two years for these life skills. Alf was also brilliant at 'playing' the system. He could outwit any low-ranking screw or top snivelling Gov. He knew which form goes where, and who to moan at to fight your corner. Like being a parent, it was all about picking your battles. I was like a sponge - indebted for his insight. If anyone needs tips in bed-making or pastry flange cooking, I'm the man for the job... and I've only been here three weeks!

Brian, like so many, had caused a nightmare for his family - far greater than mine. As well as the hurt and guilt of being torn apart, he had a Proceeds of Crime Order placed on him in accordance with POCA. It was likely 'they' would take his house to pay off his alleged 'profit' - which they literally make up. POCA is so interesting. It's not worked out based on what you profited from a crime; it's worked out on the value of the 'stock' you were caught with, added to the time they 'believe' you 'might' have been doing it. It's brutal - and intentionally destroys your family's lives forever! So, in other words, you might be paid £1,000 to drive £1m worth of fags. However, the government is entitled to claw back the £800,000 (for example) of profit from the fags, not the £1000 YOU profited. If they 'believe' you did it ten times, that equals £8 million! This shit BLEW MY MIND. Brian's POCA was £130,000 - his house wasn't even worth that, he told me! (To London readers: you can buy a four-bedroomed house in Mansfield for £85,000 - with room for a pony! You can't even get a garage or parking space for that in Sickdiq's destroyed Crapital). I've since met one lad with a £20,000,000 POCA... over a £50,000 drugs deal. Brutal. (As intended). If you can't pay, you do more time. Just like my cowboys in blue, they're ruthless and want to finish you off - crippling you financially is a great way to do it! They claim it's to be a deterrent to other dealers... the big boys at the top are never caught, of course. Once you go bust, you're homeless and dependent on the state. Despite us picking up the bill, .gov can now monitor and control your every move - and every penny – 100%!

I genuinely found all these situations and circumstances fascinating. When you have a POCA, they freeze all your accounts and assets. This INSTANTLY destroys most people. Imagine the impact on your wife and kids! Brian was going out of his mind with desperation. Not only was he penniless, but he was powerless to try and sort it out. Remember, once you're in here you can't do ANYWHERE yourself. If you're alone, you're finished. I believe 'the system' loves that. I know that's what they prayed would happen to me. Surely, there has to be a better way of reaping revenge on fraudsters and smugglers. Of course, they should be punished and all profits removed. However, I've come to realise that POCA is entirely onerous, malicious, and only designed to destroy you......which is cool, if the taxpayer didn't have to pay for the criminal when they are released! Think about it: once he's lost everything and been bankrupted, it's the taxpayer (you) who has to pay for his council house. How is that a victory for society? Surely, making them work to pay tax is far more logical. We should force them to give back to society, but what do I know?

Thankfully, I didn't have this added financial pressure - although I still had several High Court blackmail 'shushy' claims brewing that would need to be resolved. Fortunately, because the High Court system is so corrupt and only intends to profit lawyers, it would cost the claimants a hell of a lot more than it did me, as I had NO intention to engage whatsoever. It appears, for around £250,000, you can gag anyone in this country - thanks to this crooked and bent, China-esque state we live in. It's a one-horse race. The layman cannot compete against those with infinitely deep pockets. The maximum 'defamation' (shushy) payment is about £25,000 (but most are £10k), so the lawyers will always get at least ten times more than the claimants - in the best-case scenario anyway. It's INSANE! This ain't justice on any level - it's blatant intimidation and extortion. Thank God I knew the pitfalls of walking through these crooked High Court doors. Thankfully, my issues were all budgeted for months ago via the business - but with POCA, you will never pay the bill or avoid bankruptcy. It's a very dark game, isn't it, on all fronts?! I'll go to my grave believing that once you're convicted, THEY want you finished forever... never to return.

So, believe it or not, I counted my blessings. It could be a lot worse! On the wing, I was totally off the radar and completely left alone. Officers didn't even notice me. Resentment behind the scenes at HMP was growing bigger and faster than Nigel Farage's bank balance, as I hadn't flinched, had been totally compliant, was mentally well, and wasn't dead. A BIG FAIL by the establishment!

For me, prison politics is dull. I just wanted to keep busy and avoid the incessant imbeciles in and out of HMP costume. I just don't care, and I refuse to take it seriously. The chapel had become my favourite place to escape any reality of prison and its restrictions. It didn't look, sound, or operate like the rest of the building. No cameras. No officers. I could have been anywhere in the world. Vicar Tim had two very chatty and kind chaplains called Simeon and Paul. Paul is an ex-con - he served years for violence and drugs in Strangeways, a slammer as rough as arseholes! He did 'proper' prison with seriously dangerous men - and none of the 2020+ luxuries like phones, canteen shopping, or even a toilet! Paul's story is astonishing, and makes you realise how our 'Shithouses for Scumbags' are now a poor man's Alton Towers. He is a true asset to the Prison Service... you don't hear me saying that very often! He found God, and he's gone from armed robbery to golf - and to inspiring men to turn their lives around. An extraordinary human who should be the template for all HMP staff. He loved to chat politics, and I enjoyed our conversations greatly. To be around 'non-operational' (keys but not officers) staff was so refreshing. Civvies are nothing like brainwashed willy wagglers. No judgement. No agenda. Just a great human with undeniable empathy. I added in Thursday mornings for 'Bible Study' - simply to be in the company of other decent, real, normal people. I was doubting, but open to learn. Every week, four volunteers came in who were lovely. Add that to Angel Anne, who lit up the room with her ebullience, boundless energy, and sheer joy and hope - I was in my filament. Anne motivated me to fight to my next oasis of music and calm in God's waiting room - only several days away. One week began to roll into the next with these godly appointments. Bible Study left me more confused than before I started. It turns out you can talk about religion and the Bible until the cows come home - but, at the end of the day, you often end up with a house full of cows! Everyone just appears to come to their own conclusion, with their own interpretation, depending on their own agenda. Either way, it kept my mind active - and my insatiable need for human connection fulfilled. It was a glorious two hours sat next to dear Anne, surrounded by decent people. I was happy to listen and learn even if I didn't understand or agree. We all used to do this before cancel culture. It's all very evolved and grown up – lefties can't stand such compromise. You can't say rehabilitation isn't working.

Chapter 20

The Worst Thing About the Slammer

The very worst thing about jail is not SPICE, men peacocking 24/7, or being locked up from 5pm at the weekend until 9am the next day - no, no. I LOVED being banged up because it was quiet, and I could get on the blower and read and write in peace. My bachelor pad was perfect - befitting any showbiz dressing room I'd been flung into for the last 25 years! I had total privacy, something most grown men in jail will never get. Most entertainer types, especially comedians, are pretty solitary at the best of times, and thrive on silence - to think and create in between showing off to the masses.

You may be surprised that, for one so often accused of being loud and noisy, I devour silence - my best friend. Imagine cohabiting with an incontinent smack addict. It can - and does - happen! You have absolutely no say. It would be worse than sitting next to Ed Balls on GMB. Poor Suzie! Thankfully, Safer Custody and Security added 'no cell share' to my file. I'd never have to worry about this again. The biggest <u>blessing</u> of my life behind bars.

The WORST thing for me about the slammer was waiting for the servery and walking past the Mogadons and shrieking imbeciles along the corridors. This is the only point in my day where you have no choice but to stand amongst the unspeakably crass, loud, thick, uncouth inmates - and the great unwashed (literally), mostly under-30s. It's also the most dangerous point for crap to kick off, as it's the best opportunity for lunatics to recoup revenge, whilst everyone is milling about en masse. Honestly, I'd rather go to a Taylor Swift concert with all those flag-waving oddballs and outcasts than walk through these packed corridors ever again! Painful. You have to remember, a lot of these lads - especially the druggies - have no one and nothing. This is their home, life, family, and ultimate destiny. This social intimacy is their only form of humanity. My contempt was palpable from day one, so I'd find ways of being either very early or very late to avoid the 'bruv brigade.'

I have to admit, on my less patient days, these group moron conventions wore very thin. The rudeness from some of the scum was enough to make you want to stick your head in a George Formby grill. I learned to enjoy Stella Virgin's Catering Asylum, as it was generally quiet. Hysterically, she'd say, "Make me an omelette - you've got three hours starting now." I'd go into the lovely, warm office, with a fab padded chair, and sit next to the radiator writing letters and the book for two and a half hours. Then at 11am, I'd get a few eggs and whip it up (literally) in five minutes, eat it warm, and go back to the pad for lunch. Security was watching me on the cameras – they couldn't do bugger all, but they were fuming. There are no rules about words. I don't know why they didn't invent some, like the Clown Court - just like my charge. If a screeching willy obsessed self-touching troglodyte interrupted my scribbles it was insufferably aggravating, so I'd move to a different office. They quickly got the hint. I can hardly claim I'm in Wormwood Scrubs. In the real world, many people have to endure fart-heads within a factory environment - day in and day out for fifty years of their life. The willy-grabbing <u>REALLY</u> was annoying though! No, it's a real thing! There're poseur prick exhibitionists everywhere you turn. Do these luddites have no social graces? I suppose willies and vapes are the comfort blanket of the clueless missing their mother's jelly wobblers. If they're not groping one for reassurance, they're sucking on the other for comfort. Thank God, I do neither – knowing my luck I'd get them in the wrong order and get a nicking! A self-touching, thirty-year-old man is the most depressing and pathetic thing I've seen since watching the showreel and reading the CV for Jeremy Kyle.

The mix of lads in the kitchen was fascinating! I found it unbelievable that there were two murderers mincing around with twelve-inch blades, and no one batted an eyelid - least of all Stella Virgin, who could easily fend off any stabber with her grimace and cutting tongue alone. Obviously, these killers were decades into their sentences and were now trusted prisoners... but you take my point. It still amazes me how 'high' security is in certain parts of the slammer, yet not others. It's entirely based on trust, goodwill, and one box-ticker's opinion. Would you work in a kitchen in a slammer? I never flinched or gave it two thoughts. Imagine the consequences of an argy-bargy - with a cheese grater, boiling hot pans of soup, and carving knives as long as their charge sheet - on every table! Astonishing... oh, and a bit terrifying. I'm used to fear. I've played loads of

Working Men's Clubs in Yorkshire. I suppose none of this could be more dangerous than the current Mrs B's cooking. She uses the fire alarm as a timer. Her vindaloo is the best detox your sphincter can buy - outside of the Colon Oscopy Spa in Wigan. You should try it, if you can be arsed!

Within weeks, I was getting more mail than I could cope with. The boost was phenomenal. I was in my own little world where I've remained ever since. Every moment was consumed with my replies. The bosses had got wind that I was not only enjoying VT, but had my own office. They were spitting feathers! Of course, there were no rules about fan mail, but the sandal-wearers upstairs wanted to put a stop to it - out of pure spite. Bollocks to them. I was up for a scrap, surrounded by homegrown carrots I could use as weapons, and had nothing to lose. Once you're in jail with HMP terrorists, negotiating becomes tricky for the *Guardian* types in charge. I'll write my letters in the soil from our homegrown beetroot, if needs be. The volume of disdain rose from annoyance to palpable, apoplectic rage from them upstairs.

I'll be honest, I never understood why the vomitus probation Celia Imries in OMU (= Often Minging and Underwhelming) were so pissed off and took my contentment and happiness so personally. It's not as if I've ever said anything rude about them. These 'offender managers' seemed obsessed with beating me down. My boundless optimism did not fit their funeral like temperament. On reflection, spending half an hour making a fallen flan (mine never rose in the first place) and sitting at the director's table being egged on, was not the punishment the dark forces had hoped for. They were hoping that, by now, I'd be rocking in the corner - off my tits on Prozac. One afternoon, the toffee-nosed education manager, who looked the size of a double fridge freezer, was sent over to scare me into compliance. It approached me like a rhinoceros tentatively avoiding a crocodile on the bank of the Nile. By the end of our chat, she was in de-nile! I was strictly warned NOT to write letters during course time. I said, "Well what do you suggest I do for the two hours when I'm not cooking? Would you prefer I play cards, like the other lads, or deal drugs like everyone else?" This Peppa Pig face was speechless and slithered off back to the Toby Carvery red-faced. To quote one good egg officer, 'They've never had anyone causing them this much work – the one thing they hate!' You see PPU (Public Protection Unit) <u>are OMU</u>, and these tyrants are ultimately responsible for checking all of my insults and jokes about these sour-faced Biffas! No wonder they wanted to dissuade me from writing to my adoring public. Having me land -along with the notoriety, public interest, internal whoop-de-doo, my 'unique' tenacity, personality, and clear lack of respect and reverence for their self-confessed 'broken' and 'not fit for purpose' pokey - did not go down well. The hundreds of letters of love and encouragement each week made their merkins fall off in frigid incredulity! It was 'at war' - and we'd not even had our first meeting.

Anyway, this marble-mouthed management monolith returned ten minutes later. It slithered, "What are you doing?" I said, "I've completed all of my work, so I'm minding my own business, as I told you!" Agog she said, "But you can't do that in here!" I said, "Why" (off we go again). "Why What?" she spluttered. "Why can't I mind my own business, quietly, not affecting anyone else, if I've completed all the work Stella has given me?" "I'm not following you" it said. "You're the head of education and can't comprehend simple English? "OK, how can you stop my creative writing -maintaining my mental health - affecting no one else, if I've fulfilled your directive of the session?" She stared at me with a look I would see so many times during my time at HMP. These people think they're clever and smart because, generally, they're talking to imbeciles - who are up to no good and can't link a sentence when faced with someone in authority - so they fall to pieces. Surely, she wasn't going to walk out AGAIN to think of an answer? I could see steam coming out of her ears. I'd got her on the ropes. Then came the usual twenty seconds of stony, cold silence - where her brain was saying, 'Why the fack did I start this?' "OK Alex, carry on." Next, Stella rushed in. "Alex, please don't think I complained about you. What did she say?" I replied, "As always. I explained I wasn't smoking crack - I was writing words on a piece of paper, quietly. So she cleared off with her tail between her legs." Stella smiled, "As you were." Sadly, this wasn't the last of it. The frankly vindictive and utterly charmless, power-crazy OMU box-tickers would try and stitch me up at every opportunity - over my refusal not to be dead... or at least

284

invisible over the fence. Most disappointingly, it was later disclosed in an email from Stella Virgin: '8/11/22 Report text: A4747EW started 17/10. Since then, every spare moment he will take himself away to write letters - his fan mail. He said he had to answer each one, and was unsure why he was in prison. I'm not sure why he writes these in the workshop. Most sessions, he makes up excuses to leave early.' Sadly, you can't trust anyone in jail. I was very disappointed to see this sabotage - and stab in the front - by a woman I thought I could trust. This would be the first of many three-faced Judases I'd encounter at HMP. The joy of SAR (Subject Access Request) disclosure is that, even in jail, you can (eventually) get to see who the snakes in the grass really are.

The notion that I wasn't suicidal, depressed, not coping, or desperately needy drove them insane. Sadly, when the MOJ hire people with no people skills, even fewer qualifications, the communication skills of an over-boiled cabbage, and literally no training... when they come across a smart arse like me, it does not end well. Bullies only thrive on intimidation behind your back. I made it my job to know all the rules better than them, and intimidation is not an emotion I have ever been cursed with. There was no doubt they were already plotting to sabotage anything that they could control. The only place they have no influence is in the chapel – thank God! They simply cannot cope if they don't outwit morons and baffle boneheads with bullshit. Everything in prison is about BLIND COMPLIANCE. Ask 90% of officers (politely) 'why' - and they buckle. They have orders to bark, but no answers when you politely challenge. You can't PAVA (spray) someone for asking a question. From time to time, I would ask for the PLIs (prison law) on whatever bollocks they were trying to convince me of. It's a brilliant way of undermining them. They go very quiet when that happens - and quickly head for zee hills. They couldn't touch me and didn't catch me out on anything! This sent them even more crackers. So, for three months, I baked Bakewell tarts, almond cakes, sausage rolls, and learned how to make a lentil dish, carrot soup, and endless other pies, sauces, and pastry delights. Eventually, they gave up complaining about my letter writing - as the Biffa from box-ticking admitted, there was nothing they could do about it! Don't worry - I got my own back by writing down, repeatedly, in all replies to my fans - <u>everything</u> that I wanted them to know. Well, they started it. I may have been a little derogatory towards them – slap my legs, I'm such a tease.

<u>REAL</u> clink was revealing itself to me - daily. It's 100% algorithms and box-ticking. If they can't fix you, they don't know what to do with you. Druggies are their favourites, as they can highly medicate them and send them on a 'crack, sniff, or smoke' two-day course - and piff paff pouf, they leave the room cured and 'rehabilitated' - simply by turning up. Once they have the green tick, rehab is complete - and they're good to go to CAT-D to start dealing back on civvy street. Equally, if you're in for domestic violence, you're sent on TSP (not the antiseptic) - the 'Thinking Skills Programme.' That's presuming these men have the capacity to think... and not give their missus a slap! I'm

not convinced. The top course for seriously violent re-offenders is KAIZEN. After years and £100s of millions, it is about to be scrapped - as it doesn't work. Turns out, after six months of listening to how the most horrific crimes were committed, lags either ended up traumatised, needed therapy, or used the tips from the confessions of the other cons to commit crime better. FAIL. All in all, people who do courses at HMP are officially 12% more likely to re-offend in comparison to those who do nothing. What a huge own goal and ridiculous laughingstock this foolishness is. To make matters worse, you can't fail or pass any course. You just have to turn up. You can fall asleep - as long as you attend. It's ludicrous.

I also worked out that prisons are social clubs for aspiring career criminals who want old dogs to teach new lags tricks of the trade. Look, if you put a load of radio DJs in a room together, they'll talk about radio. And if you put a load of Christians in a room, they'll talk about Jesus......and equally, if you put a load of ego-driven petty criminals in a room, they'll talk about crimes - and how to commit them better, quieter, and more profitably! They're shameless and do it openly, in front of screws who say NOTHING. Kangas often join in - remember, it's their 'trade' too. They're all wannabe Danny Dyers. Sadly, they're more Diar-Rhea! This is a whole other level of mind-freak! You cannot possibly compare a first time gobshite, white collar Del Boy, or fraudster, with such criminals as Wayne Couzens, a nonce, or even a repeat smackhead dealer. Yet the system immediately puts everyone together - and follows the same process to progress for all. This identikit prison life is intriguing... but utterly depressing and confusing. The 'one jail fits all' mentality is flawed on every level! I think this might explain why the Prison Service is broken - and rotten to the core.

CAT-Cs function on compliance, born out of the men's willingness - and desperation - to get out. Sadly, with short and determinant sentences, the whippersnappers just don't care, because they know they are going home - and no one can stop them. That is not the case in CAT-As or Bs, for example, where men have years and decades in front of them, and often need good reviews at parole to escape. This totally changes the energy of the entire establishment. Other than gang and debt-related argy-bargies, there is almost no serious violence at HMP Stocken. Because it's 'high security,' it's nipped in the bud immediately. So far, I've rarely met genuine evil, though.......maybe they're all in CAT-As and Bs? You know 'that' look. Have you watched BBC News? Regardless, all courses (including rehabilitation) are bought in! It's one big business from day one. So, if His Majesty's Government pokeys are making a fortune for private companies - who are 100% run for profit - what about private prisons, that are also a business... entirely for profit? There's only a few of them - yet they cost YOU £3.2 Billion per year! That's an identical budget to the entire BBC rape tax. Who knew?!

What I love is that, every day, I'd find myself learning more and more about this disingenuous prison sham. I had an insatiable

288

need to talk to other fellas, who had their own take on life and the system. They'd been around a lot longer than me. Frankly, a lot of men claim, 'This is the worst jail in Britain' - but I couldn't see it myself. Every single slammer I've been to, they repeat the same old crap... even in brand-new super jails that operate like HMPontins. I genuinely don't know what they expect. I've never been a fan of entitlement, even in my darkest hour in the dick head dungeon of HMP. I don't think I deserve more than five options for lunch and tea every day, do you? People are my fascination. You're never going to find a bigger mixed bag of nut cases, loose cannons, loony tunes, and window lickers than a penitentiary! My curiosity was always: How did they get here? Focusing on others was total distraction from my own predicament. I was on the job. I never allowed myself the fatal question of 'Why me?' - instead, I asked: 'Tell me about you...' Self-pity in jail is a road to ruin and insanity. A cul-de-sac of self-indulgence is a guaranteed way to end up stark raving bonkers. I was having none of that. Instead, my energy was on learning as much as I could from my co-stars - in uniform and behind the door. Bitterness in jail is prevalent. I knew my biggest challenge was to avoid any indignation or 'woe is me.' I'll leave all that guff to Meghan and Harry!

In life, mistakes do happen - and I met a lot of lads who were just young, stupid, or simply unlucky. Some were just in the wrong place at the wrong time. One lad, Jake (who was nineteen and a pro boxer at the time), was provoked into a fight over his girlfriend outside a club - and with a single punch, he gave the other lad brain damage, causing him to die. Imagine the regret. He was on a six-year sentence: IPP. This now illegal sentence meant he had to serve six years minimum, but fourteen years later, he's still behind bars - and he does not know when he'll get out. He didn't even get manslaughter, despite the clear provocation caught on CCTV. However, he did kill someone in a moment of madness, but the fight was only _intended_ to defend his Mrs - after a life of good character and one drug free night on the Jägerbombs. Tragic on every human level. Now his life is wasted and destroyed, yet still younger than me. He works in the gym and was still match fit. His fitness is all he has and is keeping him alive. I guess there's always hope he could one day return to the ring – IF he can get parole to take the risk of letting him out. Do you have a tinge of sympathy? I do! We've all been there, right? To lock a man up is one thing, but to give an open-ended stretch with no hope of release is simply cruel - especially when so young. Blunkett invented IPP. He should be ashamed - and is! Even his guide dog can see it's totally unfair to convict a person without an end date. Some men on IPP got two years and are nearly twenty years over tariff. Two thousand men remain stuck in jail on this criminal sentence - which is now illegal. Who knew that our criminal justice system is the aspiration of North Korea!

I couldn't help but ask how he gets through every day. "I have no choice," he told me - a heart-breaking answer to an impossible situation. This fella looks like he should be in _GQ_ magazine, not a CAT-C! What a waste of life over a single punch.

His friends had now moved on and deserted him. People can only hang on for so long. Of course, his adoring parents would never give up - but they were knocking on. By the time he's released, would anyone be left? By now, you have to be institutionalised. To reverse that will take years of careful back-peddling. Of course, he should be punished, but is he evil? NO! Please don't think I've gone all namby-pamby, pinko-liberal, Guardian-reading vegan type - but I think there is a HUGE distinction between a premeditated 'attack' and a moment of madness with the most hideous consequences. At this point, he's served longer than a manslaughter conviction. That can't be fair or just! I guess meeting men like this taught me that we're all flawed - and mistakes do happen. Most men understand they have to pay for their actions, but does HMP actually want to reform them and 'help' them back into society? What is his incarceration now achieving for the taxpayer - at over £800K? Blimey, we could pay for the dinghy divers to all stay in a hotel for <u>one</u> night with that type of money! I have more sympathy with this guy than some scum sucking pondlife who nicks a granny's handbag - that's for sure.

The guys I despise are the 'I'll do it again' brigade - truly the ones who should have IPP and never get out. Astonishing candour and vicious contempt for society. Maybe 10% are just shameless and total pricks. Often, though, these guys aren't doing long bird for a heinous crime - they're the bottom feeders that have no conscience for their actions, even if it involves burgling an off-licence, nicking your car, or robbing your Aunty

Fanny! They truly don't care. How can you possibly retrain such contempt? These sick bastards have ZERO compassion or empathy - two traits I hate the most. I'd make them drink three bottles of TSP, not send them on the pointless course. That'll teach 'em the square root of bugger all! Sadly, my conclusion is that they're lost causes - for the undeniable reason that they don't want to change because they know no better. It's hopeless! I have to admit, jail doesn't do a lot for your prejudices either. I guess stereotypes are often there for a reason - mostly because they're true! There's a lot of arse-showing trouser-droppers, pretending to be similar to a proper grown man by not shaving their bum fluff - which doesn't impress me one jot. Grow up! Get a life and get out of mine! Odious! BTW, even in VT Catering, they would be stirring their cake mix and self-touching at the same time. Talk about ambidextrous! I'm going nowhere near their sponge finger or cheesy puffs! Enough to make me puke all over my crab stick pie. I couldn't help but laugh as I found myself in this Partridge-esque Coogan sitcom. Seriously, some of the comedy characters - mostly YO (Yuffs) that never grew up - are the funniest. Someone once asked me if I believed in euthanasia. I said, "I don't even believe in the youth in this country!" What with being born in Stoke and being as white as a wedding dress, their OTT Jay-Z rapper talk did tickle my tits. Why me? We can't point fingers these days or laugh at the socially deficient now, can we? I can, and I do - don't you worry about that! It's the only thing to get me through the excruciating tedium.

Chapter 21

I'm Still NOT Sorry!

A huge part of jail time is victim awareness and 'being sorry.' This 'system' <u>demands</u> it! However, I <u>know</u> that I was the victim of an orchestrated witch hunt by the BBC (as was proven in court) to 'close me down' - so, would the system make me say 'sorry' before I could progress to CAT-D? If so, it's a SORRY from me……that I'm not saying it! I'm not guilty - and I'm not sorry, mush! That's that - put it in your pipe and smoke it. I might be convicted, but that doesn't mean I'm guilty. I believe probation knew that I was the initial victim, as they recommended to the judge that prison was unnecessary. The judge ignored their report - he knew better. If you don't say sorry though (in most cases) - you ain't getting out! I was not willing to have any part of this, and I'm 100% entitled to maintain my innocence.

Every experienced con, staff member, and officer (who didn't have skin in the game) said, "You'll be going to open conditions soon, you're clearly not criminally minded and shouldn't be here. Your risk is miniscule." I rolled my eyes every time, as I knew my situation wasn't by the book - and the dark forces would scupper me every step of the way. I knew that the establishment hadn't gone to this amount of effort to bang me up so spectacularly, only to then send me straight home. It ain't happening. I knew full well that they'd do ANYTHING to delay me getting home to my lovely life - and try and catch me out for as long as possible. To justify their decision to 'protect the public' by locking me up - this is HMP's only function. They desperately needed a 'we told you so' moment for their own vindication. They just needed one slip - and BOOM - another charge in the Clown Court, and headlines to justify this ludicrous sentence equal to many manslaughter cases. Remember, they still had teams of lawyers trying to find some dirt. It's almost as if they're stalking me!

You don't need to be a rocket scientist to realise that the security snoopers' binoculars and mailroom magnifying glass weren't exactly deployed to 'help' me. 'They' - whoever 'they' are - prayed I'd 'kick off,' or they'd 'catch me out,' or 'stitch me up,' and then they could paint me as the 'real' stalker... as opposed to an invented ONLINE stalker via a new crime - just for me - WITHOUT alarm or distress! Sadly for them, the goons found NOTHING. Not a word was censored, refused, or acted upon - EVER. Can you imagine how pissed off they must've been - after months of prying and thousands of trappy letters? And trust me - I didn't hold back. I said everything I wanted them to know - to grind their gears. 'He'll slip up eventually.' No, I facking won't!!! OK, I admit - the devil did get the better of me. I couldn't help but bait them by writing the gossip I knew they wouldn't want made public. In hundreds of letters, I'd say FACTS like: 'Another screw arrested for shagging a Muscle Mary. Apparently, she brought him in steroids for months. What an idiot - she'll get longer than me!' Or I'd say: 'Another day at Stockings, and another teacher arrested! Utterly corrupt, and more criminal than most lags in here. They'll have to recruit more Kangas for a new wing full of screws.' The lack of reverence and blind respect sent them wappy upstairs. They couldn't touch me for it, and they certainly couldn't stop me writing it. On the phone, I was even worse. I'd say, 'To those tuning in - stick a cactus up your balloon knot!' Sadly, for all the prison law (PSIs) - bundles thick - there's nothing in them for an annoying twat who couldn't give two shiny shites and writes down every dropped bollock the clink makes. What do you expect if you incarcerate a journalist? The truth HURTS, doesn't it? More history repeating. Oh God - now they'll say I'm 'offence paralleling' for exposing them! Next, I'll be 'stalking' the post office for buying too many stamps. I made personal comments, making matters worse. Boo hoo! Not my fault if my OMU has bingo wings like an ostrich and halitosis like an open port-a-loo door at Leeds Festival!!! In revenge, my mail got slower and slower. Five weeks for a reply. Childish, immature, vindictive, clueless pricks. BUT absolutely predictable. The only bit of control they had left. They HAD to send them.....but in their own time. Fair doos.....my revenge is THIS book - and there's nothing they can do about that either!

It's this defiance and ridicule that blows their little, tiny, badly dressed non-binary minds. All they want is submission and admiration. You came to the wrong gobshite lovey! Sorry sweet cheeks, it's not in my make-up. It's all identical to the noncy BBC, the evil Cop Shop, and the clueless Clown Court: 'Why won't he take this seriously?' No tar - I've got books to write and a life to live! I was aware, though, that this decision would come at a price. Don't get me wrong - I never looked for trouble. In fact, I avoided all suits and officers like the plague. But some things you just can't back down on. Most were as smart as a monkey on a rock. The 10% of legends - those who were the full shilling - tipped me off to the dark force's dirty tricks. My tactic was, ironically, the dictionary description of 'stalker' – stealth — which was the opposite of my offence. How can telling the world (and 350,000 punters) be stalking? Yep - they'd put me in prison to be the very thing I was sentenced for: totally unseen and hiding in the shadows. My approach in this den of iniquity and Cuckoo Coo was just to glide past with a smile - say nothing, and keep moving swiftly.

I was increasingly made aware of the volume of chatter online, over the fence, via my producers Tarquin, Network Nick, Hayden and the two James' who kept me up to date daily - along with my punters. Everyone was astonished by the sheer amount of clickbait - weeks after I'd last spoken. The mentals went off their rocker with all manner of flights of fancy. I was meant to be forgotten. It was very clear that a small number of highly medicated, fixated, obsessed, and consumed numpties were self-touching to my memory - all day, <u>EVERY DAY</u>. They all had a very similar style and narrative. There finger's smelt of a fishmonger's gloves and they had the maniacal look. It was almost as if they were all connected. Do you think they had a WhatsApp group on the dark web??? It appeared they all missed me - and somehow were keeping me alive via their ludicrous fantasies. My YouTube channel was still busy despite my silence since 16th September 2022. In my absence, the Lords of Onanism were effectively my PR machine. Normal people - those without noncy, fixated tendencies or a vested interest -began to realise how insidious this takedown was. The darkness of my kidnapping overtook the shock and disbelief. Even now, jail wasn't enough for the wackos. New crackpots came forward to say I'd told a 'knock-knock joke' in 1973 - and they've had PTSD ever since. Oy vey... How disturbed are these people's unhinged brains? They wanted me back - so that I could once again become their punching bag for their ostracised insanity. They, as I'd said from the beginning, clearly wanted me dead... yet were keeping me alive. What irony. What kind of sickness is this? Their infatuation and analysis of my every move revealed a worrying insight into their warped, unbelievable, and highly alarming devotion to my entire public life. Sadly, this wasn't real life, though.

It was their jaded perception - based on their closeted paranoia and presumed knowledge. One toad-faced, boggle-eyed freak pretended he was my friend! I hadn't had <u>any</u> contact WHATSOEVER since I worked with him in 2000! A total whack job, but dangerous, as he'd convinced himself we are friends, having not clapped eyes on his morbidly obese corpse - let alone commented <u>ONE</u> word in twenty-three years!!! He later said my family deserted me, my hair fell out, I was down to seven stone, and my house had been recovered by a debt agency. Naturally, he proclaimed (and hoped) I was banned from ever going back on-air. TOTAL fantasy! What became concerningly apparent was that their imaginations were so in overdrive, they were creating whatever they didn't know. It was like the court case all over again! There's a pattern here, hey? People often say to me, 'You're an enigma' - well, I am... to nosy bastards who are mental with no life! Piss off. Leave me alone. It's NONE of your business! I don't want freaks, sick saddos, and bipolar lunatics having any insight into my private life. Would you? If you think the answer is 'yes!' - I dare you to set up a channel, get 500,000,000 hits, and see what happens when the basket cases start obsessing over you 24/7. No. No, I'll pass. There's enough curtain twitching. I'll stay as I am, thank you! My incarceration exposed a whole new level of crazy. This has to be a serious medical condition.

As I said at the beginning of my autobiography: 'When the front door closes - it closes!' This entire sick 'let's catch him out' shitstorm of five arrests and three illegal raids was only designed to find something that never existed. They HOPED for dirt and found bugger all - the square root of nothing. Now these loony tunes were just creating lies from nowhere, in some sick fixation in their heads to keep me living rent-free. Five and a half years in the slammer just wasn't enough! Even Notts Corrupt Police were still plotting behind the scenes and working on a final nail in my coffin. This was <u>PERSONAL</u>! They'd been punting for people to come forward with wild accusations after my incarceration - but got nowhere. This is the old trick that the Met pulled with the Yewtree lot. More recently, they used this tactic with Al-Fayed, Greg Wallace, and the hundreds of other accused

- without proof. Sadly, my private life is A LOT much duller than theirs! They bait any nutter to create a story and hope for the best on these vile fishing expeditions.

The mincing mentals wouldn't stop on-line, creating their own narrative. Bizarrely, three of these wannabe YouTubers admitted they were abused as a child. Ermmm. Am I the revenge for their inner demons? Am I to blame for their inadequate, failing, disturbed, and abused lives? Does my act trigger their baggage to vomit all over my success, making me their punching bag for their 'daddy' issues. Curious hey? Nothing gets past me. Freud would have a field day with that. From lies that my brother was in court (doesn't exist – don't have one), to the extremes that I'd been killed in the prison shower and was dead – nothing went too far for these lunatics, all for a few thousand clicks amounting to 80p. Surely, this can't be about the money. Even the most jealous head the ball can't be this insane? Why would this give them a kick and boost? Colleagues I'd not met or spoken to in twenty years jumped on the bandwagon, and, of course, the odd bi-curious, bipolar, and presumably bifocal Mogadon loser came out of the closet to insist I was everything - from being sectioned under the Mental Health Act to being buggered by Billy from Bradford on B Wing, wearing a G-string. The lies don't bother me, but it's not fair on those around me, and even more worrying for their inventers. Thankfully, my folks and family knew the deal and don't listen to any of the noise! You must never engage with this level of fixated loony tunes – it's unwise on every level. Eventually, you'll risk catching their cuckoo terminal disease! IGNORE. It worked. The more they lied, the more it exposed their madness and the injustice of the witch hunt. My gang were having none of it. They can spot a whacky troll from a thousand paces. I was proven right. The more these highly creepy gimp mask wearing cocks, cucks, and cuckoos came for me, the more the fans (and most importantly not fans) saw the light. The sheer disproportion, desperation, and exaggeration of these warped and evil minds led to more questions than answers. The first conclusion from my people was 1) 'You're getting 100% of your hits off Alex's name. 2) You're way too stalkery about what you've noticed, watching far too closely - and 3) Why do you look like you're on heavily sedating psychotic drugs, with rings around your eyes......and sat on an inflatable cushion? Couldn't have asked three better questions myself! Bravo! Top rate journalism!

I remember in court, someone saying: 'I had to watch every video Alex made, in case he mentioned me.' WOW. Who's stalking who?! You see, as time goes on and these people confess their own conscience - exposing their broken minds - I've taken great peace and solace in their confessions. I only have pity. It says everything we knew about this circus and the troll life online: keyboard warriors jizzing over their tippy-tappy, like insatiable, consumed addicts. I've paid the price for some very broken and damaged people who believe they'll get reflective glory from my demise. Their palpable delight in my hostage situation screams more about them than my unfortunate book-writing sabbatical. What lonely, empty vessels.

One fruitcake suggested I was a fraud—stealing money from my fans. Do you not think the cuntstables have looked over every account? One penny out of place and I would've got another fifteen years. Only an imbecile would suggest such crap, considering the scrutiny I'm under. The universe doesn't give goodness by heaping bad on someone else - yet this gaggle of gormless gonads were loving it. It's all projection. It's all deflection. It's all hairy bollocks. The lies get so outrageous, and more and more ridiculous and preposterous, that all of the credibility was gone. You literally have to let people burn themselves out. It's a bit like great sex. It's a lot of huffing and puffing for 99% of the time (with a lot of downstairs chaffing) - but in the end, it all comes good and is forgotten in seconds. As we know, the trolls have never had sex... well, not with grown-ups or anyone consenting anyway - so they have no idea about this level of ecstasy. People started writing with the greatest line ever (and my personal fav compliment so far): 'I don't like you but...' You see, a stitch-up can only go so far. When a paedo gets a suspended sentence, a rapist gets two years, and a killer gets four - thanks to whatever bullshit mitigating 'mental elf' excuses - yet I get five and a half years for words... sensible people can see the flaw in the matrix. Let's face it, everything is relative. The public aren't daft. I truly thank all the crazies, who continue to remind the public why I should be in the pokey forever......not realising what they're actually doing is underscoring why I should not! Priceless batshit bonkers backhanded PR.

As time has passed, truths have come to light bit by bit. The bigger picture of two-tier policing and justice in the UK is now undeniable - and it's clear that free speech is the new terrorism. I was the first to take the big hit and became the poster boy for shushy UK. It was finally time to file my appeal against the Clown Court sentencing, with the help of my Public Protection KC. When a judge tells a jury to 'forget what you've just heard' over blatant perjury, you know a trial is on dodgy ground - where witnesses are making up any old shit and being allowed to get away with it. BTW, why did the then Home Secretary write back 'Keep out of it' to a top MP when asked about my torture from the pigs at Notts Police? Bomb squad my arse. No further action, hey? Remember the strip search before the 'No Further Action.' Wretched, stinking, crooked, corrupt arseholes - the lot of them. I had to simply wait, be patient, and know that my time would come to write THIS book. You can sue over liars, but most mental trolls are homeless, penniless, and on PIP. The lesson I've learned is they'll bankrupt you even if you win. The costs run into hundreds of thousands of pounds, yet the most you can claw back is around £20K. You can't get blood out of a stone - so what you end up with is a financially devastating Pyrrhic victory. The law is beyond an ass; it's an enormous donkey's cock. Stephen Fry said, "The doors to the court are open to everyone......as are the doors to the Ritz!" Knowledge is power. I see so clearly now. I've learned so much. I've worked it ALL out......albeit too late. It took me a long time, relentless introspection, and a five-and-a-half-year prison sentence - but I've never seen more clearly. You <u>HAVE</u> to wait, let them eat themselves alive, before the chickens come home to roost! I guarantee these unhinged YouTube liars and snakes will delete their bile before I'm out. There's no point in me spending good money on folk who don't have a pot to piss in - or a loved one to send them to Dignitas.

Within a couple of months, I reconciled what really happened - who was involved, where, and when. I finally had total clarity and perspective. Most of the rats have already abandoned ship and disappeared into the mesosphere. I now have 360°, 20/20 vision of what happened. Times have changed, and my political 'influence' came at totally the wrong time. We now know free speech is dead. From me to Katie, Piers, Russell, Tate, Tommy, and even Dan, Barton, and Lawrence - anyone who isn't lefty is now hiding behind the paywall of protection, clenching their arse (like a blood orange), waiting for a knock on the door from the Old Bill. What happened to me could <u>NEVER</u> happen in America. If only Trump could become President again - maybe that would push back the wicked, radical far-left shushy brigade. 'It could be you!' Be under no doubt: this is all tactical, designed to scare my peers into silence. As my judge said, 'This is not about Mr Belfield's journalism or free speech.' What a crock of shit! As far as I was concerned, I simply had to endure this process - for <u>now</u>. But I could never have imagined the strength and fortitude I'd need to survive the next set of attacks and sabotage that was about to come my way via lawfare. YES - they were out to bankrupt me and take EVERYTHING.

Notts Police were not done. Various shushy-shushy folk wanted to get me extra time - on top of the three years behind the door. They held a secret hearing that I didn't find out about until afterwards. Even Judge Saini had to throw out the prosecution's request to up my sentence to ten years. Blimey - I must really have pissed someone off!

HMS Stockings were intent on breaking me, stopping me smiling, preventing me writing the books and letters – oh - and under no circumstances would I be progressing to open prison despite being legally entitled! WOW! Isn't progress and rehabilitation at HMP fun?

Chapter 22

Heartbreaking, Hopeless, and a Changed Lefty World!

It didn't take me very long to work out that prison is not torture - it's an asylum for the dregs of society. It's a warehouse for wankers, a hotel for the homeless, and a hostage centre for those (like me) who 'they' want hushed, silenced, or removed from public life. The notion that I was a 'risk' to society - which was the defence used to keep me there - was ludicrous. I'd been on bail, under strict restrictions regarding the 'victims', and nothing had happened in 2+ years. However, I desperately needed the Prison Service to complete my 'OASYS' file and officially confirm their position - after analysing me with binoculars, a magnifying glass, and a microscope.

Within weeks of settling into my new career as an author, I have to confess - there was one MASSIVE drawback. People! I don't mean the imbeciles and morons I had to live with (or be governed by). No - I mean the endless people in my life I now couldn't be with. The reality was, most would be fine, like my sister and friends my own age. The incredible heartache for me came from the kids I was missing watching grow up, and the elderly and ill I couldn't care for anymore. Contrary to the belief of the medicated mentals in their mother's back bedroom, my life is full of love. It's riddled with incredible people all over the country - and in fact, the world. I drown in human connection.

I now needed a mental strategy to park the loss of hugs and begin to cope long-term. This wasn't five and a half months!

Some people (abroad) I wouldn't be able to see until 2028. It could be longer - if the evil establishment have their way. Love is the most powerful drug in the world. Who knows what they're capable of next? Love is equally draining when crushed, and inspiring when present. Unless you're utterly unshaken or lost in a haze of SPICE, the weight of guilt and mental turmoil - echoing in your inner dialogue within this Campus for Cunning Stunts - comes from knowing that terrible things can happen. And if they did, I would be completely powerless to stop them. This was an emotional strain I'd never felt in my life.

I've been so blessed to travel the world continually for thirty plus years. I'm a modern-day Judith Chalmers! I've met some incredible people! As a critic, I hit the heady heights of #1 gobshite online which caused crocodile tears from a lot of loathsome, lonely, and jealous luvvies. I always avoid drains, as they stink of shite. Instead, I migrate towards the radiators of love, fun, and warmth at the very top of the sanity pole. In terms of brands in showbiz, comedians have always been my absolute favourites to be around - and I've been so lucky to know many of the greats. I adore controversial funny men like Jethro, Jim Davidson, Chubby, and Jim Bowen - all of whom I was lucky enough to know well. When Jethro and Bowen passed, it left a huge hole in gags for grown-ups... and for those who write to *Points of View* if the hurty words made them feel anxious. In one way, I'm glad they passed at the top of their game - because they'd be cancelled now anyway. Their bravery - and the willingness of the likes of Jim and Chubbs to take the relentless flak from snowflakes - is inspiring. The pile-on for satire always astounds me. It's entirely political, of course - just like my ejaculation from the airwaves. I started in showbiz with Sir Ken Dodd at 14 years old and worked with him for twenty-plus years. He never offended anyone! I adore those in between - like Pasquale, Brian Conley, and Bobby Davro - who might be from a different generation but are all masters of their craft. Davro is truly one of the most brilliant, hysterical, and killer turns that I've ever met - and with whom I became great friends. Bobby's wife was an incredible lady called Vicky Wright - whose dad was a legendary footballer, and whose mum was part of the iconic group *The Beverley Sisters*. Vicky and I became close during Covid, when I started working for Jim Davidson on his Ustreme TV channel. Vicky was fun, gorgeous, and full of life - the epitome of an eighties' vivacious stunner. She loved my VoR success and hated the hideousness of the trial. We spoke almost daily. Like so many, she couldn't fathom the injustice. Little did we know... her personal trial would be far worse than mine.

In 2022, I'd bought a charity auction prize for 'Care After Combat' and naturally wanted to share it with my loved ones. On Good Friday, a group of six of us gathered at a suite in the Dorchester. We had the best time - eating a buffet of their finest scran whilst drinking obscene amounts of gin and vodka - bought from Tesco's (I'm not daft) - £22 for a G&T in hotels? Are you sure?!!! Balls to that. I'm off to the corner shop for a litre for less! My working -class roots never leave me, even in the most swish of circumstances. It was perfect being surrounded by dear pals - Nick, Andy, Mark, and Alice. They, like me, knew what was coming. This was my posh swansong, courtesy of VoR, as a tax write-off to charity. There's got to be at least one perk, hey? Vicky looked fabulous - hair as big as her personality. Bobby was working, but we all had a hoot, with an amazing dinner delivered to the suite by immaculate foreigners in white gloves. Thank you, YouTube!

Little did I know that it would be the last time I'd see Vicky - ever. We spoke throughout the trial, and even the night before sentencing. I loved the bones of her. The biggest frustration -unique to me - about prison is that you're limited to twenty numbers. For most normal cons, that's eighteen too many - more than enough. But for me, it was excruciating. To put it into context: I had seven best mates who worked for VoR, before I'd even got to parents, sister, godsons, lifelong friends, and my dear Big Boned Jean - who I talk to five times a day to sort out all my guff that needs sorting. This angel has passed on more messages than a Soho hooker to her pimp. It's really been a team effort. I infuriated the lazy turds in OMU by constantly changing my numbers, but what choice did I have? They even went to lawyers to find a way of stopping me - to no avail. You only get new rules when someone's broken them. I think there'll be quite a few 'prison law' updates after my temporary visit. So, I deliberately changed five numbers a week, in rotation, just to get on their dreary, hairy-lipped, Brut-wearing chesticals. Pissing them off gave me a glorious sense of satisfaction. I'll never change. Small pleasures...

In late October 2022, I found out that Vicky had a very very serious cancer – horrifically, the same cancer that killed her father a decade before. Vicky went on my list permanently - and never came off. When she wrote to me to tell me, I wept out of pure despair. Now I realised the ONLY torture of prison... heartache and powerlessness like I'd never felt before. At the time my loved ones needed me the most, I was useless. The first time Vicky and I spoke, we promised we'd get each other through our undignified woes. We'd need tenacity, strength, and fight. 'IT WOULD PASS' and 'IT WILL END' became our nightly sign-off. Barely an evening passed without mutual words of encouragement being shared. We were so proud of each other. It was such a beautiful friendship. It's said that the average human life is about 650,000 hours long. It was now my job to make the most of my time - regardless of the squalid location - knowing that there's always someone else with a bigger fight. Millions are in shitty jobs, living the same existence on the treadmill of life. We all have - on average - 74.5 years each on this mortal coil. I suppose two years and nine months to be humbled and gain this education is a small price to pay for my forty-plus years (so far) of pure indulgence of my passions and meeting diamonds like Vicky. I've fought back every time I've been sacked and cancelled... this time will be absolutely no different. My point is - life is too short! Vicky's wake-up call, along with my Auntie's MS and Uncle's MND, was a devastating reality check - to pull my socks up and get on with, and through, this challenge without <u>any</u> self-pity. The sheer frustration of not being able to help her was excruciating. Bobby and Vicky both tried to comfort me. I was having none of it. I'm far from a victim. It became a pissing contest of who was more genuinely sorry for whom. I refused to drain her of any sympathy for this silly situation. I have my health, and this will pass, but for Vicky it did not look good. Even at her lowest ebb I <u>tried</u> to make her laugh! We loved to reminisce ......but Vicky was in excruciating pain, facing the battle of her life. Platitudes no longer cut it.

At exactly the same time, my aunty with MS was also struggling. She'd declined big-time since my disposal from public gaze. She'd been bedbound for about a year, and her angel carer, Maria, was finding it harder by the day to cope. Having spent a lifetime as a teacher, this country rewarded Dorothy with a £5,000 bill a month for live-in home care. The dafties in luvvie land always got me wrong. I couldn't care less about reimagined shitty shows in the West End that I was no longer able to annihilate - where a woman plays Phantom and a Buffalo identifies as the Lion King. All of this stuff is just fluff, filler, flotsam, and jetsam. My only regret of this fabricated fackdupery is the people I'd abandoned - who were paying a huge price in my absence. I would have helped with hospital visits. Don't get me wrong - I'm no Marie Curie (I don't do personal wiping or bodily functions). But I'll wait all day at a hospital if you've got a blue badge and a discount card at the NHS café! This all weighed heavier by the day. It was times like this that I wished I was a thicko whippersnapper - who didn't have a care in the world and could get off my tits on spice. It's a much less emotionally painful, suffocating, and debilitating life. I'm sure the Lord Chancellor stands proud of her 'family ties are our priorities' HMP horseshit. It's a national disgrace. As for Vicky - what a stoic and brave lady. The definition of resilience.

Chapter 23

How The Other Half Live

December arrived, and the final rehearsals for the two carol concerts were on Wednesdays at 3pm - my safe zone! This was truly my #1 hour of the week, to share with Anne at the piano and be in the presence of genuine hope and support. I never took it for granted.

I was well aware that I'd got it relatively cushy on F Wing. K and M Wings were seemingly the ghettos – all hell was breaking loose between gangs and lads being encouraged to get into debt. I had my first taste of the risks of prison life when I heard the emergency button pressed by an officer, and all available screws scrambled to the corridor between H and K Wing to assist. A man had been seriously stabbed while returning from work. Debt in jail is a serious business and can escalate fast. This was revenge - over vapes! They're £2.89 a pack, for avoidance of doubt. It can easily spiral over something so trivial. One of the things I loved (for the purposes of this book) - but found outrageous - was how indiscreet the system is. 99% of officers don't have earpieces, so you can hear <u>EVERYTHING</u> that's happening everywhere in the slammer - by just standing next to a screw with their radio blasting out. I still find it extraordinary that - despite their claims of high security and privacy - you get a running commentary on every single event in prison life. Riveting! The nosy parker in me never got bored of the drama and relentless 'content.' Far better written than

Corrie. Anywho, I heard a 'Code RED' on the radio = blood. This is second only to someone being found dead in terms of urgency. That's Code Black: ten toes up! 'Code Blue' is not breathing. Akin to watching those cheap 'we'll catch 'em' Channel 5 police shows - that prove 50% of cops can't link a sentence or find their arsehole with two hands - I remain staggered at the ferocity of real criminals and their determination to get revenge, knowing full well they'll get caught. No fear of consequences for stabbing someone. It's fair game to them. Their immaturity and baby-faced looks can be very deceiving. I've got meat in the freezer older than most of this lot -both running the jail and causing havoc within it.

We knew it was serious as the prison was put in lockdown. No one could move anywhere as the main route was now a crime scene. Stabbings happen all day, every day in prisons......but rarely in a security CAT-C. This almost never happens. The entire jail was sent behind their doors by order. You can have banter with the kangas, but when they say 'direct order' - you know they're not pissing about. Shortly after, the sound of the air ambulance got louder and louder as it landed in the front car park. A gentleman of colour had been ferociously stabbed in the ribs and neck. This was about as serious as an incident could get. But how? Could it be one of our meat cleavers from VT Catering or the Bistro? Absolutely not. They're meticulously counted in and out by Stella Virgin, who won't miss a trick. If her stats (rightly) didn't add up - you weren't getting out of there if anything was missing... especially a knife. This is <u>exactly</u> why!

You don't mess around with weapons! IT'S PRISON! This chap used a home-made weapon - a 'SHANK.' I'd heard of having a 'Sherman Tank' when bored with Tug TV - but never a shank! This is a homemade knife. One of the unavoidable health and safety disasters of the nick is razors. You're given them on request. Unless you're suicidal, you can help yourself and collect them up - as many as you need. In the old days, they were handed out and collected in to avoid incidents like this. These days, they can't be arsed. If you're feeling flush, you can even buy Gillette Mach 3 blades for £7.99 on the canteen. The inventive, violent scum of HMP take the free toothbrushes - snap them clean in half - and carefully affix a razor blade, stripped from a cheap yellow Bic, right onto the jagged end. They don't just use one. They'll glue several onto the end of the stab stick, which causes even worse life-threatening, disfiguring scars. This is not a Harley Street plastic surgery - it's intentional butchery at its worst. That's exactly what happened on this day. It's terrifying how these can be made overnight and carried anywhere. HMP are powerless to stop it.

Look, the reality is: the average prisoner like me - just minding my own business - will never get caught up in anything like this. It's all pre-planned revenge over debt or ghetto wars by gangbangers. However, there's an underlying risk, especially with so many unstable lunatics on every corner, where you could easily get caught in the crossfire. A lot of prison assaults and stabbings are now gang- and turf-war related. It's childish and silly - with devastating consequences. The new 'mixed' nonce jails will fall foul of this, I guarantee you. Eventually, a lunatic con will get revenge on a child rapist, paid for by the person who wants to teach them a lesson. This happens all the time in high-profile cases, where the worst cons have a price on their heads. Attacks are rarely carried out by the person behind it. It's prison - you will NOT get away with it. Remember: snitchers get stitches. You pay £150 for a druggy to do your dirty work - it's almost impossible to prove who's really pulling the strings. I never allowed myself to get paranoid about such incidents, but the pure evil and determination of some of these men is not to be underestimated.

How many times have we seen a deadly stabbing on civvy street recently? At least we've got guards and a doctor waiting to help here…. not that they will necessarily save your life. You'll have to wait thirteen hours for a policeman on the outside, as they're too busy arresting people for offensive posts online. I couldn't help but think, 'I wish I could interview this moron!' Seriously - you're in a cushy jail, and now you're going to be arrested, shipped to a CAT-A, and slapped with another ten years on your sentence for attempted murder… with no hope of parole. They don't care. They know no better. This type of evil blows my mind. Literally zero conscience. This is a mindset a normal person could never comprehend. In jail they stab you in the front, but in showbiz they stab you in the back – a sobering reality! Serious mental illness either way, right? 'Mistakes' can happen in the nick, only today a good man in his sixties was headbutted by a scumbag who was out of his mind with rage. Colin was totally innocent.

He was simply the victim of an unmedicated lad - and in the wrong place at the wrong time. It's sobering and shocking. So, you can never fully relax - you're always on your guard, as are all staff. Often, they pay the price for the vengeance of sickos. Such serious incidents are few and far between. However, about ten officers are assaulted a month in Stocken alone - some seriously. It's much worse in CAT-Bs, and private jails appear to be lawless. Why anyone would choose to put themselves in jail for a living - they either need a medal or sectioning immediately!

Finally, my three months 'jail probation' was coming to an end. OMU (the people who would ultimately decide my open jail release) arranged for my OASYS to be done on the 9th of December. This document is crucial to your development and, most importantly, reflects your official 'risk to society.' It's paramount that it's accurate. If some Celia Imrie has a grudge and gets it wrong - purely by accident, you understand - the consequences could be fatal in terms of progress for years to come. My cynicism kicked in big-time. All faith had already gone in the system after my Clown Court experience. My teeth started to itch when I was told that OMU (= Ostensibly Moronic and Unattractive) at Stocken were 'too busy' to do it themselves. This was a HUGE red flag. They instructed someone to do it remotely from London - over the phone. Not my cup of tea, and a clear, intentional way for the conspiring Government agencies to say whatever they like - by an ANONYMOUS person I would never meet. I want to see the whites of your eyes! I don't want an AI 'probation' - I'll never be released (even though they didn't believe I needed locking up in the first place!). I literally counted the days down until the scheduled phone call. Would I get a human with clarity, perspective, and common sense? Please God, take me now! I rang the number from my pad and waited online for ninety minutes for them to pick up and join the conference call. They didn't. Back to square one. By law, this crucial document has to be done within three months of arrival into custody, but this doesn't happen. 99% of men I have met behind bars don't even know it exists. It's almost never done on time - some men never get it done at all! Probation is broken - and they shamelessly admit it. This leaves a lot of good men floundering when they should be home. Can you imagine the frustration? Prison probations are more overworked than Ant and Dec's accountant. They're busier than the BBC cover-up department! I was naturally crestfallen, as I knew this only meant more delay - at least a few weeks. Cock-up or conspiracy? Delay meant ZERO hope of release. Most convenient hey? I also knew this would mean war with OMU - whom I christened Overpromoted, Menacing, and Underqualified - in my hundreds of letters (which they read). Every single one I could defend in a court of law. EVERYONE I met slagged off these blundering Biffas. No one had any faith or a good word to say about prison probation. I found it terrifying that it was universally accepted that the most important people at HMP were the least trusted - and, more importantly, the least respected. The ineptitude and contempt are staggering, which was confirmed by every con I would meet. These highly powerful (mostly women of a certain size) would become my nemesis, and have my balls and freedom in their hands. Their arrogance and ability to distort ANY reality is staggering. Why shouldn't I be pissed off over their 'unfortunate' mistake? My liberty was at stake, but they intentionally did not care. I was back in BBC middle-management HELL! They operate with complete impunity and believe they're God. I guess they are. No formal qualifications and often ZERO experience - but they wield more power than a Clown Court judge! Welcome to the embarrassing joke of HMPPS...

I was still a 'standard' prisoner, days away from being enhanced. Prison is entirely run as a hierarchy of trust and prominence, based on your job, pay, and security level - which determines your freedom and the wing on which you'll live, categorised by your 'incentive' status. 'Enhanced' is the only place to be! I had to push to make this happen. I had never before asked to speak to a three-band Senior Officer, but this day I did. I managed to get to an SO, and we had a friendly chat. He may have known about my reputation. I explained what was going on, and he was not at all surprised by OMU. His despair and frustration were palpable: "OMU don't even reply to my emails; they're literally a law unto themselves." This was my first experience of prison life boiling down to 'of course it didn't happen' – it's prison. The Gov sent an email fighting my corner, and a few days later, my call to the anonymous London OASYS box-ticker was re-scheduled for the following week. So, the manipulators had now bought a month pissing about with this nonsense. This is their raison d'être. I used the opportunity to beg for enhanced status, as it would grant me a third visit - allowing Mum and Dad to come twice over Christmas and New Year - to soften this festive Scrooge blow. December is a five week-end month, so a third visit would make so much difference. I owed my folks everything after a lifetime of devotion and judgement-free support. Christmas was never going to be easy for any of us, but the thought of only seeing them once was unbearable for all sides. To be fair, the boss said to come back next week, and he'd sign it off a week or two early, as my behaviour had been exemplary. I knew he thought my situation was one big stitch-up - but he had to play the game. It didn't take long for senior screws to slip out: "This place isn't for people like you," or, "If you weren't famous, they wouldn't have even arrested you, let alone sent you here!" He also knew OMU shipping out this crucial document was NO coincidence. Another example of passing the buck on this hot potato. A lot of history repeating again, right? I was officially in a vortex of imbeciles - who not only didn't do their job properly, but didn't care that they didn't do their job properly. Nor did anyone around them. These ignoramuses were clearly on a mission to long-grass everything and distance themselves from the ensuing shitstorm. The lovely lady from upstairs in Resettlement DID care. She was spitting feathers at the ineptitude. She personally emailed the 'Offender Management' boss and my OMU - neither replied. They're intentionally Teflon and deliberately flaky... just like their skin.

It was a long six days before it was re-scheduled. The note read: 'We're sorry you didn't call Tara as requested, Mr Belfield. Try again at 9am on the 5th January.' You can imagine the steam coming out of my ears. Cheeky bastards! What do you do? I'm powerless, remember. If you kick off (as they've baited me to do), they'll say I have anger issues and they're too in fear to engage with me. They distort and pivot all truth and reality. The following week, I called London for the second time. I waited - once again - for ninety minutes on the conference call, with no answer. Again, I went back down to talk to the Gov - and, as before, he was not shocked, surprised, or remotely alarmed by this unforgivable sabotage. It's just the way it is at HMP. I cannot describe the palpable exasperation - KNOWING I'd once again been screwed over, and they'd bought another month to reschedule it yet again. This would define my entire HMP experience. It was another cruel lesson of prison life. These people thrive on 'accidental' mistakes. 747 Alf said, "If you're smarter than them, they'll make your life a misery." He's so right - they hate anyone who can outwit them. They only thrive against thickos: those they bully and intimidate, who blindly follow their bullshit and give up before they get what they want.

Liz upstairs called my OMU directly - who didn't answer. I was a number - a very high-profile number - who no one seemingly wanted anything to do with. I wonder if this was the directive of the MOJ mafia? Wish I could say this is personal. Sadly, I've since learned that thousands of men are treated exactly the same. THEY DON'T CARE. My time would come. But they knew, for thirty-one months, they had me captive - handcuffed, gagged, and under the dictatorship of their authoritarian control.

If they didn't sign me off, I wouldn't progress. Who would want the blame and notoriety of signing me off? THEY WIN. I'm stuck behind bars, despite being entitled to open conditions. No wonder they didn't pick up - it's all a charade. This was the beginning of the end for me. And my faith, trust, and entire respect had gone before we'd even started. Of course, they're never <u>sorry</u>. No institution or mafia will utter those five letters, as it leaves them responsible in law. After several 'COMP1s' (Official Complaints), I was told my OASYS would now be written in my absence. An even bigger DISASTER - a euphemism for 'we'll make it up.' AND THEY DID! Intentional sabotage? You decide. This document should <u>never</u> be written by osmosis and guess work. They're legally bound to involve you for accuracy. This was a proper indefensible stitch-up. What a great ruse to scupper any hope of progress. The platitudes of 'it'll be OK' didn't wash with me. I'd trust Kim Jill Ill more than these creeps. In fact, his brother Menta Lee Ill would give me more hope.

Connie Lingus, who I'd liked just ten weeks ago, was mysteriously quiet and evasive. She was now only noticeable by her absence. She'd been warned off - and was soon to be replaced entirely. 'Keep your head down,' was her advice - and I'd be back home. This was now clearly not going to happen... even though statistically it should. Her false promises were clearly going to be denied. Within days, I was given two new OMUs - one, the head of the entire department; the other, sporting a nose piercing and flip-flops... in December. This did not bode well.

Despite the blatant, immoral, and crooked actions of OMU, the Senior Officer finally gave me enhanced status - giving me an extra visit every month, plus £33 in 'spends' (money available for phone, clothes, and canteen each month from my private account). Small mercies. I immediately called Mum and Dad about the extra Christmas visit - I had to give them some good news, which cheered us all up. These small boosts made a major difference. It now also opened up the opportunity to get on Newton Wing - the Ritz of HMS Stockings, with underfloor heating! The extra cash did feel like a double-edged sword. I'd got £1,600 a year for 'luxuries' - but what about those lads who had nothing? Life's not fair. Sadly, this was not the time or place for my soap box. Even in jail, there's elitism and a class war. Regardless, I was still about to spend £2,400 a year on phone calls alone! Scandalous profiteering from HMP. They should hold their heads in shame.

To keep me grounded, whilst I was in the office with the Senior Officer, it was made very clear that it was frowned upon that I was getting so much post. In fact, he clarified: "You're pissing off a lot of people, wasting HMP time on your fan mail. We're not your personal secretary!" Ouch. I responded: "Well, give it me unchecked then - I don't care!" Wrong answer!!! They also wanted me to know that changing my numbers regularly was causing 'too much work,' and I should 'refrain' from calling so many people. He said: "The prison doesn't have the resources to cope with your hundreds of letters, plus a hundred-plus hours of calls a month." I enquired, passive-aggressively: "What is prison law on these restrictions?" He went bright red. "There aren't any." AWKWARD! This was clearly sent from above. It was a hint to rein my neck in – bit late for that dear. I'm not breaking any rules - so do one! They couldn't punish me or stop my enhanced, but this was a HUGE red flag from upstairs to comply 'or else......!' I couldn't resist: "Sir, can you print off the prison law confirming my entitlements to calls and mail?" Silence. I never received this paperwork - just idle threats that this mob thrive off, demanding blind acquiescence. My curse of communication would once again cost me dear. My final shot to the bows was: "Look, if probation doesn't play by the rules, how can you expect prisoners to? You chose to kidnap me - this is your problem. I'm very happy to go home if it makes all of your lives easier!" He said, "Mr Belfield, life can be made very difficult in jail!" How's that for a threat, hey? I smiled, stood up from the cheap office furniture and said, "Sir, I'm a hostage here. They started it, tell them to do their job and I'll do mine." His flabber was gasted, "I'll let them know Mr Belfield." As I walked through the office door he said, "Belfield, don't shoot the messenger" – blimey, what a confession. Almost as if he knew this book was writing itself. Bullseye!

Chapter 24

Condiments of the Season

A Fisted Chicken and a Festive Portion in the Pokey

What was already blatantly clear was that I refused to respect the corrupt establishment that incarcerated me. They knew this - and saw it as war. 'We'll crack him!' Only a nobhead would be grateful to have their life, freedom, and career taken away in such a crooked manner, and then show reverence and grace post vendetta. I was now in survival mode. Why surrender after three relentless years of .gov, police, and court tyranny? Nothing to lose... and don't tell anyone, but the daily energy fighting the battle keeps my spirit and soul alive and kicking. Stocken had been instructed that they couldn't get rid of me. I found this out through a secret SAR email disclosure, which confirmed a block was put on 'all prison transfers.' This was entirely to keep me under these 'high security' conditions. No other CAT-C could monitor me this relentlessly to hopefully 'catch me out' - good luck with that! After posting out the first bundle of transcripts to my manuscript mule, BBJ, word spread that I was now 'profiting' from my £48K-a-year sabbatical to write a book I'd never have dreamt of doing in real life. The irony: that 'doing time' created the time to do it! I was told that OMU had contacted MOJ lawyers to prevent me from doing so. FAIL. Unfortunately for them, you cannot lock a man up and then stop him writing (in his own time) about the experience they forced him to have whilst hostage - just like Lord Archer! I no longer kept schtum in letters - I would repeat, over and over again, all of the things I wanted 'the system' to know, including my plans and even what page and chapter I was up to. Stick that in your 'surveillance' pipe and smoke it. I documented every fack-up I'd witnessed and would say, "All good content for the book," simply to get on their tits. Over and over, they went via their lawyers to 'get me' on breach of this and that. However, they didn't get one single infringement, as journalists cannot be prevented from documenting what they see - no matter how unedifying or embarrassing for the kidnappers and establishment. Just like with the cuntstables and evil BBC – they'd got bugger all on me, making them even more incandescent with rage! Once a week, I'd post BBJ (Big Boned Jean) the book, in twenty-page bundles, to keep safe - just 'in case' it mysteriously disappeared in transit. This was the autobiography - so all they had so far was hundreds of pages about how fab I am and how lucky I have been. Can you imagine how much this must have boiled their piss? In fairness, nothing ever went missing - other than one section... about OMU. What a coincidence.

The pressure was building from the 'shushy' operatives, as Network Nick was spreading the good news on SVoR. They couldn't stop him either. I am prevented from using social media, but my team are not. Madame Katie Hopkins was the straw that broke the camel toe's back, after she decided to make yet another YouTube video asking my punters to send letters and Christmas cards to give my morale a boost. ENTIRELY LEGAL - but when hundreds of cards landed on HMS Stocking's poop deck, the box-ticking cuntsultants' heads nearly exploded!

You'll never know the uplift and joy this gave me - matched by the tsunami of HATE it generated at HMP and from the mental, medicated trolls online. I was meant to be persona non grata... not the talk of social media. I bet Johnny Vaughan's sack wasn't bulging like mine! Naturally, they maliciously withheld hundreds of cards until after Christmas. Strange coincidence, that - hey? That's exactly what a petulant, slightly backwards child would do, right? You have to understand: this takedown was designed to kill me and 100% intended to destroy me publicly. Horseface Hopo created an avalanche of love and support. They wanted stalkery revulsion and cancel culture fury - not unwavering affirmation. I wasn't going away, giving up, or going on the roof - so finally, they got the memo! Furthermore, after three months onboard, the hate police couldn't find a SINGLE member of staff (kitchen, library, gym, chapel, or officers) who I'd had a single crossed word with. My file was flawless. Better still, I hadn't had a single issue with any con, lag, or even spice-head breadbin - so I was more squeaky clean than Huw Edwards' diary. They had no stick to beat me with. The belief I was a madman or loose cannon was dispelled.

OK, I'm not soft. I knew that my letters were actually being read by a crack team of security geniuses, with a GNVQ in woodwork, trying to find anything they could construe as 'stalking' - to continue and cement this fabricated foolishness. One word about a single victim and - BINGO! Extra charges and a lot of press publicity to vindicate their witch hunt. It's known as 'offence paralleling' in the biz. Balls to that - I was just ripping the piss out of HMP shitheads, none of which they could deny. I hadn't any ink to waste (or facks to give) on my so-called victims. FAIL. The mob didn't stand a chance. The volume of love and support crescendoed as word spread in the clink - and all sane kangas realised this was the stitch-up of the century. My replies got longer and longer, exposing everything I could think of to throw the key-turning mafia under the bus. They believed (I was told) that 'his audience will get bored, and it will stop.' WRONG! As five prisons can testify, I've never had a second without a VoR angel to reply to - EVERY SINGLE DAY. Ouch. They wanted me isolated, miserable, alone, and devastated - yet I was applauded, supported, and almost revered by cons, screws, and fans alike. This had gone very badly for the .gov goons. It was now a total impasse, and I still hadn't met the box-tickers in person. Crackers! At least I was now 'enhanced,' so no one upstairs could argue about my exemplary character or behaviour. They all think I'm daft as a brush - but you should never underestimate a working-class ginger kid from a pit estate. We're not all a few prison officers short of a slammer.

In fairness, the F wing staff were brilliant letting me out. Truthfully, they couldn't be bothered to argue. Far too many arseholes, off their nut on spice, to bother worrying about me. Most had the approach 'treat as you find.' I was always respectful....no matter what was going through my disbelieving mind. VT Catering would end at Christmas, which was a shame - I'd got on great with the lads.

I'd now found probably ten chaps, mostly older lifers or lags on a decent bird, who I could chat to, talk about the news, and pass the time of day with. The chapel was my natural home, as Anne and Tim had become my confidantes in this unbelievable reality show. I was later told that a top Gov was forced to announce at the staff meeting, the day I arrived, that 'we have a very high-profile prisoner joining us. Please be on your guard what you say.' Blimey - that backfired. I was now in the chapel more than my pad. Officers across the jail were like a leaky tap - and couldn't wait to tell me <u>everything</u>! By December 17th, we'd finished Christmas rehearsals and were about to do two carol concerts for the men. The first show had the mayor, clink top brass, and necklace wearers. I'm sure OMU are a fan of the odd pearl necklace from time to time! The brilliant orderly for the chapel, Chris, had decorated a beautiful eight-foot-high tree. It really was Christmas. Anne brought in refreshments - as she did every Sunday. This was the most fit, active, energetic, and inspiring, eighty-year-old on earth! She'd carry twenty pints of milk, ten packets of biscuits, and twenty-five books (containing every church song ever printed) - all in one go - for the three miles from the car park to Stocken's holy haven, like the original Mrs Claus! What a privilege to be around her irreplaceable energy. The warmth in that room was like *Home Alone 2* on acid. It was like *'Driving Home for Christmas'* playing as you pull into your mother's back passage on Christmas Eve. They managed to create and share the Christmas Spirit - a whole week before the Big Man emptied his sack in the Chaplaincy for convicts. Having toured for thirty years, performing three

Christmas shows every day in December, this had piercing importance. I love Christmas - and for one hour, it was the most wonderful time of the year.

The following day, I received even more unexpected kindness and fortuitous festive glee when Stella and Danny prepared a full three-course Christmas dinner for the Bistro and VT lads - as a final goodbye at the end of the course. They went to massive effort. Danny was Stella's right-hand man, and a former military chef. We had some fascinating chats. Top man! This is true compassion. You certainly didn't get this at DHL or in garbage disposal... sorry, 'waste management.' How the other half live, I suppose. I truly counted my blessings. They had cooked roast potatoes, parsnips, carrots, peas, Yorkshires, and pigs in blankets – I couldn't believe my eyes. It meant the world to me that they were so human, and cared. Imagine if you're a lifer: no visits, no calls, no hope. It must be mind-blowing to receive such love and kindness - way beyond what any of us could expect. Twenty out of the twelve hundred inmates got a lovely home-cooked meal, a mince pie, and some Christmas cake. What compassion. What luck to be involved. Maybe someone is looking down on me.

I made sure, every single day, I called Mum and Dad - at lunchtime and 8pm - to update them on all this POSITIVE stuff. They're ordinary, normal, kind, beautiful people, thrown into this insanity, having NO IDEA that this is what jail is in 2022. They rightly thought it was 'throw away the key' - being banged up

23.5 hours a day, in silence, probably in a cell with three men. <u>WRONG</u>. I went to HUGE lengths to paint the gorgeous Christmas tree picture, to explain how preposterous the system is, how it doesn't work, how it fails on every level, and costs <u>YOU</u> a fortune - ending no better than when it started. Every day, I'd find something surreal and magical to tell them - to prove I was OK, and keeping faith in this futile situation. Carols in the chapel and this festive feast were two huge highlights. Christmas makes you look back. I'm an optimist - a pint-half-full kind of guy - but even a hard-nosed tart like me couldn't help being reflective, as every TV ad was a punch in the guts and kick in the balls... over a 'dream' Christmas at home with the family. Which, this year, had been stolen from me by the establishment Grinch.

I'd already learned that not all people who'd done 'bad' things are bad people - but equally, some people are simply born evil and deserve their just deserts. Equally, there are plenty of criminals living next door to you, who just haven't been caught yet - and should be feared more than us lot in CAT-Cs. I disagreed with the Bible that 'all' should be forgiven, but will never be able to explain my gratitude to 'God' for bringing Anne, a piano, the chapel, and music back into my life. I'd learned the food is no worse than Butlins, the pride most men take in their cell is astonishing, and the ONLY punishment and torture of prison is passed on to your family and friends. My family - including VoR - ran into the thousands, and I'd never felt more loved. My pad was piled high with love - with every wall and surface plastered with well wishes. What more could I want at

Christmas? There was no way I could polish the reality of this turd of festive solitude – I just had to get through it. This was my lot for 2022, so I owned and accepted it. I said a prayer for those seriously ill, and wondered if I'd ever see them again. Gut-wrenching. Meanwhile, I counted my blessings - I didn't have to eat a Morrison's fisted turkey, cooked in an air fryer and drenched in Bisto mud granules, like so many of this once Great Britain.

Fatso's and A Festive Portion!

Each week, we are given a paper copy of the menu to fill in with five choices for lunch and dinner. Yep, for those wondering -diabetics, celiacs, and glutose-intolerant windy pops types are all catered for individually too. I find it hard to believe that anyone could get fat on the volume of food supplied by HMP. However, you'd be amazed how many big-boned fellas there are wombling around the corridors. Obviously, they're not as big as the lady garden vagiterian OMU types, but that's a given! Imagine if they fell on you.... By now, I had lost a few pounds - but it's not surprising, with such dramatic changes to my circumstances. I came in at 86 kilos (whatever that is) - I was now 81 kilos and was cock-a-hoop. The pokey is a great diet - no Uber Eats here... unless you pay a bent screw a couple of grand to sneak in your weekly big shop via the back passage or a restricted area! For so many of the lads, especially those without external funds to buy extra food, their menu on a Monday is the most exciting time of the week - despite it almost never changing. It worked on a four-week, respective rotation.

As well as lunch and dinner, you get a small 'variety' pack of Kellogg's (oh yes, not Aldi discount crap): Coco Pops, Cornflakes, Bran Flakes, or Muesli for breakfast. No one could survive on this though - it's barely enough to feed Victoria Beckham! HMS Stockings also included a 'breakfast bar' as well as bread (that is quickly nicked by the chosen few on the servery). I found the odd vape got me a loaf every two days, no matter which wing I've been on! Again, we are not all born equal - money talks!

The Christmas and New Year menu is the most exciting revelation of the year to most lags, as it has an extra zing - with the budget being at least thirty pence higher than the average £2.80 per day! The choice of roast beef or half a fisted chicken was the festive fayre. I'd never risk the beef curtains in jail - I'd hate to add to the farting cow's fiasco that is destroying our planet. Heaven forbid! Not really slammer gruel though, is it? I always ordered safe bets to avoid schnitzel or faggot ear holes, eye holes, or arse holes. I'll pass! Since those BBC auditions in the '90s, I'm very particular about what I shove in my gob! It's obvious that the salmon fishcakes, for example, are going to be 99% not salmon. Nothing gets past me!

You do get a 'Christmas' pack, if you tick the box, which consists of a mince pie, chocolate bar, iced Christmas cake, and bits and bobs - all high in sugar. Perfect way to get the ADHD lot bouncing off the walls and whizzing their tits off on Boxing Day. I was grateful, as I could swap it for things with sustenance.

Sadly, my Waitrose roast ham hock and Heston's 'Minge and Gunt Pie' were conspicuous by their absence. Again, I couldn't help but gratefully accept, but think about the cost - times twelve hundred cons -during a devastating cost-of-living crisis, where most pensioners are using foodbanks and freezing their bingo wings off. <u>Should</u> we really be eating half a chicken and a bag of festive luxuries - with Freeview, heating, and the security of no council tax, tv rape tax, or the obscene heating bills that are currently crippling the nation? Oh BTW, did I tell you, we don't pay council tax when we're banged up! Not a benefit if you're homeless and down on your uppers, but you take my point! That's another £3,000 perk in my back pocket, totalling my annual cost to £51,000 (to the public), before you add on tens of thousands for lost tax and VAT that I could have paid. HMP truly is the Christmas gift that keeps giving.

Christmas Eve arrived, and I'll be honest: I was dreading the next 48 hours. Not for me, but for all of my friends and family who would be feeling dreadful that I was eating porridge while they were munching on a turkey twizzler. BTW, I've never eaten porridge in my life - let alone in here. Another prison myth. We all have a routine at Christmas, and in the real world, I was like a little elf - flitting between houses, delivering gifts, and eating as many slices of M&S Panettone as humanly possible. For years, I'd conducted the Italian choir at Midnight Mass and the Christmas morning service, which had a glorious sense of tradition. Thankfully, I did have the service to look forward to in the chapel here, but nothing could take away the heartache of letting down my godkids, nephew, and neighbour's babies with Uncle Alex's boot full of goodies. Thankfully, my angel sister had packed a ton of cards with a few quid inside to soften the blow. Kids aren't daft. I remind myself, even today, that kids are like dogs - they have no perception of time; they're entirely in the moment. The heartbreak of missing these moments is the hardest thing about the slammer. Of course, when you ring everyone, it's like you've never been apart. I focused on the calls, not the separation.

This Christmas was an especially tough Yuletide, with Vicky, Dorothy, and my uncle Derek so poorly. You'd have to be a total prick not to wonder if this was to be their last Christmas. So, how do we cope? Well, for most men, they simply don't engage. They've got their Xbox and TV and just view it as another day ticked off. Which is true - it is. Millions do this who are alone (or miserable bastards) by choice. The way I coped was telling myself repeatedly that I wasn't in Ukraine, I wasn't doing a twelve-hour shift in A&E, and I wasn't one of the above angels who had little hope left through no fault of their own. Levity is key! Christmas would be my biggest test of perspective.

The wing camaraderie was quite extraordinary. Prison is a bubble and the 'zoning out' approach is a genius, and far less painful, and emotional way of surviving the slammer. Rise above reality and exist in a fake bubble. They are a brotherhood and family. Sadly, I felt more like a Jehovah's Witness - knocking on the door and chancing my luck. 'Living over the fence' and reliving, in my mind's eye, all of the gorgeous events I was missing was painful - but it was also the motivation to make me fight to get back to it: as strong and fit as possible. So, I kept busy and waited to get on the blower once banged up. Consumed writing is a marvellous distraction. Hours flew by. I'd got my useless City and Guilds in Fanny Craddock's master baking - so what had I got to worry about? I'm set for life with my large chopper and various misshaped root vegetables. I knew January - March would be depressing - exactly as it is on the out - but what new job would I get? Unfortunately, this year I wouldn't be checking in at Trump Miami like I had for the last decade. You can't have everything.

How I miss DJT's hot tub and Ivanka's bistro.

Part of Stocken's strategy is that all men **must** work, so retiring or doing nothing was not an option – even to be an author. I can't see them encouraging that 24/7! You're immediately put on basic, behind the door 23.5 hours a day if you opt out (which many do!). So, it was now all about 'make the best of it'......like the rest of the world had to do in every shitty, mundane, and tedious job. This must be what they call the real world, hey? The only job I fancied was the library. Helen and Marie-Anne knew I was no bother, so I asked if they'd have me. They were delighted and said they'd get me scheduled via allocations. Only six lads work in there, out of twelve hundred cons. It's a 'trusted' position - away from all the shenanigans and knuckle-draggers. It was going to be a long ten days betwixmas awaiting 2023. Staffing at HMP is a mess at the best of times. Christmas would make the place a ghost town. I prepared myself for a lot of unscheduled bang-up. At least I wasn't sharing with 'Norman the Nonce' like so many have to. Small mercies!

I'd become friendly with two decent Officers who had been very kind and generous in keeping me stacked with paper and pens. It's like being a toddler. You have to pick your moment and judge the mood. There's a lot of headless chickens in jail. If the mood looks dodgy, come back later - or ask someone else. 'No' never means no - it just means you've asked the wrong person at the wrong time. The times I've gone in the office, turned round, and walked straight out...I was also lucky to get self-addressed envelopes to write back to my angels. Must have cost my punters a fortune. How will I ever repay them? You're also entitled to an 'OL' - one free stamp each week. Another acronym - no, me neither! Why not just call it a stamp? Some generous, nice lads would give me theirs. From time to time, an SAE would go missing or they wouldn't include one - so at £1.25 a stamp, this was a blessing. That's a full day's work at HMP. I've never had to buy a stamp; the lads were so generous. They didn't care as they'd no one to write to, so they gave me theirs.

Christmas Eve was spent walking around the yard. There was no bravado - we were all sanguine, but pissed off we couldn't be with our people. But our countryside walk in the sunny Leicestershire hills was perfectly normal on this frosty but bright morning. We were all in it together. The definition of solidarity, right? My cruise ship experience was truly hitting the high seas.

There were lots of laughs and jokes in between Christmas memories. It certainly wasn't maudlin - but we knew there was an elephant in the room the size of Adele (pre-fat jab). Joking aside, HMP suicides spike big time during this week. I was very aware that, for some men, it could be too much. Remember, hundreds of men kill themselves in jail every year. They're never reported. Meanwhile, homeless co-stars are obviously overjoyed to be there and not on the streets freezing their nut off. Three meals a day and a roof over their head is not to be scoffed at. I guess you could say it's a Merry Christmas in the stable for the unstable. F Wing had a pathetic, threadbare tree in the entrance. It was as ramshackle and stripped as the prison service itself. I haven't seen such a depressing bush since my night at the Tory Annual Conference. I couldn't help wondering if one of the many tainted and cynical officers had put it up as some kind of piss-take. I asked Alf to sneeze all over it, so it would appear to have some tinsel. I'd not seen anything this embarrassing since my one-night stand with Sonia from *Eastenders*. I chatted with Jules, who was approaching his final six months. He could see the light of freedom - despite a divorce and impending bankruptcy. Hardly cause for a paper hat and party poppers, hey? Maybe my situation wasn't as grim as most others. Freedom is pointless if you've got no one and nothing waiting for you.

What I had noticed on F wing was the increasing number of crackpots, making the place look even more shabby. They didn't shower or feed themselves and were left to rot. I saw zero intervention. No one cared - it was horrific to see. I knew I had to keep busy, or I'd go down like a ton of bricks, just like these basket cases. By that point, it's way too late to put on big shoes and a red nose for my punters, for the media circus.

I woke up on Christmas morning and told myself (like every other day) that 'this too shall pass' - both Christmas and this ludicrous hostage situation. Like half the nation who hate Christmas (for so many reasons including loss and isolation), you just have to get on with it. It's just another day! Why do we put such importance on days that are effectively identical to every other 24 hours? Non-Christians - of which there appear to be increasing numbers in the UK (and jails) - couldn't care less. Equally, adverts seemingly have no Christ in Christmas, so what's the point? It's all a charade! Some highly religious types don't believe in the 25th, as it's possible the baby Jesus wasn't even born in December. So, to cut a long story medium length - I treated it like any other day. After half an hour in between TVAM and *Manshushy* on the evil BBC (bring back Anne and Nick), I stuck the kettle on and enjoyed my Nescafé Gold. After washing my face with Dove moisturising wash, I had my Bran Flakes, Kellogg's Crunchy Nut, and Alpen all mixed together - because I'm very cool....Yep, all ordered weekly on the canteen. Hardly a refugee camp in Gaza now, is it?

Like any other day, at 8am the doors crashed open, and - as usual - I was the first to mince, in my St Pancras flip-flops, to the showers before anyone else had even put down their crack pipe or joined the endless queue for morning methadone meds. What a bunch of characters, hey? They're collectively worse than the audience for *Jerry Springer*, or the box office queue for *Eurovision*. You could start a conference on that collective of cuckoo clocks. Anyway, I've always believed you should never start the day with mucky private parts. I brought my Teresa May (TREsemmé) PooCon two-in-one, so I was washed and dried before the officers had finished their clattering of doors and swept the corpses off to healthcare - those who had succumbed to their fentanyl suck sticks. Thankfully, with it being the Baby Jesus' birthday, I was busy in the chapel from 9am, so I still had an agenda on this holiest of Sundays - I even had a spring in my step. Today, more than ever, I'd need this team spirit to get me through the harrowing abandonment of not doing 'my rounds' before the King's speech and lunch at 3pm. This year was all change. I wasn't the only one mourning nostalgia. The Queen was dead, and I was at her pleasure. Wonder if the newly crowned King Charles III would give me a mention in the King's speech?

The commonality amongst men is that we're all abandoned and convicted. We all don't want to be here, and we're all desperate that our loved ones will carry on regardless and have a fantastic day without us. Remember, a huge proportion of men have young children or grandchildren that they love. Thankfully, I was surrounded by gammons - many of whom were in the same boat. I spent half an hour before church calling my parents, sister, nephew, godkids, friends, and silver-tops. Normally, I couldn't afford or justify this indulgence before 6pm, but today was different... needs must. Thankfully, everyone was in good spirits and despite the whopping elephant in the room, we all pretended we were fine. The kids are the most resilient. Their joy was deafening and utterly wonderous. Their excitement was palpable.

The bon ami and bravado in the nick is remarkable during your toughest times. I've never been mardy or one to boohoo. I equally used my intuition to see who else was struggling and try to give them a few pearls of wisdom. I convinced myself I was working, as I had done for two decades in December. Seriously, this psychological trick is the best bit of advice I can recommend - if you're in any extreme situation, isolation, or time away from the ones you love. Just fake it. Convince yourself that you're simply on a job, and you'll profit from the experience afterwards - and celebrate then. Delusion is much better than depression! It silences the torture, stress, and inner dialogue demons. Literally turn it off - not happening!

I went downstairs to the fellas, and they were all in great spirits. Oh yes, none of this mincy handshaking - it's all pump-pump festive fisting, and you're officially best bros for life! Maybe it was the holiday hooch that had pepped up their peccadillos. For some most peculiar reason, a lot of the lifers seemed to feel sorry for me and were more than affectionate - and overfamiliar with their fisting. I've never been one for unnecessary physical contact -especially with hairy-arsed men in their fifties. A 'hello' is more than sufficient, thank you, dear boy. Each to their own. Over time, as people learned more about me - and saw the odd turd twatting on in the 'medyar' - the notion that I was a deranged monster and the worst criminal since Bronson was dispelled and immediately dismissed. Their compassion grew greater and greater - as they knew it was total rhino cock! I grew to have huge respect for lifers, and especially those on IPP. Again... one wrong move. There, but for the grace of God, go all of us. Remember, lifers are statistically the least likely to reoffend! Once I got to know some select lifers, I upgraded their butch fisting for a gentleman's handshake. Each to their own - overfamiliarity blurs lines.

By 9am, I arrived at the Chapel, and I was at peace. The beacon of love and light - Angel Anne - greeted me with the biggest Santa-sized smile, a handshake, and a hug. It was like a Christmas onesie of comfort and protection had been draped upon me. She epitomized the spirit of the season. Her huge smile and double handshake were better than any Ferrari on Christmas morn - for me and the other 70 or so lads. I never would have thought that I could (or would) buy into this life, way of thinking, or forced lifestyle... but I had! I had no choice. Tim had arranged coffee and Christmas cake afterwards, and as I saw the chapel fill - I couldn't help but laugh. From twelve hundred sold-out seats on Blackpool's North Pier to a Sunday Service on HMS Stockings - showbiz was still a big part of my life... just on a different scale. My career had come full circle. This is how I started at fourteen years of age... playing carols on an old organ. I've long thought that vicars are twirlies. It's 99% theatrics and showing off. Come on - it's a performance. It's 100% charm, personality, and 'selling it.' Surely, at the very least, we can agree it's entertainment? What I do know is the team in Rutland were worth their weight in gold - priceless to so many. Tim, Anne, Pete, and Dan in the band, had formed a team for years - an impressive one at that - and I'd been welcomed to join them. From *Away in a Manger* to *Merry Christmas Everybody*, we did it all. The seventy or so men who packed the service were in seventh heaven and hugely uplifted. We'd taken them away from the heartbreak of the day for an hour of escapism found nowhere else in the slammer.

The Christmas tree was beautifully resplendent and decorated to perfection. Unlike the insult and slap in the face to the baby Jesus on F wing, this symbolised the class and finesse of that chapel. I blurred my eyes to maximise the multi-colours of the fairy lights. Quickly, the moment of realisation came that the service was over - and for me, like the other men, there was nothing to do for the next week, when we would return to the normal regime and 'work.' When I say NOTHING in the diary... well, other than the gym. Increasingly, I'd found the gym had become my second spiritual home - up to five times a week. It got me off the wing, on the cross-dresser (arms and leg trainer), and became my place of free thinking and inspiration ......previously only found in the shower. I'd now managed to get in almost every day - through mentor groups, over-forties sessions, and wing slots. I was desperate to leave healthier than when I came in. Maybe I could add on years that were lost by this corrupt kidnapping? The gym was back open tomorrow. Thank God!

I got back to my pad just after 11.30am, as lunch was being served. The palpable excitement of the men being offered half a chicken (left side only - as the right side is 'injected,' I shit you not!) was incredible. There's no doubting this is the biggest meal of the year. I tried to have humility and realise that, for the majority of the socially retarded and financially inept victims of Broken Britain, this could well be the best Christmas lunch they'd ever been served. The 'buzz' was electric. I tried not to sneer -the donkeys in the stable wouldn't approve. The amount of food we were given was preposterous. It was another kettle of fish compared to the usual portion size and gastronomic insult. The only 'gastro' at Stocken is enteritis! There were pigs in blankets - WOW - not to mention Brussels sprouts, peas, carrots, roasties, and cauliflower cheese. This was a far cry from my traditional gift to the family: an M&S four-course spread with the four-fisted bird, leg of lamb, salmon to start, desserts to die for, and cheese and biscuits three hours later... My sister Veronica loves anything with a blue vein in it. This year? This'll do.

I sat in my chair at my desk and put James Martin on ITV. He's like Nigella - without the knockers, pouting lips, wiggly tongue, and purring. I asked myself how I felt. 'You're fine, Belfield -they've still not won,' I told myself proudly. Lefty types tell you to check in with yourself regularly... For years I thought this was self-touching, but apparently, it's far deeper than that. You have to use a mirror. Next came Christmas Day *Loose Women* - how could anyone moan as I tried to digest half a gobble gobble while staring at Street Porter's turkey neck?

I shit you not - the average prisoner could throw away more food than so many could afford outside this Yuletide. Tough on the causes of crime, hey Kia Cars and Rishy Washy? I saved half of my half of chicken for a sandwich at teatime. You gotta have leftovers at Christmas - even in the hoosegow! Lunch always passed quickly, and before I knew it, we were all back out. This was my time for a walk at 2pm. I togged up, as it was bitterly cold, and made my way down the stairs to the playground, which was empty. I was still using the 'Dolce Gladys' - inspired prison wear, so I worked out that one jumper on, one jumper using the arms as a scarf for my old back, and another on top would keep me toasty.

Talking of clothes, I'd saved up a few quid and put in an order for T-shirts, trainers, joggers, and sweatshirts - so I could regain a little of my demure personality back. We're not talking Zara, but J&J will do for now. Maybe if I wore my trousers round my arse and called everyone 'Bro,' I'd fit in better with the chaps. It's no coincidence that HMS Stockings didn't allow clothes parcels for 'security' reasons... unlike every other jail in the UK. Another control measure, inconsistent with everywhere else, solely intended to keep you in your place. Two months later, they still hadn't arrived - which, I was assured, was perfectly normal.

I spent a good ninety minutes walking and chatting with various jail-mates. Birds of a feather flock together, and I found myself intrigued by so many lads' stories - some quite horrific. I felt such pain oozed from so many; I don't think anyone had ever asked them how they were feeling before. On days like this, having camaraderie is paramount. You'd have to have Morbidly Obese Morgan's rhino skin not to be affected by the reality of the circle of life - on this special family day, with so many absent friends. Heart-breaking. One lad, about thirty years old, told me he'd set fire to a man's house and got eight years for arson and various other crimes. This wasn't any random house - it was the house of the man who raped him when he was seven years old. The same house where this now local councillor attacked him. I repeat - there are two sides to every story. They clearly put the wrong man in prison, in my view. I was humbled by his honesty. Again, how can I moan when you hear stories like these?

By mid-afternoon, I sat and focused on the end of the autobiography, which was very cathartic and gave me a completely positive and uninterrupted mental escape. I was well over three hundred pages, so I hadn't wasted a moment of my first three months in the pokey. You can't double-think when writing - it's a glorious way to let hours fly by in your own world. Along with the letters and emails, these beautiful, immersive, and all-consuming 'jobs' got me through - with my head held high. Such a blessing. I felt for those with nothing or no one. Many have their phone hidden away under the bed. Their ghosts of Christmas past must have weighed heavy. About 4.15pm, a knock came on my door. A lifer called Daz banged on my cat flap and offered me two huge pieces of cheesecake he'd handmade - one mint and one chocolate orange. He said, "Alex, this is your first Christmas. It's not easy. Please have this, mate!" I was blown away. What kindness! How do you put into words the thought, compassion, and sincerity of such a beautiful and generous gift? How did he know mint and orange are actually my two favourite first choices for chocolate or cake? What a legend.

Daz was always polite and would say hello, but I don't think we'd ever properly spoken. Lifers are the smartest, as they've seen it all and have the most justifiable baggage. But Daz was part of the IPP group of men - who I can't help but sympathise with more than the rest, regardless of their crime. This indeterminate sentence is beyond torture. To lock men up who have no hope -or an end date - is unfathomable to me... and evil. Imagine how his parents must feel? Let me be clear: these are not men given life. Not at all. They were given a sentence like mine with the added 'IPP' status, so that the system could determine when they're fit to leave.........even though many were on 'tiny' sentences for non-fatal crimes. It was misused by judges - often for repeat offenders they wanted to teach a

346

lesson. How can a system that's not fit for purpose, and is self-diagnosed as broken, make this decision and stand by it - despite IPP now being banned and deemed inhumane? Hideous. I've met men who committed attempted robbery - who got eighteen months - and are still here fifteen years later! This cannot be right. Eighty have committed suicide, and two hundred have been sectioned. You can be sure - as eggs are eggs - that if IPP could have been given to me, they would have! I'd never be out - EVER! 'The risk is just too high Mr Belfield.' Nobheads! I can see the headlines in the NLTP (Notts Live Toilet Paper) already!

Give them 150 years if they're scum - no problem! Chop their heads off if there's undeniable evidence of crimes against kids. But this is inhumane mental torture - deciding every two years if they can finally be released. So many have simply given up and lost all faith. This barbaric government disgrace has to be abandoned! I believe, like the Royal Mail scandal, the government are too scared to admit that they were wrong - and don't want to compensate these violated men. Pete (on drums in the chapel) got seventeen years and is about to begin his twenty-eighth year incarcerated. How can that be right? Parole, have a LOT to answer for, in this sickening broken system. It's absolutely disgusting and indefensible. Akin to probation and HMP itself, it's a self-confessed ticking time bomb - so woefully under-resourced that thousands of men are having their liberty taken away through no fault of their own. I still can't find a single person who has one good word to say about

OMU/probation - or the parole-based guesswork, hatchet jobs, and personal opinion. None of the above is a science. DO YOUR JOB PROPERLY! That's all we ask!

I would, over many months, build rapport and trust with men like Daz, Clint, Andy, and Pete - and ask them how they cope. I've only got less than three years behind the door, and sometimes it can feel interminable. I'm not asking you to sympathise with the very worst criminals; however, surely, we can all agree that an end date is the only human right every prisoner deserves - even if it's never! Daz's kindness genuinely blew my mind. I was totally humbled and awestruck by his unbelievable and classy generosity - he didn't want anything! Firstly, it cost him a couple of quid (a fortune in here). Secondly, he took a lot of time and care to do it. And thirdly, he thought of ME. WOW. What a gent. Finally, it was bloody delicious! Worthy of any farm shop or garden centre café. He didn't make a fuss, but I can tell you it was the kindest thing that anyone ever did for me. From others, I would never have eaten it - but I 100% trusted him. Since then, I've had other kindnesses and compassion from the strangest places you'd never expect. I never got a chance to underscore to Daz how much this moved me. I genuinely hope one day I can meet him again and tell him to his face. Top man. Legend.

The 5pm bang-up came and went. You're never going to struggle for something to watch on Christmas Night. So, I blindly ignored what I was missing and focused on my blessings.

Sadly, HMP don't offer iPlayer (yet). Thank God, most men have an iPhone 69! I do feel this is a violation of our rights - not to be able to catchup on all the repeats the BBC trot out - that we paid for thirty years ago. Twunts! Don't get me started. Morecambe and Wise must be turning in their graves over Mrs Brown's Boys. Good lord, 'it'/'she' is to comic timing what Russell Brand is to monogamy. Anywho, I split up the various shows with my calls, and for some bizarre reason, I felt elated - genuinely lucky. Weird, right? Daz had blown my mind. Anne and Tim had offered the true essence of Christmas in the chapel, and I'd got through the day with no problem - with my pals in the playground. By the end of my three hours of blower chin-wagging, gobshiting, and chit-chat, I had a ludicrous euphoria that I truly wasn't expecting. The love, warmth, and support I received from F Block was dwarfed by the joy that came down that phone from my family and friends around the world. As long as I have my phone, I can survive anything.

Boxing Day, for a lot of people, is long, dull, tedious, testing, and pointless - identical to how I felt during my tortuously tedious days in court, trying to stay awake. Inbetwixmas, I churned out thirty pages a day of the book and kept the demons of insecurity and loneliness far away. For the last twenty-five years, I'd spent Christmas Day recovering from the Live shows - and by the 26th, I'd be driving up and down the motorway: seeing the God kids, passing by friends, and having a family tea and party. Between Christmas and New Year, I'd be reviewing pantos twice a day and seeing my pals like Davro and Pasquale - whom I adored.

For twenty years, from the age of fourteen, I'd be with my hero and mentor on the 29th/30th December at the Royal Concert Hall for Sir Ken Dodd's Christmas Show - boy, do I miss that. So, I've never EVER experienced the post-Santa blues... It was literally my most wonderful time of the year, ahead of a holiday in January. I can't see that happening either this year! The teamwork on the wing was jolly through New Year's Eve, although I continued to be an enigma to most. I had little to add to conversations about the best way to smuggle coke through Eurostar customs, so I kept my gob shut and kept walking -whistling Roger Whittaker's greatest hits. Each to their own! Fitting in - isn't always easy, is it? I worked my arse off and finished book one, four hundred plus pages, on New Year's Eve at 5pm. Poetic. Lovely. No moping, just cracking on with my comeback. Even if my return is a fallacy and no one ever reads this unpublished book, it's making the days fly by. For that, I'm eternally grateful!

Similar to Christmas Day, we were given a bag full of calories to keep us grateful, quiet, and compliant, on New Year's Eve. Everyone excitedly lined up like retarded Oompa-Loompas. I just couldn't be part of it. This circus of infantilisation was over for 2022. The lads were as happy as Larry, as if they were queuing at the Harrods sale waiting for 75% off a £300 Dyson or a £10,000 mattress. If ever you needed proof that prison is designed to regress you back to being a four-year-old moron, this is it! As grateful as I am for a kiddie's goodie bag full of lollipops and Monster Munch, I'll pass. Not meaning to be ungracious, I politely declined and told the awkwardly genderless screw - with half a moustache under her teardrop tattoo and stubble, wearing reindeer ears and a Christmas jumper - to share mine with the other officers when they were playing strip poker once we were banged up. "If not," I suggested, "my sack of cack should go to a hotel for famished and starving dinghy divers in Dover." I just got a shrug of the shoulders, zero levity or humour. This braindead troglodyte will be the top Gov by Easter with these communication skills. I took my coronation turkey baguette, bag of prawn cocktail crisps, strawberry yoghurt, and a banana - and buggered off back to my sanctuary. I ask you...

I was excited to hear the door open moments later, and the screw spewed, "Are you sorted?" I've often wondered what would happen if you said 'no!' - it's not as if he's going to leave it open, pop a set of keys on my desk, and order me a taxi, now, is it? Anywho, the lock-turning executive gave me my cue to get on the blower to my pals and sit in blissful safety and silence - for this New Year's Eve party of one. Dorothy had been quite unwell over Christmas, as her MS was getting the better of her. This had played heavy on my heart for many weeks, and I feared the worst. My absence didn't help. This wasn't just a 'normal' blip, this felt a lot more serious. I was powerless and racked with guilt. Neither of us let on, and we continued the pantomime that I'd be home and back to my old tricks - sorting the garden, filling the freezer, and putting out the bins before you could say 'probation imbecile.' Equally, Vicky was well into chemo, and I could tell by her voice that she was struggling bigtime. Both calls were very short, but I tried to crack a couple of funnies to lift the mood. Neither of these two poorly angels had the energy to talk for long - but the comfort I got from their presence was enormous. I just wish I could have taken away some of their pain and taken on their fight – let's face it, I'd got nothing else to do. We ended with the pointless platitude of 'Happy New Year' - ironic for one of the most reflective and depressing nights of the year. During my time Pleasuring His Majesty, I've had hundreds of letters from people feeling desperate after a diagnosis or loss. As I spent more and more time in the chapel - never missing a service - I couldn't help but question why life is so tough for so many people. Why are our lives littered with so much tragedy and challenge? Honestly, one of the most important lessons I've learned in custody is that there's always someone worse. Being useless is a far worse sin than being a convicted talker. As bad as it is... at least I'm not Gary Lineker.

Next came the fun calls to my mates who could gossip for hours. Especially BBJ, Nick, Jan, Claire, Anneka, Steve, Stewart, Giles, Hayden, Anne, Kev, Clive and the three James', Alice, Anna, Bobby, Jon C, Andrew, Karen, Nicholas, Robin, Viv, Miles, Dean, Helen, Johny, Charlotte, Emma, Robin, Fred - oh, and of course Horseface Hopo, who could talk for thirty minutes and never draw breath. She, indeed, could talk the hind legs off a well-hung donkey. 'Why the long face, love?' It was only my limited £5-a-night budget that cut the blither short. That's still a good two plus hours. OK, I upped it to £7 on such nights. You have to throw the boat out sometimes......ask the French in Calais. We laughed every single night as I called these angels in rotation. I especially loved slagging off HMP and .gov parasites - small pleasures to entertain the snooping 'Public Protection' mafiosi. They were my energiser bunny. My sister, parents, nephew, and godkids were always the fireworks display in my heart. No words can explain how these people collectively kept me alive on every human level. I endured the pitiful New Year's Eve TV - and, at exactly midnight, I called my mother and wished her a Happy 2023. She was over the moon that I'd called. She cried like Jimmy Carr getting his tax return. It's moments like this when, on the one hand, you feel the power of love... and, on the other, digest the wicked and evil dark forces that created this bullshit. It was a magic call - underscoring that love always outweighs sick liars and cheats. We win! Light always kills darkness. Happy New Bloody Year, dear!!!

New Year = New Start (Wish me Luck....)

2023 started on a Sunday, so I had an appointment in the chapel - which was a brilliant distraction from the laborious repetition of the wing, especially during a long weekend. The service, like all others, was uplifting, thanks to Tim's delivery and Angel Anne's boundless and supreme optimism. He'd mastered the art of 'less is more' - your only option in this

ADHD-infested asylum. I, of course, was buoyed by the joyful noise of our little band, which inspired me greatly - unlike some of the readings that I could barely comprehend. You need to be Stephen Hawking to keep up with the goings on of the Thessalonians and Judas. Did you know Judas was the first chairman of the Labour Party? The 1st January is always a new start, and I tried to reflect on my achievements of surviving the slammer and 'the system' for over three months, but more importantly the previous two years of relentless establishment hounding and take down. I don't believe my assassins and saboteurs thought I'd be alive by 2023, let alone sat behind a wooden aging upright (think Rees-Mogg) in a Christian rock band!

You spend a lot of time, in this dumping ground for depraved douchebags, questioning your own integrity. You have to reconcile your actions, choices, and your moral compass. The world was changing faster since Covid than ever before in history. Politics was now as PC as comedy. You can't even raise your voice without being accused of inciting a riot. No one has an honest conversation - and if you put your head above the parapet, you're racist, sexist, homophobic. And dare mention Transformers? You're instantly cancelled! The brainwashing 'group think' had become an epidemic......even in jail! After my obliteration and galactic take down, I realised we HAVE to question the agenda behind all convictions. So, preconceptions are risky. Did I want to go through the next years blind to the humanity of my con colleagues? Already, I'd changed. You cannot judge a book by its conviction. Poetic, hey?! My job was now to <u>understand</u> these people. Pointing fingers only leads to three more pointing back at you – look at my case. My can of worms is still wiggling. My story is far from over.

The New Year's Day service was very pleasant and passed too quickly. We had a cup of coffee and some biscuits afterwards...then back to reality. Time had passed and only the positives were stored and remembered. My edit muscle is in overdrive - to cut the crap and drink in the deliciousness of my experience as and when it came, even if momentarily. I've come to realise that 'negative' time in life is simply endured and then instantly forgotten by the brain - just like a flight, sitting through an episode of *EastEnders*, or watching *Harry Potter* in the West End. Zzzzz. The brain is INCREDIBLE! No matter what torture you may feel at the time, the brilliant brain excretes dullness almost immediately once it's over. Remember when Oprah interviewed Harry and Meghan? Nope. You see - ta-da! GONE! I already understood 'the game' and realised that prison is a circus. It's all fur coat and no knickers - an artifice that is not real. Half of the screws are more crooked and criminal than most cons. Why should I invest in this façade? I have to remain stoic and rise above the noise. Everyone is faking it. Officers are often more flawed than the criminals they're 'looking after.' They certainly don't worry about their hair or personal hygiene! For me, I'd seen the pitfalls - and it was eyes wide open. Most officers were absolutely great and quickly realised that I just wanted to be left alone. I had no interest in these penguin-dressed cuff holders -and most were too busy with numbskulls to bother with me. I was thrilled to be in my own little world. By now, it was clear that I had become entertainment for staff and officers via YouTube, which, of course, was on fire with the loons. My 'star' was rising as high as Uranus... but this then caused a backlash from the Celia Imries upstairs.

My twenty-year media archive was still available for the world to watch, much to the fury of the mentals. YouTube and Twatter are alive and kicking, as they couldn't find a thing wrong, isn't it curious that the Clown Court did......with exactly the same material! We know various senior BBC gobshites tried relentlessly to get me closed down on all platforms - to no avail. There was not one breach to justify it. Many at HMP let their curiosity override their clear directive not to Google any prisoner whatsoever. This is, in fact, a sackable offence. Who can blame them? In a sea of bland, I was the most fascinating and exciting thing to happen at Stocken - having interviewed Peter Andre in 2005! What they do on their own tippy-tappy is their business, right? You can sense when someone knows you. Having fame (or notoriety) is peculiar... especially in the pokey. It becomes a sixth sense when you know they know. They can't help reacting slightly differently - and hold eye contact a few seconds longer than everyone else. I've had the odd officer and civvy just come straight out with it, but most are cautious. Often, it was more a nod, a wink, or an 'Alo, Chunky' that would give the game away about my infamy. Other old-school screws (men of a certain age) didn't give a fack. 'Can't wait for you to be back Belfield.

"Whatever you did, the trolls will regret it when you come back bigger - and then you can set the record straight!" This always made me ten feet tall... enough to get me through another day.

F wing did feel like a drop-in centre for whack job......officers. Screw Singleton (who I called Simpleton) was chief head the ball, who made my inner thighs chaff! You know the type. The first in the shady local pub and the last out – always alone nursing his pint of the cheapest shandy. The type of boozer where you wipe your shoes on the way out. Clearly, issues with medication. Appeared to cut his own hair. Loved the barman's apron. Licked his own teeth. And literally stunk of a Glastonbury Festival port-a-loo on day three - after the *Barron Knights* legends slot! Deeply disturbed. This officer was proper nuts. I never had a cross word with 'it' - I wouldn't even look at it. But, being a nosy parker, I don't miss a trick. Like a lamb to the slaughter, all he wanted was my attention and for me to engage. Why can't these oddballs leave me alone? One day, good cop: 'Do you need anything?' The next: 'Hurry up, Belfield!' - when I wasn't going anywhere or doing anything. IGNORE! Totally off his head. RED FLAG CRAZY. A 5* douchebag of epic proportions. He opened a pad directly opposite me and snooped around - knowing the kid was at work. He banged the window (pretending to do AFC's = security checks), then proceeded to inhale smoke from the fella's vape and had a drink out of his cup on his desk. How creepy is that? Makes my skin crawl. One day, he brought me a pile of letters two inches thick. I said, "Can I have a pair of gloves, Gov?" He said, "Why?" I replied, "You can't be too careful when officers have fingered my punters' lovely letters." He slammed the door and stormed off. Zero humour or levity.

After Katie's third video to 'big me up,' I had three bosses come to my door asking me about Hopkins. They all had different excuses. My reply infuriated them. All I said was, "Oh, isn't she lovely, you'd love her if you met her. She's a hoot. One of us, Gov!!!" They didn't know what to say. Of course, they'll never meet her, and if they did, like me, she'd give them a wide berth and short shift!!! They couldn't bait me. This ain't my first rodeo. These halfwits can't, won't, and didn't, catch me out. This pissed them off even more - that I wouldn't engage. Woeful mind games by humans with the communication skills of a jelly fish fart. Pfft.

<u>A New Job – A New Year</u>
Good news!!! I got the gig in the library. Best gig of my career! A note came through via an 8am wakeup call from a joyful kanga. "Helen says can you go to the library if you want the job." I was as pleased as punch. It's the warmest and most civilised place in the entire 'B&B for the Braindead.' It was known as being the most cushty gig, as it's not only a piece of piss, but you have the most freedom and comfort, away from all screws and prison politics. The library is a kanga-free zone - identical to the chapel - and was run by two diamonds who were just 'normal' women (of a certain age), who avoided all of the crap that the Prison Service throws at its staff daily. They were

totally immune from the politics. I was working half a day, like everyone else. Due to staff shortages, full-time jobs were part-time jobs - to give twice as many people an opportunity to get out of their pads. This is the same across most jails, whilst the estate is on its arse. Clever box-ticking to make it look like twice as many men have 'purposeful activity' whilst in custody. Another fake, disingenuous mirage by the authorities - to make them appear more noble than they are. They said I could come in full-time and help out... or just write my books and letters, just like I'd been doing for the last three months. Someone was looking down on me. Helen could see I was no bother and brought an element of serenity to her palace of words. I'd be working alongside three men whom I became very fond of. A man called Alfie was truly the most positive and smartest man I encountered in the system so far. He, like me, could see through all of the bullshit and lunacy of the broken system. Equally, he had a fabulous family and missus, and he wisely viewed this as a pointless blip - a waste of a very small percentage of his life. He masterfully kept the slammer in perspective; and being only in his thirties, he had his life in front of him. He was well educated and very successful. He'd driven some drugs for a pal and had the book thrown at him for a first offence because it involved 'Encro' - encrypted phones... the hot potato in the war against drugs. He got ten years. Brutal - but a risk you take if you want to profit from sniff. Unlike me, he owned his crime and accepted his wrong-doing - but could also see that he was the fall guy for some very rich and powerful men above him, who will never be caught. He just got on with it. The Colombian marching powder barons are always a step ahead!

I also worked with two brothers who were in for cooking the books. They had a building company which cleverly bought and sold jobs and products, avoiding tax - and were facing an eye-watering POCA (Proceeds of Crime Act) that could floor, break, and destroy both of them. Both men had wives, children, jobs, homes, family - perfect lives. These men weren't bad people; they'd simply made very bad choices to benefit their families. They chanced their arm and got caught. Fair dos. None of them were a risk to society....... but they had to be punished. The system had chosen to pursue them, but instead of letting it go -knowing that their lives were destroyed by their freedom and liberty being taken away (at huge cost to their families) - now they wanted them bankrupt and homeless, to put the final nail in the coffin. I found this astonishing as we (you) will pick up the bill. Force these very smart men to work for society on restrictive tags under defined house arrest. 'Victimless' crime - as it's known - takes up years of cells all over the country, at huge cost. Alfie alone will cost you £500,000 simply to hold him hostage, for no benefit to society. He's a smart man! We could profit from his degree and save £50k a year in the process. Victimless? That stinks of horseshit more than my prosecution file. They go straight to CAT-D with no courses, as there are no identified victims boohooing at trial. Ermmm... Surely, those who are owed money, or druggies whose lives are ruined, ARE victims - just like the little old ladies they mug to feed their habits. Not in the eyes of the court, probation, or the Prison Service. Victimless crime? My hairy white arse!

This pattern is repeated throughout every prison: the smartest (most sensible) lads get the best jobs - and are punished even less than average men, simply because of the privileges tied to their 'position.' To me, this makes a total mockery of the entire system... of which I now include myself. We were in the warmest, quietest, safest, and easiest job in the slammer. Two fraudsters, one drug dealer, and a convicted talker! I'll accept, thank you very much. Wouldn't 24/7 house arrest on a tag be a better punishment for 'victimless' crimes - and make them do an online job for .gov to literally pay back society on minimum wage? I, for one, would have hated that far more than pissing around with this merry dance of a façade. Alfie, Tony, and Gareth were funny, very smart, and big on news - it was a hoot going to work every day. It won't get better than this. The two other orderlies on the other shift were true characters as well. One was a lifer who had zero ambition to ever leave the glamour and comfort of his cell (or indeed HMP). And the other chap – Swifty - was one of the cleverest but most flawed human beings I've ever met. I loved his candour. He knew every prison law off by heart. He infinitely entertained me. He loved my story and found the insanity intriguing. Lee is a gent, but a huge victim of the system. They had screwed him over from arsehole to breakfast time. He always had a genuine smile after nearly twenty years in almost every slammer in the UK. I have no idea how he kept his composure.

The library is required to have a full copy of prison law PSI's. Swifty knew every page - to the fury of the bosses. This document is thousands of pages long and is the only way that smart inmates can fight the system - by reminding Govs of their own rule book. There are very clear rules - that 99% of officers and staff have never heard of. I've had a lot of run-ins with 'You can't do that'... to which I reply, 'What is the PSI number?' You're always met with a blank look - and never hear about it again. How can 99.99% of staff not know the law they're governed by? At the HMS Stockings library, you didn't need the three large lever-arch folders full of blithering legal babble. You simply needed to ask Swifty. He's the oracle - having been away a VERY long time - and frankly has little hope of release. He's also IPP, with no end date. Every time he gets close to the finish line, they trip him up. He's failed several paroles, yet appeared to me to be simply too smart for the dopes trying to manage him - most of whom are one-tenth his intelligence. I saw zero risk in him at all. I would trust him implicitly, something I never found at the BBC, let alone with the police knuckle-draggers running this entire sham. He was renowned for suing HMP for their failings and they hated him for it. 'How dare he?' = He dare! I love him for that. I couldn't help but see a little bit of him in me - and vice versa. We're virtually the same age, but he's spent half of his life in this HMP vortex, trying to seek sanity and freedom. This guy was totally fearless, unthinkably smart, and switched on. He knew how to play the system and could outwit almost every ignoramus running the asylum. As soon as he had them on the ropes, they'd shanghai him to a new pokey. If only he could be given the chance to focus his genius mind and memory on something positive, he could be such a valued member of society. Sadly, like so many, his temper always gets the better of him - after being mercilessly provoked - leaving him trapped in the matrix of the baiting slammer. It was their revenge for him constantly outwitting the system.

A Year Older and Probation HELL

My birthday came and went on the 14th January. It had mostly been around this date for most of my life, so it didn't come as a shock or surprise. Hopkins had rallied the troops again to send more cards - causing even more palpable fury from the Celia Imries who needed me persona non grata. The messages were gorgeous; the heart-warming sentiments of hope were inspiring. And the fact everyone now knew I was forty-three (not twenty-seven in showbiz years) was the most devastating disaster of this entire captive situation! I'm not a birthday guy - couldn't care less, to be honest. I shudder at the idea of a 'surprise' party or a birthday 'do' - gives me hives. Being protected by prison doors from party poppers and cheap Pissecco was a big relief. I'm as youthful in my head and uplifted in spirit as Sharon Osbourne's face... She'll probably have had another two new ones before this goes to print. Didn't she get the memo about Joan Rivers?...Anyway, that's not why you called!

Of course, psychopath Officer Shifferbrains pounded in on the 15th with a huge pile of cards. "Sorry they're late," he said. I replied, "It's most curious that you know the date of my birthday. You aren't stalking me, are you, Gov?" He went bright red, threw a hundred-plus envelopes on my bed, and stormed out. Twat. Almost as if this Poundland PCSO and his bunch of badass wet-wipe suppositories choreographed the delivery after my big day. You see, this is how thick and vindictive the troublemakers and shit-stirrers are in jail. The gag, if you're that vile and manipulative (with an unfeasibly small man sausage), is to play stupid. Pretend you know and ask, 'When is your birthday?' I, of course, couldn't give two shiny shites - as long as I got them. I just LOVED reading my incredible letters of positivity - and spent most of my day, for the next two months, replying to them. What a blessing. I left them hung up all over the pad for a month, and then posted them all back out to my parents for them to enjoy. Who knew the second bundle (probably 80 cards) never arrived?

Jealous, scum sucking pondlife clearly threw them in the bin. At least it kept waste management busy shredding them. I hope it made Officer Nobcheese and Gov Clayballs happy! I'm a big fan of being green. I've been recycling gags for thirty years - so this is old news to me. Karma will get them, like the duplicitous snakes they are.

By the end of January, I had sent various requests to see my 'offender manager' about my progress - to no avail. These weasels were frantically avoiding me in the corridor, as they knew what was coming. I don't blame them. I wouldn't want a rollicking from me when I've got a bee in my bonnet over the two cancelled OASYS calls and radio silence from the box-tickers. For some reason, the perfectly reasonable Connie Lingus had disappeared. My demands were apparently simply 'overwhelming her' - despite never seeing her since the day I arrived. This is .gov speak for 'bring in the big guns to try and piss him off'... and they did! Look, I've worked in communications all my life, and I'd like to think my ONLY talents are reading the room, intuition, and my instant perception of a situation. Despite everyone telling me to keep the faith, I knew these appalling people were totally disingenuous. I couldn't have been more right - it was a brewing shitstorm, designed to prolong everything indefinitely simply to buy time. Nothing makes my piss boil more than lying, cheating, disingenuous, front-stabbing civil serpents. The ogres would, sooner or later, have to show their pimple-filled, wrinkly, haggard two faces.

However, one of the advantages of having a 'trusted' or top job in the clink is that you get to see, meet, and talk to people who ordinarily love to hide behind bars... and locked doors. On Mondays, at the happy ship Stockings, they do OMU induction in the library. Well, I was like a praying mantis, waiting for my opportunity to slap it on the table and find out what the hell was going on - and why Connie Thunder Thighs is avoiding me like a bout of syphilis. I saw the fear as they walked in and saw me sat at my library reception desk. I could hear their internal dialogue: 'How the fack did he get this job?' They clearly had no idea about my promotion and must've missed the memo. I was courteous, of course, but after they'd finished their talk - which included, 'Sadly, there's nine-month delays for top courses and three-month delays on sentence plans and OASYS' - it was a devastating blow. It confirmed that prison probation is hapless, hopeless, broken, and entirely unfit for purpose. In one sentence, this woman had confessed to a year's delay for every man before you even start to progress - through no fault of their own. It's a total outrage to prevent the human right of liberty for a year, simply because 'We're drowning in work, as we have a hundred men each' - their next public confession. Shameless! This marble-mouthed, mardy quiche eater confessed, "Sadly, the system is broken, but we're doing our best, so please be patient."

I was facked, just like everyone else! Patience? Patience?! This is prison not the bleeding post office queue! Afterwards, I asked Alfie which one of the rainbow flag flyers was the big boss. He pointed to a Hilary Devey lookalike… just without the finesse, posh accent, or stunning looks. I minced over like a cheetah pursuing an obese rhino in the Serengeti. It appeared she was wearing a dead beaver on her head - not dissimilar to Cupid Stunt in the eighties.

We'll call this bingo-winged, ham-fisted, and aggressive (not smart enough to be passive) boss woman Fanny Schmelling - as she had a Bavarian accent, a moustache, and looked identical to an ex-girlfriend's lady parts after having her sixteen babies. RIP.

Fanny had a Claudia Winklebottom fringe - deliberately intended to prevent all eye contact, as she was a typical government-employed liar. It was likened to having a conversation via a parrot's cage - bet she'd had a cockatoo over the years, judging by her limp, cold sore, and shaky wrist. This breed of hideously unattractive, brainwashed, and corporate munter use their hairline to cover their putrid, sour-puss features - often powered by the stench of their cheap B&M perfume, called 'Au De AZ Juice.' Thank God I saw this beast coming... well, you couldn't miss it, what with the fire coming out of its nose and the broomstick attached to its unfeasibly enormous anus erectus. "Hello, Alex." Oy vey - it talked at me. 'We'd never met before, so how does this slapper know my name?' I thought.

Good lord, this creature made Jo Brand's gunt seem attractive. The biggest joke of all is that I ended up with a second OMU bird, as I was such 'high risk' Fanny clearly needed backup and protection – 'in case I misquoted her.' Sadly, I don't speak with a stutter, as if I've got two plums and a chipolata in my mush. We'll call the other nose-pierced, Doc Marten wearer Lotty Beaverhousen, to avoid yet another High Court writ! I suddenly started getting letters from Fanny saying, 'Please stop requesting phone apps,' and, 'Please don't send another app until we've replied to the last app.' Being me, I, of course, replied with: 'Thank you for your reply. I won't write again until you've replied... provided that is within seven days.' Then the daft heifer would send another app saying, 'I've told you not to send an app until I've replied.' So I'd reply back: 'Dear Fanny, I hope you're well. Apologies for replying to your reply. I assure you I won't needlessly reply to your reply again... provided you reply within seven days.' <u>FURY!!!</u> Can you imagine how incandescent with rage this imbecile was? Talk about hoist by your own retard. They do not have a button for such confidence, lack of respect, and intentional insolence.

My worst default position is contempt. I truly couldn't care less - and that left me with nothing to lose. I already knew I had as much chance of imminent CAT-D as Kia Cars Starlin has of winning a second election. I'd been here before - many times in life - where the writing is on the wall, like a dirty protest, identical to my sentencing circus. These supercilious sanctimists take themselves SO seriously and never change their opinion. You cannot win! I could see I was back in the vortex of BBC middle manager hell - or even negotiating with Police mafia cuntstables... and that only ends one way. I'm not daft, contrary to the propaganda. OMU = (Overweight, Mingtastic & Ugly) - the gatekeepers for whoever was puppeteering this captive witch hunt. You must have had those meetings where nothing you say or do is right. It's identical to arguing with the Mrs (which is like trying to go through a revolving door on skis). I can only talk to the current Mrs B one week in four. She's either 'on,' 'coming on' or 'coming off.' My instinct is never wrong – especially with lady parts when they're off on one. I knew it was hopeless from day one, and these menopausal, men-hating broads were not for turning. They could see I had zero fear or reverence, and this got right on their pendulous and redundant jelly wobblers.

They knew I was no risk and would never break a rule, so they needed to find a plan to drag this out. We now know they'd already been told that my stats were so low (and my conviction so silly) that they couldn't 'punish' me with a single rehabilitation programme whatsoever - but when were they going to tell me? Now they needed to stop me seeing this report confirming the good news - at <u>ALL</u> costs!

Obviously, my intentional gloating letters to my punters - underscoring daily that I was OK, prison was a piece of piss - oh, and OMU were now proven dickwads, devious, duplicitous donuts, and undeniably absolute thick Judas' - only poured flames on the fire for them to keep me in my place! I can only be me. They were tasked to change me and entice me TO GIVE UP BROADCASTING! Good luck with that, my dearios. They'd got more chance of making The BBC One Show entertaining or convincing Huw Edwards not to be a nonce. I'll pass! NEXT.......

Chapter 25

HMP's First Spiteful and Vindictive Revenge!

By the end of January 2023, HMP Stocken were spitting feathers. I now had an entire team of officers managing my mail in and out, under the authority of OMU - who were even more determined to vindicate their fixation and catch me out. I was their #1, most high-profile, and gobbiest 'project' yet. Every word was read, photocopied, and passed 'up' in the hope they could prove I broke protocol, breached their dopey rules - or, best of all, had broken the law, thereby extending my kidnapping to twenty-plus years on a full life sentence. My data file later proved Fanny Schmelling spent all day snooping on my private calls, with the same dark intentions: to find a crime that never occurred. Nosy hairy arsed bastards aren't they. Maybe if they spent more time going after lunatics with knives instead of potty-mouthed DJs, fewer kids would be killed! Do you remember? A 'real' stalker had been sent to HMP Notts for stalking Emily Maitlis. Within days of arriving, this prick wrote to her to apologise and explain why he was nuts. BINGO! They gave him extra time, ran a huge PR campaign, and confirmed his obsession - just to justify imprisoning that man. That's what they needed from me. The police were still working in the background to find dirt... and came up with nothing. I still think when they kept illegally raiding my house, they hoped for their 'wardrobe' moment - like in *Bodyguard*, with all the obsession sellotaped to the doors. FAIL! To finish me off and close me down forever, they needed a golden bullet. Nearly all real stalkers contact their victim whilst in jail. I was too busy writing this scribe to waste ink on such insane pointlessness.

Next, Katie tried to book a visit. This was the final straw. OMU showed their true vindictive colours and made it clear: a royal visit from Horseface Hopo was not acceptable - and they planned revenge for my audacity by forcing me to move wings, to teach me a lesson. This wasn't going to be the cushy Newton 'enhanced' - oh no, this was gangsters' paradise. It was time for some just deserts, and for 'the state' to put me in my place. 'This can be made very difficult for you, Mr Belfield,' was the menacing and sinister line vomited towards me by a screw in the corridor. This takedown had failed miserably. These vile probation thickos couldn't have done a better job of showing their true bully colours - and they'd not even been brave enough (or had the courtesy) to talk to me face to face yet!!! It's commonly known that one of the Prison Service tactics to 'break' men is a 'disruptive move' - where they shift you to another wing or jail simply to test you, provoke you, and maliciously unnerve you, as punishment when there's no prison breach or nickable offence. I couldn't be moved out of HMP Stocken, under order from the MOJ, so they found the worst wing in the clink to teach me yet another lesson — and tried to pretend this was perfectly normal and not malicious whatsoever.

Heads were exploding, piss was boiling, and tits were tingling at my continued mocking of the system - in my letters and on the blower. They hoped and predicted I'd have kicked off by now, or be dangling from the balcony. Prison is like a leaky sieve, and I'd got a lot of insider spies tipping me off daily with the secret plans of the mob. I was 'enhanced,' and I knew my behaviour was exemplary - so anything hairy old establishment heifers said was irrelevant. No amount of convincing me I was a 'naughty boy' carried any credence, considering my unblemished file. You can't be enhanced and a bad lad. Full stop! This was all manufactured bullshit. If there was any serious breach of anything leading to a formal IPF (adjudication) it would have to be put in writing - and I'd be put on 'standard' or 'basic' and shoved in front of a governor. Inviting Motor Mouth Mavis was deliberately inflammatory on my part – but – perfectly within the rules. Katie was doing gangbusters online and had an enormous following. Her allegiance was so much appreciated.

Katie called up visits and the shit hit the fan. Five gormless screws tried to get me to talk about it. 'She's a wonderful mother. Very kind to animals.' I would reply. Bye! Piss Off. You see, the biggest 'no-no' in jail is coercive behaviour toward officers - or manipulation. This comes under corruption, and you're shipped out immediately if found guilty. I never wanted to get into any deep, meaningful, or important conversation with any kanga - especially about live wires like Hopo! They'd love that *Guardian* headline: 'Belfield Corrupts Officer.' Pfft. Grow up. Funnily enough, an HMP Kirkham Gov got nine years behind bars today for schtupping a con - nasty business! A huge price to pay for a quick shag, isn't it? As I say, these prison bosses are not to be trusted. If you're not careful they'll fack you from breakfast time to arsehole…..just ask her convicted drug dealer boyfriend. I wouldn't even offer them my last Rolo, as I know it would be twisted. They're not my friend, and I couldn't be happier about that - with very few exceptions. I'm meant to be anonymous, and so are they! From time to time, I'd write 'very clear jokes' in my letters. I'd say, 'I saw Officer Beef Curtains today, and she gave me some Stilton and crackers. The kindness of these officers is overwhelming.' So funny. They'd be running around like headless chickens, trying to find Officer Pissflaps - over another gag I'd said about bringing me in a couscous salad from Waitrose. Bunch of twats! I have a lot of time on my hands! It was now red rag to a bull. The more they tried to stitch me up, catch me out, and wrong-foot me, the more I kicked back - playing them at their own game. I replied with patronising and condescending COMP1s (the official complaints process, costing them about £75 each to process) simply to play cat and mouse. Dear God, what is it with me and these ambivilacious government paid robots? So, as quick as Katie appeared on my visits list - it would magically disappear. As quickly as she booked a visit - it would be cancelled. This absolute baloney carried on until we had to give up. Horseface Hopkins NEVER made it to HMS Stockings. They couldn't tell me, but it clearly had been vetoed from the very top - and 'the powers that be' had made themselves very clear! How on earth she coped without Stocken's renowned, out-of-date, dry and crumbly bacon baps - that had about as much moisture in them as her lady garden - is absolutely beyond my comprehension! Other, less controversial stars did make it in. My buddies Richard and Fred from Right Said Fred got it past security. It was such a joy to see them. I can assure you they're not too sexy for my shirts! The boys have been so loyal and followed me everywhere. I'm indebted for their time, kindness, and solidarity. Their visit caused a nice stir around the slammer. But there was no way HMP was having Katie in! She was the mammoth-mouthed step too far. Imagine her 'downstairs piercing' setting off the metal detector - I've heard she's got a hanging basket down there, it's so big. Naturally, Katie made a YouTube video telling our punters that our visit had been sabotaged. That didn't go down very well either. I don't think Katie and I had the reverence and respect the establishment were hoping for.

I'd been working in the library for a few weeks, and I quickly worked out that one way to get prison-wide access and exercise was by regressing to age fourteen - as a paper boy. Every day, about fifty newspapers were delivered to the wings, and one of us had to take them. The other lads didn't like the cold, but I'd got a huge grey-and-orange-rimmed jacket, a pair of gloves, and two jumpers - so I was as happy as a sandboy. Every morning, around 10am, I'd get a two-mile walk through the covered outside corridors (I don't do getting moist), and I'd take my time touring the entire nick, top to bottom, at my own pace - gossiping with any nice people as I went about my business. It was not dissimilar to my morning mince around the country park. It was magnificent. I laughed so loud at myself in my minds' eye - thinking I'd gone from a $1million YouTube career to paper boy for £1.25 a day. I loved it - as it gave me (relative)

FREEDOM! I didn't need money – but I was a millionaire again in spirit. This was the best gig in town. I delivered the Daily Sport to K Wing with great flag waving pride!

I dropped our papers off at F Wing, and the tattooed, dark-souled screw - who was regularly found in tears in the office, moaning about his life and cheating girlfriend - said, "Bad news. We need your pad. You're being moved." I asked, "Where to?" They answered, "Not sure." So I asked the only thing I cared about: "Is it a single pad?" They looked at me and sarcastically said, "You're high-risk cell-share, so you can't ever share with anyone." I said, "Oh yes, very risky messing with me. I might write about you in my autobiography." Touché. Then I asked, "Is the Gov available? I don't want to get anyone into trouble if they've made another mistake." He screamed, "Mistakes? Mistakes? What the fack do you mean?!" I said, "Nothing Sir, your reputation goes before you!" I walked into the SO Dan Gleeball's office and stood on the naughty mat, as he played tapes of Hitler's speeches through his Walkman. I asked why I was being moved. "It's come from above," he said. I said, "Who? God?" He snapped, "Don't be sarcastic. It's security. Intel." I said, "Oh, does this place have intelligence? I hadn't noticed. Where can I find this intel - can I send an app?" You have to know when you're defeated. This was OMU sabotage. I'm not daft. Screws can get away with anything - hiding behind 'security' with impunity - as an IR (Intel Report) on your file can't be revealed or even removed, even if it's a lie. I got one of my spies to check my file - nothing on it. No bad behaviour - let alone an accusation or evidence of wrongdoing. It's just bullying and intimidation tactics from weak, pitiful, undertrained, young, thick staff, who needed me to rein my gobble neck in. 'We'll get him!' This is not unique to me; it happens all the time. Most men kick off, get a nicking, and end up in the block after being baited over lies and misrepresentation – then 'they've' won, and the system has got you by the balls. I was too busy writing all of this down to cause a fuss. I was sanguine that 'a cell is a cell.'

They ended up moving me to M wing. I was warned this was Gaza and very violent, mostly inhabited by young gentlemen of colour (with a lovely Amsterdam aroma through all spurs). It was also riddled with rats on the 'ones' and smackheads on the 'twos.' Don't ask about the 'threes.' I packed up my bits and bobs – cereal, mayo, cookies, milk, shampoo - and took down all of my hundreds of pics, cards, and letters. You can kick off, but that's what they wanted. Refusal would get me a nicking, giving them the right to take away my enhanced status and visits, as I'd be ignoring a direct order. We didn't give them what they wanted! I had to play the long game. As long as I had a phone, I was OK. I was secretly glad to see how bad M Wing is - for the purposes of this investigative book project. The lads popped in and said goodbye. What was unsurprising about this 'we'll teach him' event was that one-stripe 'Officer Unstable' had told the lads before he told me - another classic tactic to create embarrassment and a scene. It totally backfired. I'm shameless. I'm certainly unembarrassable. I'm 100%, undeniably unflappable. They all liked me on F Wing. Everyone knew it was a test of my nerve - I'd had it too easy for way too long. "Now let's send him to 'proper' jail for trying to outwit the pokey with what he was entitled to. Nar nar nar nar nar - playground crap." The plan to break me in the first three months had failed. So now, the trick was to get me to be in fear - another doozy. Big time. So now what??? They <u>had</u> to turn up the volume!

The horror stories about M Wing began with the single most creepy and disgusting officer I've ever met in the entire system. He looked like the Fat Controller, and had 'nonce' written all over him. I've never said this about any officer before or since. Proper evil dark web perv - the darkest soul of anyone I've met in the entire circus and system. We'll call him Hermon Monster. I cannot express how odious and unnerving this fat pig was. He'd certainly beaten his anorexia - that's for sure! Officers and prisoners alike despised and ridiculed him, before he stood there licking his own teeth and rubbing his own thighs. He was universally avoided - yet, by chance, he escorted me to my new abode. Coincidence? He was the creepy uncle no one would invite to the wedding. It was no accident that <u>this</u> piece of work was hand selected. He tried to talk to me and get me blubbering. That's not happening Dr Shipman! Akin to when the bomb squad goons wanted 'banter' in the back of the police car - I, in no uncertain terms, told him to shut the fack up and do one. Isn't it strange how we have a sixth sense for weirdos. Homosexuals have Gaydar. I have Twatdar. This paedo pouter had been moved jobs so many times at Stockings that he might as well have been given the paper boy gig in the library - just to keep him off the wings. It's very rare I feel such instant disgust for such a repugnant human being, but I couldn't help impulsively telling this deviant to get on his bike! He walked three steps ahead - and completely got my drift. Smart man.

We made it to the West Bank. "You're on the twos. The guy left quickly, so I'm not sure what the pad is like," Wayne Couzens' twin spewed. This is prison talk for: 'It's a shit hole, and we made sure he didn't clean it.' I snapped back, "Oh brill - that happened to me on F Wing, and I got two pairs of trainers and a load of vapes. Kept me in chicken legs for weeks, Gov." He went bright red, then said, "We ain't got no phones." I said, "What you say? You ain't got what, Gov?" Silence. Is this a tactic for retarded kiddie-fiddlers to buy time for their next lie or sabotage? He replied, "I ain't got no phones." I said, "Pardon?" It puked, "Belfield you ain't getting a facking phone!" I said, "I'll never cope Gov, this is awful. You've got me this time!" In blissful ignorance, I didn't fear anyone or anything now. Once you see the bait, you'll <u>never</u> be triggered. There was a buzz on the wing that the 'YouTube gobshite' was on-board, but that was about the size of it. I never had any trouble on there at all - as I was back to obscurity - just like being a Sky News presenter. He opened the pad, and it was filled with more crap than the Labour manifesto - but it makes no odds to me, as I clean everything top to bottom twice regardless. Who wouldn't, in the Marriott for Morons? It wasn't actually filthy - just a mess, which put me in mind of David Walliams's career. The walls were clean, and the view was over the fence. It'll do me. I knew in my heart I wouldn't be here long.

Unbeknown to Officer Ian Huntley, I had pre-planned the phone issue and got one of the lads to give me a spare for a pack of vapes. You <u>HAVE</u> to be a step ahead when dark forces are at play! Clay Balls on F Wing made a point of taking everything off me that I'd openly left on my desk. Again - he wanted a row. The phone was my nemesis. This was provocation - the 'intended kick-off incendiary device.' There ain't no flies on me, dear heart!!! All old-school escalation tricks to get you started. 'I'm not banging up without a phone' = instant nicking. This ain't my first rodeo with spiteful and vindictive shitheads - remember, I was at the BBC for fifteen years! What was brilliant in this pad was the fella had made four sets of shelves out of boxes and meticulously covered them in A4 clean white paper. It was brilliant for my 'cocoa butter' moisturiser (I shit you not), deodorant, 'Easy Slide' wisdom toothpicks, and Alberto hair gel – all ordered on the canteen. The creativity of some cons is inspiring. I enjoyed making the pad sparkle again. Look, no one is going to be as fastidious as me, however, most lads are very proud. It's very rare a pad is totally trashed - unless it's a dirty protest. That has to be cleaned by the bio team, who get £25 a job. They'd have to pay me £25,000 for that gig! I've never encountered a prison 'smearing event,' although I know it does occasionally happen. Last time I encountered a dirty protest, I heard the 'two-way' between Zoe Ball and Vernon Kay! There was, of course, sixteen tons of it during my trial. This pad, though, was no bother at all in comparison.

By 4pm, just before dinner, this was once again my home, identical to the last padded safe room. Seriously, what's the difference? I always took this approach. If I'm not in my own bed, I might as well be anywhere. Years - decades - on the road in entertainment equips you perfectly to adapt immediately, cope, and get on with it. So... was M Wing something out of an Eminem video? Would I end up with a Jamaican lilt by Easter? Only (doing) time would tell! Truly, it wasn't too shabby. I'd been in worse B&Bs in Ingoldmells. The lads were OK - generally less smart, younger, and definitely of various shades of grey - but, as I've found ever since, I'm invisible to druggies and troublemakers. I was still far more scared of the paedo monster screw than any con I met at the servery! There were two very nice officers on 'M' - I presume 'M' is for 'Moron Wing?' One had been a fan, and he suggested putting in an official COMP1 to Safer Custody, explaining I felt 'at risk' and 'in danger' from the gangs on the wing. (Not only was this not true, but I wasn't even aware there were gangs). I was too busy watching *Loose Women*. I filed my chitty, and SO Priscilla called me into the office the next day. This typical type - whose hair made me question whether her dad was a pelican or a drag queen - was very nice, and put me in mind of a young butch Dame Kelly Holmes, or an aging, plain version of Gok Wan. You wouldn't want a smack in the gob from her, put it that way! She had a fabulous spiky hairdo, befitting a cockatoo in the Australian bush. I liked her. She knew I'd been <u>screwed</u> over.

Priscilla was so kind and lovely and said, "You shouldn't be on here, let me call Newton and get you on there." WOW – as easy as that. What an angel. What a godsend. What a bright woman to spot the stitch-up. From the manipulation of the unbalanced F Wing - F stands for Freaks? - I was now on Gaza, and found an angel to get me to the Ritz in the blink of an eye. The Freak Wing kangas would be apoplectic with rage - clearly, Priscilla didn't want my presence on her conscience. Smart lass! After just ten days (with no incident), I was moved to Newton West and became 'super enhanced.' Signed off by Safer Custody - who have the final say and generally aren't involved in the politics - they couldn't be overruled. F Wing's vile plan had failed! It turns out that 'induction' culture is the worst in <u>EVERY</u> prison. It attracts the most malevolent of key turners. For every corrupt or mental .gov operative I've encountered, I've almost instantly been saved by a passing angel like Priscilla. Incredible. So, once again, I packed my stuff and ended up in the relative peace and luxury of the no-BS (zero tolerance) enhanced wing with the elite of the asylum. Priscilla was smart - pass 'the problem' along, keep me quiet. A wise owl! If only her mob colleagues were this evolved. I'll always be grateful to Cilla.

OK, M wing was not an afternoon tea at the Dorchester. However, it wasn't half as bad as I'd been told. I hadn't realised how strong and resilient I was until now. I genuinely didn't flinch. I was expecting a thousand times worse - and this was the *One Flew Over the Cuckoo's Nest* of HMP Stocken. The odd inbred would knock on the door for a squirt of my Hellman's, a few roast almonds, or cookies - this culture of 'Hi Alex, can I borrow...' is prolific in the penitentiary. Of course, they have no intention of giving it back. I go back to my days on my knees in the Catholic Church - 'tis more blessed to give than to receive! Despite the lack of toilet rolls, toothpaste, and ketchup - coke, ket, and even steroids are all widely available at Stocken. Many had mobiles. I knew at least ten lads, everywhere I've been, who could get me one. This doesn't say much about their highly converted 'top security' CAT-C - now, does it?

This is literally as bad as it got. One look at me, and they headed straight for zee hills. Culturally, it was no different to Leicester Square on a Saturday night - but in a prison, you're statistically less likely to get stabbed. Bravo, Sir Sickdiq! Lord of our Crapital! Clearly, the odd corrupt bent screw was at work, as the stench of weed outshone the soup dribbles down their dickies. If you suspect a screw is a druggy, you pick up any internal phone and press the hash key to report them - at any time. When you set your expectations at zero in the Big House, you're never disappointed. There's no question I was very grateful to say toodaloo and pootle down the ramp to 'N Wing.' Look, you make your own jail. You can sit chatting shit with imbeciles all day, play snap - or you can keep yourself to yourself and be invisible. I did miss talking to the lads on F Wing, but hopefully, on Newton, I'd be even better - with the library lads and most decent cons all piled onto one big unit of the best-behaved elite.

My new pad, N97 on Newton, overlooked the Leicestershire countryside. I could see for miles. This is something that means the world when you live for 'real' life - not jail bummocks. I couldn't see any of the prison. This was all luck, BTW, but a huge blessing. By far, it was the best countryside view. Your pad allocation is totally random, but to be able to watch the air display of military planes one minute, and the huge birds of prey the next, was a massive Brucie bonus. Instantly, I found a lot more older, smarter, and interesting people I could talk to. Unlike M Wing - which appeared to have a yard littered with the living dead auditioning for Stormzy's new video - Alfie, Gareth, and Tony from the library were all on Newton Wing, so it was perfect, along with Chris from the chapel. The point of N Wing is that it rewards you with the most privileges and playground time in return for best behaviour and doing the top jobs. I was cock-a-hoop, as there are two benches perfectly positioned for the sun - where I could write my novels. Ideal for the spring and summer. I spent hundreds of hours, like a pensioner in a park, sat pontificating over these epistles. Marvellous. Ultimately, with my 'profile being so active' - the last thing they needed was me being attacked or (worse) whilst detained at His Majesty's Pleasure at the HMP... no matter how much the MOJ, Police, and BBC would have loved it. So, finally, I had protection via Safer Custody, and nefarious dark forces could no longer pull my plonker or tweak my nipples of vulnerability. For the first time, I felt a 'level' of true safety - surrounded by the very best men in the clink, away from all druggies.

Prison is weird. Most lads believe that officers will do anything to get one over on you. I disagree. Most are too thick to even know how to do it - even if they tried. F Wing's attempt to piss me off was ham-fisted and failed spectacularly. The malice was absurd and obvious to all - simply because I was coping well and not defeated. I made it my business to now fly under the radar. The best screws are on the best wings, although I still found notable exceptions. I guess they're a product of their environment. Newton had a 50/50 mix of legends and ego-wanking officers - looking to whack you over the head with the threat of kicking you off, should you put a foot wrong. This was a constant 'sword of Damocles' - it was instant eviction if you misbehaved, which makes a lot of lags never want to come anywhere near this poisoned prison chalice. Sadly, the carrot of 'enhanced' is often used as a stick many men won't be part of. Their mentality is that you can't have it taken away if you don't accept it - their way of keeping control in a system built to take it.

I quickly found there were three great officers on my wing. Mr Jeffco, Miss Philipps, and Mr Ellis. All real names. I can't mention the arseholes as their lawyers (or union) will pay £300,000 for yet another gagging order. However, I will celebrate the good eggs -surely, they can't sue me for a compliment. On Newton, I was referred to as 'Mr Belfield,' and the respect was reciprocated. They'd all go above and beyond if you needed something - 5-star screws. I was low maintenance, but they were great when needed. 90% of officers just say they'll try but do bugger all! Sadly, another gem ended up arrested and sacked for corruption - but more on her later. Her penchant for six-pack muscle Marys got the better of her lady juices! That's prison. A few lads were initially furious that I'd jumped the queue to N Wing... which was fine. Listen - prison, like life, is not fair or democratic. 'You're on a list' doesn't exist......unless it's the sex offender's register! A single pad on Newton was gold dust - I was thrilled to have it, on the 'twos' - away from the roaming rats popping in from the ghetto block.

The only bad thing about enhanced wings is that, every day, you're aware of other men going home or off to open jail. I must have said, 'I'm so happy for you' a thousand times. It's like being the bridesmaid and never the groom - what's that song? *'It Should Have Been Me!'* All you can tell yourself is: 'It'll be me - one day!' I've always been an optimist (nothing to do with your eyes)! After six months, I'd worked out my 'progress' was about as likely as Greg Wallace, Scofe, Gino, or Huw Edwards making a media comeback.

By March, I'd settled in completely, loved the library job, and most importantly knew it wouldn't/couldn't get any better than this. Or could it? There were kitchens on Newton where men made three-course meals in slow cookers and air fryers – I couldn't believe my eyes! We got another hour of 'SOHA' (still don't know what that means) in the yard at 6pm, which would be brilliant in the summer.

No one in this ridiculous system speaks English - everything is acronyms. I guess 'SOHA' stands for 'Shitheads Outdoors Having Antics!' The whippersnappers didn't care. They were too busy playing pool, Xbox, table tennis, or cooking - none of which I gave one second's interest to. I loved being in the yard, in the countryside - and with summer coming, this could be a very soft touch of a stretch!

Chapter 26

At War with the Celia Imries

Prison is normally 'shushy shushy,' but HMP Stocken was a leaky sieve. I was surprised by the jungle drums beating of screw sackings - and even staff arrests over drugs. This ain't exactly a whacky warehouse in Beaumont Leys, but it appeared to be toy-town circus behind the scenes. The turnover of staff is immense. The profit from drugs (£1,000s a week) has huge allure to many - tempted by the infinite number of lads who will pay them more than a month's salary to shove a bag of smack up their crack. No one is trusted in jail - not anyone. Literally everyone - from security, staff, officers, to management - don't trust each other because of corruption. Awfully toxic way to work. A cesspit of distrust, as it's often the quiet ones who are up to the most scandalous shenanigans. I was so lucky to be with civvies in the library, catering, and the chapel - who just did their job, took the money, and ran - treating the institution with the contempt it deserved. OMU (prison probation) has real power and sit above all - with total sanctimony. They're rude and threatening towards screws, so it's not surprising how they treat cons. Despite the disproportionately female and big-boned, plain-faced demographics of OMU, their tricks were far more devious - catching a lot of men out during regular one-on-one (intimate, private, and camera-free) meetings. It appears if you're a stud muffin with a six-pack, flirt, and call munters 'babe' - suddenly, exit doors and legs appear to open wide.

The dysfunctional relationships between these 'Ugly Bettys' and the bad lads (with arms bigger than my legs) are shocking. These women, in my experience, are generally social outcasts and man-hating feminists - who love power and control, despite having no experience or qualifications. Lest we forget: two years as an officer qualifies you to move to OMU and effectively become a Clown Court judge overnight - keeping men in jail for longer than the Lord Chancellor in many cases... simply because they don't like you, or because of your political bent. I'm sure some are professional and have integrity - but I've never met <u>anyone</u> within the Prison Service who has a good word to say about these menacing mingers with more chins than a Chinese telephone directory. The bag of chips on each shoulder can be very misleading to hung and horny men who haven't got laid in a very long time. This isn't sexist, BTW - there are almost no men in the box-ticking and sabotage department. This is totally wrong, as in my opinion, men are far less dramatic, highly strung, or likely to be influenced by the man package - and tend to stick to facts, not the emotion and drama of the case.

As a breed, OMU only want subservient, compliant, reverential, grateful, and durable men... errrr... not me. I haven't met one who's read my file properly - they seem to prefer the *Daily Mail* version! I saw endless examples of many female prison probation clowns crossing the line - as things got way too personal and intimate. As you can imagine, I was having none of this nonsense, as one word and I'd be up for stalking them and blacklisted, like Russell Brand, from the 'Shag-a-lot dating agency' website. I kept demanding my OASYS (their assessment of me) and my sentence plan - which should have been given to me back in December. It was already deliberately three months late. What didn't they want me to see? Conveniently, they refused to answer the request - until I collared them in the library, during one of their induction vomitus rants - to their palpable disgust and fury.

The library is located next to OMU, and they had no choice but to regularly fly by on their broomsticks. Ouch. No longer could they hide behind their locked door - like the enigmas they are, and deliberately try to be. Their big blue door had a sign on it saying: 'DO NOT KNOCK! SEND AN APP.' As big as this door is, most OMUs still had to reverse out sideways. I'd tried sending 300 Apps - to no avail. So, in for a penny... I'd knock on it every time I passed, just for the shitz and giggles. What arrogant pricks! It's so passive aggressive. This is PEOPLE'S freedom that we're talking about. I wanted a face-to-face meeting to see the whites of their bloodshot eyes and the jaundice in their slithery skin. I'd grab the boss for a chat, let's hope it would go better than last time - hey?! On Tuesday, about 2pm, I sat at my reception desk, peeping over a fake pair of glasses (for effect), and awaiting the OMU royal visit. You never get a second chance to make a first impression! I looked like I was on the checkout at Aldi - behind my tippy-tappy for book worms. I even had a scanner to swipe the barcode - so some heroin addict didn't pinch the entire Encyclopaedia Britannica. OMU were doing their weekly induction 'fob 'em off' event and 'don't bother us' crap -

with repeat reminders of the broken system and 'unprecedented pressure.' One fella said, "I'm out in five months - so you won't even have time to start my paperwork?" - everyone laughed. Fanny Schmelling said, "Sadly, you'll have to bear with us." Bear with what? He'll be back robbing little old ladies for a fiver - before you've had time to assess him, to find out he's a flaming shuttlecock! They also do a lot of 'looking into it' at HMP. I wish they'd stop looking and just do something about it! Give me strength! This is people's lives - careers, children, and families. I was gobsmacked by the sheer disregard for liberty. By pure chance, Fanny stood behind the desk, so I said, "Alo." Dear God, I'd not felt this level of negativity, animosity, and palpable disgust since my last hideous BBC boardroom meeting - when I asked why so many journalists are hideous nonces! Ever had that feeling when an assassin is waiting for a row and ready to kick off? It was all too familiar. I said, "Hello, I'm Alex Belfield. I've been writing about my OASYS and Sentence Plan for three months - where is it?" Then it seethed back at me: "You'll have to be patient. There are more important men than you, who are a higher priority. We're sick of the amount of time you're taking up at OMU!" Oy vey - she's as bold as brass, this dope!

Wow! What a charmer! This human colostomy bag didn't even try to be professional or civil. I couldn't resist upping the stakes, I had nothing to lose - "Well why don't you send me to CAT-D and then I'm not your problem?" She screamed back with her greasy, nit ridden mush covering merkin, "You're far too high risk to go to CAT-D, you'll have to wait!" BOOM. I'd got the nasty cantankerous imbecile on the ropes and her true colours were clearer than the space between her rotten yellow teeth. "Oh, so I'm not eligible for CAT-D then – you've already decided!" I sarcastically pouted. This walking Anusol went as red as her psoriasis. "How do you know I've done it?" she fumed. I said, "Because you've just said, 'I'm too high risk to go to CAT-D,' how can you know that if you haven't ticked your boxes for the report?" "What," it snapped like a toddler spitting out its rusks. I continued, "If you haven't done the report, you've just revealed your personal prejudice. You're not another incompetent Civil Service assassin are you, who has gathered your judgment from the *Daily Mail* or mental bulldog-faced loons on YouTube? That would be gross misconduct, Miss!!" She literally stormed off with a trail of cheap perfume and the stench of Gregg's steak bakes wafting behind her hippo-sized posterior. BTW, can anyone tell me why OMU's arses hang six inches lower than proper biological women? Asking for a friend at HMP Belmarsh. I'll leave it with you...

I knew I was facked - in that moment. I'm not even six months in - it's game over. I felt it in my bones! I was straight back to 'that feeling' in the Clown, where I didn't stand a chance. It was all pre-decided. Little women, with no talent, skill, passion, or experience - wielding their personal vendetta to cause you misery, backed by their over-promoted entitlement, government protection, and impunity. I don't know what was worse - her inner thighs chafing together, or her double chins dangling like stalactites. Never seen so many arms flapping since Windy

Miller. What had I done to generate such a disproportionate overreaction? Where had this vitriol come from? Why is there such paranoia towards me from goons paid by the state? Regardless, they ALL appear to believe they're beyond reproach! Wonder if it was that time of the month again? Just my luck, hey?! Here we go again....

The following day, the nose-pierced and sandal-wearing wonder slithered into the library with two bundles of A4. Piff, Paff, Pouf. This was Lotty Muffdiver, now replacing the repugnant - sorry, redundant (and AWOL) - Connie Lingus. She apparently had greater priorities... or was it that she'd dropped a bollock by telling me I would go to CAT-D if I kept my head down when I walked through the door on day one? Lotty came bearing gifts: my OASYS (official Gov stats etc.) and their manufactured Sentence Plan -created on the back of a fag packet, manipulated and engineered without any input from me, and distorted by AI dark forces. The plan was conspired alongside the creative imagination of a civil serpent gatekeeper, whose sole function seems to be keeping me gagged, silent, and behind bars indefinitely. All while they try to convince the system that I pose a genuine high risk to the public. What a stitch-up! Oh, this would be fun. I said, "I'll read it, but how can you write two reports having never spoken to or met me? This is very curious." She shrugged her hunched-back shoulders. Speechless and embarrassed, she left in a hurry - dragging her dungarees along the corridor whilst clutching her pearls and 47 friendship bracelets, humming Taylor Swift anthems. Lord, take me now.

Are these clowns incapable of answering any questions? Fortunately, Gareth and Alfie both heard the conversation. Both were absolutely gobsmacked. Alfie, in his usual ebullient way, said, "You're facked, mate." He nailed it. This was a new level of disdain the trolls would love to aspire to. Everyone could see this was a total impasse before we'd even started. It was hopeless - and intended to be so.

That afternoon, I sat at my tippy-tappy in the library and made notes. The good news was my official and now undeniable recidivism (chance of repeat offending and risk to the public) was officially 0.19%. That, by definition, excluded me from every single HMP course available, however, on my Sentence Plan old Narky Nickers had written I had to complete 'KAIZEN' – this is a course for violent reoffenders with a risk over 60%. Ahhhh......I see what Fanny Schmelling has done here. A less than 1% chance of re-offending gave her zero, nil, nada, zilch scope to mess with me. I qualified for nothing - so all she had left was dirty tricks. This blotch on the contract would take months to correct. Pfft. I counted 86 lies, inaccuracies, mistakes, and general horse shittery in these documents - conjured from the fantasy of a 'person' in London who I'd never met. I think most lies had been copied and pasted from Lucy Letby's file for a laugh. You've never seen such foolishness - but it's entirely to be expected from a mafiosi with nowhere else to go. How could my 0.19% get any lower? Finally, the chickens were coming home to roost. It was laughably ridiculous - but entirely to be expected. Obviously, this situation was absurd but spoke volumes. I could only laugh. Because my actual crime (in reality) was a first offence not involving drugs, weapons, violence, or sex, I didn't tick a single box to require ANY rehabilitation... BUT they didn't want me to know that. Most morons would get pissed off and do nothing. OMU do this all the time. I'm not the only one - thousands of men face the same unforgivable lies but are unable to defend themselves. IF caught out, OMU simply say, 'It was a mistake.' Algorithms were 100% on my side for CAT-D. Now it was one seedy game of delay to keep me captive. Then came the killer blow: 'You must engage with the National Stalking Hub.' Blimey, if I contact them, they might accuse me of stalking them! What could possibly go wrong? It later became clear 'the stalking hub' DOES NOT EXIST - it's psychology. But they didn't want to call it that! They now wanted to diagnose me as mad, in a fishing exercise akin to the three illegal police raids - hoping to uncover some dirt to prolong and justify this hostage situation. Cunning. It felt like they'd stop at NOTHING to wipe me out forever - or, at the very least, keep me captive until the very last day of my sentence.

The mistakes on my OASYS report were endless, they hadn't even got my address right. I was signed off as homeless – they can dream.... I sent a list of every lie to the OMU boss. She hit the roof, writing back 'I'm a professional. How dare you undermine my authority, questioning my decisions, OMU stands by both documents.' A few days later, at the OMU induction in the library, I once again approached fire breathing Fanny. I said, "How can I qualify for a repeat offender's course when I'm a first offender which was non-violent?" It replied, "Well, Mr Belfield I believe words are weapons and therefore you used them repeatedly to be violent!" I laughed in their face. What else could I do? How do you even communicate with such an odious and vitriolic sphincter? I said, "So, if you walked in my pad and I was watching The Tellytubby's on CBoobies, you'd write on my OASYS that you think I'm a paedo - based on ZERO evidence?" She rolled her eyes and stared at her colleague. "Now you're being ridiculous Mr Belfield." I said, "You started it dear." Then this marble-mouthed Mogadon screamed, "DON'T CALL ME DEAR." She's right. I shouldn't have called her 'dear' - I should have called her 'Babe' – it's a great film!

This had not gone well. Her steadfast arrogance and defiance said it all. Alfie was right, I was fooked! You can't argue with stupid. They knew they were exposed and caught out, but in typical authoritarian style, they weren't budging, because that would give the game away. This was the only option they had left – more establishment lies and figments of imagination to make the clock tick down. Hijacking them in the library for the third time would once again lead to revenge. They answer to no one! I was back in the vortex of wicked box-tickers - clearly willing to cheat and distort all reality to buy time at any cost. All those around me told me to keep the faith, play the game, and join the circus. I knew it was pointless.

Since arriving, I'd written several letters to my OMU on the library computer, which I was perfectly entitled to do. My spies told me it left them incandescent with rage! 'Who does he think he is?' was the identical line used by the 'close him down' bandits, the BBC evil bullies, the corrupt cuntstables, the Clown Court……and now His Majesty's Prison and Probation Service. Ohhh God. Back to square one. This could be a new Elton John musical - 'The Circle of Shite!' Just like always being right makes you enemy #1!

At the end of March, they called a meeting with Jo Nulty, the top Senior Forensic Psychologist for HMP, and her deputy, Jenny Bradbury. Those are their real names - unlike Fanny and Lotty, who, like all establishment crooks, will be protected by expensive gagging orders should I name them. Boy, would they like to get these six books banned. Jo confirmed, 'The Stalking Hub' doesn't really exist - it's HMP psychology dressed up as another quango. They couldn't tell me that, as I've never had a pill for anything, no history of any psychosis, and no concerns in forty-two years WHATSOEVER to justify me requiring a psychologist costing you over £500 an hour! Being so overstretched as a department - with year-long waiting lists - Jo and Jen are generally only called upon in the most extreme circumstances: when the criminal was medicated, had previous psychotic episodes, or was a murderer being released on parole. Even OMU didn't claim that was the case…..yet! Everyone was speechless at this crude attempt to misrepresent me again - in the hope the shrinks <u>might</u> find something. Oh, but one wouldn't be enough – NO. NO! I'm a terrifying monster remember. I needed a second cuckoo inquisitor. This is the deputy senior forensic psychologist for His Majesty's Prison and Probation

Service, called Jenny Bradbury. I went to 'Equalities' for the meeting and the atmosphere was frostier than a divorce sign-off in the Arctic - in January. I was on a 12-week assessment, with the threat that if I didn't engage - I would not progress to CAT-D. You can't be blackmailed into psychology, BTW. OMU at HMStockings don't care about the rules or the law!

I have to admit, Jo seemed a very nice lady. She was, by far, the most qualified and smartest person I'd ever met in this entire three-year witch hunt. The two front bottoms from OMU sat opposite me - spitting feathers and crushing stones into their pint of stout. "Right, Alex, thanks for coming. You go first." This is a woeful management trick - it's a deliberate trap to get you to spill the beans and rant and rave. I'm far too long in the tooth for this bummocks. I snapped back, "No, you invited me, go ahead." SILENCE. A very bad start FOR THEM. It's all a control game and they'd lost it in second one. Ouch. A pissing-contest had begun. Jo could see I was repulsed by these two devious and unqualified morons, and stepped in. "Alex, I'm Jo, and I'll be working with you - but sadly"... wait for it... "the system is broken, and it's going to be three to six months to fit you in. You are a priority, though. How do you feel about that?" I said, "This is the perfect .gov cockamamie scheme to prevent CAT-D, isn't it? Well done! I expected no better!" The divey, dead-behind-the-eyes PMT probation piss-take chimed in, "Alex, we need to lower your risk to be sure you won't commit your crime again. Also, bad news, it's likely we won't let you broadcast again, how do you feel about that?" I laughed, "You obviously haven't heard of Human Rights Article 10, now, have you? You can't stop me talking or breathing love." Both Lotty Beaverhousen and stinky Fanny's heads exploded! They went BRIGHT red - like a pulsating haemorrhoid that had just been popped by their gynaecologist!

Again, Jo stepped in just like Kofi Annan, "Yes, she's not suggesting you can't ever broadcast again, just whilst in custody." Oy vey. I said, "Listen, I'm a professional communicator of thirty years. I don't play word games. I heard what she said, and it was deliberately intended to provoke. I'm a 42-year-old man, this nonsense won't wash with me." Jo backtracked for Pinky and Perky, "No it wasn't clear." I continued, "Of course, I can't broadcast in jail, I'm captive for a reason and a hostage in prison by design – that's the whole point. I won't be borrowing one of the hundreds of iPhones in this high security jail, don't you worry about that!" Then Jo (so smart and avoiding the gag) said, "You feel you're a hostage?" - looking concerned with her head tilted like the confusion alpaca. I replied, "Well, what would you call it?" Silence. "If you're kidnapped and taken somewhere you don't want to be, I would suggest this is the dictionary definition Jo." Have you ever been in a situation where you know whatever you say is wrong, and no matter what your position, demeanour, or answer is - they'll find fault and argue with you? Well, this meeting was exactly that. Jo tried her best to defuse Rose West and Myra Hindley's bile, but I'd had enough. I was having none of it. Walk all over me but don't jump!

Doofus Beaverhousen wanted me to believe that I was finished - and would, therefore, explode in rage - to prove to Jo I was a raving crackpot. She wanted me to get angry, cry, and lose it. It's an obvious tactic to justify what she'd signed off - to waste Jo's precious time. Lest we forget, this woman is at the top of HMP psychology and signs off (releases) murderers and paedos, so she's got much better things to do! This was a vicious tactic of the state - a final stunt to prove me unstable and unhinged. BTW, Lotty remained schtum throughout. Not <u>one</u> syllable. She was more attuned with watching *'Made in Chelsea'* or *'Naked Attraction'* than mass debating with me. I bet Fanny the mop haired pen pusher said 'leave it to me Lotty – I'll show him' – snore. Look, I know I'm not average, but the sheer lies these people expect you to swallow is unbelievable. I had this for two years from the police, five weeks in court, and now these ugly sisters are at it too. It's like a mucky panto of Sinderella! Let's hope Jo takes me to the ball - not the funny farm. What sickens me about civil serpants is that they want you to be grateful for the diarrhoea you have to swallow. Tosspots. The excruciating, devil-like provocations they hope will ignite your reaction are laughable - but sadly, they do work on highly addicted or abused men, which accounts for most of the prison population. It's cruel!

So, more than six months had passed, and I'd got nowhere! All a game to long grass <u>everything</u>! I would need the grace and patience of Mother Teresa to get through another two years of this incomprehensible bullshitery! For all these people's protestations about safeguarding, wellbeing, and development - this prolonged torture of the clock ticking is enough to send the strongest of souls off their rocker and over the edge - AND THEY KNOW IT! Their bullying and intimidation were a red rag to a bull-sized box-ticker. Next, the Achilles heel - a kick in the nadges - came.

The evil and despicable walking funerals opposite me said, "I have bad news. We're taking you out of the library because of security, it's not appropriate for you to work in there." I knew this was a lie, and clearly to stop me seeing them. This pair of human sewers did not want to be held to account - and a weekly 'audience with' for the entertainment of my lads? This was not going to happen on their watch. The two hairy cornflakes lied. If there had ever been any security breaches, I would have been told, suspended, given the accusations in writing, and then investigated by a Gov during a prison court nicking. I said, "What on earth have I done?" Mavis Minjita replied, "We can't tell you. It's intel." Again, this was the guff they spewed when I moved off F Wing - that was never put on record either. It's the get out of jail (if you pardon the pun) for any dopey, vindictive, and cunning saboteur that wants to screw you over, hide behind 'shushy' security and hope you don't catch them out. These people only survive on control, and they hoped it would be the straw that broke the camel toe's back. Then came the most ludicrous accusation of my four-year legal circus.......

These two dreadful women had come in armed. Next, they said a line that was intended to blow my mind and trigger me bigtime! "Alex, you are writing to us too much. We believe you are stalking us and if you continue, we intend to escalate it to a formal security issue." I laughed in their face. This was hysterically ludicrous. I genuinely couldn't believe my ears. They'd weaponised my conviction to protect their incompetence by threatening me into silence. How do you 'stalk' a bloody department? It is impossible! Akin to THE BBC, Police, HMP and Court - they are 'unstalkable' - as you and I fund and own them. I couldn't resist having a little fun and said, "So let me get this right - you are OMU, the Offender Management Unit, right?" "Yes," it replied. I continued, "And you believe that I am stalking you by asking you to do your job properly - after a litany of mistakes you've already admitted... along with the confession that your department is 'broken' and 'overworked,' leaving you incapable of doing your job properly? Are you serious? This is a joke, right?!" It replied angrily, "Mr Belfield, accusing you of stalking us is a very serious accusation. You cannot write to us more than once a month." It's all just a little bit of history repeating. An absurd misrepresentation, deliberately intended to maliciously prevent any progress home. These two are about as straight as the M25! Jo looked agog, like she'd been asked to do health and safety checks on *Top Gear*! I couldn't help but call these two devious and scheming snakes' bluffs. "OK, so what is on my NOMIS? Where is the paperwork regarding your insane accusations?" Then the gigantic buffoon began. "Well, well, well, that's how it is Alex. You cannot repeat your criminal behaviour, we call it 'offence paralleling,' we won't stand for it. This was the reason that you were kicked off F wing, you wouldn't stop harassing a prisoner on that wing, someone we had to protect." WOW. Here we go. "I beg your pardon - that's the first I've heard of this. Why wasn't I told of this lunatic accusation?" At which point Jo Nulty - the top shrink and smartest person in the room by a mile - said, "Hang on, this doesn't seem fair. Why has he been moved if he doesn't know anything about it? Why is there nothing in writing?" BOOM!!! You see, the problem with crafty wolves in sheep's clothing is that they're crap at covering their turgid stench. They're not used to dealing with rational people who have <u>logic</u>. Fanny Schmelling and Lotty Beaverhousen were speechless. I simply said, "I can't win. The witch hunt continues. You are willing to lie and cheat to prevent my progress, and now you've wasted six months - just so I could be seen by a psychologist I don't need, hijacked with preposterous accusations you cannot back up. It's pitiful." Silence. Stone cold silence. I said, "Where is the evidence of any accusation that a prisoner led to me being moved?" They looked at each other. Jo was eyes wide open speechless. She's no fool. They'd exposed themselves. Hairy said, "We don't have it, but you're finished in the library, we'll get you another job." Unaccountable. Liars. Odious. A vortex of sickening crooked shite! I made a very quick exit - I didn't need to indulge in this insanity for a second longer. Arguing with these people is like trying to eat soup with one chopstick. This was the biggest letdown, flop, and anti-climax since I last tried to knock one out to women's weightlifting at the Olympics (needs must in jail). It was blatantly obvious what was going on. Jo would not deny the clear sabotage and had to remain on 'their' side - but she's no fool! It was totally pointless trying to rationalise their corruption. The decision had been made. You can't unpick this level of sleaze. They weren't even clever at it. THEY DON'T CARE - they're 100% protected. Round and round in circles we go. Seriously, why do I attract this identical breed of pricks - so personally aggrieved, put out, and undermined - that they feel the need to maliciously attempt to destroy me, so viciously, just to score cheap points on behalf of others, every single time? My only conclusion is two words. No, not those! Two words: TRUTH and FACTS. They're incapable of living by them. They're so riddled with duplicity; their only form of defence is attack. I can't help but feel that all of this was a test - a deliberate push to tip me over the edge. Without hope, you can lose your marbles. You can easily go doolally. Many would not have the tenacity and strength to keep fighting back. Most would give up, lose faith, become angry, or hit out... I, of course, went back to my pad, got my spies to check my file, and called my lawyer. The truth - surely - would be my saviour! Nar... This is Grate Britain.

There was nothing on my file ANYWHERE! Impeccable - that's why I'm still 'super-enhanced' on Newton. Not one scintilla of anything: the library, stalking F Wing, or OMU crap. It was all bollocks. I was negative-free, still enhanced, and a 'model' prisoner with an unblemished record. All total lies and orchestrated twattery from .gov funded probation. So, once again, off we go to legal land. I hadn't got £300,000 to waste this time on fruitless court hearings, but let's see if my civil lawyer, Al, could make them see sense. These vomitus, vitriolic, and vindictive trolls of HMP had only one hope left... to get me sectioned under the Mental Health Act. If you can't beat someone and they won't give up - paint them as stark raving bonkers! That old chestnut, hey...

So, now I'm unemployed - and could be stitched up by the two most revered and senior government-funded shrinks, who could medicate me and keep me under the thumb of the establishment forever. Marvellous! Just my luck. Were Jo and Jen 'in' on this conspiracy? Well, Jo certainly gave the OMU imbeciles short shrift in the meeting, so <u>MAYBE</u> not. Their core values are to be entirely independent. I guess I'd have to wait until the end of the summer to find out. We all know what can happen with 'impartial' judges now don't we? All I know is that the only thing uglier than OMU's two faces is their relentless jiggery pokery and piss-taking catheters full of dirty tricks!

Chapter 27

Thick As Mince

I couldn't help but smile at this ridiculous meeting. Even by March 2023, I had told myself that the only way to survive the slammer was to see every single argy-bargy as content for these books - and dismiss every imbecile as a clown in this circus. This 'meeting' wasn't real; it's all just a mirage to shroud this mental conviction in a veil of credibility. As far as the two septic Celias were concerned, they'd won. They'd got what they wanted - peace and quiet - and kicked me out of the best winter job in the jail. Sadly, though, their malice outweighed their smarts, and they hadn't dotted the i's and crossed the t's. They'd banned me from contacting them - which is totally unlawful - but that didn't stop me formally challenging it and getting the lawyers to send them a ditty or two instead! A lawyer can't 'stalk' a member of HMPPS staff, surely? Equally, they can't stop the prison 'COMP' system, as this is totally independent of these Judases. There are many ways to skin CAT-A or pussy - Schmelling Fanny and Muffdiver were about to see Belfield's stiff upper lip and fortitude.

An officer came to my door shortly after and said, "They've got you the best job at DHL." I've mentioned before that HMP Stocken was a hub for the canteen (shopping list) for a ton of prisons. It paid £40 a week - which was three times more than any other job. To most men, this was a dream. You could buy a week's worth of SPICE or weed with that! DHL were making a fortune - the markup on a lot of the items was enormous, and they had a monopoly. Whether prisoners should be able to buy hundreds of items is another argument, but for fellas with no money, this job was nirvana. For me, it was a nightmare. You're cooped up in a factory environment, working with a lot of butch men in a very tight space. Not for me, dear. I haven't done twenty-five years in showbiz to pick and pack other men's shopping. I don't do nonsense chitchat, and I certainly don't do banter whilst fingering other men's Curly Whirlies! I sent an app to Gardens - this, for me, was the summer dream gig: fresh air and freedom. Let's see how risky I really am. This is the toughest gig to get in the slammer for obvious reasons - you're outside the two fences, with only one to go. It was still chilly, but soon it would be suncream, fun, and running the odd vine up a trellis all day long. I went to the office to speak to SO Rachel Slurrs, but unfortunately, there were two hideous oafs on duty. I'll pass! I did an about-turn and ran for my life to avoid a conversation with these two tattooed Shrek tribute acts.

I'd promised myself I'd <u>never</u> engage with such numpty pub doormen, but I had no choice. "Alex, what do you want?" PCSO Wayne Rooney growled. "Alo Sir, can you check my NOMIS for me and confirm there's no issues or negatives please?" He couldn't wait, "What for?" Here we go, more Belfield shenanigans. I said, "I want to get a job emptying the bins on the wing, so I need to check I'm clear to apply. I've been sacked from the library and I'm heartbroken. OMU have ruined my life, so I need a wing cleaner job." He laughed. "How has it come to this Mr Belfield?" he mocked whilst tittering like an old retard on coke! "Yes Sir, I got sacked from the library for reading the Kamasutra, so I want to find a position less complicated." This douchebag didn't even know I was taking the piss. I could already hear him bragging to his co-pricks, whilst eating Pot Noodles and playing hopscotch in the playground. DOPE. He fiddled on the tippy-tappy for a minute. "No. Nothing on at all," he chuntered. "You're 100% clear. Just positives. I'll see if I can have a word. I might be able to make you a shower cleaner," he joyously crowed. I said, "Oh, thank you. That would be tremendous!!! As long as I can wear gloves, I'm up for it! Does HMP supply marigolds? Thanks, I Appreciate that, Sir - so kind." What a prized pilchard. I went straight upstairs and applied to Gardens, and wrote to DHL to decline their 'incredible' opportunity. I wrote: 'Wing staff confirm I'm a model prisoner with no issues whatsoever on file. Therefore, please can I be considered for the highly prized gardening job?' I'd now wait a week to find out if I was through to the final round - having missed the golden buzzer (more like a golden shower).

The next day, I had the misfortune of meeting a corpse who claimed to be my 'key worker.' You're meant to see these 'intel collectors' each week to make sure you're not dead. I nipped that straight in the bud - don't you worry about that! We got off to a VERY bad start. It was 7am on Thursday morning - I wouldn't recommend knocking on my cat flap pre-*Lorraine*. Whilst Ed Balls is stuttering his way through the GMTV autocue, I'm renowned for being very grumpy! Look, I believe I'm an affable guy, but <u>NEVER</u> open my bedroom door at silly o'clock and ask for a mass debate. We shall call this extra from Eurotrash - Afelia Bhigkok. Straight out of an Amsterdam window - she decided to crack my door open before unlock and introduce herself. I'd been tossing and turning all night over OMU, and now this lap dancer from foreign parts (with an incomprehensible accent) sees that I'm asleep, then proceeds to come in and says, "I'm Afelia, your key worker. Can I turn your light on?" I nearly knocked her lights out for such an uncouth indiscretion. Listen, sugar tits - at 10pm at night, there's nothing I like more than a good old chin wag with a slapper like you banging on my knocker, but before *This Morning* - I'm schtum! "Turn the light on?" I said in fury. "Are you off your rocker? Come back when it's daylight, I'm up, the light is already on, and you can clearly see if there's someone home." Ouch. I don't think this modern-day Linda Lusardi with a filthy lilt had been turned down before. She started coughing - she was so taken aback. I said, "You defo need something for that cough! Go and suck on a Fisherman's Friend and I'll come and see you at nine!" She slammed the door.

Cheeky bitch! I've not had an unsavoury offer like that since I stayed at Hooters and forgot to hang a 'DO NOT Disturb' sign on my nob! I now believe this was the first trick by OMU. This was <u>totally</u> inappropriate and unacceptable. If she'd have turned the light on.......what fantasies could she have written on my file about what she didn't see. Outrageous! BTW, what's the difference between light and hard – I could never sleep with the light on! I thank you! Never mind key worker, this one looked more like a street worker. I'd deal with this gobby harlot after my coco pops.

Naturally, I avoided Afelia at 9am, as she triggering my acid reflux with her untimely invasion into my private parts. Instead, I went about my business, but before I could even digest my croissants (yep, they're on the canteen too) I had the cab off the wank trying to cause trouble. A very weird screw collared me on the way to chapel and said, "Alex you're not allowed to go to the library." I raised my eyebrows and nostrils and chuntered, "I know. Only this prison could ban a journalist with perfect behaviour from a library" - and carried on walking. OMU had obviously called down, trying to incite more trouble - having missed out on the Dover Dinghy Diver bait incident at 7am. I wonder if my key worker is an illegal immigrant, looking to move into Alex's Acres whilst I'm pre-disposed? For the record, the question this kanga twunt should have been asking me was: 'Where are you going?' Again - if you're trying to be a smart arse and catch someone out, get your ducks in a row. Curiously, this fruit was wearing a hat, big jacket, and hoody thing – INSIDE - when it was over twenty-one degrees. I noticed, for weeks after, that he was always dressed for a snowstorm - unlike his more sensible (and less creepy) colleagues, who simply wore a shirt and trousers. My suspicion is that, like so many corrupt screws, all of those layers were covering 'something' he would deliver on his rounds, hoping it would go unnoticed. They don't call me Miss Marple for nothing! The dullness and darkness outshone his acne. Poor dear... try Clearasil - or a Brillo pad, for the love of God!

He obviously didn't get the reaction he wanted, so the soft sod called security - who sent five officers to the library to 'nick' me and bring me back by <u>force</u>. You cannot ignore a direct order and be somewhere you're not allowed to go - especially in a 'security' jail! The goons from the mob can use any 'reasonable force' to remove you if you're in the wrong place - and then hit you with a formal adjudication. If this happens, you're back on basic, kicked off the enhanced wing, and ordered to stand 'prison trial' in front of a Governor, who decides your punishment. They'd love that now, wouldn't they? This would have been a <u>dream</u> for OMU! I'd be heartbroken, humiliated, and back on the ghetto wing - and all the people I've made look stupid - from lying F Wing officers to OMU, and now this new gang of gormless halfwits - would get bonuses and celebrate that they'd got one over on me. I've seen it a million times with less equipped men who fall at the last hurdle. Alfie (who'd been in the library at the time) told me that the library door flung open as five black-clad thugs stormed in, looking for trouble. "Where's Belfield?" one screamed. "No idea," Helen said. "Well, he's in here - where is he? He's getting a nicking!" Good Lord, you'd have thought I'd knocked one out in the Gov's office. Five minutes later, after a forensic search, they realised they were on a wild goose chase. Red-faced and embarrassed, Officer Meeskite radioed the clueless, Eskimo-dressed 'key' mobster on Newton. "He's not here - you said he was in the library!" barked the furious lynch man. Eskimo mobster replied, "Oh, he's in the chapel." The furious lynch man said, "But you told us he was in the library, he's allowed in the chapel, oh for fack sake...." Slam dunk! Mic drop! Wounding! They minced off like a pack of penguins, tails between their legs, never to be seen again. Can you see the relentless games these idiots play? It's all about 'Let's catch him out.' Fail 101.

I, of course, was having a lovely time fingering my organ and singing 'God Save Me Now' with Angel Anne in the chapel. I wouldn't give them the satisfaction of ever going near the library again - in fact, I never did. I, obviously, knew nothing about any of these shenanigans, and it was certainly not mentioned on my return. I hope this unedifying story doesn't end up in print to mock these mental morons! Alfie and the lads were speechless - shocked by their indignance. They were looking under tables and in cupboards. Gareth and Tony were pissing themselves. Helen and Marie-Anne held their head in their hands. Nothing was ever put on my record. Not one word. All of this was instigated by the bitter OMU crooks who wanted the upper hand. Definition of weakness. Like before, these vengeful creatures want any distraction to avoid exposing their incompetence and dumbfackery, with the hope of anything to avoid them doing their job! What a total own goal. I feel like I'm in an episode of *The Sweeney*.

It would be another four months before I'd hear from OMU again. I'd already lost the will to live with them. I gave up and left it with my lawyers. I might be many things - but naïve, I'm not. This situation was untenable. Karma would kick in once I released this book. As with the trial, the public will decide - and the truth will set me free! But, in the meantime, I will not surrender. Until then, I had to take it all on the chin - like Stormy Daniel's last mucky movie on Tug TV. More and more letters were piling in, keeping me motivated. My replies documented all of the above - simply to underscore that I wasn't scared, intimidated, or remotely concerned by their ignorant stupidity. I continued to tell them what I needed them to know. So, what now? Well, my KC had been so supportive since the trial. Ironically, this man works for public protection. He didn't appear remotely concerned by my 'risk' at all. He was in disbelief at the litany of 'incidents' that I was enduring after the criminal court farce. I think it's fair to say that Mr A was as confused, disheartened, and shocked by all elements of my prison experience as I was. He'd obviously lived every second of the trial and knew it inside out. He was a huge comfort in keeping clarity on what REALLY happened - opposed to what they wanted to pretend COULD have happened, which seems to be the basis of my entire kidnapping. The shenanigans of the establishment were alarming. He'd very kindly also agreed to represent me as King's Counsel in the corrupt Nottingham Police's final attempt to stitch me up, which he brilliantly thwarted simply by stating THE LAW. If only that would have worked in the Clown! As we know, the Nottingham Police Mafia - cuntstables like OMU - seemingly believe they're above the law, as they've proven since day one.

Meanwhile, another YouTube wannabe resurfaced - someone who I have never met, don't know, and who had sent over five hundred tweets about me, despite being asked to stop by police. He had pulled out of the criminal trial back in September. Curiously, he was close friends with one of the BBC 'not guilty' female types who no longer work for the corporation. Most peculiar set of affiliations, right? He had been warned - unlike some others - that what is said in open court is legally reportable in its entirety... as I proved in the daily court reports. He chose not to be involved. Just after Christmas, my lawyer was contacted by the goons at Nottingham Police, who said they were going to return to court to get a stalking order for this fella. My KC, Mr Aubrey's advice was akin to the other shushy 'situations': who cares? I have no interest in them, don't know them, and have NEVER met or contacted them - let alone gone near them. This man, who I'd never heard of, approached me via Twitter - and I replied. Stalking? You decide. If it gave them 'peace of mind' to have a worthless piece of paper, then so be it - that was the boiled-down advice from Mr A. In other words, I couldn't win. It was just another attempt to blacken my name, as the Clown Court case had clearly failed.

So, they'd try again to assassinate my character with more incomprehensible allegations. Makes no odds to me – these people are of no interest whatsoever and never were. Totally worthless. This was clearly a gagging order, and in my view, a totally onerous abuse of the SPO 'Stalking Prevention Order' and another slap in the face to real stalking victims. Again, how can you stalk someone you've near heard of, talked to, or met? The notion of being bullied into silence is outrageous and stuck in my craw – but I had no choice! This feels identical to all of my legal woes.

However, what was FAR more devious was Nottingham Police's outrageous five-part gagging order – they were CLEARLY working as the mafia and private security company for the evil BBC. This is all they really wanted. Two of the most outrageous demands - hidden away in this 'smoke and mirrors' hearing for the next 'Alex is still a stalker' headline - were that I'd agree to: (1) never go near a BBC building, and (2) never contact anyone at the BBC ever again. Now, what's hysterical about this nonsense is that I've NEVER been accused of going in or near a BBC building - EVER - since leaving BBC Leeds in 2012, when I resigned. Prior to that I had no HR or security issues whatsoever at the BBC. Indeed, two independent reports in 2018 confirmed: 'Alex Belfield is of no risk to anyone at the BBC.' I have no interest whatsoever in penetrating the nonce factory or engaging with any of its complicit operatives. Heaven forbid!

The second police blackmail was far more ridiculous, unscrupulous, and totally impossible to enforce. It was blatant establishment interference to gag my journalism FOREVER – all they really wanted from day one! To enforce not contacting 'anyone' at the BBC is impossible and ludicrous, as there are 22,000 people who work there - some of whom are dear friends I've known for two decades, since I started my career at Aunty in 1994 - without ANY controversy until 2020. My entire career was unblemished, and I was respected, admired, highly regarded, and sought after. I worked there for fifteen years - for the love of God - all over the country, without ANY issues! How could an order be enforced to not contact, or not go near, people you didn't know... or equally, not talk to top friends of two decades whom I adored? Only the police farce - responsible for ignoring the nutcase who killed three Nottingham angels - could concoct such absurdity. Maybe if they hadn't arrested me five times, they could have locked up this monster and prevented the massacre in my beloved hometown. They did have a warrant for his arrest – unlike me! Not to mention the right to burgle my home three time. To adhere to such a lunatic order would require the names and addresses of every member of the BBC - just to know where not to go and whom not to contact! Hysterical! Can you imagine them updating that list every month to ensure I don't inadvertently breach the order?

Notts Corrupt Police's next demand was a hysterical clause: that I'd agree never to cause 'alarm or distress' ON-AIR again. How could that possibly be managed? Jesus, I wouldn't even be out of the jail car park before being re-arrested for 'visually offending' some lefty do-gooder with a hatred for common sense and the truth. All of this was totally ludicrous and legally untenable. The day before the hearing - which was listed for two days - the two KCs agreed to drop all of the unbelievable mob gagging orders, which were in total contravention of the Human Rights Act. Who the hell do these people think they are? Oh yes, the Notts Police Mafia Security Services for the BBC. All of the Beeb's outrageous 'close him down' clauses were scrapped in entirety. Can you imagine how their piss must have boiled.

This is so transparent! As the #1 BBC whistle-blower I believe they didn't give a fack about their 22,000 staff, or indeed this extra victim they needed to 'protect'......even though I've never met him and have no idea who they are! They didn't want me to contact foi@bbc.co.uk, who are legally bound to send me FACTS and the TRUTH - to expose, ridicule, and humiliate our national broadcaster's indiscretions. These emails gave me the evidence to eviscerate the credibility of the BBC for ten years in the press - the REAL reason they needed to 'close him down.' Remember: you CANNOT stalk a government department, so there was nothing they could do about my legitimate journalistic request. This court order was SHOCKING and laughably far reaching! I averaged three hundred FOIs per year – as I will in 2025 - the second that I'm back on my tippy-tappy. So welcome to China, people. If you don't believe the mob at .gov operate in collusion and a collective mafia to gag, silence, and intimidate their critics – there's your proof!

The 'threat' that I couldn't go in or near a BBC building would have prevented me from working for ITV - which is based within Television Centre, inside BBC-owned studios at White City. Identical restrictions exist at Media City in Manchester. This was a VERY clever way for the establishment to secretly restrict my practice - protected under the ECHR - and effectively stop me working for almost anyone, as the BBC's private business and cockamamie schemes own, manage, or are entangled in almost everything in the media! It felt like the Notts Police wanted to 'close me down' - both in showbiz upon release, and on-air with the Voice of Reason - to prevent me from exposing them and their undeniable corruption. Who knew? Surely this wasn't the motive all along? This order would have also prevented me from going near BBC Broadcasting House, blocking my efforts to continue the appeal to axe their emblem and the paedo statue by Eric Gill on the front of their HQ. He raped his two daughters and the family dog. I shudder to think why our national broadcaster would want a CONVICTED NONCE AND RAPIST on the front of their flagship building. You can make your own mind up about the above insanity. Before I was ejaculated from jail, the BBC used £500K of your TV rape tax to upgrade 'Ariel' - and put it behind bullet-proof glass! And they wonder why people can't wait to cancel their direct debit for the licence fee.

Can you believe the relentless horseshit I was facing, day in and day out - seven months after I was silenced and in prison? My public demise still wasn't enough!!! They knew the public were 100% behind me, and they knew this entire witch hunt was total BS. All of this is so dark. So evil. I couldn't believe their audacity. Now say I'm paranoid. They'd given me a preposterous five and a half years for a first offence of words. And now they were even more petrified about what I'd say when I came out, knowing the ONLY two things licence conditions can't cover are speaking and breathing - the very two things they prayed would stop! It's almost as if all of this was designed to finish me off - to wipe me out, once and for all. Surely that couldn't be their ultimate agenda? Totally onerous. Unjust. Outrageous. In its breathtaking (and illegal) audacity. Another final nail in the coffin that was <u>way</u> beyond the bounds of any court under Article 10. However, I believe they thought I wouldn't be <u>able</u> to defend the order and it would be signed off in my absence - as I was A POLITICAL PRISONER and HOSTAGE in prison. NOT A CHANCE! They hoped by now my public assassination would have bankrupted me - that this would be missed and swept under the carpet. SHAMELESS. And beyond crass.

The fact I hadn't topped myself by Christmas left them incandescent with rage - desperate to get one last bite of the cherry to push me over the edge. FAIL. This nibble was needless, and openly malicious. They hoped I'd now be a lone wolf - that no one would defend me - so this would slip through the net, giving the authorities an indefinite ban on me, my voice, my words... and ultimately, The Voice of Reason. Outrageous! Under these shocking clauses, I only needed one offended vegan and I'd be off to a CAT-A to begin a life sentence. Even their KC knew it was a croc of shit. He agreed to drop all of the bizzies' preposterous demands. Thankfully, Mr Aubrey, my KC, was all over it. This was a huge legal heist too far. I had an application made to the judge to appear via video link. It would only be a ten-minute sign-off anyway, as all of this was pre-agreed, and I had very good reasons for not wanting to leave HMS Stockings for the hearing.

When you go to court from prison, you're back to square one. The worst thing about the slammer is uncertainty and the unknown. No one wants to be shanghaied to somewhere new. It's a horribly unsettling feeling. Once you're comfortable and have a decent pad on a good wing, you don't want to find yourself back in a CAT-B -for a ten-minute court hearing, waiting with the roaming rats at HMP Lincoln. On court days, you're picked up in the bus and taken to the cells in the court - early. It's the prison's responsibility to get you there on time, so they don't mess about. If they're late, the jail gets fined, and you'll have to go through the entire charade again. You can refuse to go, but unless there's a very good reason, you'll get a nicking and possibly end up in the block or taken by force. I think, in years to come, they'll get tighter and tighter on these rules, as cons know exactly how to avoid their victims and the media spotlight. I don't blame them - it's not nice in the headlights! You can imagine the fuss if I refused to attend. So, if you have a court date, you pack up your stuff, go to court, and are then returned to a CAT-B local remand - HMP Lincoln, HMP Nottingham, HMP Leicester, etc. - all of which are a nightmare in comparison to this holiday camp. It's all relative. Then, you have to wait weeks for a bus to take you back to your jail - and start all over again in induction. Hideous! It's soul destroying. I did not want this to happen. Some lads go through this excruciating nonsense time and time again. Remember, hundreds of cases a day are cancelled or adjourned. I've (so far) avoided it. I was so relieved that I could stay on Newton wing and pop to visits to do the sign-off and be back in my pad for lunch. This local

Nottingham judge clearly did not have skin in the game. Despite the press baiting their breasts for two days of solacious gossip - we knew it was a pre-arranged five-minute rubber stamp.

Nottingham Police, I'm told, were once again furious! Oh, come on let's be honest, we know they don't care about SPO (Stalking Prevention Orders) in my case. I was never a risk as is proved by my 0.19% official file. You know I didn't 'stalk' anyone as do they. It's politics. One big game. My 'threat' is exposing inconvenient truths that the powers-that-be want hidden. Shushy Shushy! All they wanted was me gagged indefinitely, not even about them... but about <u>EVERYTHING</u>! This was a major failure for the cuntstable turds, who once again achieved nothing - despite spending months setting up this latest vendetta. Even they can't argue with their own KC! I wonder if OMU have told them about my books? I guarantee these will cause the establishment serious alarm, distress... and embarrassment. Fear of guffawing from my audience, I suspect! No amount of vitriolic bile will stop two KCs doing a pre-arranged deal to avoid court time. Remember, they're signed up exclusively to the court...not their client. They work in their interest – not the paying punter! You must never forget their allegiance is to the Clown! This was a massive own goal and back-fire for the mob. Yep, thank God I dodged this latest bullet.

My hearing was set for 10am at Notts Clown Court, so at the very last minute (deliberately), I left to go across to Visits, where a very strange officer sat in the room, gawking at me like a gerbil waiting for a passing carrot. This fella looked the spit of Jeremy Corbyn - my caution was raised before he even spoke. This was another snake who wanted to 'chat' – <u>NOT</u> happening. I'd heard rumours about this one, but had managed to avoid him until now. It was blatantly obvious he knew way too much about me. "It's two days, Belfield. Must be serious?" I said, "Two days? I'll be back in the chapel by 10.15am - it's all sorted." He said, "That's what you think," as he laughed like Gary Glitter hearing his hits on a BBC Four *Top of the Pops* repeat. I gave that one short shrift, don't you worry about that. We sat in a small, studio-sized room with the court camera and waited for it to start. It was like the good old days of the VoR phone-in. Within a few minutes, it was all signed and sealed. I really wonder if the general public realise that 99% of court cases are decided by the lawyers - way ahead of the trial? Shifty deals, done on the phone days in advance, are all part of this secret legal world. This was not made clear in the press or on the news, of course. Oh, the press once again had a field day - no context, no truth. No media covered the fact that the BBC gagging orders were laughed out of court. You can't trust anything .gov, media, or court-related. Ask the Post Office or blood scandal victims... still waiting for their dosh, 20-plus years later. To me, all of this is totally unimaginable, not justice, and it's certainly not in the spirit of the court! The notion that all of this time and public money is wasted on trials that were already sorted before they'd even begun seems obscene to me... but speaks volumes about the power of your representation. It truly is a pissing contest. The law, more than any other facet of life, is riddled with hierarchy, and status is driven by how rich and connected you are. Reverence is key. I respected Mr A. He could see the wood for the trees. Finally, I'd found a silk I could trust, which is harder than finding a needle in a haystack. I wish I'd met him in October 2019 when this 'close him down' BBC choreographed circus began. Would've should'ves, hey?"

During my five-week trial, he had to play the game for which he was engaged - simply to cross-examine the 'victims' on my behalf. He did much, much more than that. He was a confidante and a leveller, cutting through the rigmarole and court bollocks. However, from the moment he wished me well in the bowels of Notts Clown Court on sentencing day, he didn't need to speak to me ever again. But he did. Mr. Aubrey's class and sincerity shone through. To continue to be a guiding hand and legal mentor was invaluable. He doesn't suffer fools gladly. He could see through this insanity in seconds - but, as I've learned to my cost, the law is an ass and is mostly about long grass and costs. We won't fall for that mistake again! This wasn't my only legal woe pending. Would I ever get a clean desk, which I hadn't had since 2019?

On top of all this noise the first civil pay-off had gone public. It's almost as if the capital PR ballet to 'slam Belfield' was all pre-arranged. It had cost 'them' hundreds of thousands of pounds in legal costs to win a £10,000 settlement. Only God knows how that is a victory. Another legal angel had come into my life prior to the trial called, 'The Blackbelt Barrister' on YouTube. We had spoken quite a lot, as he was so curious and fascinated by my case. Daniel is a very clever family man, who I have grown to hugely admire. He became a great friend and confidante. He can smell bullshit a mile off and was dismayed about the 'substantial' settlement quoted in the press regarding our mutual agreement - along with many other inconsistencies in my absurd case. Now, let me be careful how I say this: to most people, £10K is a life-changing amount of money. However, to a wealthy person who has spent £300,000 on lawyers' fees, for example, you can't possibly suggest this is a 'substantial' settlement. 'Substantial' surely infers £1 Million in such a case? Let's face it, at this point you're buying a gagging order for a £290,000 loss - possibly more. It's an outrageous abuse of process, surely? Was this not to simply generate sexy headlines in the press? As well as all of the other lessons I've learned about the crooked legal system, the wording of any legal 'mea culpa' is laughable. Basically, it seems to me the High Court is designed for obscenely rich people to buy apologies and humiliate those they want to teach a lesson - despite knowing full well they'll lose a fortune. In this twisted world, the victory is in the 'I'm sorry'... even if you're not, and it's written by someone else - which is what seems to happen in nearly all of these cases. Of course, I will not say those two words regarding my Clown takedown, as I'm not sorry - so deal with it. If you want to buy a 'sorry' - that reveals more about you than me. These are called politicians' apologies: 'If I offended you, I'm sorry.' Hey-Ho, I kept my house - I win. They could have bought their son a flat in Soho, instead of buying their lawyer a holiday home in Puerto Banús. Total insanity!

I'd taken a lot of advice over my various civil actions, and my conclusion is that you're forced to settle. Ninety-nine percent have no intention of airing their dirty laundry (even in my extraordinary case), but simply want to look like they've won... despite losing the equivalent of a three-bedroom house in the north. Mental. Blackbelt very cleverly explained the law on YouTube - for total transparency and to dispel any myths. People were astounded! Few could believe it. Nothing is what it seems - it's all a game. 'I'll show him. I'll close him down!' Oh, do bore off!

I can't deny that the relentless 'lesson teaching' was getting old and tiresome. I've directly, and indirectly, made lawyers over £3,000,000 since 2020. Where is the victory for the individuals or indeed the public interest? Nottingham Corrupt Police paid MILLIONS, all in all, to send me down via 'Operation Orchard' - as my kidnapping campaign was called. These lawyers must be richer than Matthew Perry's pharmacist! Pitiful. Battling one twat or troll after the next was exhausting on so many levels. Mostly because I genuinely couldn't care less about any of this circus and could see it was all bluster and tomfoolery - and one long press release to beg the public to hate me. Another fail! You will never hoodwink the punters - they're far too smart. To now face the same level of stupidity from within the Prison Service was a step too far! And alas, they'd achieved nothing either. Where's the victory? Oh yeh, I'm in jail to write this book. Ouch. I can't help but go back to the bomb squad - they found nothing......not because I was tricky, not because I was lucky and 'got away with it' - but because <u>I'M UP TO FACK ALL</u>! I truly believe the mentals are still convinced 'they'll get me' in the end.

In between the library gig and awaiting 'gardens' (if I got it), I refused to go to DHL. Balls to that. I don't do manual work - not for me! They were staggered when I called their bluff. Mr. Ellis said I'd need a job, or they 'could' kick me off the wing. I wasn't leaving the Caesars Palace of the Stockings Penthouses, so I said, "Put me in tea packing." He said, "It's the worst job in the jail!" I said, "I know. Where better to write my books under the radar?" He laughed his head off and went to sort it out. Always keep them guessing, my friends! I didn't need a job - I wanted somewhere warm, with a desk, where there were no screws sticking their snotty noses in. I'd done my due diligence. A desk each, coffee machine, and decent civvy gaffers. That'll do me! Sadly though, my luck ran out, as I had to see my 'key worker.' With her eastern European long black hair, mid-twenties twinkle, and endless tattoos - this slapper demanded a meeting downstairs. Afelia Lottacock is the officer who is meant to be on 'my' side. Everyone told me 'new start' - be nice!' Oh, do fack right off! I'll punch the next person who says that! How many more chances do you give these brainwashed institutionalised loons, before you realise it's a waste of everyone's breath and you're just a beaten wife? "Hello" I said. "Alex, I'm Afelia your new key worker. What can I do to help?" she said in a comedy eastern 'Allo 'Allo accent. I thought to myself, 'you can try and do your make-up with a brush, not a trowel, for a start.' No no - I said, "Yes, get OMU to do their job properly!" She hit the roof.

She was furious...almost as angry as the tiger tattooed from the top to the bottom of her arm. She was half call girl and 50% docker on the Mersey! We shall call this box-ticker 'Tiger Lily' from now on. Blimey, this doll (blow-up) would make a fortune on Boobstation - or even CBoobies. I couldn't understand a word she said. She looked nice, if you're into that sort of thing... (nice until it opens its gob, that is).

Tiger Lily roared, "I have just spent the last six months in OMU having to deal with your facking mail! You can't blame them for being pissed off when you say such awful things about them!" Ouch. Bullseye. Here we go…...another Judas sent in to tame me and try and reel me in with loose lips (judging by her trousers two sizes too small) and inadvertently spill the beans. Once again, it's personal. Despite her palatial jelly wobblers and blow job injection teeth coverers, I can assure you I wouldn't risk it with yours. Even her Rabbit lady tickler resigned saying, 'I'm not up to the job!' Anyway, she continued, "Sadly, your gardening job has been turned down by security. Sorry Alex, I understand this is bad news." I said, "Most peculiar. I'm told my file is clean and I'm still enhanced." It replied, "Intel Alex. Sorry I can't tell you. But we won't kick you off Newton – keep your head down and time will pass." I smelt a rat stronger than her BO of Big Mac stench. She'd make a good drag queen though, maybe rebrand as 'Tickle my Tiger!' I don't know if she was a dinghy diver, but she'd not been long off the boat. Talking of oars, I wonder which 4* hotel she's staying in? Don't look at me for benefits. I'm in no position to make a food parcel donation. I thought I'd have some fun after her OMU rant: "I can't remember a single offensive thing I've ever written in my letters. What exactly did I say to offend them?" Tiger walked into the trap. Her raging eyes spluttered, "How would you like having to read hundreds of letters where you made us look like twats?" I said, "Oh no, my dear, you don't need my help to look like twats. That was me giving you a compliment." She snapped, "What did you say?" I replied, "It's so lovely to meet you, dear." "DON'T CALL ME DEAR!" she grizzled. I said, "In England, 'dear' is a compliment, dear. Our cultures must be very different."

It turns out that Tiger Lily had once been an officer. She was promoted - thanks to her vagina, which apparently helped boost diversity - and then ended up in a compromising position. Demoted down the chain to the lowly dungeon, she was tasked with checking the mail in 'Public Protection'...where, unfortunately, she had to deal with my bulging sack of Belfield fan mail. I was shocked - she could even read. Why would you assign a 'lady part' who can't pronounce her T's or F's, and who never made it past Year 5 English, the job of deciphering MY waffle? And now - would you believe it? - she's suddenly reappeared as my key worker. Uniquely hand-picked and promoted to 'help' me. What a coincidence, hey? As I stood up to leave, she repeated, "Can I help you with anything?" I said, "My life is perfect. You can't help me with anything other than getting OMU to do their job properly, correct the mistakes on my file - of which there are eighty factual errors - and help me 'progress' to CAT-D, as I'm entitled." She spewed back, "You won't be going to CAT-D for a VERY LONG TIME! You are the worst stalker I've ever met, and it's very serious." Here we go... "Oh really? You've read my file as well as all of my letters, have you?" I enquired. "No!" she aggressively replied. "So you read it in *The Sun*, or heard the moronic tittle-tattle from OMU halfwit colleagues? Which one is it?" Then Tiger Lily made the fatal mistake - "We have every right to talk about you; I'm your key worker!" I said, "You may well be a key worker, but you've just exposed yourself as one of the most unprofessional, stupid, and rudest people I've ever met. Thank you for showing your true character in less than five minutes. My only request is to <u>never</u> speak to you again! You've helped me more than you could ever imagine!" Oy Vey - put that in your pipe and smoke it!

I was genuinely shocked. The venom and sheer arrogance of this trumped up eighteen to thirties holiday rep was astounding! They all think they're so clever. This pattern happened over and over again, 'I'll be the one lads!' - Good Lord, it's so pathetic and draining. It was always the same type of snake. If only their intelligence equalled their confidence, audacity, and bra size. They clearly understand as much about 'dignity' as GDPR and data protection. They just don't care! Have they never encountered anyone who knows the rules of the game we're playing? Every single time, within sixty seconds, they reveal their modus operandi. I have to admit, even I was speechless at her sheer brazen balls out boldness. All this dope taught me, within the first two minutes, was that she was not to be trusted and was only to be avoided at all costs. She was absolutely one of the most heinous, wolf ugly, and socially retarded twunts I've met whilst in custody - including prisoners!

Sadly, Tiger's skintight trousers - showing all and sundry - don't impress me, unless I'm in The Mary Hinge Strip Club in Swansea or trying to visualise a hippo's undercarriage. I think Lily Loose Lips would be far better suited to mounting a pole than talking to the likes of me. Fag Ash Lil won't last. I walk around prison all day, seeing twentyish-year-old female screws looking important - all fur coat and no knickers. They're a magnet to a certain type of demographic: easy to manipulate, destined to end up corrupted. This always ends in tears... and not tiers of wedding cake, either!

This confirmed that the OMU numbskulls were on a mad tear, and no amount of common sense would win them round. This was, once again, personal - and now another group of goons were fixated on reaping revenge. My instinct and premonitions were correct. Identical to the BBC androids, you cannot argue or reason with saboteurs driven by a vendetta. Tiger Lily was sent by OMU to spy, and to get me to spill the beans. She's so thick, she spewed her motherlode in the first three minutes. So... who would be the next cab off the rank?

At this exact time, Stocken was changing and seemed to have an influx of drugs. Standards had slumped lower than Lily's mum's pubis. It was virtually impossible to get anything through visits, so that left only one other route - bent staff and screws. Security were constantly playing cat and mouse, but they had a grip on Stocken - unlike private prisons, which are flooded. Spice and coke are ten times more expensive here than in the new 'super' jails, as security is so tight and effective. You can get MDMA easier than a toilet roll in these new super prisons, but this 'secure' CAT-C was coming a cropper to corrupt criminal kangas. I wonder whether this new breed of 'Girl's Aloud' officers like Tiger Lily explains it!

Last year 160 prison officers were sacked from the prison service, so with only 120 jails, you can see this is a fight across the board.

At lunchtime, security locked down the staff in the bistro, as it was a great way to get stuff to dodgy prisoners - no cameras, very informal atmosphere. Everyone was searched. Two screws were caught with drugs. There's always someone up to something at HMP Stocken. Female screws 'crossing the line' was becoming a bigger issue for security than drugs. Having met Tiger Lily, Beaverhousen, and Fanny Schmelling - with the collective crumpet IQ of a ringed donut - I was very happy to avoid all temptation. I'm fed up, not hard up! I don't do charity work, and I don't need another unsightly rash.

Chapter 28

The Heartbreak of the Slammer!

You might find it hard to believe, but everything in my life depends on the weather. Because of insatiable global warming, March to May '23 was unbelievably cold. We were below freezing until lunchtime. I don't think God got Greta's memo. I desperately wanted the freedom of the gardens, but I'm not chilling my nuts off for the sake of trimming His Majesty's bush. I decided to 'COMP1' my security refusal for gardens - alleged by Tiger Lily and OMU. To their annoyance, my file was still squeaky clean, and the Head of Security had no choice but to confirm in writing: 'We did not refuse your job. You're very welcome to apply.' I'd spent a few weeks in 'The Noddy Shop' doing tea packing, as I just needed a chair, a desk, and no one snooping - so that once I'd done my forty minutes of work, I could get on with my scribbles. The people running it were fab. They got me a heater to keep my feet warm (under my wooden desk), and I was as happy as Larry - on £1 less a week than the library. HMP do not understand the first thing about motivating or inspiring people. Whether I did education, a workshop, or the easiest job in the jail, it only served my purposes - which were to give me freedom around the pokey, provide a decent regime and schedule, and allow me to gather gossip from the looney bin for lags for these epistles. Money was irrelevant to me now. I don't think £2 a day makes much difference when you get £33 enhanced per week, plus a £100 Newton bonus per month.

'Tea-packing' had some right characters. One lad had just come back from open prison at HMP Sudbury. I'm told this is an odious shithole that, frankly, should be condemned. I was very interested to talk to him, as I (naturally) hoped to go there - it's very close to Notts. He confirmed my worst fears: that it was old, cold, riddled with YO's (Youth Offenders), and flooded with drugs. A lot of men shared pads, too. Dear God, it sounded hideous. 'Be careful what you wish for,' hey? My idea of hell! "Why have you come back?" I asked. "A package," he said. "What Royal Mail?" I stupidly and naively replied. He said, "No numb nuts, a package of drugs over the fence." Of course! Silly me. You see the 'criminal mind' is fascinating. They never learn and never change. Sam was your average turnstile con. This is his life and world.

Open jail has virtually no external security. There's just a fence like your garden fence. They almost tempt you to escape or get stuff thrown over – it's all a test. You can get anything over the fence……. it's four foot high, but you almost certainly will get caught by CCTV. This dope would have made £1,000 for weed, but landed himself back at CAT-C for at least six months - due to being twenty-five stone and not exactly inconspicuous. He didn't seem bothered – it's the risk you take. All he knows. He told me his brother was also in another jail. I liked the cut of his jib - he was very nice to me. Little did I know, a year later, I'd be in his bro's jail - two hundred miles away in Wiltshire. Small world hey! This chap would come to Bible Study and offer to read. He was clearly struggling and obviously dyslexic, but had a profound sense of family and a good heart. However, he couldn't change his ways. I suppose he's in the category of lovable scoundrels that are so often found in the nick. After hearing about HMP Sudbury I did more digging around. North Sea Camp is an open jail, but is used for a lot of nonces, whilst HMP Hatfield is only an hour away and has CAT-D next door to CAT-C Lindholme. HMP Hatfield only has single pads, so would be perfect for me. Ironically, fifteen staff just got a hundred years collectively for dealing drugs in the clink. You couldn't make it up. Can we trust any of these asylums?

By May, it was finally warming up, so I applied to Gardens again. I wrote: 'Despite OMU claiming I cannot work in Gardens, the Head of Security says I can. Which one would you trust? When can I start?......' Pete and Aidy ran the huge compound - two old-school, 50+ legends - who could see the wood for the trees. Literally. Two days later, I was in. I wrote to Fanny Juize and Lotty Lickapuss saying: 'There appears to be another OMU misunderstanding, mistake, and cock-up. I am eligible to work in the gardens, in fact, I am eligible to work ANYWHERE - including the library! How on earth did YOU make this unbelievable mistake, claiming I was not? Thank goodness the Head of Security slapped it on the table and cleared everything up. Anyway, I'll start handling my hoe and grabbing my chopper on Monday. I'll be sure not to get a prick off a cactus - unlike that lazy-eyed key worker you sent to spy on me! These sickening bullies are a breed: sly, underhanded, and protected by a 'system' that encourages and promotes pitiful, pathetic, weak, conniving cheats, freaks, and bullshitters! What this, once again, has taught me, is you can't take <u>anything</u> for granted or believe a word that <u>ANY</u> goon from the Prison Service say. Challenge <u>everything</u>! 'No' is their opinion born out of malice, not the truth. How many more times do I have to learn this lesson before I get it into my thick head? I'm waking up slowly...

Everything was going great. I've still not had an issue, row, argument, or argy-bargy with a single prisoner. I doubt any of my assassins could have predicted this. I actually feel a hundred percent safe. My only issue was OMU - or those curiously connected to them. KC Aubrey had written to the prison to get my OASYS corrected via Al Robertshaw, my civil barrister. Lotty Beaverhousen replied, claiming to know more about criminal law than a silk. Good luck with that! I'd given up, honestly. I'd learned the hard way that these dysfunctional players will distort until their death. They're never wrong. Their conduct is the definition of a narcissistic psychopath. Total brick wall of impunity. They will lie their way out of any situation - including a brown paper bag! They have no fear – even of a KC or barrister. She didn't even have the class to check her reply with lawyers! They will defend the indefensible – even to the highest-ranking legal operative. They believe their own bullshit. It's not an act. Prisoners are helpless and hopeless. It's a sickening culture to deny them legal assistance. Their windy pops smell of Ambi Pur bed sheets. YOU CANNOT WIN! I made it my business to tell everyone possible about their childish games. No one was surprised. Total fart heads. This is decades of trained contempt and arrogance in front of my eyes. No prisoners or staff were remotely shocked by their contempt.

Privately, Mum and Dad were well (which was my only big paranoia and concern); my nephew and godkids were brill; and I'd convinced everyone to get a landline - meaning I could ring for two to three hours a night for the same price as thirty minutes on mobiles. Nothing gets past me! Visits were still a joy, and I slowly was seeing everyone via the 'three-adults max' policy. My delivery of T-shirts, joggers, trainers, and jackets had finally arrived, so I felt less dehumanised and more 'me.' No sign of my Trump polo shirts, but you can't have everything. These are all very small but hugely important steps forward in jail. I'd found my rhythm. Nothing made me flinch. I'd worked it all out. I fitted in well on Newton - with not a single issue with any con. I dare say I felt popular and one of the gang - something I've never felt in the toxic, jealousy-ridden mental institutes of radio and showbiz.

The longer my sentence went on - the more ridiculous my stretch became. Most days there would be a paedo on the news who had done something unimaginable and got a suspended sentence. Equally, a three-year stretch for death by dangerous driving or a rape (plastered all over *The Daily Mail*) doesn't seem very fair or just to me. It was a running joke with the lads that my words made me a far bigger risk to society than any of the above. Finally, the notion of 'two-tier policing' had become part of the lexicon - and was now an undeniable UK phenomenon.

Suddenly the only crimes of 'public' interest were political. This certainly worked in my favour to rally the troops online and underscore the lunacy of this incarceration. People were waking up - becoming increasingly infuriated by the hypocrisy of the establishment. Our country was changing. It was now undeniably clear that my sentence was simply a PR exercise by the authorities: a warning shot to dissuade any wannabe YouTubers from slagging off the high and mighty - for fear they might gain traction and end up with the 'influence' my jealous attackers so massively feared. People would update me about Andrew Tate, who was being character-assassinated by the media (on an hourly basis) for simply being a man with a penis and getting laid more than they did. Still no charge or conviction, as I write. He's identical to Russell Brand, who has endured similar slurs for being a comedy stud. Of course, Tommy Robinson was banged up again for trying to protect under-aged white girls from being raped and groomed by specific, demographically sensitive gangs of monsters. And finally, my dear MP pal Andrew Bridgen was being obliterated on all fronts for being RIGHT and fighting for the TRUTH. The only man left standing was our Katie, who was smashing it - mocking the afflicted and poking fun at our corrupt politicians on ALL sides.

It is a sickening situation - BUT the public were joining the dots and seeing the wood for the trees. It's very hard not to applaud Tommy, since the various Rochdale, Rotherham, and Telford reports have completely vindicated him - confirming sixty-plus towns in England have rape gangs who appear protected and thriving. Who knew the police would lie to bring someone down and stitch them up - simply to cover up their own crooked incompetence? Talking of which, the police were having a terrible time, being exposed as nothing short of despicable across the entire country, at almost every force. Six hundred cuntstables sacked so far THIS YEAR, as I write. Good Lord, how can we keep the faith? Anyone would think my own corrupt force in Notts were about to be exposed - and put in special measures!

Looking back, I still wonder if I was on a 'watch list' because of the theatre paedo I wanted to out in Yorkshire. Why did South Yorkshire Police threaten to arrest me in 2019 - for naming a nonce who sexually attacked <u>ten underage girls</u> in a dance school? He was protected and 'No Further Actioned' - without any searches of his house or tech. Why do .gov quangos go to such effort to protect paedo's??? Most peculiar. I was threatened with jail for protecting a girl that he grabbed around the throat - having driven her to a car park at midnight. Surely not every force can be as sick, broken, and crooked as the MET? Ermmmm... weren't the Yorkshire Cop Shop involved with the BBC and the Sir Cliff stitch-up... not to mention protecting Sir Jimmy in Leeds? Need we say anymore? Goodness gracious! Howz about that then?!?! There appears to be so many inconvenient tentacles to this octopus of civil serpent noncery! BTW - the paedo I tried to out is now working at a holiday camp... with kids!

Despite the world going to shit, my only heartache right now is for my three legends battling cancer, Multiple Sclerosis, and Motor Neurone disease. Vicky was absolutely drained by chemo. I'd call her up every night, but often she couldn't answer. My Aunty Dot was fading away, ravaged by forty years of MS, and my uncle Derek is being decimated by the worst illness of all – MND. I had to do something, so I arranged a 'purple' visit - the stupid name for the most complicated 'video visit' in the world! A nightmare to arrange, even more complicated to set up - and once all that bureaucracy was complete, often the person who connects you would be off sick, had pissed off home early, or was too 'busy to put you through.' This caused huge distress to five men at a time, per thirty-minute slot, who - like me - were desperate to see loved ones, unable to visit in person. These visits were all they'd got if they'd been shanghaied to somewhere like the Outer Hebrides. Most men simply gave up, unable to be bothered with this endless, aggravating farce. People have literally thrown the laptop at the wall in frustration. I got my sister to set it up. It took well over a month - back and forth with ID, blood samples, and rectal examinations from the Home Office - to finally get it approved. Exhausting. We finally managed to get connected, with all the family surrounding Dorothy in her chair. It was only eight months since I'd seen her, but her decline was shocking. She was clearly fading away. You know 'that' look - drawn, gasping for breath, and clearly 'buggered' - as my old gran would call it. I've seen it too many times over the years. There's a greyness in the skin, and the face seems to eat itself from within. Heartbreaking. She laughed and joked but my old Dot had gone – a pale imitation of her former confident and courageous self.

"Alo, my love," I opened with. "You look fabulous." Even Billy, her canary, nearly fell off his perch with cringe. Then the worst thing possible happened. My sister had rested the laptop on the table and put it on loudspeaker. Right in front of my eyes - centre stage - suddenly Doddy jumped up to see her old dad and find out where his voice was coming from. It broke my heart. She was the only one who had no idea why her best mate had buggered off without explanation. Everyone else had reconciled and was fine. It was a big punch in the gonads. Those glorious puppy eyes of love, joy, and adoration were suddenly flung in my face. I have to admit, it was a sickening moment that truly underscored the hideously cruel reality of my hostage situation. The moment passed, and we all carried on as if nothing had happened. I simply had to put it to the back of my mind. Every single night, I call up to chat to the princess at her various royal residences. That kid is the luckiest pooch alive - and a ray of light for anyone she meets. Let's face it: it's a bit of 'me' in the room when she's there with the family, especially Mum and Dad, to focus on positively and distract from this temporary cruise and prison research project.

Doddy has kept them both focussed, fit, and 100% alive, since this ghastly witch hunt and nightmare began. I repeat – the slammer is far worse for family than the con behind the door. We just go into our slammer bubble and get on with it. After thirty minutes, I said goodbye to everyone - no problem. We all knew this would end, and our love would return stronger when I was back - just like any extended contract to foreign parts. However, in my heart, I feared... well, I knew I would never see Dorothy again. A dagger through the heart. I told her I loved her, and said, ta-ra.

Chapter 29

Gardening, Sun Cream, and A LOT of Tomatoes

Finally, after the longest winter EVER, things were warming up. 2023 had got off to a disastrous start, with two of my comedy heroes passing away - closing a final chapter on variety that actually made you laugh out loud. Paul O'Grady and Barry Humphries were pros - and both fearless! The absolute best. What a loss to the business we call show. Britain was enduring unprecedented high inflation, mortgage rates off the scale, and the most bonkers heating bills in history. I should really send a letter to Judge Saini, to thank him for removing all of my cost-of-living expenses. Loopy Liz Truss's tax rises epitomised how shambolic the fabric of our world had become. Brits had realised that opinions were banned, and that you daren't sway in an imaginary breeze - for fear of being locked up for three years by the thought police. I had thwarted my saboteurs and could begin the dream slammer gig in Gardens... so things were looking up for me!

I set my alarm for 7.30am, had my Crunchy Nut cornflakes and a banana (external use only), watched the filler bilge from GMTV with Anne and Nick, and - at exactly 800am - put on my boots and made my way to the F Wing security gate, where Pete and Aidy stood waiting for their fifteen handpicked men with squeaky-clean reputations. Gardens were universally deemed the best job by a mile. The main obstacle to get the gig (literally) is that HMS Stockings has three perimeter fences and gardens is on the outer fence. Last year, one green-fingered genius decided to try his hand at hurdling over the thirty-foot barbed-wire entrapment cage. Miraculously, he did make it to the top... and then got stuck. Unfortunately, the twenty-five officers waiting underneath didn't have reverence for his *Krypton Factor* skills and kept throwing things at him until he fell off. They did 'try' to catch him, of course. Poor dear got another five years for those gymnastics. Security checks were (allegedly) much tighter after that. What staggered me about my daffodil-loving crim colleagues was that one man was highly medicated - and clearly stark raving bonkers. Thanks to his condition and meds he could now mow half the grounds before the screws had done their 9.30am corridor sweep. He was like Linford Christie......just without the baguette sized bulge. This chap had been sacked the year before for 'borrowing' a mower blade - which was found under his bed. Most disturbing (more than what he was going to do with it) is HOW on earth he got it out of the gardens and past the pat-down at TWO gates. Prison never ceases to amaze... and yet they're worried about me writing letters! Naturally, he was re-employed - for his mental 'elf! Speechless.

We walked through four security gates to get to the compound located behind F Wing - where I'd lived for the first four months. It was a fresh but sunny morning, and past gate five, we came to the pond. It was glorious. I couldn't believe my eyes: a pond, fresh water, tons of very expensive, huge fish (donated), two lovely benches... and then the mother lode! A mother and her seven ducklings came waddling towards us - like eight fat lasses in OMU pouncing on the all-you-can-eat buffet in the staff bistro. As anyone who watched VoR knows, I'm a sucker for nature. I'd rather be in the presence of animals than humans any day. They're consistent, always happy to see you, and give you more free love than you could bank in a lifetime from a moody millennial. You have absolutely no idea the endless joy those gorgeous bundles of fluff gave me over the next five months, as they grew to be bigger than their mam. What is most extraordinary is that the other lads cared even more than me. It was a massive lesson to see a triple murderer, who incidentally couldn't have been nicer, take responsibility to make sure those ducklings were the size of swans by St Swithin's Day! Within a week or two, the seven ducklings were waiting for us outside the compound - impatiently pacing backwards and forwards, excitedly awaiting their buffet of muesli, biscuits, and proverbial porridge. It was truly adorable.

Sadly, a week or two later, only five ducklings greeted us. We were all heartbroken. The lads were 100% convinced it was the prison sniffer dogs who'd maliciously been allowed to chase them during a post bang-up search. I have to believe that isn't true - but these lads know the 'system' far better than me. Who am I to disagree? Several of the chaps have been through double CAT-As to Open (and back again), and have experienced first-hand the very best and worst of the Prison Service. The two dead ducklings were lying next to the pond. The lads literally gave them a funeral, and made even more of a fuss of the five remaining (ever-expanding) brothers and sisters - plus Mum. It didn't take long for them to feed out of our hands. That was the cutest thing of all. Amidst all of the hideous negativity and toxicity of prison life, this was a God-given gift as far as I was concerned. Glorious! For months, they brought me - and many others - infinite joy. Proper cutie patooties!

The fellas running the gardens were salt of the earth legends. They put me in mind of my dad. No bullshit, completely aware of the failings of 'the system' - but just kept themselves to themselves and made their world the best it could be. They were respectful to everyone, but no fools. They'd seen it all! I've got a feeling they may have heard of the Voice of Reason. I'll never forget Pete's kindness - and the chats especially. I truly looked forward to going to 'work.' We'd walk around 'pruning,' whilst gobshiting about the news and politics like gammons always do. I made it my place to take charge of the top garden. This was over the grounds of the old H Wing, now demolished and covered with four polytunnels and a greenhouse. The gardens hadn't been dug or fettled in years, so - bit by bit, over many weeks - I made my way through the plot, enjoying every single second whilst listening to *Gold* on the DAB wireless, which was shoved out of the portacabin window. This was like any other 'proper' job. I was blown away how professional, well organised, and lovely it was. I had peace and quiet, a polytunnel full of tomato plants, fresh air, and sunshine. They even provided sun cream – essential for a ginger to avoid self-combustion. I'm not kidding, I was so happy to have sun, fresh air, and nature every single day! You have to count your blessings; I knew I'd got lucky.

To find serenity and calm in the slammer is unheard of. Now, twice a day, I'd leave the privacy of my pad, from the decadence of Newton and head for the oasis of nature, ducklings, and virtually no morons! Quiet. Still. Calm. Beautiful things growing. OK, there were a couple of pilchards - but they weren't in my huge section, and I was busy with a strimmer, keeping out of mischief. I was left alone. OMU was furious and humiliated that I'd got my own way - a pattern that would define my incarceration. Same as medicated trolls - their venom outweighs their smarts. It always ends up with egg on face! Basically, OMU were spitting more duck feathers than the security dogs chasing my chicks. At least three times, they caused trouble with Pete and his boss. "He's writing letters," Smelly Minge said - both on the phone and in writing – "If you catch him, sack him." Twats. These bosses were dealing with smackheads and violent murderers, and were being asked to worry about my pen by the box-ticking TK Maxx wearers. No class. Even less social grace. Bollocks to them!

I spent my stunning summer writing hundreds of reply letters, having the best time ever in the sunshine - singing along to The Chiffons, Dusty, and The Shangri-Las on *Gold*. I truly was! It was unspoken, but my gaffers let me do what I needed to do, as I did more work than most, was trusted, and no bother to them whatsoever. I proudly transformed three big areas and worked on my tunnel of red spherical wonders like they were my own.

Pride - few have this anymore. If I do a job, I do it properly - even in the clink. Days and weeks passed by, and it almost never rained. I loved it. This is my dream retirement on the out! The sun and those beautiful flowers lifted my heart. I'd got pigeon chicks in my bush and great tits would pop by each morning to say Alo…...no, no, I'm not talking about Officer Gloria Stitz, she was in the doghouse for shagging a butch lad called Chinzy. Must've had a huge chin, I guess??? Stitz was led off the premises in cuffs (not for the first time!) - I bet she didn't go down well at Stamford Police HQ. Regardless, I was in my element. There's no doubt this was the best time I'd had in years. I could actually relax. I began writing material for the comeback LIVE shows. I felt funny again. I felt like the old me. This was definitely not what my assassins hoped for. The darkness of the years of shit had lifted, and the insanity of this heist became clearer and clearer. In life, all you need for sanity is to see the wood for the trees. It's ironic that I was a top executive in the prison gardens. It turns out you do your best thinking and most positive creative and ingenious planning whilst gardening or exercising. This grounded me. This inspired me. This recaptured the old Gobshite Belfield.

I was back!!!

Chapter 30

Box-ticking Insanity and Evil Madness!

Every day is a mental challenge in the slammer. Ninety-nine percent of the time, I'd be busy writing or working and just got on with it, but occasionally, I would see myself through my mind's eye and laugh at the sheer absurdity of the situation - especially at moments with the ducklings or stood amongst my fifty tomato plants, which were now raging towards the roof of the polytunnel. Prison is about compliance and control - two things that take discipline. Everyone, from screws to my co-stars, knew that 'two facks I couldn't give,' and I wasn't about to get an epiphany to change. In the gardens, there were no kangas and 100% trust to get on with it. I've always been a realist about my situation. I never wanted to be in prison, but I had the mentality of 'make the best of a bad job' from day one. With the chapel being my ray of spiritual, human, and musical light, the freedom of nature all day in the gardens, and finally being on Newton - it truly couldn't get any better. I trained myself to have gratitude that I wasn't in the Seg at Belmarsh, like other free speech warriors. I had zero issues with a single prisoner or staff member, and most screws liked me - who, by now, had realised I should never have been here in the first place.

The human brain can only cope with what is real and tangible. You can convince yourself of any nonsense, but in the coldness of night, alone in bed, your conscience will always get the better of you if you're living a lie. Thankfully, I was at total peace psychologically - I had no guilt or regret, and was certainly not sorry - thus taking away all of that usual convicted guilt. The injustice, disproportion, and pure lunacy that I had been dealt could only be processed as foolishness. Everyone knew my sentence just did <u>NOT</u> add up. But to now be faced with OMU Celia Imrie's facking around with my freedom (as instructed by the MOJ) was much harder to deal with. Why? Because it directly affected my loved ones.

According to OASYS, I was regarded as 'high risk' to 'known individuals' and medium risk to the public, but what does that mean? Who decided that? Some twat - state-funded, of course -decided it in London, having never met me or even spoken to me! I was even labelled 'medium' risk to staff, despite not a single incident - proved by my continued enhanced status, which is undeniable. How is any of this possible with an ultimate 0.19% risk? That kind of rating should only be given to a prisoner who's physically attacked a screw. It was about the risk of me quoting them, and the danger that could have on their reputation and career, right? Laughable. So, I was being forced to wait to see the state-funded psychologists - having cleverly wasted a year achieving nothing. Now do you see I'm a political prisoner? Could they all be complicit? I'd noticed, on Newton, that there were two snakes in the grass, who were increasingly frustrated - because they couldn't bait me. One was a hairy, tattooed, foreign woman (who looked like she was on loan from the Richmond Rugby Club) and seemed intent on provoking men by nicking them or handing out negatives over nothing. Nonsense like 'Mr Smith had toilet cleaner in his pad. He knows it should be in the cleaning room.' My mate Mark genuinely got that. This puffy-faced, sour old bag was on a mission to start a riot. My spies made me aware that Officer Emma Royd had put a 'negative' on my NOMIS file, implying I'd waited for her to look into my pad 'whilst naked.' In fact, after I challenged this Bernard Manning lookalike with a Bernard Matthews gobble-neck, she conceded (in writing) that I'd had my back to her - facing the window - and wasn't naked at all. I was simply getting ready for work at 7.30am, when she shouldn't have been perving through my cat flap (obs panel) in the first place. However, the sheer claim gave OMU the opportunity, later, to quote this incident on my paperwork - implying I was some creepy Wayne Couzens who had waited for her to turn up just to see my half an inch and a dozen wrinkles. So stupid, but clearly intended to cast doubt on my 'risk to lone females.' Would this be a new trick? To allege nobjockery behind the door - something I couldn't even disprove?

Of course, officers like Emma Royd see men a thousand times a day in all kinds of inappropriate and compromising situations and circumstances - because screws can look in whenever (for 'welfare checks') through the pervy peephole into what is effectively your home, bedroom, and TOILET! What a genius tactic: accuse men of something they can't disprove in the privacy of their own clink cupboard. This over-zealous battle-axe was kicked off the wing days later - which is ironic, as all she wanted was promotion. Bad lads simply won't stand for such crap. When they've collectively had enough - kangas are finished. There's far more of us than there is of them. The irony - that she was dismissed to the chaos of F wing induction to 'learn her craft' - is delicious karma. Emma Royd can now go and be a pain in the arse somewhere else. Tatty bye, dear! Another fraud, caught out and dismissed.

My best advice to cons is: don't allow probation to get in your head, control your emotions, or play with your liberties. They have no training and even less social skills. All they have is bully tactics, intimidation, and condescension. If you remove their power, they're facked. By proudly telling these dopes the rules, I'd found their Achilles' heel - it was almost exciting. Identical to the BBC, the Police, lawyers, court, and now the Prison Service – it's all bravado. Trust me, this book will BLOW THEIR MINDS, and they will do ANYTHING to get it pulled and banned. They can't bear being undermined – let alone exposed as the inept imbeciles they are. They'd naturally (and instinctively) claim everything is a lie and deny, deny, deny! They cannot stand a mirror (as is the way with all .gov monoliths) ……that's why their eyebrows are channelling Denis Healy's Brazilian! If you think I'm lying, ask my 90,000 con colleagues or the 20,000 screws, who can confirm exactly who these wicked saboteurs and snakes truly are.

There is always hope! Visits are still my joy and entire path to happiness. I'd heard private jails give you five visits a month, ten hours, which is brilliant! I had FOMO over that. Two new Boris Johnson 'super jails' had opened in Leicestershire and Wellingborough. I applied for a transfer. It took seconds to get an 'it's a no,' as I had to remain in a 'security' CAT-C- not in the chaos of the Alton Towers of HMPontins! So, I carried on as is. On the wing, I'd watch with such curiosity at the way lads passed their time, especially the long stretch dudes. Sadly, it seemed gambling was a massive hobby. I was riveted by how seriously they took it - and how loud they became - right in front of the screws' eyes when they won or lost. Gambling is strictly forbidden – everyone turns a blind eye. I guess, like with a kid, you pick you battles. The toddlers were occupied, so - no trouble (yet). They would run out of their pads to play cards and wouldn't stop until the very last second before bang-up. No money involved, just matchsticks -which you can buy on the canteen. Don't be fooled: the matchsticks are 10p, 50p, or £1. One fella had sheets of chitties like John McCririck at the races! They all had each other's bank codes and would pay their debts direct into each other's accounts. Debt unpaid can lead to serious injuries! All of this is illegal - as are the mobile phones they used to do their bank transfers on in their cells. However, most believe they'll never get caught. Most do not. Welcome to prison!

Every single day that I've been in custody I've done my exercise. I'd walk for whatever time they allowed in the playground - my fitness was improving, and despite only losing a few pounds, I was stronger physically than I'd ever been. In fact, I was now 80 kilos - of pure muscle, you understand. You could crack walnuts between my inner thighs. On Newton, we could go in the yard most of the day. As the weather improved, I'd become legendary for sitting on the bench with my letters or books - ferociously scrolling away whilst taking the peaky whiteness off my ginger skin. I loved it. I positioned myself to look into the countryside, to avoid any vision of the slammer. So relaxing and peaceful. I'd never had time to just sit before in my life, so this was all new to me! I counted my blessings. Best of a bad job, I guess. I loved watching the red kites, young bustards, old bustards, and any silly old bustard walking past.

The first true prison kick to the knackers - and reality check - came when I called my friend Vicky, who could barely speak. This angel had been ravaged by cancer and tortured by chemo, all within just six months, and I knew the end was nigh. Her fiancé, Bobby Davro, dashed back - but we all knew it was desperate. For the first time in my life, I was trapped, with nothing I could do in this hopeless situation. She had fought like a diamond to shine through the treatment and pain, but alas, she was exhausted. Meanwhile, my Aunty Dorothy had become very confused and weak. She'd virtually stopped eating, and I would ring every night to beg her to at least try and devour something nutritious. Her fight and spark had gone. She was now on those high calorie milkshakes, which were her only means of staying alive. As any carer or family member will know, you can see the tipping point - where it's gone too far. I knew I couldn't save her. She'd had many 'blips' over the years, but this was all too much. She couldn't fight anymore. Dorothy ended up in hospital and deteriorated fast. I'm told she would come alive when I'd ring or loved ones would visit - but it was momentary. She was exhausted. Her time had come.

The trite line is always 'they had a good innings' – far too flippant for me. To see a loved one deteriorate in front of your eyes is one thing, but to not be with them, be powerless to help, and have no way of picking up the slack with hospital visits doesn't even cover it. Frustration pales into insignificance. It's nothing short of torture, and the ONLY true price I've paid for my saboteur's take down. Bravo! These people must be proud of their achievement! I was useless. The day before Dorothy passed, Big Boned Jean managed to get her to listen to me on the blower. Jean said she smiled momentarily, but she couldn't speak. I told her I loved her many times. Both Vicky and Dorothy passed away within weeks of each other. Two of my twenty prison phone lines were now available - through the worst possible circumstances. I guess this is the punishment that the 'system' claims it tries to avoid. Family ties are their priority and the key to rehabilitation. What crap. They delight in stealing your remaining moments together, it's evil. By the way, you are only allowed to attend parents, siblings, or your children's funeral - not even grandparents. Heartless! If you do go, you are handcuffed to two screws! Imagine the indignity and humiliation of that. No thanks. All I needed now is the prison mafia tipping off the paps or paedo trolls to proudly publish photos of me putting a rose on a coffin - with two kangas cuffed either side.

I'll pass.....in fact, I rather die before I do that! That is the end of a huge chapter in my life. Dreadful.

As for Vicky, I adored her. She was a ray of light and hope for me and many others. Only the good die young. This was so terribly cruel. She was a radiator of joy. All I can do now is try and be there for Bobby – on the phone.

All of this lose heightened my paranoia over my parent's health. Nothing prison related could ever compare to this hideousness of abandonment and grief. All I could do now was pray this would be the last of the funerals I cannot attend. Well done HMPPS – you win!

Chapter 31

Mental Summer and the Shrinks

Let's face it - the entire purpose of banging me up was to, firstly, silence me (achieved); secondly, destroy and bankrupt me (failed); and, hopefully, make me kick off to end up in the Seg, on basic, and mentally broken, to prove their misnomer that I'm 'off my rocker.' After ten months of incarceration, I didn't have a single issue. I was 'super' enhanced, on the best wing, and doing the best job in the jail through the summer. I'd met many friends across the jail who were smart and interested me. The rest of the moronic imbeciles I simply ignored - and they returned the favour. My biggest amazement on Newton was the number of foreigners cluttering up our cells. Send the buggers back – they want to go back! This isn't a joke. Foreign nationals (not British passport holders) fill our jails in the thousands - and we have to pay for them. There are over 10,000 currently in custody! One in nine prisoners are NOT British - costing you! £4.8 MILLION a year! Send them home! 99% are desperate to return. I would suggest there was at least fifty on Newton alone. No wonder the jails are so overcrowded! Why are we paying for them to remain on British soil? 'Guilty' = off you pop back home chunky – just like the illegals, hey?! Never mind tents in the 'departure lounge' – offer them a dinghy and get those windmills in the Channel to blow them back to where they came from.

I loved spending my downtime in the yard, sat on the benches with the old fogies (over thirties), who would sit and chit-chat in between my writing. I met an old Muslim fella called Mo, who would sit in the sunshine, listening to Classic FM whilst reading *The Times*. My type of con. We spent weeks over the summer together, talking politics and enjoying Mozart - slagging off the likes of Kuntsberg, Derbyshire, Myrie, and other BBC sanctimists who blindly vomit the .gov mantra on behalf of the state. We both agreed that the volume of numpties in the asylum of sin was the only real punishment. We'd both found ways of avoiding all clusters of those with bovine intelligence. Our little literary oasis was a huge blessing. We'd join other lads like Chris, Mica, and Greg – all top fellas ranging from murderers to drug dealers. You quickly learn to put aside their crimes….as long as they're not nonces - we're all in the same boat. Mo had issues with his wife that, to me, appeared <u>very</u> trivial. He got five years IPP. Yep, that now illegal Blunkett disgrace. Mo can only be released when the establishment/parole decide he is fit. Nearly <u>two decades</u> behind the door, he's still being pushed from pillar to post. Mo is just like me, a total gobshite, who is <u>way</u> too smart for the overpromoted fart heads in OMU and Parole. Sadly, because he's degree-educated, they can't stand him. He intentionally runs rings around them and loves to correct their spelling, grammar, or just their lack of social graces. His supreme intelligence - a thousand times greater than mine - left his twelve-year-old key-turners undermined and willing to do anything to prevent his justified freedom. Mo and I had a fabulous summer in the glorious sunshine. His serenity, clarity, and sense of humour was so very much appreciated. We were defo the odd couple. I had my folder of love under my arm, whilst he had his battery radio banging out Chopin and Tchaikovsky – both dead now. I suppose you could say they're de-composers. I'd walk for an hour with Alfie, Tony, and his brother - whilst a hundred lags lay topless auditioning for GQ magazine. Between us, we'd keep each other's spirits high and more importantly keep perspective on how utterly ridiculous and pointless this circus is. We all had families, love, hope, and a future. I'm indebted to these guys for their civility and 'normal' conversation. Birds of a feather I guess.......

I'd met other guys on the wing who were fantastic. Kev worked the servery and was my eyes and ears. He kept me in a fresh loaf of bread every day. Titch, Ash, and Lee were always around with a smile and a handshake. Believe it or not, collectively, it inspired me to carry on. It meant the world that they'd got my back.

I'd long ago given up hope on the legal appeal, as I was warned in no uncertain terms that the Court of Appeal would never overrule a High Court judge. Furthermore, if I did pursue an appeal, they'd start my sentence again - which they CAN do in rare cases - to teach me another lesson... after procrastinating due to court delays! It was, frankly, hopeless, as they could make me start my sentence again. We don't want that now, do we? Meanwhile, a dear 'friend' of mine insisted a lawyer had cracked the case and was willing to help for free - as she was outraged by the injustice. This pal we'll call 'Cunning Cathy' was 100% convinced this top barrister was going to be my saviour -

and I'd be out and exonerated in time for Halloween. We had spoken daily for months - she'd been a rock, and I had known her for years, so had no reason to distrust. She had even visited me in jail just before Easter. We had a fab time drinking mochas and eating shit food on the HMS Stockings' 'poop deck.' Why wouldn't I believe her. We were true friends – I thought. That's showbiz – one minute the Ivy, next minute the clink. Anywho, she filled me in on daily developments behind the scenes, but all cloak and dagger. This went on, day after day, for months. She couldn't tell me the lawyer's name and was paranoid about the prison-recorded phone calls and the dark forces tuning in. I never gave two shiny shites, of course. She remained schtum whilst dangling the carrot of, 'I'm going to get you out before Christmas!' WOW - a hero at last!

I had to believe this could be real, but I knew deep down it was never going to happen. Cunning Cathy would ban me from mentioning names etc and got furious if I did. In hindsight, I guess I was being groomed. No better ploy to craft than promising you freedom - with so much tragedy going on in the family (that she was fully aware of). For months, this dragged on. She heard about the blackmail gagging orders and insisted I shouldn't pay any. 'I'll get it thrown out,' she said. I do love confidence. After a couple of months, she needed £3,000 for court papers. A week or two later, another £2,000 - for specialist advice. In this moment, I knew exactly how those morbidly obese, desperate, divorced, or widowed women feel when they go to Greece - at twenty-two stone - and get wooed by twenty-six-year-old stunner 'Alonzo,' who wants to take them up the aisle, provided they can hand over their pin number and two blank cheques. You so easily get caught in a vortex of hope above common sense. The 26-year-old, 'six-pack Alonzo' is, of course, genuinely aroused by 75-year-old Tess Tickles' bingo wings, back fat, and drooping mouse knuckle - don't you worry about that! You're so far in, and invested in the scintilla of faith that 'this could be the one - surely it has to be worth a shot' that you blindly carry on depositing £5K and £10K - then you end up bankrupt and homeless, whilst he's back in Zante, living on a yacht. Look, I had a few quid, but I was still spending tens of thousands on lawyers and bullshit gagging orders. I didn't need this. It was another leak in my dwindling coffers.

Cunning Cathy had been going through a hideous time with a failed project abroad and her mum passing - which I did believe, and is true. As usual, being a dopey dick, I put my hand in my pocket and paid £5,000 worth of her rent over the summer. What a tit, hey? Hook, line, and stinker - I guess I'm 'that' mate who falls for any old gobbledegook or sob story. Am I a wonderful, kind, and generous guy... or just a total mug? I couldn't see her on the street which I had to believe was possible - no?! Imagine if this angel had freed me, and then she ended up in a sleeping bag on Charing Cross Road? OK, I'll fess up. I knew deep down it was all a scam, despite twice daily assurances. I knew I was being royally fleeced/facked, BUT I wanted HOPE and a ray of light. I basically bought faith, which passed several months and kept me going with almost electrifying excitement. I'd finally convinced her to get a 'legal' letter to the prison - which was sent from a PO Box in Wigan. The letter had the wrong Governor, wrong spelling of my name, and simply demanded......'You are to release Alex Belfield immediately. He is being held illegally as a political prisoner. He is a hostage.' As profound - and indeed accurate - as this may be, I could have written that myself on a fag packet. I can't imagine the guffaws they must have had in the Gov's office and Parliament dungeons! This 'dear friend' meant well, I do believe that... but enough was enough. I'd paid her the equivalent of two years' mortgage. The scam was over. She'd profited quite enough.

I beg of you, if you ever have anyone in a hideous situation like prison, <u>NEVER</u> tell them that you're going to get them out. It's torture if you're not 100% grounded and sane. I dare say this would be enough to push someone over the edge if they were cuckoo and it didn't happen. Add that to duplicity and fraud - it's enough to send you over the edge in sheer fury, in the face of such devious duplicity, at your lowest and most desperate ebb. It ended up costing me £20,000, all in all - money I have literally no paper trail for, let alone anything to show for it. I didn't (and still don't care) about the money, but <u>a lot</u> of people did. I saw it as a legal expense, but it was still my hard-earned cash - wasted on a con artiste. Having already spent way more than half a million on tax and legal bills, I needed the remaining dough to pay off blackmailers, keep my mortgage paid through to 2025, and finance opportunities like this book - to get published.

Cunning Cathy eventually contacted my sister to offer to repay £2,000. Maybe, just maybe, her conscience got the better of her. Maybe? We've heard nothing since. Do I think she knows what damage she did – absolutely not! She is delusional and wanted to help - and thought 'he can afford it' – the common reaction a lot of people with a few quid experience. She went about it totally the wrong way. Do I hate Cathy? – nar – she's got enough going on in her head that you could start a conference. Will I fall for this nonsense again? Once bitten, twice shy! However, none of us knows what rot we can fall for in our hour of need - to motivate us to get to tomorrow. Will I ever forgive? Absolutely not. I place this entirely on her Teflon conscience, equal to the other liars, cheats, and frauds before. In life, I've learnt you have to let go. I know Network Nick was fuming; my Big Boned Jean was incandescent with rage at what she'd done to me. Others were in shock and disbelief that someone could be that cruel - including my sister, who I insisted paid the woman. I can assure you my blood pressure never raised. My sister was disgusted, and lawyers flabbergasted that someone could be so cunning. Listen, it was worth a shot. I was £300k deep in legal costs so far, another £20,000 to give a few months of false hope couldn't hurt. People mean well, but that doesn't mean they're right. A good lesson learned. Onwards and upwards mush......

From Ripped Off - to Pissed Off!

So, I was back in OMU <u>hell</u> with yet another tortuous meeting with the two mansplaining heffalumps. They put me in mind of the sumo wrestling final at the 1979 Bushey Olympics. Off they went! "We've been reading your letters" ....I interrupted, "I'm sure you have. Haven't you got anything better to do? You told the induction lot you have a hundred clients each. I insist, I mustn't keep taking up your precious time with my nincompoopery!" – not a good start, right? "Mr Belfield" .....I interrupted again, "Listen, are we going to talk about something productive or am I going back to talk to my tomatoes in the poly tunnel?" BTW, they were magnificent. I'd worked my artichokes off to grow those whoppers - six rows of my spherical wonders! I was already picking two or three bread baskets full a week. I was the talk of Newton - bringing back fresh fruit and veg daily for the lads to enjoy. OMU just looked at me like I was an alien. Anywho, pig nose and shifferbrains realised that once again, I was not going to be baited into some pithy promise to stop my beloved epistles - so they moved on to my OASYS car crash. "You should never have been put on Kaizen".....I interrupted, "What the violent reoffenders course?" "Yes" it said. "No shit. Any more revelations?" I churlishly spluttered. "Mr Belfield, we're only human, mistakes happen." "Well dear," I patronized, "You two seem to be record breakers at mistakes and delays, you should win the HMP Olympics for procrastinators of the year!" Listen, when you've nothing to lose, fack it. I wish I'd have said a <u>LOT</u> more -not just here, but in court, to the press, and on-air

- from day one! I'm done with this Mr Nice Guy crap - it's getting me nowhere!

I beg anyone reading this: when you're in a position of being emasculated, subservient, and desperate - say what you think! If they're going to help you, they will... and if they hate you and want to screw you over, they will. Enjoy the moment. Revel in the serenity of the truth. It sets your soul free. Facts don't have feelings. Remember: how they 'feel' is not my concern.

Over the next two hours, these two brainless Biffas and I went through every single one of their <u>eighty</u> mistakes, as the Clare Balding doppelgangers - with the personality of Amy Winehouse's corpse - gormlessly stared back and recoiled deeper into their seats, unable to defend a word of this anonymously written hatchet job, curiously concocted in my absence. "How is my crime racially motivated when my so-called victims were all white men?" I asked these two nonbinary, vegan, ambivilacious dopes with cracked, 'do-your-own' purple nail varnish. Silence.

I can't help but pity the majority of prisoners who have the reading age of an eleven-year-old - FACT! To deal with these appallingly clueless, protected, utterly vacant, homogenized, and institutionally contemptuous characters must be devastating. They don't stand a chance. How can the 'system' give such power to such bottlenecked cretins? Reverence is the root of all evil. Once people in power smell fear, they'll take advantage -

and ultimately corrupt. A bit like if the police ever question you: Say NOTHING. DO NOT HELP THEM. They're your enemy, and they're only pretending you're their friend so that you blab like an incontinent baby. They want you put away, so <u>they</u> get a result. They will lie to your face - identical to probation. Their crooked deceit, lies, and bollocks will <u>all</u> be forgotten - <u>BUT</u> every word you spew will be taken down, distorted, manipulated, and used against you. All civil serpants are the same. Identical group-think reptiles = cold, heartless, and completely self-serving!

Their last lie was: 'We'll get your file updated in the next two or three weeks.' Three months later, it still hadn't arrived. I didn't want to see the putrid two-faces – each - of Fanny and Beaverhousen EVER again. I knew further engagement was just self-flagellation - punishing myself. I knew the game was over, and they'd planned everything. They're deaf! Nothing I say or do matters, as has been the case from day one. Curiously, all of these awkward pilferers of reality want small talk at the end of the meeting. "So, is gardening fun?" I couldn't resist: "Not as much fun as trying to stop you getting me fired every week." It said, "No we haven't." I just laughed. They are to the truth what Meghan Markle is to sincerity. "We hear you're doing great in the chapel. Your piano playing is wonderful," the inbred puffer fish face said. "Yes," I replied. "Playing at the memorials of men who kill themselves because of this evil system - and your department - is devastating. I don't know how you lot sleep at night!" Ouch. Ridicule is my only weapon of defence at this point. I wasn't joking, of course. I had to play for several men who literally lost the will to live - two of whom were going home shortly. They had been drained of their humanity and existence by probation, which made their reintegration into society so difficult that, latterly, they couldn't carry on.

Despite all of my gags and flippancy, prison is dangerous - life or death. Probation and parole are the biggest provocateurs in jail, without a shadow of a doubt - leading to hundreds of deaths and self-harm incidents.

I couldn't wait to get out of that bottom burp stenched office, away from these toxic turds of fake hypocrisy. They made my toes swell. "Any questions," it asked. "Yes, so, on record - once psychology has finished - I have therefore completed my sentence plan and can go to CAT-D. Is that correct?" This was the only question I cared about. "Yes, we'll ad hoc you immediately once the twelve-week assessment is over - IF they don't recommend courses or therapy." Another revealing premonition, exposing their true intentions. They'd now put all their chips on one number and backed this lame horse. It was shit or bust - I'm either loop-de-loop and they win, or I'm on a bus home. We'd wasted <u>NINE</u> months waiting for a psychology slot and next week it would begin in earnest!

Chapter 32

So, am I Bonkers, Crackers or a Head the Ball???

The following week, at 9 am, I was finally scheduled to meet with the Senior Forensic Psychologist and Deputy Senior Forensic Psychologist at HMP. This wasn't local wannabe quacks - they'd hired in the big guns! Jo and Jen were waiting for me behind the 'activities' locked door. Unlike the OMU tosspots, they didn't smell of tinned salmon and cat litter. The relief was palpable. I was pissed off, though - Wednesday morning was band rehearsal. Could this be another unfortunate coincidence? Ermm... my diary wasn't exactly packed, yet this booking clashed curiously with my date with the piano. Grumpy Alex can give a very cold shoulder. This was not the cozy, rosy-glow start that my two loon analysts - looking for trouble - were hoping for!

Jo and Jen were literally driving over from Birmingham to see me - at mega cost to HMP - pulling their resources away from proper criminals with a risk above 1%. Three hours in the car for one hour with me? Shameful. We ended up missing two weeks, as Jo and Jen didn't make it from Birmingham. Surely, they could've found someone local who could stitch me up at far less cost to the public - and with way less inconvenience to themselves.

Jo put her hand out, and I did the same. These two ladies had my freedom in their hands - we both knew it. I'd phoned a lot of mates, like Emma Kenny, who is a brilliant psychologist. She's also an amazing broadcaster and stage star. She promised me that, if I was just me, they'd give up immediately and see that this whole thing was a stitch-up - a total waste of everyone's time. She had total confidence that these two pros couldn't be corrupted and didn't have any skin in the game. I wasn't as confident - for very obvious reasons. She, and endless others, did not believe they could be 'bought' by the system or would lie about my mental stability. It was a stretch too far - even by .gov standards. My devoted KC, David Aubrey, had worked for years on various panels overseeing approval for being sectioned, and he said it would literally be impossible for them to even get 0.19% close to insinuating such a theory for me - as I've never had a single mental health episode in my life, let alone taken any pills for anything other than a paracetamol for ball ache after ten minutes in the presence of OMU! Unlike most wappy, testicle-touching trolls in their mother's back bedrooms, I've never had any of their common conditions whatsoever - including any insinuation of even an ingrowing toenail!

So, I went in 'trying' to be open - despite knowing it was a total hoodwink wankathon! Not engaging would have been an OMU dream, as they could say I refused to join the circus, and therefore my sentence plan was incomplete. They win – no CAT-D. They know there is ZERO justification for this, but it's all they've got left. We sat down and immediately I asked, "Why am I here?" Jo said, "We're here to get to know you." Immediately, paranoia raised its ugly head, as I didn't want them to know me - why should I open myself up like a Gen Z on Onlyfans? I said,

"Look, I am being forced to be here, and blackmailed into attending, which totally goes against your founding principles of psychology. I don't want or need to be here. They even lied that you're the 'stalking hub' - which you are not – your psychology! I know you know this." They had a look of shock and were taken aback. Jo said, "Well Alex, we appreciate your honesty. Why do you feel you're being blackmailed?" I said, "Well, the OMU liars say that unless I sit here wasting both of our time, I can't progress to CAT-D, so I have no choice – which is blackmail." Jen looked at Jo in disbelief at my candour, they stared at me in shock. I knew it was shit or bust. I continued, "Ladies, I'm probably the most honest person you've ever met - that's why I'm in prison. I'm fearless. I do not fanny about, filibuster, or tell lies - let alone butter parsnips. I'm passionate, and I'll risk everything to expose the truth. I've been this way for twenty-five years, and you can't ask me to change who I am." Again, I could see a fear of 'Who the hell have we got here?' come across their faces.

This entire system is about saying sorry (for normal people). However, you are also entitled to maintain your innocence. They are fully aware of this - having actually read my file (unlike OMU who couldn't be arsed). I think my two poor shrinks knew this was nonsense, but - being on the government gravy train - they had no choice but to continue the pantomime. It's all just ANOTHER box-ticking exercise - that had to be completed. "Alex, you seem to be resistant," Jen said. "Resistant?" I replied. "This is a joke. I have no history of any mental health issues - never taken a pill in my life. You've made me wait six months, yet you're the two most senior psychologists in HMP, claiming to be overworked with parole. And now, you want me to trust you - and invest the next three months (at least) in this lunacy - based on nothing but the desperation of OMU (to leg me over), despite admitting my risk is a laughable 0.19%. I don't qualify for a single course, so they are stitching me up with this tomfoolery - in the hope you'll diagnose me with the monkey aids or PTSD from BBC middle management!" I got a semi smile. I then asked my killer question, "What would you do if you were me?" – the best question ever! Jennifer calmly replied, "Why do you hate OMU?" Here we go – now we're getting somewhere. Clever pivot and distraction. This wasn't about my mental health – it's about hurting the feelings of more brainless establishment muppets. I said, "Ladies, my job is to smell bullshit. I didn't survive twenty-five years as an investigative journalist walking round like a SPICE zombie with my eyes closed. The imbeciles running this place have lied, and wanted to put me on a year-long 'violent reoffenders' course! It's preposterous. When they were caught out, it was just another mistake. Again, what would you do?" I, of course, knew they wouldn't answer this question - but it's a brilliant way of getting them to backtrack and see the sabotage I'm up against. "Alex, you make these claims about them, tell us what happened." This open questioning and willingness to listen was a revelation to me, as it was the opposite approach to the aggressive, defensive, talk-over, odious bullshit I'd endured with the Celias - whose communication skills resembled those of a hibernating tortoise.

They (rightly) wanted to hear my thought process and the reasoning behind my strong opinions. They'd been told I was a maverick big mouth who spouts lies to stalk shrinking violets. Jo and Jen were calling my bluff. Smart. I explained the system had failed me. No one turned up -TWICE - to do my paperwork, then guessed what I'd done, why I'd done it, and who I was. They'd copied and pasted from 'The Stalker's Handbook' for effect and presented it as my OASYS case file. I calmly expressed that my career had been defined by fighting injustice and battling frauds like the morons in probation at HMP Stocken. Jo and Jen didn't jump to the defence of the Ministry of Justice whatsoever......or indeed HMP Stocken. To my amazement Jo said, "Alex, the system is broken. OMU is completely overstretched and can't cope with their workloads." Her candour is only to be admired, but how does that help me? I can't believe that - once again - I'm the enemy of the state, simply for asking people to do their job properly. She continued, "You're a smart man, Alex - someone who deals in clever use of language and nuance - and they simply don't know how to handle you!" Wow. I hadn't been in the room five minutes, and they'd more or less conceded that His Majesty's Prison Service is a joke - and the very people who determine your freedom are Over-promoted, Moronic, and Underqualified = OMU. Which is exactly what I'd accused them of being a thousand times - in my letters and to their face! Oy vey - what a shit show. History won't stop repeating, will it...

For the first time, throughout the entire three years of legal hell and terminal bullshitery, I finally felt I had met two people who could see the wood for the trees. We carried on chatting and established what I was - and wasn't - willing to talk about. Because psychology HAS to be voluntary - it's a mutual commitment - which of course this wasn't. However, their own rules worked in my favour. I set the boundaries, not them! They rely on loose lips. I was too long in the tooth for these games. They had tried to get me to sign a 'I agree and consent to be here form.' Fack that! I was all over it, and wrote: 'I am being blackmailed by OMU to be here against my consent.' This was an untenable position for Jo and Jen. They were very gracious - considering what a laughingstock this is. I refused to talk about anything that wasn't relevant...for which I'm perfectly entitled.

I quickly realised sixty minutes goes quickly when Belfield's off on one. We spent the first session establishing the prison service has gone to shit, and it's run by imbeciles. We left the meeting cordially, and I churlishly asked, "What was the point of that?" Jen said, "Just relax. All we want to do is get to know you." For the love of God - why me? This is the worst Tinder EVER! "We'll see you next week." Next week didn't happen. These very busy women had been called to an emergency parole. Marvellous. They'd already bought another seven days of achieving nothing - whilst keeping me excreted from the public gaze and shushy. I want to be very clear: they're powerful. If you're a murderer and have served twenty-five years, these ladies will sign on the dotted line to open the cell door - or keep you banged up for another three years until they have another say. They literally free rapists or paedos with one swipe of the pen. It was like being on an episode of *Loose Women.* We talked until the cows came home... and ended up with a house full of cows! They're more powerful than any Clown Court judge. Terrifying reality. I cannot deny - all of this fake chit-chat was making me lose the will to live.

Prison is Life and Death

One of the magical things about prison is that I could never have predicted the solidarity amongst 'good' men. The first person I met at HMP Stocken was a giant of a man called Jock - who, unsurprisingly, was very Scottish and a veteran. Jock ran induction singlehandedly and had free reign in the jail to go anywhere. He'd work fourteen-hour days if guys came in late, and wouldn't settle until everyone had what they were entitled to. He was a star. He was especially kind to me, and could see this clearly was not my world. He got me a jacket, clothing, and all the bits and bobs to clean and sort out my pad. From that moment on, he kept an eye on me and literally advised me on any issues or questions I had. Shortly after, this twenty-stone man started to lose weight - big time - and by Easter, he was down six stones. Something was seriously wrong. He had faded from a strong hero in his sixties to a withered, tired, and clearly very unwell man.

Being ill in jail is the absolute worst. To begin with, getting medical attention is not easy. What's more frustrating - and even life-threatening - is that healthcare in prisons is so stretched with self-harmers and drug addicts that they struggle to take seriously men who complain about 'invisible' illnesses, as so many cry wolf. After months of begging and complaining, Jock finally got a scan - after being taken to hospital cuffed to two officers. By the summer, Jock was down to twelve stone and could barely walk. He'd been diagnosed with terminal cancer. Within nine months, he'd gone from pushing huge crates for miles to becoming a man I would see holding onto the wall just to stand. We would all try and help him, but he was too proud - until it was too late. One day, I was going past the Seg, and Jock looked like he was about to collapse. It's a mile from Newton to healthcare. Finally, he needed a wheelchair. He couldn't battle on any longer. Prison had broken him - and in his hour of need, it was all too late, even for compassionate release.

What I hadn't realised is that, a few months after I arrived, Jock had been unceremoniously sacked from his beloved job. He'd been in jail twenty years and had lost touch with a lot of his close family - so his job was his entire focus. They claimed he wielded too much influence at Stocken and needed to change roles for 'security reasons,' based on intel. That old chestnut again. It broke his heart and spirit. This happens all the time in prisons, where they give 'trusted' men very 'powerful' and important jobs - running around like blue-arse flies for £15 a week - only to rip it away from them when they become cosy and settled.

By June, Jock was in a wheelchair. It was horrific to see his inhumane decline in such a short time. He was on such a high dosage of medication that he told me he'd wake up in the morning, having eaten all of his canteen food in one sitting - a week's worth - and remembered nothing about it. It's so cruel that prison doesn't give dignity to terminally ill men. Lest we forget, about 400 men died in jail last year - many were terminally ill. Jock had managed to rebuild a relationship with his mum and sister on his deathbed. They were given special permission to come in together, along with eight other family members - for a double visit one Saturday. I was seeing Mum and Dad the same day. It was heartbreaking to see the long-lost family reunite - and, of course, the heartbreaking goodbye. So dreadfully cruel and unnecessary. What possible risk could a dying man in a wheelchair, unable to walk, pose to society? The inevitable drew closer, as Jock faded away in his remaining moments.

In July, I'd been asked to play the piano at my first suicide service in the chapel. A man had taken his own life with an overdose on H Wing, and his family requested a service for the men, which they would attend. The man had just been turned down for parole after almost two decades behind the door. He literally lost the will to live. Simply awful. I've played the piano and sung at many funerals over the years. It's mostly 'a job' - you just get on with it. But this was different. Prison is a dark and seedy world of depression, mental illness, addiction, and often severely broken men. As I write, HMP Lowdham (just moments from my home), have had five suicides (hangings) in the past year. It's shocking! Suicide is inevitable in prison, especially with certain offences dripping in shame - but it is still a human life. Remember, at least a full 747's worth of prisoners die each year within HMP - that we know of. Tim asked me to play the piano, as Anne was away. His family were so grateful, as a hundred men turned up to fill the chapel. Tim is a pro and got the tone absolutely spot on. He's a terrific Chaplain, and the heart and soul of HMP Stocken - through good and bad.

Only a matter of weeks later, I was at Jock's Memorial. He had been taken to a hospice just 24 hours before he passed. Anne played the piano beautifully for his family, who attended. Sadly, there's no common sense or dignity within HMPPS. If you're in custody you die a criminal. I'm so glad he was able to be with his family as he passed. What a hero. What a gentleman to me. Prison isn't all air fryers, gym, and spice. So many don't make it out alive. Even more leave a basket case and end up on the merry-go-round of the HMP. Tragic on every level.

RIP Jock, you were a gentleman. I'll never forget you!

Chapter 33

The Top Story on the BBC (Again)!

My tomato picking was a hoot - it was a glorious July! My relentless sunbathing made me go from translucent ginger death tone to blancmange pink... or lobster. Week after week, I picked bread baskets full of tomatoes. In between, I'd pull up the odd weed to try and look busy. I'd basically been rehabilitated into Alan Titchmarsh! I had three gorgeous raised beds I watered twice a day - simply for the fun of it.

The highlight of my summer was being the top story of *East Midlands Today* - <u>AGAIN</u>! The summer is known as 'silly season' in news, but this was more lunatic asylum. It's never normal seeing yourself on TV, let alone on the news, when you're least expecting it......but this was a topper! Why now? Who was pulling these puppet strings? All very fishy......

Can you imagine how utterly vindictive it would be for the BBC to promote a 'GoFundMe' for a 'victim' to get civil damages, simply because he was offended that I'm not sorry – seemingly the basis of his claim. This was <u>11</u> – yes eleven months after my conviction for Stalking <u>WITHOUT</u> fear, alarm <u>or</u> distress (which was never mentions in the article)! Curiously, the word WITHOUT was never mentioned by the police, in court, or indeed, during this article on the BBC. I've never met this man ever! I'd never heard of him before my witch hunt began. This openly penniless man (the reason for his appeal) was given six minutes at 1pm, 6pm, and 10pm on BBC1, plus thirty seconds every half-hour from 6am to campaign for donations to sue me in the High Court. He admitted he'd borrowed £6,000 so far, and to date has borrowed another £10,000 - to hire the same solicitors of another 'WITHOUT FEAR' victim. Nobody had told him that it costs the shushy gag brigade £200,000+ to win a £10,000 settlement. The precedent has been set many times, and payouts - if successful - are around £20K, so the claimant is looking at a jaw-dropping six-figure sum... to win a tenth of the costs. Cuckoo! This doesn't seem great maths to me, does it to you? He openly admitted he hadn't got any funds to do it himself - let alone the finances to cover the cost and a countersuit, should he lose. Why were so many people so fixated and resolute on continuing the very public campaign to destroy me professionally, reputationally, and financially?! I feel like I'm being stalked! This hysterical article was akin to a mass murder report - with lines including 'he hurt my feelings' - which caused much hilarity the following day across HMS Stockings and social media. When twelve hundred cons are coming up to you, laughing and absolutely dumbfounded as to what I owed compensation for - you know this was utter bummocks. BTW, I wasn't stalking him to find out this information - it was on MY TV, in MY prison cell! This is arguably publicity money can't buy. The power of public opinion far outweighs - and outlasts - a news article. The thing that has become clearer and clearer as the months progress is that no one can work out what I've actually done - and, moreover, what these people want... other than cheap publicity and me incarcerated, gagged, and hopefully dead. Even with six minutes of 'top-drawer' BBC journalism - by a hack who doesn't work for the BBC and seemingly filmed it on a Nokia 10 - the public were none the wiser. The journalist doesn't have a social media footprint anywhere. Most peculiar. Curious, hey? Maybe this hack was AI.

This piece (paid for via the TV rape tax) crystalised everything I believed. The dark forces were still at work to destroy me in entirety - and furious, after a year, that my audience, friends, and family were still 100% behind me. Not only is it unethical for *BBC News* to promote, endorse, and advertise a fundraiser for a legal action against an individual - but it's TOTALLY in breach of every *BBC News* editorial guideline to use news time for a personal vendetta and targeted campaign. The person claimed I'd destroyed their career - but admitted in court their career had ended because of Covid and lockdown. If your showbiz highlight over twenty-five years is defined by six minutes on *East Midlands Today* - I send my condolences. It is unbelievable that the BBC broadcast this with no editorial justification (as the top story) - let alone allowing me a right of reply. Proof of the ongoing witch hunt. I'm told this 24-hour BBC campaign raised £0 from the public. Ouch. These people will never realise that all these articles do is ask more questions than they answer. Bizarrely, I'm told this person has made more than five hours of video about me on YouTube since I've been held hostage. Good Lord - who is stalking who??? What is most curious to me is: WHO signed this off at the Beeb? I will go to my grave knowing this wasn't a 'local' decision. Can you imagine how hurtful it must have been - that nobody cared? No leverage at all. Thank God it was on BBC Local! If it hadn't been made by the nonce factory and instead aired on a credible news channel, someone of importance might have seen it - and donated.

What is magnificent is that no one now believes or trusts the old, established legacy media - let alone 'invested' journalists - because of incomprehensible guff like this. News is now political. We know they're biased, prejudiced, bought, and controlled by the institutional gatekeepers. But an appeal for legal fees? That is truly hysterical!! Their agenda and alliances are screaming. We see thousands of newspapers, TV stars, and stations vanishing around the globe, as people now consume their news differently - through standalone producers like me - online - simply because our independence and integrity are more appealing than establishment mouthpieces. Even Wootton and Morgan have ditched TV for YouTube and paywalls. We can't all be wrong? Surely? When the BBC's highest-paid journo was a paedo, and their building mascot was created by a child rapist, it's hard to take these people seriously - no matter how much their boss, Tim Divy, bangs on about 'trust!' Who is left that's credible? What's delicious about my endless MSM character assassination is that, within minutes, someone on YouTube fact-checks the lies and manipulations - and it's immediately discredited and debunked. Imagine if the BBC had been fair and balanced – their founding principles – and said, 'former BBC journalist of fifteen years who wrote for national newspapers for ten years as a whistle-blower of the BBC, became one of the biggest names on YouTube with half a million viewers and 500,000,000 hits……' – how differently that would have painted their version of 'help fund the bankrupting of Alex Belfield, sentenced to 13 weeks for stalking a fella he's never met WITHOUT fear, alarm or distress…..' Both stories are true - BUT one gives context, and the other deliberately does not. It misguides the viewer through manipulation and lies - not truth. This word vomit is everything 'news' should not be. Thank God, I rose to success at the exact point old media was on life support. Twenty years ago, I would be finished, and the haters (who still love me and miss me more than the fans) wouldn't be able to read this very book, that their half an inch is currently aroused over. I wonder how many truth-tellers were wiped out back in the day - unable to defend themselves, and without social media to expose the truth. Terrifying. Thank you, BBC, for the publicity. That laughable piece of gutter guff - colostomy bag hackery - epitomises who and what TV news has become! I send all your entitled staff good luck in your new careers, when the TV licence fee is finally scrapped. Over 250,000 households stopped paying last year alone. A million licences CANCELLED overall. You're DOOMED! The clock is ticking my friends. Let's see if you can get a proper job when the gravy train hits the sausage in the Yorkshire Pudding Valley - and you all drown in sanctimony, not the gravy train of state-sponsored broadcasting. You're all toads in a hole! Karma!

Chapter 34

Shrinking my Patience

Back to the shrinks…..

By my next meeting with the cuckoo investigators, we were going around the houses, deliberately avoiding the elephant in the room. There was still no mention of my crime whatsoever. I read the notes from week one, and it was like we were in two different meetings. I felt totally misrepresented - intentionally - so I slapped it on the table. There was no mention of the chapel, gym, job, or my infinite support inside and outside the prison. I said to the girls, "You have not represented me fairly, either you didn't listen to a word I said, or you've deliberately chosen to edit it out. This does nothing for my confidence in you as professionals!" Jo quickly replied, "You're absolutely right. We should have included that. Yes, it needs explaining how comfortable you've made yourself in prison, despite making it clear you feel you're a hostage." Blimey, that was easy! "Thank you," I said. To be fair, the following week those notes were corrected. You cannot rest on your laurels for a second in this conspiracy commune.

This was a turning point for us. They realised I was no fool and probably, for the first time in my prison history, they'd met someone who had a better memory than them - with nothing to hide! To out communicate me would be difficult. Words are my job, life, love, passion, and entire being. I remember minutia that others forget. It's my job to cut through the crap and boil down what people say in real time. I've dedicated my life to perfecting this skill.

These two very clever women didn't try to cover up, double-speak, or argue with me. They wisely accepted my rationale, and we moved on like grown-ups. Unlike the odious derelicts in OMU, this wasn't a pissing contest of bearing grudges and using their power and venom to eviscerate my existence - to squash my soul and will to live. Next, they asked me about my contempt for authority and my alleged 'hatred' towards the Celia Imries with folders under their arms. I made it very clear: I don't have hate in my bones. But I believe 'the least a human being should expect is respect, common decency, and professionalism.' I had an astounded look back of 'WOW!' Jen looked at me and said, "And you feel you haven't been given that?" I replied, "No. They couldn't be arsed to turn up for my official report – <u>twice</u> - then made it up! Then Cissy and Aida refused to correct their mistakes, and when I wrote to them politely, asking them to sort out the eighty lies, they said if I wrote again, they'd accuse me of stalking them! How could any decent human being deal with these impossible and exploitative people?" I could see the shock on their face at my principled clarity. Jo asked, "But this has happened before, hasn't it? You have accused the police of similar injustice." As quick as a fart after cabbage soup, I said, "What would you do if the bomb squad smashed in your door - having removed their ID and collar numbers - and then raided your house ILLEGALLY, without a warrant? They searched my baked beans for four hours, then released me with no further action - four minutes after they found fack all. Would this endear you to the police?" Jen was clearly astounded and said, "That must have made you angry?" I said, "No - it made me a fortune on YouTube - exposing the moronic, disgraceful, criminal, disgusting, and corrupt creeps who did it!" I did get a smile, but she's no fool, so she repeated the question. I confirmed, "I wasn't angry - I certainly wasn't even surprised. They wanted to pin something on me to <u>shut</u> me up. I was disgusted that we live in such a pathetic country where this could happen – signed off at the very top level like a Chinese dictatorship!" This was a massive turning point with the shrinks. They now realised that I <u>could</u> rationalise and explain everything, but every single one of my answers opened up a can of worms that they didn't want wriggling all over their hideous 1970's prison furniture. The only job of psychologists is to work out if you can reason and explain your actions. If you can – their job is done. Nothing to see here!

In these short few minutes, I knew that they knew this wasn't the story they'd been spun by OMU. I was embroiled in something way above their paygrade that had nothing to do with me being ill, dangerous, or a risk to the public – their <u>ONLY</u> concern. I felt the atmosphere palpably change. The pressure dissipated. We were all FINALLY on the same page. I then asked them the killer journalist question. "Can I ask you an honest question?" They can't say no, so it gives you carte blanche to vent your spleen. 99.99% of civil serpants will never allow you to take control, as their feigned power only exists in the artificial constraints of them controlling the narrative. Jo was gracious and said, "Yes of course." I then asked, "Have you actually read my file? Not the Disney-made-up, bullshit, nonsense version that OMU want to believe - from the BBC Verified website?" Jo replied, "Yes, Alex." And I said, "So, you know I'm the first stalker who has never met, been near, or threatened his 'victims'? I just wanted to know who wrote the email 'to close me down' from the BBC." Agog, Jen confessed, "We know this is complicated. Did it make you angry?" I replied, "Angry? Why would it make me angry? I just wanted to know who wrote the email. I believe this is perfectly rational and reasonable. Neither he, the publisher, or his bosses – the BBC - would tell me who wrote it, which ultimately got me five years in jail! You know I wasn't angry. I wasn't accused of that. You read the file." Blow my bloomers, this was getting good... "If someone wrote an anonymous email to 'close you down,' what would you do?" Jen and Jo stared at me. "Did the house raids make you angry?" Jennifer enquired again. I reiterated, "It made me more determined to expose their blatant, corrupt stupidity - and total abuse of my human rights! The 'no further action' was all the vindication I needed to ridicule them."

Clearly, psychology's fixation and agenda (knowing they couldn't get me on anything else) was to focus on 'anger issues.' I'm a satirist chief piss taker - I don't have the energy for anger. Nor have I ever been accused! Now they really were scuppered and clutching at straws! Sadly, just as we were getting somewhere, that was session two sorted. I was having a hoot, but the clock had beaten me again. It was a jolly joust. We'd have to return for next week's episode; this was like a real-life BBC *Traitors*. I left feeling like these two smarty-pants had finally cracked the egg. Now it was my job to turn it into an omelette....and not over-egg it into a custard. As for 'Mr Angry' - a preposterous claim that anyone who knows me would deem ridiculous. My only curiosity is who's driving this narrative? This is the only coat hanger they have left to hang me on. It's all just woke, namby pamby, tomfoolery, and mumbo hairy bollocks – not to mention, a complete waste of <u>EVERYONE'S</u> time.

Meanwhile, wing life was getting saucy. I love a mucky screw!!! The very well-endowed female officer, Miss Stitz, had got a mouth full after being caught on her knees polishing a prisoner's belt buckle. Gloria's jelly wobblers were the talk of the slammer. Like most millennial women, she seemed to think lip fillers and the silly 'shave off the eyebrows and paint them back on' look was appetising. Of course, for 90% of the prison lads, a post box with a skirt on is positively erotic - so this was a walking 3D Tug TV with cuffs, a truncheon, and PAVA spray. I got word that Gloria Stitz had been unceremoniously led out of the building 'in cuffs' - by the rozzers - after being found with a Muscle Mary in an uncompromising position... presumably missionary! This wasn't the first Kanga (Kangaroo = screw - <u>literally</u>) to be arrested during my time in the slammer. Old MJM - 'Milk Jugs Mavis' - had been getting very familiar and friendly with a very butch lad called 'Tim' - who was far from tiny (if rumours are true). Anywho, Tiny Tim was actually a good lad. Built like a brick shit house, he used to be my barber, and we'd have very nice chats during a short back and sides and a blow from the front. Sadly, he always seemed to fall at the last HMP hurdle. For three vapes, he gave me a perfect trim -considering he couldn't use scissors. Well, he DID use them, but he shouldn't have. Perhaps security in reception isn't as tight as they'd hoped - as he sneaked them in! Officer G Cups seemed to be spending an awful lot of time popping in and out of his pad - presumably getting tips on blow-dries... or blow jobs. But she stupidly got caught on CCTV, in and out of the laundry where he was 'working.' Apparently, as he was folding boxes, she was dropping her drawers. There were no cameras in the laundry or the 'equipment' cupboard next to it. It appears 'Randy Rita from Rutland' regularly needed to assist with his equipment! Those bottles of fabric conditioner need a woman's touch, and Gloria Stitz is the screw to give him a hand! I'm going to guess there's a hundred cameras on each wing. You can't get away with anything. They might not film 'what happens' - but they ain't going to miss you <u>coming</u>…...and going (literally). That night, Tiny Tim had his pad spun (turned upside down by the mufties/security/goons) and he was taken to the block (Seg). They found a piece of paper with her telephone number on - and a mobile was found shoved up his arris when he was put through the scanner. Unfortunately, her number had been called hundreds of times. Talk about dropping a prison bollock on both sides!!! That is VERY rare. They must've found something serious - and undeniable proof. What was most shocking was that, six days later, he was meant to be out on his tag. A total disaster that would set him back six months... at least. He'd once again gone arse over tit (if you pardon the pun) crossing the finishing line - all for a quick one, two, buckle my shoe on the washer during fast spin. He'd only told me the week before that he was desperate to get home - and now he was in the block, likely to be shipped to a CAT-B (even higher security) for corrupting an officer... until the very last day of his sentence. If he'd only waited two weeks, he could've banged her like a barn door in the car park - and no one would've cared less! What a disaster. Officer Mega Mammaries was bailed to appear in court. I'm told she was sacked and received a suspended sentence. Gloria Stitz can never work for the bang-up society within the Prison Service ever again. How on earth these people think they'll get away with it is beyond me. Two nice people. Two good people... Two flawed people... Two horny millennials... Two very silly and short-sighted randy buggers who will pay dearly for their hanky-panky. Welcome to the circus of prison! It feels like everyone is getting a portion other than me. Why am I always the bridesmaid and never the groom?

I've noticed a lot of this lately with the young women EVERYWHERE in jails. The average age of a new recruit now is twenty - I've got socks in the drawer older than that. The staff canteen now offers Happy Meals to keep them quiet. A lot of these peculiar, damaged, and odd whippersnappers - who draw all over themselves - cross so many boundaries that would never have been acceptable, even pre-COVID. They don't understand where the line is drawn. They have no social graces and seem desperate for affirmation and attention - especially from the well-endowed randy lags. These ill-equipped, inexperienced, and immature girls - are the very <u>worst</u> type of human to put in the sin bin. Desperation for staff is dropping standards lower than their gussets and under crackers on the cleaning cupboard floor. Talking of which, I bet that dreadful Tiger Lily will want another welfare check any day soon!

The following week, during bang-up, a knock came on my knocker. Three officers were prowling. Mr Smarts was a young new officer - a former soldier and salt of the earth. Mr Ellis had been very kind to me. And that vomit-face life drain - Cruella De Villas - was stood there too. Vomit-face said, "We're doing a random search Mr Belfield." I said, "Oh really. Strange coincidence after telling psychology about my police raid six days ago." I wonder if OMU read Jo and Jen's notes and planned this PTSD reminder - of having my pad soiled by their mucky .gov fingers - to make me ANGRY? Mr Smarts said, "Are you compliant?" I said, "Yes, but whatever you do don't look in my second draw. Please don't go in there or you'll find it. I'd be very embarrassed." Of course, Smarts (brilliantly named) and Mr Ellis knew I was taking the piss. Smarts said, "You know you can take all of your legal documents with you." A brilliant wink to the prison laws about 'Rule 39' - officers can't read lawyer's letters or court papers, etc. I said, "Well, that's a flaw in the system. If I were going to cover my paper in spice, heroin, or Viagra, I'd use legal notes - which you've just told me you're not allowed to touch, read, or test. Whoopsie." The fellas laughed. Cruella growled like a Bulldog having its arsehole sniffed by a Bichon

Frisé. Old taint face Cruella Deville didn't see the irony of my humour at all, let alone the funny side of this latest sham. She became excited - like Doddy when I head for the biscuit tin. She is more of a long-faced bloodhound or XL Bully than a cockapoo. The opportunity to poke around my pad, perve over my pants, and prowl around my particulars was just too much for this neighbourhood watch Keystone cop. This daft cow needed a mop. Dripping with 'I'm going to be the one to get him' energy, this soft, simple slapper couldn't wait for the wild goose chase to begin. They took me to a nice office to wait while they searched my room. I wasn't worried, of course. This was deliberately designed to unnerve, frustrate, AND MAKE ME ANGRY! Do you see what she did there? Cruella's plan was so obvious. If I'd refused and kicked off, they could've given me a nicking and booted me off the Ritz wing for refusing a direct order - this wasn't my first rodeo. I sat in the office and scribbled a couple of pages of the book. Less than fifteen minutes later, they came and got me. Smarts said, "All good. What a waste of time that was." I laughed. Cruella was stood there with a face like she'd just sat through two hours of Jason Manford singing live. "You didn't find it then?" I teased. "What are you hiding?" it spewed. "My KitKats. You get two fingers, Miss." Everyone laughed... other than Cruella. She'd been worked from behind by OMU, all in cahoots, and achieved bugger all. But the fellas and I were having a laugh at her gormless expense. What 5* pilchards. Utterly malicious but totally pointless. Here's what I don't get. Why bother? All they've done is given me another story for the book and actually put the power back to me. She looked stupid and they found the square root of fack all. I have to say the chaps were <u>VERY</u> respectful and openly embarrassed. In fact, as fastidious as I am, my pad was tidier when they left than when they came in. I got a COMP1 complaints form. Scribbled 'COMPLIMENT' at the top 'FAO GOV' and wrote; 'May I thank the three courteous officers who spun me today and couldn't have been nicer. I thanked them for so studiously fingering my inner sanctum, without causing any damage within my private parts. I am reassured about OMU's and Newton's staff's devotion to wiping out drugs, weapons, and hooch on board HMS Stockings. Please offer Cruella a promotion for her generosity of spirit and grace.' I didn't get a reply.

The following day, I was back with the shrinks. Jo and Jen were as chirpy as ever. As always, they began by asking, "How are you?" I had previously been somewhat sarcastic and facetious - something along the lines of, 'Considering I'm kidnapped in prison...' They'd tilt their heads like kittens after you raise your voice... and sit in feigned pity. I'm sure, with your average crackpot, this would pad twenty minutes moaning about the crap food, dirty showers, or rude staff. I couldn't be arsed. I wasn't going to make their job easy and waste precious (costly) time with foolishness – with them coming all the way from Birmingham. I wanted to cut to the chase. So, on this occasion I called their bluff. "Yes, I'm OK - considering. But I find it very coincidental that, last week, I told you about the corrupt Notts police 'cuntstables' raiding my house with the STI van, and sending in the mafia bomb squad to poke through my bags of pork scratchings and sweet potato M&S crisps. Then, yesterday, the same thing happened from your lot - looking for my stash of machetes and ketamine. Strange coincidence, isn't it, ladies?" Silence. Jen then did the old line: "Did that make you angry?" I replied, once again, "Why would that make me angry? It makes me realise I can't trust you, OMU, or this prison. What kind of idiots would spin the cell of a man they know hadn't got anything?" Again, silence. Once again, they churlishly tried to butter their parsnips and threw it back: "Did they find anything?" This tennis match of tomfoolery continued. "Of course not. You know they didn't." I ended this ping pong of prickery with, "It makes me feel that I should have as much contempt for HMPPS as I do Nottinghamshire Police." Done. Touché. Look - I'd got it off my chest, with my tits tingled like Gloria Stitz in the laundry cupboard. Now we could continue...

Prior to the session they had passed me last week's notes. I noticed that Jen had picked up on my reference to the word 'delicious.' I had said that it was ironic that my assassins had stated their intention was to close me down, but in doing so had made me the most famous, successful, and high-profile of my career – 'a delicious irony.' "Why did you take exception to that word Jennifer?" I asked. She answered, "Well it's a very strange word to use in that context." I said, "Jen, I'm a forty-three-year-old journalist and entertainer who has spent his life using words as my tools. Do you want me to pretend to be as inarticulate as 99% of staff and inhabitants of this 'Premier Lodge for Prized Prats' are, or be me? You said you wanted me – not a sanitised edited prison version of me." I could see the ladies squirming. "No, no. We'll remove it from the notes. We need you to be you," Jo said. Another self-combusting fire extinguished. It does prove how forensically these two mind-readers read into my every syllable. This wasn't the best start to week three, but I'd cleared the air. Word would get back to the OMU savages via the notes they'd be reading - with bated breasts.

We were only three hours into the 'getting to know you' sessions, and it felt like we were running dry. I'd slapped it on the table about my perfect life (for me) - including no sex, drugs, addiction, or violent issues (the backbone of most of their work) - so their work felt done. Neither Jen nor Jo had encountered anyone more boring than me... which was exactly the same position Nottingham Police found themselves in when they raided my home three times and didn't get one shred of evidence. I'd told Jen and Jo about my twenty-five years in radio, ten years in print, and rise to fame on YouTube. They knew my agenda was never fame, jealousy, or profit - it was born out of entertaining my punters from day one and trying to expose the truth. The price I'd paid was obvious. The wild accusations the fantasists created about me being racist, sexist, and homophobic were all conjecture and nonsense. Just a lefty, woke, virtue-signalling attempt to destroy me and get me cancelled. Who do these people think they are - the mainstream media? Zero evidence. Just more unsubstantiated hearsay. Homophobic? How dare they! I love my home. At no point did they even attempt to go near 'why did you........' or 'you said......' It was a hot potato - way too scalding to touch. Instead, it felt more like a Piers Morgan Life Stories. We waffled on about nothing - but, as the notes prove, they would clearly see I was a family man, devoted to my job and audience. And then, the most flattering of lines: 'Alex feels he has a vocation to hold to account and expose corruption.' BINGO. They'd got me! I'll accept the verdict, Your Honour. If only Jo and Jen were the judge in the Clown!

Whether it's with dodgy Covid companies, Handcock's landlord, Baroness Mone - or politicians lying, cheating, and screwing the very people who elected them - I'm not exactly renowned for keeping quiet for an easy life. A smaller example was my exposé of Phillip Schofield and his 'ITV right-hand man' - eighteen months before *The Sun* threw him under the bus. Shush shushy! From exposing paedos or convicted fraudsters on their latest con, to revealing public figures living double lives paid for - and protected - by public money, I will always fall on my sword of free speech. I used my platform and influence to expose the stories others <u>intentionally</u> covered up. I sleep very well at night knowing I compromised my own freedom and safety for the greater good. What a price I've paid - but finally, for these two HUGELY influential and powerful 'forensic psychologists' to get my character - true character - in a matter of minutes was incredible. A weight was lifted. Why were the police, Clown Court, and OMU, so resistant to see the real me, yet these ladies got it - in less than three hours! Perhaps my style touched a nerve? Finally, vindication, albeit way too late, but nevertheless vindication. However, hopefully this could be a turning point of common sense! I'm only joking....even I'm not that naïve. This <u>was not</u> the result 'the state' was looking for! It was inevitable that they'd double down.

We're now in early September, and I'd had no word from OMU in months…...despite their promise to update my file in two weeks. The silence was intentionally deafening. By pure chance, I bumped into the nose-pierced sphincter, who desperately tried to make a quick about-turn and escape when she spotted me - ironically leaving the chapel. Thank You, God! I said, "Miss Beaverhousen, you said you were going to update and correct the eighty-plus mistakes on my file in July, yet I've heard nothing." Then it started to stutter – LIAR ALERT – "Well, err, well, well, well it needs to be signed off." I was straight in - "By whom?" Here we go again, "Err, err, I, I, I, he, or he, or." I said, "He or, he or, he ought to know better! So, who is signing it off?" (I'd got the big boned bumbling buffoon bent over backwards – most off-putting). She spouted, "Management." Straight back, "Who in management?" You see the problem with lying is that you have to be quick, smart, and able to double lie to get yourself out of the triple shit. This turkey necked foul piece of work couldn't find her enormous arse hole with both hands, let alone think on the spot. "Urggg" - it stammered! At this point, the reversing spineless jellyfish couldn't get away quick enough. They're so powerful on their tippy-tappies and in packs of OMU hyenas. I don't know about you, but when someone squirms and lies to my face - I'm out. There's no way back! It's hopeless and pointless. As it slithered down the corridor <u>trying</u> to answer, I said, "I think psychology is coming to an end, so I'll need my paperwork doing correctly - as it should have been done nine months ago." This walking incontinent nappy replied furiously, "What do you mean, coming to an end?" I chirped like a canary in a factory shithouse, "Like I just said, I don't think there's a lot left to say. We're done!" Then came the most telling revelation ever: "Well, I thought it would take a lot longer than this!" What an admission, hey? I snapped and snarled back with my acid tongue, "No, dear, you hoped it would last a lot longer." BOOM!!!

Exposed. Caught out. True colours. When you catch these passive aggressive suppositories alone, they're not so smart, cocky, or confident, are they? This woman(ish) was on the ropes. She knew my next question would be about an immediate 'ad hoc' to CAT-D, as they promised. She 'thought' and hoped I would be diagnosed with IFD - 'Indefinitely Facked Disease' - by the shrinks. Sorry about your luck: it's not happening, you Judas! To cut a long story medium-length - Jo and Jen couldn't find a thing wrong with me, so had no grounds to humiliate me further. Lotty Beaverhousen slithered off to crush stones with the other OMU demons.

<u>Surely now I can Progress to Freedom?!</u>
The summer progressed, and I was spending hours pottering in the gardens like a retired silver-top - five hours a day. I loved it! I am a modern-day Monty Don Juan! By the end of September, I'd picked five hundred kilos of tomatoes. I'm not shitting you - I

had enough to chuck at the entire terrorist group behind the OMU door of impunity! Seriously, some weeks there were so many bread baskets full that we gave prison visitors free tomatoes on their way out. I arranged for Mum and Dad to get some on Saturday morning. They were more proud of my greenhouse growths than me selling out Blackpool! Funny old world, ain't it? Imagine the value for 'Belfield's Convict Plums' on eBay! Del Boy would be proud! If Gregg Wallace (sentenced by the woke police) ends up in here, he could open another veg stall to keep him busy! Occasionally, I'd be asked to do some mowing in the grounds, which I enjoyed, as I got a 360° suntan mincing around the slammer with my strimmer. I haven't used one of them since I did some personal grooming for Susan Boyle in the nineties. To have such freedom during the summer - free exercise and screw-free liberty - is a massive 'privilege.' Look, people can't believe how grateful I am for these 'ordinary' and silly little things, but remember: ten years ago, prisoners at HMP Stocken would never have been allowed to do this job. You'd be shoved behind your door with a radio 23.5 hours a day. Imagine if it was tuned to BBC Local Radio? TORTURE! I still recoil at what the lads went through during Covid. Hideous. Twenty-three and a half hours lock-up for nearly two years, for absolutely no justifiable reason. They were even threatened that if they didn't have the prick injectable, they'd never see daylight again! I've always counted my luck and blessings from day one. I'm an optimist. On my worst day, I'd tell myself - 'At least you're not Angela Rayner's make-up artist or speech therapist!!'

I could never put into words the joy of watching my ducklings grow and fly the nest. Hand-feeding these bundles of joy sent my heart into overdrive. I'd sit by the pond for hours, writing my book whilst they puddled around me. Pete, who ran the place, was a diamond and I'll never forget his kindness and humanity. He got very poorly before I left, and I never got to say a proper goodbye. I hope someone will show him this one day. I'd send him a copy, but I can't see it getting past security at HMS Stockings - do you? Do you think in years to come they'll allow this book in the library – or will it be banned and cancelled for no reason – just like me? Irony hey?! My time at HMP Stocken in the gardens was like that ABBA song (no not Chiquitita), I mean 'Our last Summer!' It was perfect! There were some really nice lads up there and we had <u>freedom</u>, unlike the other 1,185 Stocken asylum victims stuck in a dopey workshop pretending to be rehabilitated. What a load of old shite. The weather was remarkable - I had the best tan of my life growing radishes, cucumbers, peppers, onions, herbs, carrots, and the odd kumquat, which was a privilege I'll never regret. Who would have the time and inclination for this in real life? Maybe I needed time to be 'off grid?' I was living like one of those scruffy 'Just Stop Oil' whackos, with all the muck over my trousers. The Lord works in mysterious ways!

On 17th September, it was my 're-categorisation' day - and my first anniversary as a political prisoner and hostage. Every six months, every single prisoner gets re-assessed for which CAT prison you need to be in, according to your risk. 100%

algorithms - and not prejudiced by box-ticking opinion, apparently. They'd dodged my first one back in March by simply not completing my paperwork. You can go straight to CAT-D, but it never happens nowadays - certainly not in cases as 'high-profile' as mine. Total Radio SILENCE, despite my less than 1% risk! Instead of turning me down, they just did nothing - breaching all PSI. No meeting - just totally ghosted. Despite their aspersions, they had no justification to detain me. I was automatically kidnapped for another six months. They are required to give you a written reason why you haven't gone to 'CAT-D' - and why closed conditions are required. I didn't get that either. Must have got lost in the post too! My two front-stabbing Vagisil pen-pushers had not only maliciously lied, cheated, and manipulated my official 'OASYS' file, but had forced me to waste nine months seeing the shrinks for no reason whatsoever. Now, after twelve months In custody, they very conveniently overran my next CAT-D opportunity - pushing me back to March 2024 to get home. That totals eighteen months! Pure evil spite. The fact that a village near Oakham is missing two idiots doesn't even cover it. It was so clear. It was so sick. It was also unlawful.

Another week flew by, and I arrived for what would be my fourth and final session with Jo and Jen - the two 'Senior Forensic Psychologists.' I sat down, and Jo said, "This week, now we've got to know you, we thought we could do mind maps and use the whiteboard." Well, you can imagine my reaction to this lefty, hocus-pocus, box-ticking crap! I'd spent three hours doing the flotsam and jetsam of my career and now they wanted me to invest in some vegan, free love, #metoo, gender neutral, noncy bollocks, from the University of woke. I THINK NOT! Balls to that – I'm off! "Absolutely not, Jo," I said. "You told me at the beginning that you wanted to get to know me and find out why my crime happened. You've already (in three hours) conceded you have. We're done. All you need to know now is why I did what I did, after a BBC employee started a witch hunt to 'close me down' - right?" Silence again. This wouldn't be the last time I'd leave two HMP pros stunned, shamed, and absolutely speechless. What's really fascinating is that, at no point, did either of these ladies approach my allegation of BBC or police corruption. SHUSHY! No one in authority seems to want to address my very serious claims. I wonder why... I made it clear to them what happened to me, and how all the 'victims' were connected – something that was banned from being mentioned during my court case. I told them how the BBC had presented the entire file and how two of the 'victims' had apologised in court. I let them know how one victim had a bent cop lie on oath and another had confessed to tuning into (and taping) every broadcast I made - in case I mentioned him.

Of course, all four cases involving the women were returned as not guilty verdicts - no one believed a word of their sabotage and they no longer work for the BBC post-trial. Just days after my sentence *The Guardian* reported that the judge's wife had been given a job working for the BBC and she'd updated her LinkedIn page confirming this was true. How can anyone unpack, comprehend, defend, or begin to rationalise this absolute nincompoopery! They didn't! For the first time, I felt listened to and believed – it had only taken three years! After a lot of head nodding, we were done.

Frankly, Jo and Jen couldn't wait for me to shut up! The peculiarity of my stitch-up was of no interest to them - once they could see I wasn't bonkers they headed for zee hills. They were not going to say a syllable. Very wise! Funny how my old judge refused my request for a psychologist in the trial - and here I am, with two bobby dazzlers, paid for by you, to diagnose me 100% safe. I wanted this vindication a year ago! That would have scuppered the cuntstable and prosecution narrative - now wouldn't it! No wonder they didn't want these two sanity truth-tellers at the trial - to undermine the witnesses! No flies on these two (or me!) - Jen said, "So it feels like this has come to a natural end."

I knew OMU would be pro-nuclear and seek revenge! Those over-promoted port-a-loo cleaners upstairs would be incandescent with rage - that the game was over with the shrinks. BUT now the war would begin with the two brainless wonders, who would now have to fall on their sword and admit there is officially NOTHING wrong with me... Not my opinion. Not my half a million YouTube goggleboxes. But the opinion of the two most respected voices in the prison service! No one was qualified to argue. Their opinion was unchallengeable. I had officially completed my sentence plan. What time is the taxi then?

Seemingly, I'm the only one willing to disclose my ENTIRE medical records - proving I don't even need a paracetamol. Unlike so many trolls, who have publicly admitted they're as mad as a box of frogs, as thick as tarmac, as traumatised as a Taylor Swift fan, and as dumb as a monkey on a rock.

"So now what?" I asked Jo. "Well, Alex, we'll get OMU in next week to explain that this has come to a natural end, and we've completed our assessment." I couldn't resist - for the record: "So I am done, you are done, and they cannot continue this circus to delay my CAT-D any further?" Jen replied, "Alex, we are nothing to do with CAT-D or your risk. All we can do is present them with our findings, based on the reports you've seen week by week." Here we go: "So what's the point of all this - if they can still move the goalposts and ignore your clean bill of health?" Jen stepped in, "Alex, sadly, that is beyond our control. We can only hand them our report." Sombrely, I said, "Well, they're corrupt and won't read this, it's not the answer they're looking for. This is not the .gov narrative to keep me in jail! Now they'll feel even more stupid and get revenge to avoid the 'I told you so's.'" Silence. This wasn't paranoia BTW, it was my innate reaction based on almost twelve months of collective authoritarian ineptitude, incompetence, experience and three years of the establishment conspiracy.

Jo and Jen had done their job. I thanked the ladies for wasting their time. They didn't even disagree. It was an outrageous waste and abuse of resources and public money. So next week, will OMU turn up? I knew it was all going to kick off. I prepared for more egg on face...like a circling pigeon shitting all over you in Trafalgar Square. Lord, take me now!

THE END IS NIGH! What a riot!

HMP Stocken was changing towards the end of 2023. As prisons were overflowing in London, they were sending 'a different breed' of criminal 'up north' - and one of the first ports of call on the A1 was Stocken. You could palpably feel the demographics changing, and that led to an increase in violence, stabbings, and staff assaults. One Saturday afternoon, it all kicked off on M Wing. They wouldn't bang-up. Three lads jumped on the netting, which led to a prison lockdown - the #1 Gov was called in, and the 'nationals' were dispatched. It escalated to 'Gold Command', where the MOJ effectively takes control of a slammer that's out of control.

This is as near to a 'riot' as you're going to get these days. They had collectively smashed up their cells, broken all wing furniture, and obliterated the pool and table tennis tables. To be honest, there's not a lot else they can do. After taking to the net over the 'ones' - they're given a couple of chances to desist - and then it goes 'national,' with the heavies (or mufties) brought in to get them off using any necessary force. The big boys never lose by the way. The nationals ask you once - then your feet don't touch the ground. After our gym session, you could tell the screws weren't happy. It was bang-up - no messing about. Once in Gold Command, no staff can leave the jail… no matter how long it takes. Newton is next to M Wing, so we could hear the ranting and raving - in the hope of persuading them to get off, so they could get home to their Mrs for a swinger's party and a sniff of class A. I jest. These three gentlemen of colour were having none of it. This was now a criminal issue and could land them with up to ten years each for 'inciting a riot' and various other trumped-up charges - to send out a message that this is not acceptable, and will not be tolerated.

These London lads weren't pissing about. They wanted to be shipped out, in the hope of getting back to Belmarsh, so had nothing to lose! Being at height (anything off the floor – even an inch or two) means they're untouchable. Officers are not allowed to touch them under <u>any</u> circumstances. It has to be escalated to the mufties (tornados) at 'The Nationals.' At about 8pm, there was two <u>BIG</u>, bomb-like 'flash bangs.' You could hear it for miles. The mufties had arrived and detonated a smoke bomb so loud that there was no way the lads couldn't be discombobulated - then detained, restrained, and 'bent up' before they'd had time to shit themselves. 'The Mufties' are trained to sort anything out in seconds. You ain't getting away from them… or away with it. All three lads got years added to their sentence. The Gov HATES this stuff - it looks very bad on his scorecard. He'd have done anything to avoid it. Thank God it didn't make the press. I wonder who covered that up? Such events flag the prison as volatile, which is the last thing any Gov needs during a prison crisis. Why did this happen? The failings of OMU and probation to process people correctly.

Overcrowding is now so bad, they're turning CAT-Cs into CAT-Bs to house men who should never be in CAT-Cs. Moving them out of their local area is cruel, inhumane, and also provocative - and causes events like this. Why should they be three hours from home, making visits impossible? It's a ticking time bomb. The fuller prisons get, the further men are being sent to be housed. It's going to get worse before it gets better - but it's a recipe for disaster for the entire Prison Service.

A few days passed, and it was time for my final sign-off shrink session. To my amazement, Jo and Jen were both on time - and Lotty Mingesniffer turned up too, with halitosis that could strip the paint off a Victorian prison pad door. Not everyone can pull off a rainbow cardigan, trilby, flip flops, and hot pants - but Lotty Guntbaggage had a good try. I've been in some awkward meetings over the years, but this was colder than an arctic cruise. Obviously, she'd been told it was curtains, but how would she react? I couldn't resist: "Where's your boss, Lotty?" I sneered. I'd so missed delicious Fanny... well, it's been a year, boys!!! "Oh, she's busy today," it cowered. I said, "I can imagine. Are you sure this isn't too uncomfortable without her holding your hand, Lotty?" Ouch - "I'M FINE," it snapped, like a two-litre Bacardi drunkard at a twelve-step AA meeting. "So, what can I do for you ladies?" I said - to deliberately undermine their authority. "Well, Alex," Jo said, in her usual classy and demure way, "this has come to a natural end, so I wanted us all to sit together." I couldn't resist: "So what time is my CAT-D Lotty?" Miss Whiffgrowler was seething, "Alex, we will now look at your file again and re-address your risk now you've completed this part of your sentence plan." Snake. "This part?" I said, "<u>This</u> is the <u>entire</u> sentence plan; all I've had to do for a year is to get to know these lovely ladies for less than four hours – hardly a twelve-month high intensity therapy like KAIZEN, is it? Oh, talking of which, where is my updated OASYS, you said you'd have it nine weeks ago?" The look on this wet wipe's face, "Alex it's not all about you, I'm busy." I couldn't resist: "Well, if it's not all about me, you might as well go and see someone else. I'm done." This might be the best moment of my life. It was a proper *'Beadles About'* or *'Gotcha'* moment. This charity shop Meghan Markle went as red as her piles and was stunned. "I'm not finished" it begged. "Well, I am. You're Teflon Lotty - you can't lie straight in bed. In fact, the only time I know you're not lying is when your lips are firmly closed! I'm done. You thrive on moving goal posts, well sadly, I don't play football. I'll let you go about your business, and I'll conclude with Jo and Jen." <u>Awkward</u>. I've never heard so many squeaky bottoms – it was like *The Frog Chorus*. Look, in life, you have to know when you can't win. Why would I continue this circus? Why would I indulge this imbecile with anymore of my time? I've got pumpkins that need picking – seriously…...it'll soon be Halloween - and that's the only day in the year that she's socially acceptable! We must celebrate……..Lotty stood and declared, "Alex, I don't know why you're so resistant with me? I'm trying to help you." LMFAO. Oh please. This was delicious. "Help me? You're about as much help as a tank of petrol on a fire. Look Lotty, I've tolerated your double speak, lies, backstabbing, duplicity, fake sincerity, and crap for twelve months. Am I now going to CAT-D or not? I'm almost 0% risk, adjudication free, and have completed my sentence plan – everything you require." She said, "I can't comment until I've looked at your file." I was done. "Oh, please leave, I need to talk privately to my psychologists."

Beaverhousen did the walk of shame. Jo and Jen finally saw it with their own eyes. They said nothing, but saw everything. I had my say, slapped it on the table and they saw everything in front of their eyes. So, what now?......get ready for REVENGE!!!

Chapter 35

Revenge: The end of HMS Stockings

That night, I called my lawyers and told them about the revelation that psychology was over. They said, "I told you so." Big Boned Jean was cock-a-hoop, Network Nick was thrilled, and my producer Tarquin couldn't give two shiny shites - as he'd broken a fingernail during a dogging event near Broadcasting House and was beside himself. As I rang my beloveds, I had great reservations about showing any genuine excitement. I saw this as just another hurdle to jump - on the endless Everest-scale Mountain I'm climbing to freedom. Many were convinced this was my key to the door. Common sense would applaud such optimism. But I knew in my heart, after the OMU's backstabber's reaction, that this was the next chapter in a sickening story of the establishment's gagging order - providing absolutely no voice of reason. By the way, I know it's nothing to do with Lotty or Fanny - they're just the MOJ gatekeepers. My captivity goes to the very top of HMP... and indeed, .gov.

Psychology's report was the worst possible outcome for my saboteurs. If they could have only said, 'he's got narcistic personality disorder' - they could heckle and medicate me forever. Sadly, I'm a nobhead from a pit estate - a fearless professional tease and wind-up on the tippy-tappy. There's no diagnosis for that - YET! The leash was off. Jo and Jen could see the absurdity of the mindless, unfounded accusations the Celias had vomited over my file. These appalling lies and distortions were redundant. Their elucidations were now superfluous. Of course, they didn't update or correct the eighty mistakes on my file - in case this stitch-up went their way. A diarrhoea of damaging aspersions was now completely undermined and dismissed by two women nobody could overrule. I believe they realised my 'criminal' case had more holes in it than a colander. So, now what? A few days passed by, and I told all of my close - but loyal - that, once again, the establishment would have the last word. They weren't done yet, and they certainly weren't going to be made to look a pilchard by me!

That weekend, I did my usual routine: the gym and a visit on Saturday afternoon, and my beloved chapel piano playing on Sunday morning - next to Angel Anne. Remember, in one year I'd still not done one second of rehabilitation - mainly because I didn't qualify for any. Just twelve months of filler, procrastination, and filibustering from box-tickers. I'd also got to the bottom of the lack of any 'victim awareness' work. Almost everyone has to apologise and say sorry - even if it's to their families, the real victims of every criminal's actions. However, I discovered that OMU had worked out (very early on) that I was, indeed, the victim - due to the 'close him down' provocation before any of this started. Therefore, they couldn't even get me to do that. On top of my 'not guilty' plead - a position I maintain - they were shit out of luck requesting any sorries, mea culpa, or repentance. Total farce.

By the end of September, I'd sorted the entire top end of the gardens and was now chopping down my tomato vines after a bumper crop season. My work was literally done. I don't do cold -and autumn was literally upon us. The availability of drugs was getting really bad, and screws blamed drones for dropping them off. Bollocks. We're in the middle of nowhere! It's dopes dropping them in their work bags - that's the main problem. Stocken would be like Heathrow if drones were delivering that many packages of sniff and smoke. Whilst I was on gardens, several came and went - for drug dealing or being off their tits on spice. One guy - a very charming man in his fifties - ended up 'self-isolating' (behind his own door), as he was in debt big time for 'borrowing' spice and was terrified he was going to get the shit kicked out of him walking to work. For weeks, he locked himself away. Ironic, in prison, hey? I'd learned very quickly that you can't believe anything you see. These lads, especially at the lower end are constantly up to no good and all kinds of shenanigans. A real eye opener. They never stop.

A female maths teacher had recently been arrested when leaving the car park - after she had brought in a phone by 'mistake.' I don't think I've ever mistakenly shoved my flip phone up my lady parts, have you? What a clumsy cow? She got arrested and sacked. HMP was in focus and regularly the top story on the news - for corruption and overcrowding. Prisons seemingly have more drugs than a Soho nightclub. HMP Stocken had a dopey male teacher who went back to his car twice after spotting random checks in place at the staff entrance. He was arrested and held on remand. This shithead gave the game away. They searched his house, where he had £50,000 worth of drugs and tens of thousands of pounds in cash shoved up his anus-erectus chimney - I presume! He's looking at ten years. Very rarely do you ever hear any of this on the news – again, another strange coincidence. Do you think our regulated broadcasters do deals to cover up 'bad news' stories in return for funding? It's happening every day across the Prison Service. BBC News especially appears to be in the pocket of the MOJ - and vice versa. Most peculiar, eh?! I wonder who funds both projects....If the public knew how many dodgy, creepy, corrupt, and contemptible police constables and prison scumbags there are, they'd realise they're almost as disgraced and dysfunctional as the BBC broadcaster itself.

Monday - Tuesday came and went uneventfully. Wednesday - I was back to band practice. I turned up at 3pm and Paul said, "Are you OK?" "Yes," I said. "Still fighting the OMU numbskulls." I didn't get a laugh - or, in fact, any reaction. Weird. He walked off. It won't be my first or last awkward moment in the pokey. We rehearsed for an hour, then Anne and I shook hands. "Ta-ra, love. Bye, Alex," said this octogenarian miracle. Little did I know it would be our last ever goodbye. Tim shook my hand as I left, and off I went - down the mile long corridor to Newton. By pure chance, as I passed the Seg and I bumped into the admissions and reception orderly. He asked, "Are you OK?" I said, "Course, another day done." Silence. Here we go. He said, "You haven't heard, have you?" I said, "Heard what?" He laughed and said, "They're shipping you out to HMP Five Wells, the brand-new super jail? Oh yes, you'll be back on your vodka and coke by teatime in there, it's a private jail like Butlins."

I wasn't shocked, I'd called this a week earlier. Look, I'm a gobshite. Authorities are never wrong, when they're caught out and exposed, they have to get rid of you and pass the hot potato to someone else – it's happened throughout my career. The inbred halfwits had come to the end of the road and were on the ropes. They were humiliated that I'd had the last laugh with the shrinks, and their delay plan to detain me indefinitely was thwarted. They were never going to say, "Off you go to open jail, Alex - we want you to be happy and back with your family." They were even less likely to say, "Sorry, we got it wrong." I was so grateful for the heads-up from Gaz. I went on the wing and found out that the Gov had emailed 'to all' - crowing about my imminent ejaculation from the jail - as if to say, 'We've got rid of the prick. Tomorrow you can all relax!' Out of sight out of mind. Nothing to see here hey?......well, until this book is published.

Everything within the Prison Service is a pissing contest to save face. I bumped into Mr Smarts and said, "No way out of this right?" He laughed, "No, they've stitched you up - and if you refuse a direct order, they'll use it to bend you up and put you in the block... and then ship you out anyway." Charmers hey? In English, if I refused the transfer, I'd be physically removed under force. Like I say, you're totally powerless and emasculated once convicted. Welcome to Russia! Of course, I didn't want to go. I'd got the life of Riley at HMS Stockings. I believed it couldn't get any better. I went to see Alfie, who, by a weird twist of fate, was packing his stuff and had been told he'd got his CAT-D at Spring Hill. His CAT-D was given on the EXACT three-year birthday to release. Unheard of. His face fit. His handsome charm wooed his OMU. God bless him. He was thrilled for me about Five Wells, as it was brand new. He said, "A new start. This lot were never going to support you. You made them look like c@nts!" I said, "They didn't need my help for that - and Alfie - don't call them the C word – that has a purpose unlike those sphincters." I went to my pad to tell my 'loyals' that I was off to the Disney World of prisons - sell it as a promotion, which it 100% is, by comparison! All HMP were instructed to do was keep me behind bars and compliant, even if it was in the newest, most 'super' hoosegow in the UK. On the wing, they were over the moon, as HMP Five Wells was the laughingstock of the Prison Service. Everyone wanted to go there – it made Newton wing look like a slum. There had been a Sly News exclusive exposing drugs and booze parties that made this G4S private jail look like a Stringfellows. It was state-of-the-art pads, with underfloor heating, showers, no bars on the windows, and even an iPad - tippy-tappy - to do my emails. I went to call Mum and Dad to share the great news that, at the very least, I'd get two more visits and two canteens a week! I can PR any amount of bullshitery - don't you worry about that. 'Glass half full' should be tattooed on my scrotum! Guess what? Phone not working. How could this possibly be a coincidence? For months I'd never had a single issue. It's pitiful. Can you believe how sick those moronic, pre-menstrual, mortician-faced degenerates are? I'd had it up to 'here' with their kindergarten games. Thank God - I'm off! Utterly malicious, vindictive, and spiteful – identical to my time at BBC Leeds. I laughed. They knew my phone was my lifesaver and that I'd want to share the good news - so they sabotaged that as well.

Their final kick in the gonads was to stop my calls…..but again they failed! This was 4.30pm. We're out until 7pm – so Kev my dear pal on the servery said, "Use mine." All phones in jails are 'open' to anyone with a pin. Such a stupid and revealing last jab - to turn off my cell when the ones next door worked! Evil. Can you believe they'd ONLY switched off my floor, on my side of the wing? How pathetic, hey? Again, these pilchards can't see beyond the end of their hairy brown noses. Of course, Beaverhousen and Fanny were nowhere to be seen. The only thing that outweighed their stupidity and malice was their ability to avoid eye contact and hide - like the lefty cuckoo clocks they are! I'd love these two broke Biffas to sit with Jo and Jen for four hours, just to look into their sewer minds. I fear they'd need a lot longer than four sessions to resolve their MANsogynistic hate and demons. Urrrggghhh – enough to make you heave. However, I thank them for this book. Without the nose-pierced, big-boned bell end and the Hilary Devey lookalike (after a serious chip pan fire in a council flat), I wouldn't be able to expose the most incompetent, disgraceful, and unprofessional dopes within HMPPS. EXPOSED! I await the next defamation claim to try and gag me over their comedy names. All publicity... Please do! That can be book 13. The poor lads who can't process this stuff must end up swaying in a corner! Their evil games are relentless.

You always have to be a step ahead of snakes and vultures. Despite OMU's blackmail with psychology I'm not sorry about a second of my time at HMP Stockings.......and I never will be. Furthermore, I believe, from the bottom of my bottom, that my shrinks saw everything as clear as day. They, in fact, vindicated me - not by what they did say, but by what they didn't ask. So revealing! I made my calls - everyone was thrilled. No one could believe the outrageous reviews for Five Wells. From prisoners being called 'residents' to the 'super' executive floor, Belfield would be off to the most modern, lefty, and woke prison in the world! They've even got an LGBTQ+69s flag next to the Union flag on the front - what could possibly go wrong? This prison (like lockdown) is Boris Johnson's legacy. Need I say more?! It's a mixed NONCE nick, with paedos on every corner! Oy vey! Everyone on the wing appeared genuinely sad to see me go. Lads I'd never spoken to looked upset. My 'gentlemen of a certain age' on the benches were gutted. Prison life is all about keeping you on edge. These moves are designed to remind you that you're 100% powerless. My candour, balls, and outrageous optimism pissed them off to the core - but were ultimately admired by my co-stars. My refusal to play 'their' mind games infuriated them more than a nonbinary vegan during 'that' time of the month. They'd bitten off more than they could chew, and I hadn't snapped in the process. All they wanted was for me to lose it or worse! Now they needed to let someone else try - and save face - by jizzing me to HMPontins! Newton wing had been such a blessing. I'd met probably ten lads/silver-tops who kept me motivated, sane, and well. I'll be forever grateful! Prison is about isolation – I felt totally embraced, protected, and safe. Everyday they'd remind me I shouldn't be here......despite many of them facing a decade more behind bars. I guess this is the milk of human kindness. As long as you don't let it go sour, you can gain great strength from the rays of light. These men were radiators of hope. They encouraged me every single day to keep writing on their behalf - to expose this scandalous sham. They never let me forget that the truth would set me free. I cannot thank them enough.

At 6.55pm - I banged up for the final time. I slowly packed away my bits and bobs. I slept like a baby. I still have never lost a wink of sleep over any of the Prison Service shenanigans. Nor have I taken it seriously. My phone, purely by coincidence and chance, came back on at 10pm. I called everyone to say goodnight - as I have every single night since 'working away.' That was lovely. If I've got their love, nothing else matters in this woeful and vindictive circus.

I woke up at 7.30am, as usual, on the 18th October 2023, to begin reviewing my new cruise ship - HMP Five Wells in Wellingborough. I actually had a tingle of excitement. The door went at 7.55am. It was Tim, the Chaplain. I was so moved - honestly, I welled up. I felt in my heart he wouldn't let me leave without saying goodbye. How kind. He said he did know yesterday, but couldn't say. He thanked me for my piano playing, enthusiasm, and my smile. He told me I'd never be forgotten. What class. How could I be this ogre and monster to two women in OMU, and such a hero to a vicar? Story of my life! I thanked him. I've had a lot of letters from very religious people over the last thirteen months. Their prayers mean the world to me. I told Tim that he, Paul, Simeon - and especially darling Anne - had kept me 100% sane, positive, and focused since day one. Without them, I could never have remained so stoic and positive. I would never forget their kindness and generosity, and be forever indebted to them for making me feel supported and part of the team. What a top man.

Shortly after, I walked up to reception to catch the bus. There's no cuffs or anything like that, by the way. I've still never been cuffed. The fellas in reception knew me and trusted me. They didn't even bother checking my bags. Everyone was lovely. As I passed OMU, Connie Lingus (the Tena Lady of HMS Stockings) was walking out. She was my original OMU, who had been replaced months ago. She's a decent woman who 'knew' I'd been shafted by her corrupt colleagues. None of this was her fault. I can't help but wonder if she didn't want to be part of the foolishness. She's spineless and corporate - as all civil serpents become. She didn't speak and walked straight past. Words are irrelevant now. It's a job. I'm a number. I just pity her for having to live this vile, toxic, and sadistic life with such evil and spineless colleagues. I could have done twenty minutes, but I said nothing. Silence. Why bother? If I've learned any lesson -

it's that you can't win – you can't reason with stupid or corrupt. People have to live with their own actions, conscience, and duplicity. My power is in the pen......the very reason they hounded me from day one and fought to remove my sword.

At 12.20pm, I left HMP Stocken for HMP Five Wells – my new home. They gave us a sandwich, crisps, and drink on the 'bus.' It was far more comfortable than Ryanair. Would HMP Five Wells be less corrupt? Would Five Wells see through the bollocks? Would Five Wells finally see sense and send me home? Only time would tell......

Thirteen months ago, I was worried about going to prison - I feared I'd be passed from man to man like dysentery in a death camp, but I need not have worried - with being ginger no one cared or noticed. I left HMS Stockings fit, well and sane. I was also healthier than when I came in. You can't beat a free gym. They lose!

So, Tick Tock. They turned the lock for a year - <u>BUT</u> they can't stop the clock! It won't be long before I'm halfway through Pleasuring His Majesty. I'm proud I didn't surrender to the tyranny.

If you've enjoyed this scribe, please check out 'HMPontins' my fourth book written whilst in custody. If you think HMP Stocken was an asylum you won't believe what this offence neutral 'theme park for pricks' has to offer.

Super jail? It's a SUPER FAIL!!!

Prison Guide and Glossary

ACCT = Put on watch for own safety

`Bent Up'` = Removed by force

Canteen = Weekly shopping

COM = Houseblock Manager

COMP1 = Official Complaint Form

Con/Cons = Convict/Convicts

Cuntstable = Police

Direct Order = Disobey it and you'll get a nicking

Gov/Com/SO/AD = Senior Officer/Assistant Director

HDC = Home Detention Curfew

Hoosegow/Nick/Pokey = jail

HMPPS = His Majesty's Prison and Probation Service

IEP = Incentives and Earned Privileges

IPF = Incentives Policy Framework

IPP = Imprisonment for public protection

IR = Intel Report

Kangas/Kangeroos = Screws

Kit = Prison Clothes

Lag/Con = Prisoner

`Moves'` = When prisoners can walk around the jail

Mufties = Helmet wearing `bomb' squad of HMP

Nicking = Adjudication in front of Governor

NOMIS = Prison record/file on individual noting everything

NONCE = Not on Normal Courtyard Exercise

OASys = Prison Assessment System

OMU = Probation Managers = Liars, cheats & corrupt prison probation donkeys (Obnoxious Moron Unit) – (Odious, Minging and Underqualified)

Pad = Cell

PAVA (SPRAY) = Pelargonic Acid Vanillylamide and is an incapacitant spray used by the Prison Service

PIN = Numbers approved on phone

PLI = Prisoner Led Initiatives

POCA = Proceeds of Crime Act

POCSO = Prosecuted of Children from Sexual Offences

Prop = Your clothes and items listed on 'property' card

PR = Public Relations

PSI = Prison Service Instructions

Roll Check = Officers count men behind their doors 3x a day

ROTL = Released on Temporary Licence

Rule 39 = Legal Letter = Can't be opened by Kangas

Screw = Officers

Seg/Block/CASU = Segregation Block/End of the prison line

Servery = Food station

SOC = Time on wing with prisoners

Spends = The £33 a week you get to spend

Stretch/Bird = Your sentence

TSP = Thinking Skills Programme

VO = Visiting Order for Visits

VP = Vulnerable Person

Wrong'uns = Crimes against women or children

Don't miss the other books in the series:

Book One – Alex Belfield Autobiography

His Own Worst Enema – 40 Fantastic Years

Book Two – Locked Down: Locked Up

'Let's close Him Down'

The Evil BBC & Corrupt Police Witch Hunt

Book Four – HMPontins = Super Jail / Super Fail

Private Prisons – A Complete Waste of (Doing) Time

Book Five – HMPortaloo

A Sure Wank Redemption : All Screwed Up!

Book Six – HMPointless

5* Pokey Spa and Asylum

Therapy Horses, Pedicures and Yoga

Murder, Rape, and Suicide